A Culture of Enquiry

Therapeutic Communites

Series editors: Rex Haigh and Jan Lees

The Therapeutic Community movement holds a multidisciplinary view of health which is based on ideas of collective responsibility, citizenship and empowerment. The tradition has a long and distinguished history and is experiencing a revival of interest in contemporary theory and practice. It draws from many different principles – including analytic, behavioural, creative, educational and humanistic – in the framework of a group-based view of the social origins and maintenance of much overwhelming distress, mental ill-health and deviant behaviour. Therapeutic Community principles are applicable in a wide variety of settings, and this series will reflect that.

A Culture of Enquiry

Research Evidence and the Therapeutic Community

Edited by Jan Lees, Nick Manning, Diana Menzies and Nicola Morant

Therapeutic Communities 6

Jessica Kingsley Publishers
London and New York

First published in the United Kingdom in 2004
by Jessica Kingsley Publishers Ltd
116 Pentonville Road
London N1 9JB, England
and
29 West 35th Street, 10th fl.
New York, NY 10001-2299, USA

www.jkp.com

Copyright © Jessica Kingsley Publishers 2004

Library of Congress Cataloging in Publication Data
A CIP catalog record for this book is available from the Library of Congress

British Library Cataloguing in Publication Data
A CIP catalogue record for this book is available from the British Library

ISBN 1 85302 857 6

Printed and Bound in Great Britain
by Athenaeum Press, Gateshead, Tyne and Wear

Contents

Section III – Research Findings

Acknowledgements

Frank Margison is grateful to Professor Glenys Parry for permission to use Figure 3.2 and for helpful advice on recent policy initiatives; and to the *British Journal of Psychiatry* for permission to reproduce Table 3.1.

Fiona Dunstan and Sarah Birch would like to thank Dr Linda Dowdney and Dr Chris Fife-Schaw of the University of Surrey for their help in the preparatory stages of the project in Chapter 11.

Chapter 12 research was made possible by a grant from the European Commission Dg XII-SSMA, No. BMH4-CT-96-0688. The authors would like to thank their collaborators, who include Charles Kaplan, Department of Social Psychiatry, Maastricht University; Eric Broekaert, Department of Special Education, Ghent University; Ove Frank, Department of Statistics, Stockholm University; and Sebastian Reichmann, CNRS-LASMAS, Paris. We also thank the Royal Mail for their sponsorship of the earlier studies.

Chapter 13 was made possible by grants from the Henry Smith Charity and the Trusthouse Forte Foundation.

Introduction

Jan Lees, Nick Manning, Diana Menzies and Nicola Morant

Therapeutic communities are enjoying a wide resurgence of interest, in part because of the growing evidence base about their effectiveness for certain groups such as people with personality disorders, and in certain settings, such as prisons. This evidence base comes from a diversity of traditions. This has included researchers interested in social systems, group processes, psychodynamics and individual treatment outcomes. However, there has been little in the way of dialogue between these various research paradigms, and no books exist to date that report specifically on research conducted in therapeutic communities. Meanwhile, as emphasis on the evidence base of treatments and services increases, there is a growing need for research which can investigate the effectiveness of therapeutic community treatments, explore the therapeutic processes involved and help us better to understand the unique nature of therapeutic communities. This edited book presents a selection of research studies investigating various aspects of therapeutic community treatment environments. The selection of studies included in the book reflects two motivations on the part of the editors: first, to present examples of recent high quality research conducted in an international range of therapeutic communities; and second, to illustrate the diversity of perspectives and methodologies that can be applied in therapeutic community research.

The overall aim of the book is to bring together a set of research reports in order to contribute to the dissemination of existing research on therapeutic communities to clinicians and researchers in fields of health and social sciences. It is hoped that the book will also promote and facilitate the development of good quality and clinically relevant research on therapeutic communities. Through examples of specific research studies, the book presents a range of research methods. Discussion of more general research issues encourages the reader to contemplate the practical, ethical, social and political issues that impact upon the research process in therapeutic community settings. The juxtaposition of reflexive reports on a range of forms of research demonstrate that there are multiple ways of researching and understanding therapeutic communities, and that different research questions may be best answered using different methods. Both quantitative and qualitative methods are included, as well as research questions related to individuals, groups and collective systems. The book promotes methodological eclecticism in therapeutic community research and encourages the reader critically to evaluate and compare the various studies presented.

The target readership of the book is researchers and clinicians who work in therapeutic communities and who are conducting research, or want to understand more about the various ways in which research in therapeutic communities can be approached. The book will be of interest to practitioners from a range of disciplines including nursing, social work, psychology, psychiatry and counselling. A basic understanding of therapeutic community principles and of research methods will be assumed. For students and trainees, the book will act as a source book, which would help the reader think about and undertake a small-scale research project in a therapeutic community environment. For more experienced clinicians and researchers the book encourages consideration of various practical, methodological and epistemological issues associated with the research process. For readers outside the therapeutic community world, the book provides a window into current research practice in therapeutic communities and those interested in research on psychotherapy, group therapy and systemic approaches to mental health care environments may be attracted.

This is not a textbook on research methods for therapeutic community research. It is not a 'how to do it' manual, but a review of the body of existing research in therapeutic communities. In showing the reader what has already been done in the small but expanding world of therapeutic community research, this book hopes to encourage researchers, practitioners and service users to become involved in therapeutic community research.

Overall format of the book

Section I

The first two chapters that comprise the first section relate the history of therapeutic community research from the earliest days in the 1940s to the latest studies. Therapeutic community practitioners have not always been sympathetic to research, as a result of both a firm (and, on occasion, defensive) conviction as to the superiority of their clinical interventions, and also a perceived need to 'get on with the job' and extend the range of therapeutic community settings. As such this early suspicion was of course a creature of the times: clinical judgement was not routinely subjected to rigorous evaluation, and the randomised controlled trial had still to be devised. But it is also important to note the difficulties created by the wide range of social and psychological theory that was relevant to this 'complex intervention' (as it is now called), and the range of research methods that might be needed to understand both its overall effect and the relative contributions of different elements that made up the overall complex.

Nevertheless, the therapeutic community has now joined fully with the requirements of evidence-based practice, and has been subjected to extensive systematic review and meta-analysis, along with the growing use of complex statistical modelling, in an effort to tease out the essential ingredients and their interactions. This work continues through a growing network of research staff attached to therapeutic communities, and has been reflected in the increasing number of papers reporting new data in peer-reviewed journals, both qualitative and quantitative.

Section II

In this and the following section, we have grouped the chapters into those discussing different approaches to research questions, and designs for tackling them on the one hand, and some research results on the other. In the eight chapters in this section, the focus is on the context for research, different research designs and methods, and the process of undertaking research. There is no single best method of doing research. The choice of research questions and the methods needed to tackle them vary with the context and interest of the researchers.

In Chapter 3 Margison considers the paradigm of 'practice-based evidence', to which therapeutic communities are ideally suited, as a counterweight to the evidence-based practice paradigm. Therapeutic communities in the UK have already moved a considerable way towards the Practice Research Network (PRN) model of research summarised in this chapter, as one of the main settings for practice-based evidence. This chapter puts therapeutic community research into the context of psychotherapy research as carried out in the National Health Service (NHS). The NHS Review of Psychotherapy Services in England (NHS Executive 1996) described a model to link research with other aspects of good clinical practice such as outcomes benchmarking, clinical audit, guidelines and protocols. Since publication of that review the overall clinical governance framework has become increasingly influential. This chapter gives an overview of the links between research and clinical governance.

In the following chapter, Lees describes how therapeutic communities in the United Kingdom, particularly through the strategies and interventions of the national Association of Therapeutic Communities, have been developing and expanding both practice in, and links between, research, audit, clinical governance and quality standards, assurance and monitoring, within the national community of therapeutic communities. How do research, audit, clinical governance and quality assurance relate to therapeutic communities? Lees reminds us that a fundamental tenet of therapeutic community practice has always been the 'total culture of enquiry' as propounded by Tom Main (1989). Audit cycles, quality standards monitoring, clinical governance and research are exactly reflected in a culture of enquiry, which are all in turn examples of reflexive practice. Lees shows this through three examples of a large multi-centre comparative project on 23 therapeutic communities, the development of a standard for therapeutic community practice, and a further multi-centre 'community of communities' development for standard-setting and accreditation of therapeutic community practice.

In Chapter 5 De Leon looks at two critical contexts for therapeutic community research – the development of therapeutic communities in the USA, and their use to treat a particular population: addicts and alcoholics. In the USA the early differences between democratic and conceptual variants of the therapeutic community have receded. Development of a new generic therapeutic community in the USA has emerged from its various adaptations for special populations and settings and from its modifications of practices. The main lines of therapeutic community research in the USA fall into two phases, the early (circa 1973–89) and current (1990 to the present). The evolution of the scientific knowledge base through phases I and II has shifted the research question from *whether* therapeutic communities work to *how* they work. To a considerable extent, this shift reflects both policy and scientific issues. The weight of the outcome research accumulated over 30 years has established the field effectiveness of the therapeutic community as a *global* approach. However, identifying the 'active treatment ingredients' of the therapeutic community approach remains a compelling question for funding policy as well as science. Reducing the costs of treatment, by limiting its planned duration for example, can be rationally implemented only if the necessary and sufficient therapeutic community interventions are known.

Chapter 6 is focused on the randomised control trial (RCT). Manning suggests that knowledge is not neutral. It is a socially created and socially shared resource, which has sometimes proved to have limited shelf life in science. In the case of therapeutic communities there has been some uncertainty about what we now know about its effectiveness, and how this might be improved. The RCT is for many observers of medical and social practice a powerful method of developing a strongly legitimate means for gathering evidence, which carries extensive social power. The RCT involves the experimental allocation of patients to one of several kinds of treatment, or no treatment, to determine, by comparing the results for each group, which patients do better. The RCT has become the 'gold standard' for the experimental evaluation of medical and social interventions. However, it turns out that many medical and social interventions cannot be undertaken under the 'right experimental circumstances', and hence cannot draw upon the support of an RCT to demonstrate their efficacy. There has been a growing critical literature about the limitations of the use of RCTs in practice. This chapter also considers an alternative in which naturally occurring variations in 'real world' treatment can be modelled.

In Chapter 7 Moos continues the theme of evaluating the therapeutic community. He suggests that it is critical to measure key aspects of the treatment process and environment, to assess variations in the organisation and implementation of therapeutic communities, and to identify the influence of specific aspects of therapeutic communities on patients' change both in the programme and post-discharge. Although therapeutic communities are increasingly diverse, he offers a common conceptual framework to evaluate them, and argues that more emphasis should be placed on examining the effectiveness of matching specific types of patients to varying treatment programmes. Specifically, he focuses on how different types of therapeutic communities vary in their impact on patients who differ in their level of impairment and the chronicity and severity of their disorders. In this model, the connection between the objective characteristics of the programme, patients' personal characteristics, and patients' adaptation in the outside community, is mediated by the programme social climate and by patients' in-programme outcomes. The model specifies the domains of variables that should be included in an integrated evaluation.

Chapter 8, by Rawlings, takes a rather different approach by reviewing the place of purely qualitative methods in therapeutic community research. These data are often collected through interviews and/or observation, but studies can use other methods. Traditionally researchers have supplemented interviews and observations with examinations of existing documents or by asking subjects to keep diaries, which record their views of events and their thoughts and feelings. More recently, researchers have used tape recorders, not just to record interviews, but also to record 'naturally occurring activities' such as meetings or therapy groups, and have used these to examine how the talk leads from one topic to another. Occasionally videotape is used, so that the relationship between visual cues and speech activities can be explored. Recently, too, researchers have begun to use focus groups, which are a specialised form of group interview and which encourage people to talk between themselves so that the researcher can listen in. Rawlings reviews two well-known studies using these techniques, and discusses how these can be used in the therapeutic community and some of the problems which researchers meet; in particular the need to become both immersed in the field and distant from it.

This theme of the relationship between the researcher and his/her role in the therapeutic community is explored in more detail in the final two chapters in this section. In Chapter 9, Morant and Warren argue that therapeutic community researchers have an unusual role associated with key features of the therapeutic environment. In particular they highlight the 'culture of enquiry' and associated high levels of reflexivity, and the close integration of researchers, staff and clients/residents that characterise therapeutic communities. This leads to the researcher's position as an 'outsider on the inside', such that the dynamics of interactions and relationships with staff and clients become much more important than for researchers in more traditional mental health settings. These can impact upon the quality of therapeutic community research via, for example, their influence on study response rates. They conclude with some pragmatic suggestions for how researchers can negotiate the interfaces between research and clinical agendas and between independence from and integration within the organisation.

In the final chapter, Menzies and Lees discuss how researchers become involved in the psychodynamic life of the therapeutic community in relation, first, to the conscious and unconscious (countertransference) issues on the part of the researchers and, second, to the conscious and unconscious (transference) issues on the part of those being researched. Relevant to both groups is the desire to form relationships, but as an 'outsider on the inside' (Chapter 9) the psychodynamics incumbent on the researcher's position can result in feelings akin to living 'the borderline experience'. This chapter thus addresses the boundary between researcher and clinician, and the power differential between researcher and researched. The authors conclude that it is the researcher's responsibility to consider the factors that will influence his/her research and its findings, and to put in place measures that will minimise these, while acknowledging that obliterating them altogether is not possible. They argue that having the researcher on the staff team allows for the collective anticipation and exploration of interfering psychodynamics, helped by the experience of the clinicians, without which the project is likely to flounder.

Section III

In the eight chapters in this section, different authors present results of research projects across a range of settings in Scotland, England and Norway. It is evident from the research reports that many factors influence the type of research that is done, including the particular interest of an individual, the background from which the researcher comes and the need for survival in a changing political and social climate. The latter is mentioned in several of the studies and the authors have grasped the opportunity to evaluate their work demonstrating the consequence that, not only does politics affect research, but research also can influence politics. The research projects show a range of methodologies, both quantitative and qualitative, in secure and non-secure settings, exploring clinical outcome, economic evaluation, ideals and values, biographical details and the experience of the leaving process.

In the first chapter in this section Dunstan and Birch describe a multi-centre study aiming to examine the ideal values and practices across six therapeutic communities. Included were therapeutic communities in secure and non-secure settings, residential and day units and therapeutic communities providing all group therapy and a combination of group and individual therapy. The authors were interested to see if they could identify some core values in these different settings. They used a 58-item questionnaire derived from previous research done at Henderson Hospital. This consisted of questions enquiring about the four tenets of communalism, democratisation, reality confrontation and permissiveness; a section asking respondents to rank their groups in order of importance; and a qualitative section asking respondents to describe the most important treatment event during the last week. Factor analysis performed on the items of the original questionnaire did not support the four constructs proposed by Rappoport (1960), and Dunstan and Birch discuss possible reasons for this finding. Other elements of the previous research were supported and the authors discuss their results in the light of some of their methodological difficulties in doing multi-centre comparative studies.

In Chapter 12, Eley, Yates and Wilson report on the activities of the Scotland-based research team within the Improving Psychiatric Treatment in Residential Programmes for Emerging Dependency Group (IPTRP) projects, a three-year multi-site international programme. Their research centred on three concept-based therapeutic communities in Scotland for substance misusers. They describe how they investigated the incidence and impact of childhood trauma in this population using a semi-structured interview and a self-report-screening questionnaire. Their study confirmed the relationship between childhood maltreatment and substance misuse and they go on to discuss the implications of this in terms of the treatment provided, and in particular relapse prevention work.

In the next chapter, Chiesa, Fonagy and Holmes begin by discussing the social and political changes which influenced clinical practice at the Cassel Hospital and which resulted in a research project designed to evaluate the new service developments. They describe a prospective, controlled trial comparing two specialist treatments at the hospital, one entirely hospital-based and the other a shorter inpatient admission with community follow-up, with a group of patients with personality disorder who receive treatment as usual. Entry to each arm of the project is determined by geography. The trial used a mixture of self-rated and clinician-rated measures and semi-structured interviews, choosing measures that would allow a comparison with mainstream psychiatric research. Outcome was measured across a range of areas including symptom distress, social adaptation, internal change and cost. The results show that a specialist inpatient psychosocial approach to personality disorder is significantly more effective over time than standard general psychiatric care in many of the areas measured, and that the shorter admission with community follow-up produces faster improvements and significant reduction in self-harm and hospital re-admission.

In Chapter 14, Norton and Warren review the research done at Henderson Hospital since the therapeutic community model's inception and discuss methodological issues. Research began with a mainly descriptive anthropological approach by Rapoport in the 1950s, but his research also included an outcome study, this being the first of many in the hospital's 50-year history. Outcome has usually been measured against baseline data but in later studies a comparative sample of a non-admitted group was also included. The studies have used a variety of criteria to measure success; for example clinical assessment, reconviction and re-admission rates, symptom distress, changes in core borderline personality disorder symptomology and cost offset. Measures have included self-report questionnaires as well as the more objective measures of questioning referrers and GPs for information, and the use of data from the Criminal Records Office and the Ministry of Health. Follow-up has varied between one and five years post-discharge and a consistent finding has been that treatment effect is associated with length of stay.

In the next chapter, Karterud, Pedersen and Urnes describe the Norwegian network of psychotherapeutic day hospitals, currently consisting of ten different day hospitals. The aim of the network is to provide mutual support for quality assurance, professional development, internet facilities, research and survival issues. Being a member of the network requires a commitment to using a range of diagnostic and evaluatory procedures, thus allowing the pooling of data to provide a large sample as well as comparison between the individual units. The authors describe some of the completed and ongoing research done by the network including research into personality, pathology and functioning, outcome research, research into different therapeutic elements of the programme and into patterns of attachment. A large data set and diversity of areas of research show the advantage of having a well organised, supported and funded organisation to do such comparative work.

In Chapter 16, Davies and Menzies summarise some of the different types of economic evaluations used in health care systems before going on to discuss economic evaluations in therapeutic communities. They describe the political spur for such economic evaluation and then compare studies done across three residential units, all of which reported a reduction in costs following treatment. They discuss the practicalities of doing such research, ending with some practical suggestions.

In Chapter 17, Genders and Player describe their research into Grendon Therapeutic Community, situated in a prison. The focus of their research was on how therapy was negotiated in a penal setting and how the resultant therapeutic process gave rise to specific patterns of change amongst its participants. This was mainly a qualitative study, but also incorporated some quantitative elements. It involved long periods of observational work that extended over two years of fieldwork in the prison, as well as analysis of official records, semi-structured interviews and self-completion questionnaires. The authors summarise some of their main findings in relation to the partnership between the prison and the therapeutic community with their seemingly contrasting objectives; the specific patterns of change in the prisoners bought about by this particular institution and the process of adaptation shown by men transferred back to ordinary prisons after completion of treatment.

In the final chapter, Morant investigates the process of leaving the residential therapeutic community. She used semi-structured interviews to access the views and experiences of a cohort of ex-residents at two time points following discharge. She discusses the advantages of using a qualitative approach in accessing service users' views and gives examples of responses given on investigating residents' experiences of the leaving process, of the month following discharge and of their service needs and experiences.

SECTION I

Overview

Overview

CHAPTER 1

Principles and Practices in Therapeutic Community Research

Nick Manning and Nicola Morant

Why do research?

Research is the process of asking and answering questions using the systematic collection of data and analysis of these data. It is linked to the development of theories about the concepts of interest, and aims ultimately to further our understanding of these issues. Beyond this rather general definition, research in therapeutic communities (and other mental health services) can be conducted from a range of different perspectives that are associated with different aims, methods and underlying principles. This chapter aims to provide a brief review of these and to orient the reader to some of the basic issues in research on therapeutic communities. We will consider the aims of research, the historical context of therapeutic community research, and forms of research that are appropriate to therapeutic community contexts.

Why do research, and why is therapeutic community research important? Research aims to enhance our understanding of the world and, in clinical domains, of clinically relevant issues. In a therapeutic community context, these might include the following areas of investigation: the impact of treatment on clients' symptomatology or subjective well-being (Chiesa and Fonagy 2000; Dolan, Warren and Norton 1997; Norton and Warren this volume); factors that predict treatment drop-out (Chiesa, Drahorad and Longo 2000; De Leon 1986); clients' experiences of therapeutic community treatments (Morant this volume); economic evaluations of the cost of care (Davies and Menzies this volume; Dolan *et al.* 1996); explorations of therapeutic processes in different contexts, such as forensic settings (Genders and Player this volume; Rawlings this volume); and analysis of stress coping processes used by staff (Shine 1997). As these examples illustrate, the answers to research questions enhance our understanding of what happens in therapeutic communities and why, thus allowing us to appreciate these processes from the point of view of various stakeholders (patients, staff, purchasers etc.). Perhaps, more important though, the answers that research provides feed into clinical practice.

This relationship between clinical practice and research is emphasised in the concept of evidence-based medicine (Sackett *et al.* 1996), an increasingly important ideal within the British health system. Evidence-based medicine (EBM) aims to enhance the quality of health care by ensuring that treatment decisions are based on relevant research evidence. Within this model, the dissemination of research findings to clinical practitioners and their ability to access, interpret and evaluate this research is as important as the production of research results (Greenhalgh 1997). This places the emphasis on training in these skills for clinical practitioners and suggests that therapeutic communities need to ensure that practitioners as well as research staff have adequate opportunities to access and learn about research. EBM suggests a 'research then practice' model. For example, services should base their treatment decisions on the latest research on treatment efficacy for particular clinical populations. However, in reality, the relationship between research and clinical practice is usually more complex, with clinical practice often being the impetus for new research questions. For example, if it were observed in a therapeutic community that members of particular ethnic groups tended to do less well or drop out of treatment early, this might provide the starting point for research investigating this issue. This in turn might lead to changes in the clinical programme to make it more appropriate to the needs of certain ethnic groups. Thus there is two-way traffic between research and practice that is best conceptualised as a continually evolving process.

Having said this, clinicians or those new to research are often disappointed that research is rarely able to answer broad questions or provide definitive answers to clinical practice questions. There are several reasons for this. First, most research (with the exception of single-case studies) is conducted on large samples. On the basis of findings it would only be possible to predict that an individual *with similar characteristics to those in the research sample* would be *likely* to respond positively to a particular treatment, and *only if* it were delivered in exactly the same way and under the same conditions as those in the research. Second, as we will discuss later, there are various approaches to research amongst which there are debates about the nature of research and the meaning of its data. This means that even the most clear-cut of research findings are usually open to debate. Finally, the questions research sets out to answer are generally very specific. This is not to say that the contribution of research is trivial, but to emphasise that it is important to be aware of the approach a particular research study has adopted, the specific conditions under which the research was carried out and the associated limits of applicability of its findings. For example, research on factors associated with treatment dropout in a residential therapeutic community may not be applicable to non-residential settings. It may not even be relevant to other residential therapeutic communities because they may have a different client group, have a different clinical programme, or be situated within different social and service settings.

How does research happen?

So how does research happen, and what factors shape the way it is conducted? There is a surprising amount of work in getting from an initial research idea to a fully designed project. Once a broad area for research has been identified (usually from problems encountered in clinical practice or from reading related research literature), a literature search is conducted to establish what related work already exists. This may give some indication of appropriate methodologies or theoretical positions, and lead to the refinement of the initial question. As we will discuss below, because therapeutic communities are social systems that lend themselves to both psychological and sociological forms of research, the range of methods that may be adopted in therapeutic community research is extremely large. It might include, for example, written self-report questionnaires or psychometrically validated measures, structured or open-ended interviews, observations of clinical practice, focus groups, diary methods, or secondary analysis of existing data bases. Any method has both strengths and weaknesses, and the researcher must weigh these up in choosing a method that is most appropriate to his/her specific research question. Choice of methods is also associated with broad approaches to research and related underlying assumptions that we will discuss later in the chapter. Before data collection can begin there will be other decisions to make. Depending on the method adopted, these might include defining the population of interest, deciding how to sample from this population, operationalising concepts into measurable variables, developing hypotheses and piloting measures or techniques. Thus the stages of research design involve successive refining and specificity of the initial research question.

Research in therapeutic community settings is also shaped by factors that are external to the research processes or out of the researcher's control. Therapeutic community research, like health services research more generally, is situated within existing services and must operate within these 'real-world' parameters. For example, while a researcher might conclude that the most powerful way to assess whether therapeutic communities 'work' would be to conduct a randomised controlled trial, there are substantial ethical issues associated with the requirement to randomise clients to treatment regimes. (See Chapter 6 for more detailed discussion of randomised controlled trials in therapeutic community settings.) Other ethical issues should also be considered. For example, research should never do anything that has the potential to cause distress or discomfort to those involved, and should be conducted in a way that protects the identities of those who participate (Homans 1991; Royal College of Psychiatrists 2001). The requirement to submit research proposals to local research ethics committees can often lead to modifications of the design or implementation of the research project. The practicalities of the research process must also be acceptable to all those involved or affected by it, including research participants, therapeutic community service users and staff teams. It doesn't matter how well designed a research proposal is, if the data collection is excessively time-consuming or scheduled to clash with other activities in the therapeutic community programme, results will be compromised by poor response rates or non-repre-sentativeness. The nature of therapeutic community work means that many of the topics of interest to therapeutic community researchers involve sensitive or difficult subjects. In order for this kind of research to be successfully and ethically conducted the researcher must be skilled in both human and research skills and able to understand the dynamics of the therapeutic community within which the research is conducted (see Chapters 9 and 10 for more discussion of these issues).

The availability of research funding can be another pragmatic constraint. As most therapeutic community research relies on external funding, aspiring re-searchers must engage with the politicised world of funding councils and grant-giving bodies whose agendas often determine the type of research they are willing to fund. Research funding is often linked to wider agendas, for example the current political and legislative interest in the management of people who attract the label of 'dangerous and severe personality disorder'. What research gets funded, and ultimately what research gets done, is often a highly politicised and non-neutral process. This leads us to consider the factors that have shaped the history of research within therapeutic communities.

Why have therapeutic communities historically been bad at doing research?

Therapeutic communities have had a mixed record of research activity. In the early years they were invented and grew out of a research culture. However this close relationship declined in subsequent decades, only to become re-established in recent years. The therapeutic community originated simultaneously in two separate places, usually associated with the work of Tom Main and Maxwell Jones, both including research as an integral part of therapeutic work.

The first resulted from the appointment of J.R. Rees, director of the Tavistock Clinic, as consulting psychiatrist to the army in 1938, and as head of Army Psychiatric Services in 1939. Almost one half of the Tavistock Clinic moved with him. The Tavistock was unorthodox and independent from the mainstreams of psychiatry or psychoanalysis, and under Rees's direction developed a fundamental shift of focus: from a concern with the individual, to the larger problems of morale, and the effective management of human resources. Rees (1945) suggests that war brought psychiatry out into the world, and stimulated new ideas in psychology and sociology: group relations, personnel assessment, job analysis and placement, training, morale building, rehabilitation, re-socialisation, education, health promotion, sociological surveys and psychological warfare. The notion of a therapeutic community drew on many of these ideas and was initially explicitly designed as a research experiment by Bion at Northfield Military Hospital, then used to inform the design of 'civil resettlement units' for returning prisoners of war (Curle 1947); eventually it became the basis for the organisation of the Cassel Hospital.

The second place was the home of orthodox psychiatry, the Maudesley Hospital, where Maxwell Jones also developed the idea of the therapeutic community (Jones 1968). The context of his work was quite different: a practical involvement with a specific client group which presented symptoms of 'effort syndrome' (psychosomatic heart disease), rather than a theoretical elaboration of new ideas. Over five years from 1940 Jones developed the idea of group discussions and sociodrama, after a series of innovations in educating and informing clients of the nature of their disorder, and the use of more experienced clients as tutors for neophytes. This was a continuous practical experiment, in which Jones gradually came to see that the active involvement of clients in discussions and the management of the unit, together with continuous observation and feedback, helped to establish and consolidate therapeutic changes.

After the war the therapeutic community was consolidated in the 1950s as a new form of therapy by Tom Main at the Cassel Hospital and Maxwell Jones at Henderson Hospital, and it spread as an idea further afield to Fulbourn Hospital, Claybury Hospital, Pentonville Prison and elsewhere. However, as the idea spread, a split developed between practice and research. While publications appeared describing, or more often celebrating, the new approach, there was little attempt to develop explicit research. Where research was developed, most famously by Rapoport at the Henderson Hospital (Rappoport 1960), there was considerable tension between the research team and the therapeutic team, such that the latter initially rejected the findings of the former (Manning and Rapoport 1976).

Why did this happen? One reason is that the values of the therapeutic community tended towards the rejection of hierarchy, the demystification of medical practice and the tolerance of behavioural disturbance. These were defended as matters of principle and faith rather than reason and science, indeed the therapeutic community idea resembled a social movement rather than scientific medicine (Manning 1989). During the wider value changes that ensued in the 1960s, the therapeutic community was felt to be resonating nicely with the ascendant world; why consolidate a sect into a church? The seductive sense of messianism (Hobson 1979) and even righteous persecution (Baron 1987) ran strongly counter to the world of nitty gritty research. Another reason was the complex nature of therapeutic community treatment. It was difficult to research, given the wide range of work using this idea – some commentators even asking whether it was 'fact or fantasy' as a method (Zeitlyn 1967). In addition, the kind of staff attracted to this area were not on the whole interested in research as a significant element in their careers.

The lack of research left the therapeutic community high and dry when the tide of social values changed in the 1970s: residential care settings in which the therapeutic community had flourished were to be replaced by community care, the general thrust of psychiatric innovation moved towards the biological basis of disease and pharmacological modes of treatment, and in the UK and USA at the end of the decade governments were elected that no longer believed in the realm of the 'social' at all. Too late came the realisation that research was the only way in which legitimate wider professional and economic support could be gained (Manning 1979).

However, the therapeutic community survived. Even though there was a steady decline in the number of places using this method, a determined and committed small group of practitioners continued to work and to meet, and slowly, slowly the wheel turned. Perhaps the Rapoport study had left a cultural residue at the Henderson Hospital; certainly the results were in time accepted, and even came ironically to embody the very essence of the therapeutic community's understanding of itself (Manning 1997). Henderson Hospital kept the small flame of research alive (see Chapter 14), and by the 1990s it was ready to grow and spread.

Once again, however, it was the changing opportunities and values in the wider professions, policies and society that provided the means for this to happen. Biological psychiatry has not delivered the breakthroughs hoped for. Community care, one of the alternatives that had seemed to undermine therapeutic communities, was deemed a failure in the UK in 1998 by the then Minister of Health, David Blunkett. The category of personality disorder, for which the therapeutic community had always been considered one of the few effective treatments, however expensive, and with however slim a research base, earned a dubious but growing reputation through a number of high-profile murder cases (Manning 2000, 2002) in a society now seen as ubiquitously subject to manifold forms of 'risk'. The cumulative effect of the Henderson Hospital evidence, particularly on cost-effectiveness (Dolan *et al.* 1996), persuaded the government to set up two new similar hospitals. In addition, daytime-only communities that nevertheless were able to manage clients through their difficulties 24/7 were bringing down the cost of treatment.

This change of fortunes in the 1990s has been accompanied by a new generation of practitioners committed to developing the evidence base for therapeutic communities. Evaluation through the use of randomised controlled trials (RCTs) has been cautiously accepted in principle, even if it remains as yet untested in practice. A systematic review and meta-analysis has been funded and provided strong evidence in the appropriate language of evidence-based medicine in favour of the therapeutic community (Lees, Manning and Rawlings 1999, described in Chapter 2), and further large-scale research projects have been funded and are ongoing (www.therapeuticcommunities.org/lottery-protocol. htmb; Haigh 2002). Therapeutic community research of many different forms is flourishing and this book is one of the outcomes and signs of this change.

Broad perspectives – Psychological, sociological and 'synthesis' approaches

The Tavistock tradition that gave rise to the therapeutic community in the 1940s combined ideas drawn from psychology and sociology. It pre-eminently focused on personal change in the group context. This was applied to all kinds of settings – initially, of course, the functioning of combat and support groups for the war effort. Later this was to underpin a substantial and continuing stream of applied research on the way in which organisations functioned, and how they might perform better. The motivation of individuals and the effective working of groups are now perennial stocks-in-trade of management schools and gurus.

The therapeutic community shared an intellectual heritage with much of this work. It combined two analytically distinct fields: organisation theory (and in particular the interaction between structure, interpersonal process, and individual behaviour); and psychotherapy (the attempt to promote personal growth and change through guided conversation). Early practitioners drew upon what Dicks (1970) described as the 'invisible college' surrounding the Tavistock. Ideas were available from Freud, of course, but also from the work of Kurt Lewin on groups as 'fields', and the notion of unfreezing, moving and re-freezing groups (see his obituary in the first edition of *Human Relations* in 1947). The human relations school of management studies had prioritised the human experiences of workers as critical to the understanding of organisational change (Roethlisberger and Dickson 1939), and the Meadian school of sociology focused on the way in which people as actors developed through a reflexive approach of 'taking the role of the other' (Mead 1934, 1938).

Much of this theory asked the questions: what is the nature of the individual and his/her social environment, and how do these two interact? This approach has traditionally conceptualised the individual and the social as two distinct types of reality which, while closely interwoven, were to be understood as ontologically separate and self-contained. Within the social sciences this separation has been reproduced in the distinct disciplines of psychology and sociology. Indeed, in therapeutic community writing this has also been reflected in a separation between the ideas of psychotherapy and sociotherapy (Edelson 1970). However, this split has come under increasing criticism. Within sociology the split between individual and society, or actor and structure, has been a central stumbling block to the understanding of social action. How can an 'oversocialised' concept of the individual, as merely the bearer of social forces, be reconciled with the idea of the individual as a rational actor, in an endless cycle of calculations about how to engage in reciprocal exchange with other actors (Coleman and Fararo 1992)? Within psychology, there has been a similarly long-standing debate between those who see personality as composed of various individual traits, played out invariantly in social situations, and those who have sought to demonstrate that behaviour varies from situation to situation (Mischel 1968). Where should clinical interventions be directed? At changing those individual traits, or at managing and choosing the situations in which and through which clients' lives are lived?

Such criticisms have in both disciplines resulted in attempts at theoretical synthesis between the individual/social divide. Within sociology two key attempts have been mounted by Anthony Giddens and Pierre Bourdieu. Giddens's (1985) structuration theory proposes that the individual/society dualism can be overcome by conceptualising both individuals and society as constituted by social practices which are recursive. In other words social phenomena are continually recreated, rather than created, by people as a result of the very way in which people express themselves. Ordinary people are more or less aware of this process, and therefore Giddens stresses the importance of paying attention to people's accounts of their own motives and reasons for doing what they do. He focuses on two elements: the rules for social action, and the resources people have available with which they can follow (or break) those rules. Bourdieu (Bourdieu and Passeron 1990) has worked at the same issues through three inter-linked concepts: habitus, field and capital. He argues that individuals have various kinds of capital (social, economic, symbolic, political etc.) that they can deploy in fields of social action, but that they are constrained by the accumulated habits, expectations and normal styles of interaction (habitus) in any particular field.

Within the psychology of personality and social action, we can also identify attempts to overcome individual/social dualism. One is the analysis of groups, and the way in which individuals seek to establish their personal identity through the social relations within and between groups, and another is the re-conceptualisation of individual personality and group relations in common terms as a study of the development and exchange of social meanings through language. The question of identity was at the heart of much of the work of Henri Tajfel (1982), a social psychologist who developed his ideas through an attempt to understand prejudice, and the way in which individuals come to identify strongly with 'their' group (their 'in-group') and strongly against other 'out-groups'. Tajfel found that individuals will show preferential treatment to or bolster the status of members of their in-group in comparison to members of other groups. Groups, it seemed, were a fundamental part of a person's self-identity and an important source of self-esteem.

Harré (Harré and Secord 1972) extended this point to consider how the concepts used to understand individuals and their social settings could be redefined in common terms, and in particular whether a science of meanings could be developed to define both the individual and the social through the idea that they were enshrined in language and language use. Just as linguists had realised that grammar can be precise and account for complex speech patterns, yet not be able to predict any particular utterance, so Harré suggested that individual behaviour may follow quite tightly prescribed rules, yet be unpredictable. Moreover, those rules, like the grammar of language, were themselves subject to modification and change over time, even if only slowly, through the cumulative actions of individuals. In a similar vein, discursive psychology (Potter and Wetherell 1987) is a form of social psychology that emphasises how individuals draw upon the linguistic resources available to them to construct versions of events and position themselves in the world and in relation to other people. Another social psychological approach that attempts to overcome the individual/social dichotomy is the theory of social representations (Farr and Moscovici 1984). The focus here is on the indivisibility of individuals' views of the world and the stock of common sense knowledge that circulates in their social world. Individuals are social actors and their social representations both construct and reflect the worlds they are a part of.

How are these ideas relevant to therapeutic communities? These recent reconceptualisations of the interaction or intermingling of individuals and social environments are grappling with just those areas in which therapeutic community clients ask for help. Therapeutic communities are small social systems in which interactions between individuals and social contexts are encouraged and facilitated through intense group experiences, and are brought to consciousness through continuous feedback. The difficulties that clients of therapeutic communities typically have are those that are expressed in the interstices between them and their intimate social and work environments. The therapeutic strategy of the therapeutic community is to enable the client to reproduce the kind of interactions he/she has had trouble with in the past so that these can be observed and reflected upon.

What research questions do these approaches imply?

Paul (1967) memorably summed up the essence of psychotherapy research as addressing the question '*what* treatment, by *whom*, is the most effective for *this* individual with *that* specific problem, under *which* set of circumstances?' (p.111). The research traditions that we have reviewed imply different approaches to conceptualising the individual, psychological disorder and the process of therapy.

(They also carry with them rather different assumptions about the process of doing research that we will discuss further in the following section.) Consequently, they would suggest different approaches to therapeutic community research and would adopt different methodological strategies in answering this broad question.

Generally speaking, if we think of a continuum stretching from the exclusively psychological to the exclusively sociological, we would find that psychological research is interested in the individuals who are treated in therapeutic communities, whereas sociological research is interested in therapeutic communities as social systems. As such, in sociological research the unit of analysis is usually not the individual but the social system, be this the therapeutic community, the family group, or a particular therapy group within a therapeutic community. In between these two extremes would be forms of research that are interested in the interaction of social systems with the intra-psychic processes of individuals.

For example, in tackling the question of which individuals are likely to benefit from different types of therapeutic community treatment (e.g. residential, non-residential, democratic, hierarchical), a traditional psychological approach could be adopted, employing standard psychological measures for large samples of clients in different communities to identify the relationship between client characteristics, therapeutic community practice and therapeutic outcome. An alternative approach to this question of individual differences would be suggested by the work of Harré, who proposes the term 'persona' to refer to 'the resources upon which a person draws in giving form and meaning to their actions as social performances. These resources are the basis for what one could call their social competence' (De Waele and Harré 1976, p.193). This perspective would suggest research questions focussing on the variety of personal and social resources available to therapeutic community clients, and how clients with different resources respond to therapeutic community treatment or to particular types of therapeutic community. For example, family background, gender, psychiatric and health status, educational achievements, knowledge of social and language skills, and ethnicity will all affect the behavioural, cultural and social resources upon which individuals may draw in their interactions with the therapeutic community rules and environment. This approach recognises both that individuals are moulded by their social environment, and that the social environment is composed of and shaped by interacting individuals.

Similarly, psychological disorder itself can be conceptualised using Harré's perspective as deficits in an individual's personal, social and cognitive resources. Harré argues that human social activity consists of the performance of acts in socially recognised episodes, and the speaking of accounts so that acts are given certain meanings, especially that they are intelligible as the products of a rational being. If an individual's resources are deficient, knowledge of the appropriate style of self-presentation or of the rules for successful interaction in a situation, and consequently the possibility for contemplation and correction by self-monitoring and self-control, may be lacking (Harré 1979, p.169). The therapeutic community milieu may have the potential to remedy these deficits through the construction of a rich and varied set of social situations for the client combined with continuous feedback through interpretation, and at times confrontation. In order to investigate how therapeutic community experience impacts on psychological disorder conceptualised in this way, research might involve the recording of therapeutic conversations and their subjection to detailed qualitative analysis using techniques of thematic content analysis, discourse analysis or conversation analysis.

Research questions such as these go beyond a simple 'dose-response' model of medical treatment typical of the randomised trial of a new drug. They recognise that clients have complex biographies and different resources and that therapeutic communities have different and changing rules, cultures and social structures. Hourly, daily, weekly, monthly and yearly rounds of an intensely lived experience in a therapeutic community are difficult to capture reliably, and to represent validly. Ethnographic immersion by the researcher in the detailed daily life of the community, a technique commonly used by anthropologists in the study of pre-industrial cultures, might be chosen as a method that would allow the careful elucidation of the complex and dynamic nature of therapeutic community culture and practice. As social systems that involve the intersection of the individual and the collective in therapeutic practice, therapeutic communities are open to research conducted from a variety of perspective and employing a wide range of methodological strategies. The following section discusses issues associated with these methodological choices in more detail.

Quantitative and qualitative forms of research

An important issue to be aware of in designing and evaluating therapeutic community research is the type of data that are generated. For the purposes of this discussion, we will make a broad distinction between quantitative (numerical) and qualitative (textual or non-numerical) forms of research. (However, we acknowledge that this is to some extent a false dichotomy, and that *all* research involves – either implicitly or explicitly – both quantitative and qualitative concepts.) Quantitative data might be in the form of, for example, numerical scores on psychometric questionnaires, or the number of times a particular behaviour is observed. Examples of qualitative data would be interview narratives, written diary entries or descriptions of observed interactions. In general, there has tended to be a preference for quantitative data in psychological research and for qualitative data in sociological and 'synthesis' forms of research. However, there are many exceptions, and as researchers become more aware of the benefits of combining methodologies, and the dangers of slavish adherence to particular methodological approaches, these broad distinctions are breaking down.

Deciding to adopt a quantitative or qualitative approach to research carries with it advantages, disadvantages and implications (Bryman 1988). Quantitative forms of research usually collect data from large groups of respondents. The data that are produced have the great advantage of being amenable to statistical analyses. Statistical tests are powerful because they tell the researcher whether it is valid to draw inferences about the populations from which the data sample were drawn. Thus, if samples are both representative and large enough, and the results are statistically significant, the conclusions of quantitative research on, for example, eating disorders in a sample of clients with borderline personality diagnoses may be generalisable to the broader population of people in this category. Numerical data also allows the researcher to compare groups or to measure change over time. The classic experimental design allows the researcher to investigate causal relationships between variables (for example, treatment type and reductions in psychological distress). This design forms the basis of the 'randomised controlled trial' that is considered by many as the 'gold standard' of mental health research (see Chapter 6 for more discussion of this issue).

However, quantitative research does have some limitations. In order to establish causal relationships between variables, the researcher needs a large degree of control over the research situation. For example, in a clinical trial, the researcher must ensure that treatment is delivered by all therapists in the same way, and that those being treated show similar mental health problems. There are considerable practical and ethical barriers to conducting this type of research in mental health. In addition, these conditions are rarely representative of how treatment is delivered 'normally', and as such the 'external validity' of this type of research is often low. Put another way, there can often be a significant gulf between treatment *efficacy* (how a treatment fares in a tightly controlled clinical trial) and treatment *effectiveness* (the success of ostensibly the same treatment as it is delivered in a service setting) (Guthrie 2000; Seligman 1995; Wells 1999).

Other potential validity problems in quantitative research revolve around the difficulties of quantifying psychological concepts and the social psychological processes that can interfere with this. For example, the way that people answer self-report questionnaires can be shaped by factors other than the concepts the questionnaire claims to measure. The respondents might be concerned to present themselves in a positive light to the researcher, or might believe that exaggerating their problems will lead to access to support services. Many psychological processes are extremely difficult to quantify or to access using self-report measures. This is particularly the case in research relating to therapeutic community work with its focus on psychodynamic processes (for example, attachment, splitting or denial) and their manifestation in interpersonal and social situations. A concern with the technicalities of reliable and valid measurement may divert researchers from this task of evaluating the more complex realities of clients' problems and treatment delivery. Finally, while quantitative research is able to measure the psychosocial *outcome* of treatment for groups of individuals, it is less able to explain *why* this happened or unpack whether the same change processes occurred for all individuals. Qualitative research, with its focus on subjective experiences, meanings and processes, may be a more powerful research tool to understand the reasons why certain treatments are successful or unsuccessful for particular individuals.

There are many forms of qualitative research associated with different academic traditions within the social sciences. These include ethnography, narrative analysis, discursive psychology, collaborative enquiry and grounded theory. Similarly, there are many ways of collecting qualitative data including semi-structured or in-depth interviews, focus groups, participant or non-participant observation, and analysis of pre-existing sources such as media output or literature. The common feature of these approaches and methods is a concern with meaning and with producing rich descriptions and understandings of the phenomena under study (Denzin and Lincoln 1998). Qualitative research is exploratory – it is usually more concerned with hypothesis generation than hypothesis testing. For topics in which there is little pre-existing knowledge or that involve sensitive or complex issues, this exploratory style may be preferable to quantitative methods. The focus is on naturalistic enquiry – exploring how things are in the 'real world' and what this feels like for those who experience this world. For example, qualitative methods may be an excellent way of exploring the subjective experiences of service users or therapeutic community members (see Chapters 8 and 18). Qualitative research works with how things are defined by research respondents, not by researchers: it is conducted *with* (rather than *on*) people. This collaborative style means that the power balance between researcher and researched is arguably more equal than in quantitative research. Principles of respect and equality resonate with those of therapeutic community practice such that qualitative research is seen by many as more compatible with therapeutic communities than the scientific stance of quantitative research.

Because of its concern with understanding the uniqueness and complexity of people's experiences and of social situations, qualitative research is usually conducted using much smaller samples than quantitative research. This means that the generalisability of qualitative research is usually limited. There are also issues surrounding the analysis of qualitative data; a common critical misconception being that it is vague, lacking rigour, or reflective of the whims of the researcher. One reason for these views is that, unlike quantitative data analysis in which standard procedures for conducting statistical tests are performed, qualitative data analysis is much more fluid and can be conducted in different ways depending on the theoretical perspective and aims of the researcher (Denzin and

Lincoln 1998; Miles and Huberman 1994). Qualitative data analysis involves exploring themes, patterns and associations within the data. This is a complex process that is usually very time-consuming and consists of successive readings and interpretation of the data. That this is done in a rigorous and systematic way is vital to increasing the credibility of qualitative research in the eyes of quantitative researchers, policy makers and other consumers of research. In order to enhance validity, it is now generally recognised that qualitative research should include strategies such as transparency, triangulation and respondent validation (Elliott, Fischer and Rennie 1999; Mays and Pope 1996). In addition, several specialist computer packages now exist to aid the process of qualitative data analysis (Weitzman and Miles 1995).

Any discussion of quantitative and qualitative forms of research should consider the philosophical differences between these traditions. There is only space within this chapter to discuss these paradigmatic issues briefly, and again we acknowledge that this division into two broad camps is a simplification, and that within each one a diversity of theoretical and philosophical positions exists. Quantitative forms of research are generally associated with a natural science model in which it is assumed that human behaviour is measurable and amenable to the deductive principles of positivism (Bryman 1988). These propose that the best way to accumulate knowledge is to generate hypotheses from scientific theories and to test these hypotheses empirically. There is an assumption of realism – that what is being studied has a fixed reality that can be observed in an objective way. In comparison, qualitative research is usually based on a model that assumes the value-laden nature of all research and recognises the researchers' role in this process. Much (but not all) qualitative research is located within a constructionist paradigm that views the phenomena it studies as constructed by social, cultural and interpersonal processes such as language use, tradition and social practices. The implication of this is that research cannot claim to be an objective process as the researcher's theoretical stance and practical interventions shape the very thing he/she is studying. For example, viewing the problems of clients as 'personality disorders' or 'long-standing inter-personal problems' imply different approaches to their study and treatment. A further implication is a broader view of what is classed as data that includes the researchers' own impressions, feelings and reactions in the research situation. Research becomes a process in which the researcher is involved as a socially situated being and requires not only technical but reflexive and interpersonal skills.

Just how important are these philosophical and epistemological differences? This is an issue of continual debate within the social sciences. There are those who believe that differences in assumptions about knowledge and the nature of reality render the two types of research and their findings incompatible. As researchers working on pragmatic problems in the field of mental health, we do not subscribe to this view, and believe that integration of quantitative and qualitative forms of research is not only possible, but often fruitful. Of course philosophical standpoints are important, and it is essential that both researchers and consumers of research are aware of these and their implications for how research is conducted and its findings evaluated. But the fact that qualitative and quantitative forms of research have different strengths (and weaknesses) in answering various clinically relevant questions can only be beneficial to our understanding of such a vast and complex area as mental health problems and their treatment in therapeutic community contexts (Arnkoff *et al.* 1996; Sackett and Wennberg 1997). For example, while quantitative studies may tell us about the outcome of therapeutic community treatment, qualitative research is able to inform our understanding of the processes involved and what this feels like for those who experience it. There are also situations in which quantitative and qualitative approaches can be usefully integrated within the same study. For example, qualitative methods may provide an initial exploration of an area and point to specific key variables whose relationship can then be investigated using more focused quantitative methods. In other situations, the results of quantitative research may suggest a need for more in-depth explorations using qualitative methods.

Thus, in conclusion we would argue that the existence of a broad range of theoretical approaches and related methodological strategies can only be advantageous in providing a diversity of perspectives from which to tackle the research questions that arise from and are relevant to good quality therapeutic community treatment. We have argued in this chapter that as social systems integrating individual and collective factors and processes, therapeutic communities offer scope for research in psychological and sociological domains as well as from perspectives that recognise the inseparability of the individual and the social. We hope that the range of research studies presented in this volume will demonstrate the benefits of this diversity.

CHAPTER 2

Therapeutic Community Research

An Overview and Meta-Analysis

Jan Lees, Nick Manning and Barbara Rawlings

Introduction

In this chapter we will firstly outline the history and current state of therapeutic community research. We will then locate the undertaking of a systematic litera-ture review of therapeutic community effectiveness within this context. We will describe the current methodology used in medical research for systematic litera-ture reviews, describe how the authors of this chapter applied this methodology to a review of the literature on therapeutic communities, discuss some of the findings of this systematic review and reflect on the usefulness of the systematic literature review for therapeutic community research. We will then draw out some implications for future therapeutic community research.

The historical antecedents

The literature on modern therapeutic communities generally refers either to the democratic psychiatric settings, which began in Britain during the Second World War, or to the hierarchical, concept-based houses which began in the USA in the late 1950s. The early literature on the British communities is descriptive rather than analytic, penned by the practitioners themselves who wanted to describe and explain their radical new approach to the treatment of mental illness and be-havioural upset. Thus, in *Social Psychiatry* (1952), Maxwell Jones, the psychiatrist in charge of the Belmont Hospital Industrial Neurosis Unit, describes the innova-tive work done there in treating and resettling a sample of long-term unemployed men. Bion, who, together with Rickman, was developing a similar approach for treating unruly military personnel, went on to describe these 'Northfield Experiments' in his book *Experiences in Groups* (1960). Foulkes, a psychiatrist who joined the hospital after Bion had left, described the creation of a therapeutic community at Northfield in *Introduction to Group Analytic Psychotherapy* (1948). Thomas Main, who worked with Foulkes and later became the director of the Cassel Hospital, described this early Northfield work in 'The Hospital as a Therapeutic Institution' (1946). (See also Harrison 2000 for a more detailed exploration of these experiments and the work of Bion and Rickman.)

Thus, the first written material on therapeutic communities was produced by the practitioners themselves. This had two effects. In the first place, the writers were extremely close to the work of the organisations they were describing. Indeed, they themselves had largely instigated the changes they were writing about. Thus it was difficult for them to stand back and look at therapeutic communities 'disinterestedly'. In the second place, the books and papers they wrote were mainly directed to their own interests – bringing about change in people through the implementation of psychodynamic means. They were writing from their own particular professional viewpoint as trained psychiatrists and psychoanalysts, who wanted to improve the quality of treatment (and not, for example, as outside commentators who might reserve their judgement on the activities of mental health professionals). These initial descriptive accounts, written to open up debate about mental health practice, and take new ideas to a wider audience, cannot be considered rigorous reviews of therapeutic communities.

In the USA, a different type of organisation was emerging, also called a 'therapeutic community'. This was Synanon, the first 'concept house', begun by a reformed alcoholic, Charles Dederich, and aimed at the treatment of drug addicts. Dederich, however, did not write the first book about Synanon. This task fell to a sociologist, Yablonsky, who had inherited a new American interest in generating detailed descriptions of small settings. This in turn had developed out of the methods used by the early anthropologists, who would often spend years with 'their tribe', learning about their language and customs. Yablonsky was, like these earlier anthropologists, an outsider to his subject area. To carry out his work, he went to Synanon and spent an extended period of time there, listening, watching, asking questions and recording the things that he saw and heard. His book *Synanon: The Tunnel Back* (1965) is a descriptive account of Synanon, written not by a practitioner, but by an outsider. Yablonsky's interest was not primarily in helping drug addicts, but in trying to understand what was going on in this organisation, and how it helped drug users to recover. Later, when Daytop Village was established in New York by ex-members of Synanon, a similar research study was carried out there (Sugarman 1974).

In Britain, meanwhile, an American anthropologist named Rapoport had been hired to carry out a study of the Belmont Hospital (now renamed Henderson Hospital, and still under the directorship of Maxwell Jones). His report *Community as Doctor* (1960) provided the first 'outsider' view of a democratic style therapeutic community. It was not wholly well received by Maxwell Jones, who argued that Rapoport, as an outsider, had not fully understood all the nuances of therapeutic community life, and had thus misrepresented and misjudged some aspects of their activities. However, Jones did also comment later that 'for me to discover the discrepancy between what I thought I was doing as a leader, and what trained observers saw me doing was frequently a painful – but almost invariably a rich – learning experience' (Jones 1968). The differences between Maxwell Jones and Robert Rapoport stand as a good example of the differences that can arise between a committed staff group on the one hand, and an 'objective' observer on the other. For the staff, any 'disinterested' account may be interpreted as critical, and the researcher who attempts to write such an account may be viewed as disloyal and regarded with suspicion. The value of an outsider account, however, is that other outsiders will see it as more impartial than an insider account. (See also Chapter 9 of this volume for a discussion of similar issues in relation to the role of therapeutic community researchers.) Rapoport subsequently analysed the way in which his book was at first rejected by colleagues at Henderson Hospital, but subsequently accepted (Rapoport and Manning 1976). Indeed, Rapoport's book has since become recognised as a seminal text on therapeutic communities. Some of its classifications, for example the 'four pillars' – democratisation, permissiveness, confrontation and communalism – have worked their way back into therapeutic community practice as criteria to be achieved and standards to maintain, and more recently have been reworked and updated to fit in with contemporary therapeutic community practice (Haigh 1999).

Such descriptive work was largely aimed at getting down on paper some kind of formal outline of what these therapeutic communities were all about. They were mostly conducted and written as single case studies, although sometimes these were then compared with others, in an attempt to further refine what was distinctive about these places. For example, Bloor, McKeganey and Fonkert (1988) compared eight organisations that called themselves therapeutic communities in order to ascertain what kind of treatment could be considered 'therapeutic community treatment'. However, at the same time as this descriptive work was flourishing, a different kind of evaluative research was taking off, particularly in the USA. This research was focused primarily not on what was being done, but on whether it worked, and whether it worked any better than other forms of treatment. In the early 1970s, George De Leon began what was to become a long series of evaluations of therapeutic community treatment for drug abusers at Phoenix House, New York, beginning with evaluations of in-treatment changes and going on to studies of relapse and offending rates for people who had been through the treatment (see e.g. De Leon 1973, 1994b). Although similar studies were being carried out in the UK at hierarchical therapeutic communities (Ogbourne and Melotte 1977; Wilson and Mandelbrote 1978), the trend for such work there did not continue. In the USA, however, evaluation research became central to the therapeutic community movement in the community (De Leon 1994b) and in prisons (Wexler 1997). The positive results demonstrated through these evaluation studies have played a large part in the development of the therapeutic community into a major player in the drug treatment field.

In Britain, research into therapeutic communities has remained fairly patchy and sporadic, and has relied upon the ability of researchers to find outside research funds or on members of staff to carry out small-scale studies (see Chapter 1). Henderson Hospital is an exception, and has a long history of encouraging research and employing researchers who have produced a steady stream of work since 1980 (Warren and Dolan 2001). The evaluative work on the effectiveness of therapeutic community treatment for personality disorder in the UK largely stems from work done at Henderson Hospital and HMP Grendon. There has been a long history of research at HMP Grendon, the therapeutic community prison in Berkshire. This research has been largely carried out by members of the psychology department in the prison, and has shown that positive changes occur during treatment (Newton 1997) and that reconviction rates for Grendon men are lower than might be anticipated (Cullen 1994; Marshall 1997). (See Shine 2000 for a compilation of the research findings from Grendon.) More recently, the Cassel Hospital has also begun to produce evaluative research, which shows encouraging results for their more psychoanalytically oriented approach to therapeutic community treatment (Chiesa and Fonagy 2000; Chiesa, Iacoponi and Morris 1996).

The interest in research then has moved through a series of stages, beginning with the early informative and persuasive accounts of the therapeutic community pioneers, through the qualitative, ethnographic accounts of the early outside researchers, and into the quantitative, evaluative studies of more recent times. Therapeutic community research has become more sophisticated in terms of research designs and methodologies, and our understanding of the complexity of the issues is greater. The questions 'does it work?' and 'who does it work for?' have become increasingly more urgent as funding has become more and more tied to results. The question 'how does it work?' is still largely unanswered, since it is difficult to tease out the mechanisms at work inside such a complex and multi-faceted organism as a therapeutic community. A current study by the Association of Therapeutic Communities, and funded by the National Lottery Charities Board, is partially directed at this latter question, as well as the former two. It involves a national comparative study of the effectiveness of democratic therapeutic communities in treating people with personality disorders (see Chapter 4 for further details).

The final type of research to acknowledge here, which has been going on all along, and is likely to continue whether it is funded or not, is 'practitioner research'. This work is largely devoted to understanding what is going on at the basic, day-to-day community level and directed towards informing others of what communities are doing and improving the quality of therapeutic community treatment itself (see, for example, Black 1999 and Coombe 1995). A more detailed description of therapeutic community research can be found in Lees (1999).

Methodological antecedents

Initial research on therapeutic communities was predominantly descriptive, and therapeutic communities, particularly the democratic therapeutic communities in Britain, were slow to adopt more rigorous evaluative approaches to their work. However, increasingly in recent years, all therapeutic communities have come to realise that a strong evidence base for their practice is essential for their economic and therefore literal survival. With the NHS reforms that led to the purchaser–provider split in the mid-1990s, therapeutic communities were made painfully aware of their need for an evidence base. The prevailing opinions, particularly among purchasers, were that therapeutic community treatment is expensive, and that there was no evidence that therapeutic communities worked and no evidence that they were more effective than other treatments. This made purchasers reluctant to buy therapeutic communities' services for clients, and also made providers less willing to consider continuing to provide therapeutic community services, and certainly less willing to set up new provision. Indeed, many therapeutic communities failed to survive in the 1980s and the early 1990s, because of this lack of empirically appropriate evidence that therapeutic communities work, or indeed have any effect at all. This position was exacerbated by the publication of Report 67 in 1997 (Cornah, Stein and Stevens 1997). This report was a publication from the Wessex Institute for Health Research and Development, and funded by the Research and Development Directorate of the National Health Service (NHS) Executive South and West. It is described as an expert technical report on the 'therapeutic community method of treatment for borderline personality disorder'. Despite being limited to borderline personality disorders, and only including a small number of studies, it became widely cited and formed the basis of many NHS authorities' decisions not to buy therapeutic community treatment for their patients.

Within the research field, the medical model for the hierarchy of quality of research evidence has prevailed – with, initially, the randomised controlled trial (RCT) being seen as the most rigorous way of obtaining hard evidence of effectiveness. Subsequently, with the establishment of the NHS Centre for Reviews and Dissemination (CRD) at the University of York, and the Cochrane Centre at Oxford, meta-analyses were viewed as the apex of research and evidence-based practice. Indeed, the NHS hierarchy of evidence, as stated in the *National Service Framework for Mental Health*, is:

- *Type I evidence* – at least one good systematic review, including at least one RCT

- *Type II evidence* – at least one good RCT

- *Type III evidence* – at least one well-designed intervention study without randomisation

- *Type IV evidence* – at least one well-designed observational study

- *Type V evidence* – expert opinion, including the opinion of service users and carers. (NHS Executive 1999).

The generally held opinion, typified for example in Report 67 (Cornah, Stein and Stevens 1997), had been that therapeutic communities had at best level 3, but mostly level 4 type evidence. There have been criticisms both of the predominance of the medical model in research, and of the view of the RCT as the 'gold standard' for research. (For discussion of these issues, see Chapter 6 in this book; Seligman 1995; and Evans, Carlyle and Dolan 1996.)

NHS Centre for Reviews and Dissemination – Systematic literature review

It was within this research context for therapeutic communities that the Department of Health, through what was then the High Security Psychiatric Services Commissioning Board, commissioned a review of therapeutic community effectiveness. This review focused primarily on treatment for people with personality disorders in secure and non-secure settings, but came to have a much wider and more general remit, including an overview of an extensive range of types of therapeutic communities and their clients.

The three authors of this chapter undertook this systematic literature review in 1997–98, covering relevant literature up to 1997 (Lees, Manning and Rawlings 1999). Here, we will describe briefly the required methodology for undertaking a systematic literature review for the CRD, the ways in which we undertook our review of research on the effectiveness of treatment in therapeutic communities, and some of our major findings. We will outline the current position for therapeutic community research, and its methodologies, and suggest ways to optimise future research on therapeutic communities.

Systematic reviews are a scientific tool that provide a way of ordering, synthesising, summarising and evaluating the research evidence available in any field which might otherwise be unmanageable in terms of quantity, results and implications. They are usually designed to inform decisions about the organisation and delivery of health care. Systematic reviews differ from other types of literature review in that:

they adhere to a strict scientific design in order to make them more comprehensive, to minimise the chance of bias, and so ensure their reliability. Rather than reflecting the views of the authors or being based on only a (possibly biased) selection of the published literature, they contain a comprehensive summary of the available evidence. (CRD 1996)

When conducting a systematic review under the auspices of the CRD, guidelines are provided for use as a framework for carrying out a review – these are contained in the above report, and are summarised in Appendix 1. As will be clear from the above, what is most important is that the review is undertaken in a rigorous or systematic way; that it is carried out in as objective a way as possible; and that all decisions, assessments and evaluations are clearly enumerated in such a way that the whole process, and the findings, are easily and consistently replicable by others.

We were commissioned to undertake a systematic international literature review of the effectiveness of therapeutic community treatment in secure and non-secure, psychiatric and other settings, for people with personality disorders and mentally disordered offenders. Although the original bid called for a review of the findings for the democratic therapeutic community, which are mainly found in the British literature, this review also includes the relevant post-treatment and in-treatment outcome studies for the effectiveness of hierarchical, or concept-based therapeutic communities, usually for substance abusers, and particularly those in secure settings (although the non-secure concept-based outcome literature is also summarised in this review). Hierarchical therapeutic communities were included because of their powerful presence in the research literature on therapeutic community effectiveness in general, but particularly in the USA, Canada and other parts of the world.

The review was conducted in accordance with the CRD guidelines, as outlined above, in an explicit and structured manner, with clearly stated research objectives, and protocols guiding the work and criteria for describing the relevance and quality of identified research. Results of the literature review are presented in both narrative, qualitative form, and in the form of a meta-analysis, using summary odds ratios. The initial assumptions were that we would probably not find many studies overall of sufficient quality for inclusion in the review, and that this review would have to be in narrative form only, because it was unlikely that we would find sufficient numbers of studies of sufficient quality data for a meta-analysis. In the event, these assumptions proved incorrect and details of the meta-analysis conducted are included below. The narrative findings are extensive, the full report amounting to over two hundred pages, and cannot be adequately summarised here (see Lees *et al.* 1999 for the full details).

The review concentrates on the research literature on the effectiveness of therapeutic communities, and the main part of the review concentrates on post-treatment outcome studies of secure and non-secure democratic therapeutic communities for people with personality disorders and mentally disordered offenders. In addition, the review enumerates and assesses some evaluative studies on in-treatment outcome in secure and non-secure democratic therapeutic communities. The review also outlines briefly an extensive outcome literature on democratic therapeutic communities for client groups other than those with personality disorders, or mentally disordered offenders.

Finally, the review also contains a large descriptive section, looking at the overall background and context of therapeutic communities; the issues around defining what is a therapeutic community; the types of therapeutic communities; how therapeutic community philosophies have been modified to fit the needs of particular groups of clients, or the requirements of factors like security; and where therapeutic communities are, and have been, located internationally. In accordance with the original bid call, the review also includes a descriptive section on identifying the settings for therapeutic communities, their regimes, and the ways in which they define themselves; the populations of the communities; details of their standards, standards monitoring and outcome indicators; the catchment areas, selection criteria and links and integration with other services; the types of care procedures present in the therapeutic process, and any evidence about their effectiveness; what procedures are used to support the regime and any evidence of their effectiveness; and the roles of different disciplines, and their support structure, with reference to multi-disciplinary working.

What we found

The search of the published literature began with the Cochrane Library databases, to ensure no other similar review was being undertaken. A long historical perspective of the literature was taken, with no fixed start date, although most of the research and effectiveness literature was written after the Second World War, in the period 1946–1997. Citation searches were undertaken of a number of books on therapeutic communities, published between 1974 and 1997, and of the journals the *International Journal of Therapeutic Communities* and *Therapeutic Communities*. Inevitably, electronic database searches constituted the main source of information for this, as any, systematic review. Twenty-six databases were selected for inclusion in the review, and were searched using pre-designed search strategies, based on a pre-selected list of keywords (itemised in the review). It was also necessary to hand-search the widest possible range of journals (both English- and foreign-language); to search other relevant publications, and reference and compilation works; to visit a number of key sites (libraries and active therapeutic communities); and to perform Internet searches of the World Wide Web.

In addition to the published research literature, we targeted the 'grey literature'; identified and wrote to as many therapeutic communities nationally and internationally as we could find; wrote to known writers and workers in the field, asking for any published or unpublished research they might have and for information about their therapeutic community; and surveyed, by post and/or visit, a sample of secure and non-secure democratic therapeutic communities, and the three special hospitals – Broadmoor, Rampton and Ashworth.

All these searches turned up 8160 book, conference and journal article references, with very little of it turning up as 'grey literature'. Database searches were undoubtedly the most fruitful in terms of both relevance and volume of material for our review. However, it is important to note here that, while considerable effort was made to include foreign-language references in the review, it was not always easy to locate or gain access to these, and the preference of the majority of databases for English-language journals and a bias towards North American scholarship are factors recognised by researchers in the field of bibliometric analysis (Artus 1996; Seglen 1997). The value of journal hand-searches was negligible and its main value lay in the information hand-searching provided about the main researchers and writers in the field for the subsequent mailshot. The usefulness may have been compounded by the number of incomplete series and dearth of foreign-language journals held at institutions in the UK, and the difficulty in obtaining rarer items. Visits to key library sites did not yield much additional information. Although World Wide Web searches are now an established part of any literature review, they cannot, strictly speaking, be described as 'systematic': the quality of material on the Web is very variable, with no quality control (although a few important items were collected for our review). In addition, search engines are not particularly consistent or accurate between each other, individually or over time and, while many search engines claim to allow multi-lingual searching, in practice they often do not. Therefore their usefulness is limited at present. Finally, we sent out 296 letters internationally and got 64 replies, of which 10 produced material or references that were of direct use to our research project, but none of them related to literature or therapeutic communities that we did not eventually access through our other searches. Although we did get a lot of interesting peripheral material, we would not recommend future researchers undertake this task, and we think it is unlikely that there is a great deal of unpublished therapeutic community treatment outcome studies to be accessed.

Interestingly, most references retrieved for the review are from the UK and USA, and most therapeutic communities identified are in the UK and USA. However, if we look at the types of therapeutic community, while the UK has produced more articles about the democratic therapeutic community than the USA and has roughly the same number of therapeutic communities referred to, when we look at the concept therapeutic community, the USA dominates the field in terms of the number of articles and the number of therapeutic communities referred to. However, the number of concept articles is also dominated by both a few concept therapeutic communities, such as 'Stay 'n' out' and CREST (prison therapeutic communities), and by a few authors, such as De Leon, Wexler, Inciardi and Condelli.

These 8160 retrieved references were then examined by two of us working independently and according to our pre-determined inclusion/exclusion criteria. The inclusion criteria for the review were based both on the type of study design and on whether or not the study was evaluative, with an emphasis on post-treatment outcome studies (Lees *et al.* 1999, pp.34–40). We had set an upper limit of 300 as workable, but in fact this level of sorting actually produced 294 references for the final review.

These 294 articles/books were scanned to ensure they were of sufficient quality to include in the final report, and/or that they included information that was required by the data extraction sheets. Those articles or books which provided research information on the post-treatment or in-treatment outcome of therapeutic community treatment in secure or non-secure democratic therapeutic community settings for people with personality disorders or mentally disordered offenders were set aside for more in-depth analysis, together with those for secure concept-based therapeutic communities. These latter came to 113, of which 18 are review articles. The final number of studies included is less than the number of articles found, because some articles relate to different aspects of the same study. The spread of these studies over post-treatment and in-treatment outcome studies in secure and non-secure democratic and concept-based therapeutic communities is outlined in Lees *et al.* 1999, p.40.

We then concentrated on the post-treatment outcome findings, and found there were 10 RCT studies, 10 cross-institutional, cross-treatment or comparative studies, and a further 32 using some kind of control or comparison group. We took the latter as the minimum level of rigour that is acceptable, which left us with a total of 52 acceptable studies, all of which are discussed in some detail in the review. Of these 52, 41 relate to democratic therapeutic communities and 11 to concept-based therapeutic communities.

Although many of the findings are presented in narrative form, we also conducted a systematic meta-analysis of some of the studies, using odds ratios. Because of the quality of data presented and the quality of the analyses of these data in the studies, we were only able to meta-analyse 29 studies in total, dated between 1960 and 1998, and including eight of the RCTs. Where there was a choice of outcome measures and control groups, emphasis was placed on conservative criteria, such as reconviction rates rather than psychological improvements, and on non-treated controls. The meta-analysis is discussed in more detail below.

There were also many more single case studies, focusing on describing and evaluating single therapeutic community treatment regimes, but without control or comparison groups, and these are described in detail in the report. However, they tend to be idiosyncratic in terms of research methods, type of regime, client population and outcome measures used. More uniformity of research design across individual therapeutic communities would produce more rigorous and valid outcome findings and, therefore, evaluations of effectiveness.

Meta-analysis

The 29 studies included in the meta-analysis are listed in Appendix 2. The standard way to combine these studies into a summary measure of the effectiveness of the treatment (the therapeutic community, in this case) is slightly more complex than simply adding up the number of studies 'for and against'. The reason for this is that the importance of each study varies, depending on: the size of each sample; the confidence intervals around each result; the size and direction of the result and, most important, the extent to which there is systematic variation between the studies as a group – the 'heterogeneity' of the whole collection of studies being considered. These factors are systematically taken into account by calculating the summary odds ratio of the group, and running a number of tests ('meta-regressions') to look for and account for any heterogeneity in the whole group. The summary odds ratio can be of two types – 'fixed' or 'random' effects – depending on the assumptions made about the representativeness of the study samples to the overall population.

The log odds ratio for each study is calculated very simply by constructing a two-by-two table comparing the numbers of those with a successful outcome, and the rest, in the separate treatment and control groups in the study. A summary odds ratio combines the results of the whole group taking into account the variations in sample size, effects, and so on. This was calculated and the variance estimated for each of the 29 studies, using the Woolf method (the sum of the reciprocals of the cell counts – see Kahn and Sempos 1989). For one study there was an observed zero, and 0.5 was added to each cell before performing the calculations.

Figure 2.1 shows a 'forest plot' of the study effects – each study is identified by the number listed in the appendix. Each horizontal line represents the results of one trial – the shorter the line, the more certain the result; with the position of the black square indicating the odds ratio – the bigger the square, the more weight is given to the study, taking into account sample size, range of confidence intervals, etc.; the bottom diamond represents their combined results expressed in a summary odds ratio. The vertical line indicates the position around which the horizontal lines would cluster if the two treatments compared in the trials had similar effects; if a horizontal line touches the vertical line, it means that that particular trial found no clear difference between the treatments. The position of the diamond to the left of the vertical line indicates that the treatment studied is beneficial. Horizontal lines or a diamond to the right of the line would show that the treatment did more harm than good. The overall summary log odds ratio is

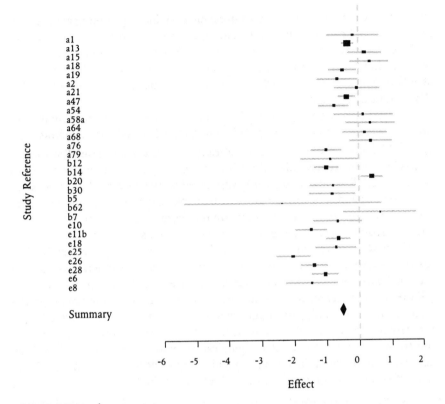

Figure 2.1 Forest plot

-0.512 (95% ci -0.598 to 0.426), which indicates a strong positive effect for therapeutic community treatment.

Meta-regressions

Two key measures of the quality of any meta-analysis are: the extent to which the variation between the study results could be accounted for by factors other than the variable effectiveness of the treatment under study; and whether there is evidence that only 'successful' results have been published – implying that there might be a hidden set of 'unsuccessful' studies that were unpublished, but that if included might reduce the overall positive outcome. If there is large variation that cannot be accounted for, the implication is that the studies are too dissimilar to be combined – for example, they may not be using the same treatment method. In this particular case, there is some possibility of this, since therapeutic community treatment is multi-dimensional and complex, and may vary from one setting or time period to another. This is conventionally examined by looking at the extent and sources of heterogeneity (i.e. variation) between the studies. We can test for both heterogeneity and publication bias through 'meta-regression'. (Where some of the technical terms in the following discussion are obscure, please refer to a standard text on statistical analysis – we have not been able to include such a detailed introduction here.)

A 'fixed effects' analysis of the log odds ratios, which does not assume they are representative of any wider population, revealed considerable heterogeneity ($\chi^2 = 170.2$ with 28 df), which is significant at any reasonable level. Rather than simply trying to accommodate this extra variance with a 'random effects' model we suspected that the heterogeneity was caused by two factors: the combination of democratic and concept therapeutic communities in the group, and the age of the studies – spread across 40 years. We therefore tried to account for it with various predictor variables in a set of 'meta-regressions'.

We used the following predictor variables: whether the study was an RCT or not (two levels); whether the therapeutic community was a democratic or concept type, and if democratic, whether it was in a secure environment (e.g. prison) or not (all the concept therapeutic communities were in a secure environment) (thus a factor with three levels); year of publication (as a variate – in years since 1960, as the earliest study was in 1960); and the study precision (as a variate – measured by the standard error – to check for publication bias). Details of the modelling approach can be found in Thompson and Sharp (1999). We present a series of fixed effects meta-regressions using each predictor singly:

- Whether the study was an RCT or not accounted for relatively little of the heterogeneity, $\chi^2 = 0.74$ with 1 df.

- The therapeutic community type (democratic, concept, secure) accounted for much of the observed heterogeneity. Overall $\chi^2 = 70.2$ with 2 df. The effect sizes are shown in Table 2.1, indicating that while non-secure therapeutic communities are slightly more effective than secure therapeutic communities, the key difference is that concept therapeutic communities are markedly more effective in this collection of studies than democratic therapeutic communities.

Table 2.1 Effect sizes from model with therapeutic community type

Effect	Log odds	se
Intercept	-0.29	0.057
Secure, democratic	Reference category	
Non-secure, democratic	-0.04	0.122
Concept	-0.86	0.106

- The year of publication also accounted for much of the heterogeneity, $\chi^2 = 42.6$ with 1 df. It is of course confounded with therapeutic community type, since the concept therapeutic community studies were in general published later than the democratic therapeutic community studies. The effect sizes are shown in Table 2.2, indicating that later studies have a stronger effect size by about 0.03 per year.

Table 2.2 Effect sizes from model with year of publication

Effect	Log odds	se
Intercept	0.30	0.132
Year of publication (per year)	-0.03	0.004

- Figure 2.2 shows a 'funnel plot' of the effect sizes, based on Egger *et al.* 1997. If there were any publication bias, whereby negative outcomes had not been written up for publication, we would look for an uneven pattern, or gap, to the right-hand side of the vertical dotted line, where those studies were 'missing'. Visually there do not seem to be any such gaps, and formal analysis using the standard error as a predictor (which is equivalent to the Egger method) showed that there was little evidence of publication bias, overall $\chi^2 = 1.52$ with 1 df.

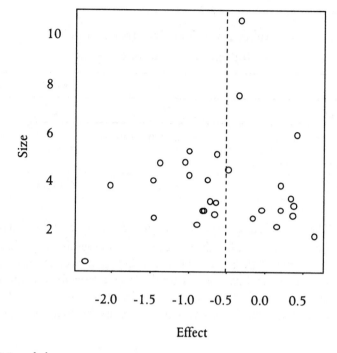

Figure 2.2 Funnel plot

In conclusion, the sources of heterogeneity are thus largely accounted for by the differences between types of therapeutic community, with concept-based studies having been generally reported in recent years. Having an explicable account of this heterogeneity allows us to conclude more confidently that the overall summary odds ratio generated by this set of studies does provide evidence for the effectiveness of therapeutic community treatment for personality disordered patients. This is Type I evidence, according to the *National Service Framework for Mental Health* – at least one good systematic review, including at least one RCT.

Discussion

Although painstaking, and occasionally tedious, systematic literature reviews such as this one provide very useful information on an overview of therapeutic communities and their literature and research, and are respected as a research tool, particularly within the NHS. The work involved in a systematic review of this kind is considerable. The number of potential sources of material, and the number of possible studies, was amplified by the wide scope of the review, since it included not merely high quality RCTs but also the many descriptive studies that have been published over the years. This inevitably delayed the speed at which we could sift through and summarise the material, but given the strict rules to which reviews of this kind must adhere, and the specific inclusion and exclusion criteria, there was no alternative but to plough through to the end.

Nevertheless, this process ensures the integrity of the final result and has made a very significant contribution to the field. We do not feel that any material, including 'grey literature' and unpublished work, exists that we have not found. It has encouraged us to work in a disciplined and systematic way, which any subsequent researcher would be able to replicate, or to supplement.

An interesting aspect of the way in which the review was commissioned was the assumption that there were very few, if any, high quality comparison studies or RCTs to find. The reasons for this widespread and erroneous assumption in the medical and psychiatric research community are explored in Chapter 1. In the event, the broad remit to include descriptive studies probably would not have been given if it were suspected that there were so many high quality research studies to include.

In terms of the general scope of the literature, we found several trends. Although there were studies from more than 30 countries, the best evaluations have come out of the USA in recent years, many of which are focused on concept therapeutic communities. Democratic therapeutic communities are more common in Europe, where the most useful studies are typically older than those in the USA. The target treatment populations are addicts in the USA and those with personality disorders in Europe. Personality disorder itself is a rapidly expanding psychiatric and forensic category, on the back of which there is now a resurgence of interest in and government funding for therapeutic communities in the UK.

Several methodological conclusions arise out of the review. The difficulties of controlled trials reported in the literature include treatment complexity, treatment dosage and treatment integrity, population selection, dropouts, effects decay and diagnostic shifts. Fundamentally, the nature of the treatment and the nature of the disorder need to be clearly understood and articulated. Evaluating the effectiveness of therapeutic communities, towards the establishment of which this review was primarily aimed, depends crucially on a clear understanding of what the therapeutic community is, the setting (whether secure or non-secure) in which it is delivered, and at which patients it is aimed. These elements are all evidently contestable, both within a largely sympathetic literature and within a smaller, hostile literature.

The definition of 'personality disorder' has changed over time. British mental health law has been ambivalent about psychopaths. Both the 1959 and 1983 Acts separate psychopathy from other conditions, and define it behaviourally, while holding a pessimistic view of treatment interventions. Gunderson (1994, p.12) suggests that 'personality disorder is a diagnosis whose construct (i.e. its meaning) has grown rapidly and changed dramatically during the past 25 years'.

Recent official reports on work in this area have reflected these difficulties. For example, the Reed *Report on Psychopathic Disorder* (DoH/HO 1994, p.34) states that, 'the diverse meanings attached to psychopathic disorder often undermined the effectiveness of evaluation of treatment'. Analyses of the way in which such definitions, especially in relation to personality disorder, have changed are presented in Manning (2000, 2002). Conceptual expansion makes judgements about research reports difficult, especially if they are more than about 15 years old. Moreover, patients accepted for therapeutic community treatment are normally both self-selected (in terms of application to join) and community-selected (in terms of the whole community, not just staff or consultants). This means there is no independent decision that can guarantee referral and acceptance, and consequently randomisation is difficult to set up and sustain.

The definition of therapeutic communities has also been difficult. There are two main types of therapeutic community: democratic and concept-based/hierarchical. For some writers these are variations on a basically common theme (Sugarman 1974), one dealing with deeper intrapsychic change and the other with initial behavioural control; for others they have nothing in common but the name (Glaser 1983). They have emerged from quite separate origins. In general the intensity, or dosage, of treatment is commonly recognised in the literature by differentiating between therapeutic community approaches and the therapeutic community proper. The former refers to a therapeutic approach across whole hospitals, whereas the latter refers to specialised therapeutic communities dealing with a defined population. In addition, democratic-type therapeutic communities developed in prisons or secure settings are inevitably influenced by the requirements of prison regulations concerning security and control.

Moreover, since one of the criteria identified above for the definition of a therapeutic community is that of self-identity, there is a difficulty over treatment integrity – how do we know that the self-identity of a particular programme is not erroneous? Or what happens when therapeutic communities, as they have been known to do, go through periods of disruption or sluggishness? At what point is the treatment itself compromised? This is a point raised in connection with the Clarke and Cornish (1972) study of Kingswood – it was not clear how 'pure' the therapeutic community house was, and thus how representative of a therapeutic community treatment modality.

Treatment in therapeutic communities takes time – typically around six to nine months. This heightens the possibility that patients will leave prematurely. In fact, dropouts from therapeutic community treatments are commonplace. Dropouts from research studies are also a difficulty. The US literature on addiction therapeutic communities contains numerous articles on such 'splittees'. In treatment terms, there is a clear association between in-treatment improvement and length of stay (Nieminen 1996), and hence a concern – almost an obsession – with retaining patients in the programme. In research, as we have mentioned, sustaining comparable dosage is an essential prerequisite for evaluation, which can be seriously compromised by dropouts.

Even if the patients are randomised, and treatment is successfully delivered and measured, there remains the problem of the point at which improvement should be measured. On the one hand, in penal research it has been possible to follow up failures over quite long periods of time through the use of criminal records; for example, for five years or more. On the other hand, many studies have been content to look at change while still in treatment, at the end of treatment, or at a year post-treatment. Clearly, given the likely effects of post-treatment experiences and effects, effects that are sustained over long periods may be more convincing even if those effects are smaller than larger effects early on which are not sustained. The solution to this problem was fairly obviously felt to be the measurement of intermediate change during and soon after treatment, and the use of cross-institutional designs (see below) to capture changes during treatment.

Although the difficulties of undertaking RCTs are widely appreciated, there is still a case for trying to undertake them for democratic therapeutic community treatment in the UK, since the most recent RCTs have been undertaken in the USA on concept therapeutic communities. The RCT is undoubtedly a powerful design, where appropriate, and has in many respects become the gold standard for evidence-based medicine (see Chapter 6 for a detailed review). The alternative, as Clarke and Cornish (1972) argued, is a large-scale cross-institutional study of therapeutic communities in the field. Such a study is now ongoing in the UK. Funded by the Lottery for four years, 1999–2003, it recruited 21 therapeutic communities treating personality disorders. This sample included therapeutic communities in secure and non-secure settings (prisons, special hospitals, NHS units and charitable sector communities) and residential and day therapeutic communities. Although most of these were democratic therapeutic communities, there were also two concept-based therapeutic communities, one secure, one non-secure, for comparative purposes, and one community also using dialectical behaviour therapy, which is often counterposed as more effective than therapeutic community treatment for this client group, and will again provide useful additional data.

Conclusions

The systematic review did furnish a substantial number of studies of sufficient quality to undertake a meta-analysis. This analysis, taking careful account of sources of heterogeneity and possible publication bias, shows a clear and positive treatment effect for therapeutic communities.

In the past, therapeutic communities have been ambivalent about the need for research, and about its usefulness; there have also been concerns about the effect of research and researchers on the day-to-day functioning and effectiveness of

the therapeutic community, discussed in Chapters 9 and 10. Our systematic literature review led us to conclude that therapeutic communities have not produced
the level or quality of research literature that we might have expected, given the
length of time they have been in existence and the quality of staff we know exists
and has existed in therapeutic communities. This may be partly due to a lack of
emphasis placed on research in the early days of therapeutic community development, and more recently to a lack of resources, in terms of finance, staff and
adequate research methodologies, designs and instruments.

However, these attitudes have changed in recent years. The medical model of
research has come to dominate this field of activity, not only because many therapeutic communities are located within the National Health Service, but also
because the medical research emphasis on evidence-based practice, in a time of
scarce resources and funding, has made it imperative for all treatments to prove
their effectiveness and efficiency in order to survive. This has meant that
evaluative research has come to take primary importance. It is clear that we need
more, and more good-quality and comparative, research on therapeutic communities, in order to counter the charge that there is not a proven case that therapeutic communities are effective, and that they are expensive. There is clinical
evidence that therapeutic communities produce changes in people's mental
health and functioning, but this needs to be complemented by good quality qualitative and quantitative research studies.

Our systematic review concluded that future research on the effectiveness of
therapeutic communities should include further RCTs. However, these have to
overcome the difficulties posed by therapeutic communities controlling their
own intake, and the multi-dimensional and volatile nature of the treatment intervention. It should also include more complex, cross-institutional studies in the
field, together with further cost-offset studies to complement those few already
developed.

SECTION II

Context and Methodologies

CHAPTER 3

The Research Context in the National Health Service

Frank Margison

Introduction

Therapeutic communities pose particular problems for evaluative research as discussed throughout this book. The difficulties are both technical and conceptual but, as this chapter argues, the areas that have been problematic have also led to innovative research methods. Moreover, many of the new paradigms for addressing the research efficacy effectiveness interface are particularly applicable in a therapeutic community context.

This chapter considers the paradigm of practice-based evidence, to which therapeutic communities are ideally suited, as a counterweight to the evidence-based practice paradigm. Therapeutic communities in the UK have already moved a considerable way towards the practice research network (PRN) model of research summarised in this chapter, as one of the main settings for practice-based evidence. However, the research base of empirical studies in the form of randomised controlled trials (RCTs) and open trials is far from negligible and this material is summarised in Chapters 2 and 6.

This chapter puts therapeutic community research into the context of psychotherapy research as carried out in the National Health Service (NHS). The *NHS Review of Psychotherapy Services in England* (NHS Executive 1996) described a model to link research with other aspects of good clinical practice such as outcomes benchmarking, clinical audit, guidelines and protocols. Since publication of that review the overall clinical governance framework (Department of Health 1999b) has become increasingly influential. This chapter gives an overview of the links between research and clinical governance.

Research and clinical governance

Clinical governance was developed as a framework for improving clinical accountability. Clinical governance is

> a framework through which NHS organisations are accountable for continuously improving the quality of their service and safeguarding high standards of care by creating an environment in which excellence in clinical care will flourish. (Department of Health 1998a, p.33)

Clinical governance can be seen in the context of several related policy issues covered in *The New NHS, Modern and Dependable* (Department of Health 1998b) and numerous specific papers covering aspects of clinical governance. Mental health has been addressed specifically in *Modernising Mental Health Services: Safe, Sound and Secure* (Department of Health 1998c), and in the *National Service Framework for Mental Health* (NHS Executive 1999).

There are two main sets of objectives for clinical governance:

- *To strengthen existing systems for quality control* by the use of clinical standards and guidelines and evidence-based practice, and by learning from risk assessment, from local and national audit and from reviews of adverse incidents;

- *To modernise and strengthen professional self-regulation* by building on the principles of performance review and continuing professional development, detecting and managing poor performance.

From the research perspective, clinical governance draws on research evidence in establishing practice guidelines, and the clinical audit cycle should identify service research priorities. Two national bodies support the introduction of clinical governance. The National Institute for Clinical Excellence (NICE) is developing national guidelines for best practice in several key areas. The Committee for Health Improvement (CHI) is a national regulatory body with a system of on-site visits envisaged to maintain high standards, partly introduced through the reviews of research but also from national policy statements.

Responsibility for good clinical practice is divided between the individual practitioner, the employer, the professional body, and the government. Some themes can be seen as primarily evidence-based practice, whilst others are primarily concerned with professional development. Both lead to the research and education infrastructure essential for clinical governance (see Figure 3.1).

These are abstract concepts and, although clinical governance is an attempt to improve accountability, responsibility may still be diffuse. From a research perspective the accountability of the research agenda can be seen in terms of various 'stakeholders'. Each stakeholder can be assumed to pose particular types of research questions within the clinical governance framework and these have been discussed in detail elsewhere (see Margison *et al.* 2000). The patient/client/

Evidence-based care

- Evidence-based practice (clinical effectiveness)
- Clinical audit
- Integrated quality improvement processes
- Collection of systematic good-quality clinical data
- Risk management processes
- Complaints procedures and feed-back into improved care
- Detection and management of adverse events with feedback to improve future care
- Rational drug prescribing
- Patient and public involvement in setting standards and monitoring care
- Clinical guidelines

Staff management, performance management and appraisal

- Leadership skills
- Clinical risk reduction processes
- Early identification of poor performance
- Job plans
- Appraisal
- Personal development portfolios
- Continuing professional development reflecting clinical governance principles
- Employment policies
- Assessing and monitoring clinical outcomes
- Maintaining standards of ethical practice

Research and education

- Evidence-based practice infrastructure
- Dissemination of good practice
- Research which is clinically relevant
- Research methods used take account of clinical safety
- Development of research-based interventions in service settings
- Using research evidence to inform clinical standards
- Using research evidence in improving care
- Linking research findings to education
- Library and information management
- Standards of teaching based on best evidence
- Providing accurate information to users and carers

Figure 3.1 Elements of clinical governance

service-user perspective is becoming increasingly important in research and project implementation groups are encouraged to have a service-user member with
an equal say. Service-user initiated research is also an area of considerable
growth. Service-user involvement has been particularly influential in the therapeutic community movement.

The levels of the individual professional, therapist–patient dyad, peer review
(clinical audit) group, organisation, professional body and national priorities
generate different types of research question although there is considerable
overlap between the levels (see Table 3.1). For example, a professional body will
need to be concerned with measuring competent performance, just as will an individual reviewing his/her own practice. However, this framework sets the
context for a discussion about the most appropriate research strategies. In the
therapeutic community setting the assumption that we are concerned with individual therapists and patients is, of course, inaccurate. But, if the table is read to
mean the therapeutic community team as well as the individual members of the
team, the concepts cross-relate well. However, the unit of the therapist–patient
dyad is highly problematic in the therapeutic community context. Here the individual therapist is inextricably part of a team, and the unit of analysis for research
and measurement has to be the team itself. From the clinical governance perspective, however, each team member has to consider his/her own personal development. The development can be considered at three levels. The simplest level is *skill
maintenance* (avoiding skills atrophying or becoming outdated). Second, each individual needs to have a personal development plan to *enhance skills* in areas which
may have been highlighted by research reviews, or through sharing good
practice across therapeutic communities. Clearly, the therapeutic community as a
whole needs to be alert to developments and to ensure that new ideas are properly
evaluated and incorporated into best practice.

At a more complex level each individual needs to have a system to alert him
or her to the possibility of *under-performance*. This is highly threatening to any
therapist, but is fundamental to clinical governance. For the therapeutic
community team it is necessary to review the performance of each member, but
also the team as a whole. It can be argued that insularity of therapeutic communities has been one of the most problematic aspects of maintaining consistently
good clinical practice.

From the patient/resident's perspective there are two distinct aspects. Prior
to joining the therapeutic community the individual level of assessment is still
relevant (although there may be some particular issues about allocation in, for
example, custodial settings). Nevertheless, in principle the individual needs to be
part of a system that can advise on the best evidence available whether this particular individual is likely to benefit from joining the therapeutic community, and
whether any less costly, more effective, less disruptive alternatives have comparable chances of success. To date, the evidence has been embodied in the clinical

assessment process. In many instances this involves consideration of the individual in his/her own right, followed by that individual's 'fit' into the community at a particular time in its development cycle.

From a clinical governance and research perspective this can be highly problematic as two distinct levels of evidence are conflated. It is difficult to demonstrate consistent practice standards if the decision to admit is moderated by quite separate matters concerning the well-being of the community. The dominant drug research paradigm is quite inappropriate to these decisions as the treatment being 'delivered' is itself part of a dynamic system.

Monitoring outcomes under clinical governance presents similar dilemmas: is measurement of the progress of any individual possible without reference to the well-being of the community as a whole? One of the most pressing tasks in research in therapeutic communities has been the development of a measurement strategy that allows such issues as the therapeutic 'climate' of the institution to be measured and be linked to individual progress. Technically, the problem is to separate the variability in clinical outcome measures attributable to group-level changes from those at the level of the individual. This is statistically possible with large enough data sets looking simply at outcome measures, but there is still the problem of understanding any worsening at the group level.

Looking in parallel at the group climate measure can make such group-level shifts more understandable. If the group climate measure shows a markedly downward shift in a particular month it is appropriate to allow for this effect when looking at change by time in a particular individual, as otherwise an interpretation of clinical deterioration may be attributed to the individual when it is better to see it in the context of more global, group-level shifts of group cohesion or morale. Some of these ideas are being addressed in the cross-institutional multi-level modelling study, started in 1999 and funded by the National Lottery Charity Board (Association of Therapeutic Communities 1999; Haigh 2002), which is described by Lees in Chapter 4.

Peer group review has a different meaning in the context of a therapeutic community. The relevant peer group is probably a group of therapeutic communities, not of individuals working within that setting. Similarly, the professional organisation might represent community approaches rather than the professionals working within communities. Recent developments within the therapeutic community movement have seen the establishment of a peer review process called the Community of Communities, in which standards are set and individual therapeutic communities reviewed with these in mind (Haigh 2002). Lees describes this in more detail in Chapter 4.

This alters the pattern of responsibility for the organisation that manages the therapeutic community. In other aspects of clinical governance and research there is an assumption that the organisation can oversee the processes involved in peer

Table 3.1 'Stakeholder' view of evidence and psychotherapy

Stakeholder	Priorities	Salient practice-research issues	Measurement needed
Individual professional/team	• Best use of time and resources • Developing clinical skills	• How to allocate time as a therapist? • How to improve 'skills portfolio'?	• Case-mix and case-load review • Specific skills • Adherence • Competence • Overall skilfulness
Patient–therapist dyad	• Allocation to best treatment • Monitoring progress • Early identification of problems	• What interventions? • Why used? • How accurate is the formulation? • How to maintain therapeutic alliance?	• Case formulation • Measure (personally relevant) change • Case-tracking method
Peer review group	• Maintaining quality within local service	• Benchmarking outcomes • Case complexity • Treatment allocation decisions	• Routine evaluation of assessment and outcome

Organisation	• Managing clinical and financial risk	• Treatment protocols and guidelines • Identifying and managing clinical risk	• Identifying outliers • Risk recognition from case-tracking
Professional body	• Maintaining optimal professional standards	• Remedy deficits • Maintain skills • Add skills in new therapies	• Specific skills • Adherence • Competence • Overall skilfulness • Ability to train others
National government research and clinical priorities	• Allocation of resources between therapies • Focus on effective therapies • Prioritising those in most need	• Evidence-based clinical guidelines • Efficacy • Cost effectiveness • Orderly treatment developments (see Linehan 1997)	• Treatment definitions and manuals • Quality, adherence and competence measures for each treatment • Generic measures of competence and outcome • Health economic measures • Population-based health needs assessment methods

From Margison *et al.* 2000

group review, but in this context the peer group may have to cover a large geographical area to be viable.

This resonates with the final level in Table 3.1, the national and governmental agenda. It has already been accepted that some aspects of provision need to be commissioned at a national level. One effect of this is the close links between those commissioning and funding service provision and those commissioning research on effectiveness. This can have beneficial effects, but the potential danger is that therapeutic communities become separated from the mainstream national peer-reviewed research agenda.

Efficacy and effectiveness

The distinction between *efficacy* and *effectiveness* becomes relevant when considering the different priorities of the different stakeholders. *Efficacy* refers to evidence based on carefully designed trials where threat to internal validity is minimised. Traditionally in evidence-based medicine the RCT is given prime place because of its ability to deal with systematic bias through the randomisation process. However, even with the RCT there is a trade-off between different elements in the design in terms of rigour and generalisability (Shapiro *et al.* 1995). In particular, the more selective the sample and the more rigorously-defined the intervention, the less applicable the treatment is likely to be to routine practice, thus threatening external validity. In *effectiveness* research the design is weighted towards high generalisability, but the price paid is in greater threats to internal validity.

Several resolutions to this dichotomy have been proposed for the strategic developments of new treatments. Linehan (1997) suggests three phases of theory generation, validation, and dissemination (see Table 3.2). Salkovskis (1995) introduced the metaphor of the 'hourglass' to describe a similar process. A relatively large number of generative and pilot studies are carried out. These are then focused through a few very carefully designed efficacy studies with high internal validity (the 'neck' of the hourglass). A larger number of studies then follow to test effectiveness across different treatment settings and for different conditions, where the balance shifts back towards maximising external validity.

Table 3.2 Developmental model for new psychological treatments
Three-phase model
Phase 1: Development • Generating the treatment • Standardisation • Pilot studies of efficacy
Phase 2: Validation • Formal tests of efficacy • Researching underlying methods of action • Testing of utility
Phase 3: Dissemination • Service development • Programme evaluation • Testing effectiveness in typical populations
Source: Adapted from Linehan 1997

Linehan's and Salkovskis' suggestions are logical, but in practice there are diffi-culties to this orderly approach. First, the need for *replication* of efficacy studies is understated. In therapeutic community research there are, also, particular practical and conceptual difficulties in setting up RCTs (discussed in detail in Chapter 6). Drawing clinical inferences from the relatively few randomised efficacy studies is difficult, but the progress in meta-analytic strategies has led to some generalisable conclusions (see Chapter 2 for fuller discussion).

Second, the time from early descriptions to full implementation of a new treatment is very long, by which time clinical practice may well have changed. This is a particular problem in therapeutic communities where new members of the community team may bring radically different ideas about practice. To some extent good management structures and clinical guidelines can control this, but the extra level of complexity in evaluation still needs to be taken into account. A possible consequence of these difficulties may be that the transfer of knowledge from RCTs has been slow and partial. However, agreement about appropriate practice standards and the key features of therapeutic communities is still possible using a consensual approach.

Third, specific findings may no longer apply when translated from efficacy studies to routine practice. The implications for services differ depending on whether those responsible for service commissioning attend mainly to the efficacy evidence or the different implications from replication in a service setting.

Changing clinical practice as a result of efficacy studies is notoriously slow and difficult, and clinicians often choose their mode of practice based on a wide variety of non-research grounds (Margison, Loebl and McGrath 1998). Clinicians, even in services that profess to use standard length therapies, actually show wide variation in treatment length. Even when good quality efficacy evidence is available, there are often difficulties in allocating patients to the optimal treatment as shown in a service evaluation in the USA (Sperry *et al.* 1996, p.160), where '62% of the patients could not be referred to the programs considered optimal to the evaluator'. Reasons included lack of treatment places at the point of referral, refusal by the funding agency, patient preference and preference for local services above optimal treatment.

Department of Health Psychotherapy Review model

Given the immense difficulties of carrying out good quality research in psychotherapeutic treatments, the *NHS Psychotherapy Services in England: Review of Strategic Policy* (NHS Executive 1996) paid particular attention to describing a realistic framework for improving clinical performance through evidence-based practice.

The review makes several general points about the components:

- Standard practice in NHS psychotherapy should be more clearly specified through clinical guidelines.

- Clinical guidelines are useful to benchmark good practice and as an aid to clinical judgement.

- Treatment-of-choice decisions should be based upon formal research findings, service evaluation, cost effectiveness evidence and clinical consensus.

- Outcomes benchmarking helps to discover how a local service is performing against research-derived standards or in relation to similar services (after allowing for differences in case-mix).

- Clinical audit is particularly useful in examining the reason for failure to deliver a set standard of practice.

- Clinical audit should link to local training, education and professional development and potentially refines the research agenda.

In Figure 3.2, the various components of the model are shown in context.

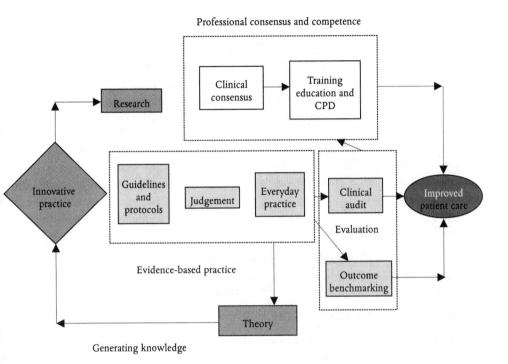

Figure 3.2 Improving patient care through evidence-based practice and practice-based evidence
Source: NHS Executive 1996, p.44, modified by Professor G. Parry

Generating knowledge

In this model, knowledge is generated by links from *theory* into *innovative practice* and *research* as described above. This area is strong in research in therapeutic communities. The literature has many examples of new approaches to therapeutic communities, sometimes linked to social theories of change, sometimes to psychodynamic or other modality-specific theory of change. The weak point of this cycle has been the link into guidelines. Until recently, guidelines that transcend the particular organisational culture of a specific therapeutic community have seemed difficult to imagine, far less achieve. Current work, as exemplified in this volume, makes it more likely that there will be models of therapeutic process, which can be evaluated in a mixed qualitative and quantitative approach. The synthesis of multiple, simultaneous models of evaluation is in keeping with the pluralistic philosophy of therapeutic communities.

Evidence-based practice

The development of *guidelines* and *protocols* is supported by a systematic analysis of *clinical consensus* to ensure that agreement is well-founded and replicable.

The evidence and consensus-based guidelines are then moderated through clinical *judgement* into routine, everyday practice, which in turn leads to revision of *theory*. The development of guidelines as summarily stated here is, in fact, a complex process with clear rules and procedures for dealing with evidence.

The levels of evidence are clearly stated in the *National Service Framework for Mental Health* (NHS Executive 1999). There are five levels of evidence considered in drawing up clinical guidelines as shown in Table 3.3 (as used for example in HMSO 1999, p.6).

Table 3.3 Evidence standards	
Type I	At least one good review, including at least one RCT
Type II	At least one good RCT
Type III	At least one well-designed intervention study without randomisation
Type IV	At least one well-designed observational study
Type V	Expert opinion, including the views of service users and carers

The level of clinical consensus in this widely used model is considered inferior, even to simple observational studies, supporting a move towards increasingly empirical approaches to evidence. In the therapeutic community approach, within and between units, discussion leading to consensus is a highly valued activity, perhaps stemming from the belief that thought and dialogue should replace action. The fundamental values underpinning the research appraisal are far removed from the philosophy of therapeutic communities, but the 'research to guidelines' link is only one component of the evidential approach shown in Figure 3.2.

Evaluation

The *evaluation* part of the diagram deals with two related topics: *clinical audit* and *benchmarking*. Clinical practice should be appraised through clinical audit to allow a service to set standards and then review practice against those standards (Margison *et al.* 1998).

The quality of a service is usually considered to be a topic closely linked to audit. Conventionally, audit has dealt with the details of inputs, activities and outputs, asking questions about the standards desired and the potential steps that might lead to change. The whole process forms an iterative loop with the standards against which the service is to be assessed being themselves continually revised.

Questions about quality have dealt with:

- How *comprehensive* is a service intended to be?

- How *relevant* is the intervention?

- How *acceptable* is the intervention?

- How *accessible* and equitable is the service?

- How *efficiently* is the treatment delivered?

Audit and quality improvement programmes in general have been viewed with suspicion by clinicians. Clinical audit has not produced the systematic re-evaluation of practice that was desired initially. Even when audit has been carried out regularly, it is rare that there is 'completion of the loop'. That is, after the first cycle of audit there should be a review of practice followed by a re-audit to ensure that there has been change towards the desired standard (see Parry 1998).

Concerns have been expressed about

confidentiality, freedom of clinical choice, untoward effects of the audit on the therapist–patient relationship; an excessive concern with costs, medico-legal fears and a lack of trust in how the information might be used. (Margison *et al.* 1998, p.79)

To deal with the different senses of the word 'quality', it is usual to distinguish several overlapping concepts:

- *Service evaluation* is a broad approach that uses concepts from social science research methods to assess the conceptualisation and implementation of an intervention.

- *Operational research* to improve cost-effectiveness by mathematical and logical modelling of a service as a system.

- *Service audit* describes and measures service processes and outcomes.

- *Quality assurance* monitors processes by which care is delivered against pre-determined standards.

- *Total quality management* is a management-led commitment to continuous improvement in quality by improvement in processes.

- *Medical audit* is the systematic, critical analysis of medical care, including procedures used for diagnosis and treatment, the use of resources and the resulting outcome and quality of life of the patient.

- *Clinical audit* resembles medical audit, but there is a commitment to a multi-disciplinary approach and there is a recognisable cycle of analysing the current situation: setting standards; measuring against standards; reviewing processes in the light of findings; reviewing standards etc. (see Margison *et al.* 2000).

Clinically, there are substantial problems in ensuring comparability as the audit standards are difficult to specify in a therapeutic community setting. Some questions are, however, still open to empirical scrutiny. For example, the proportion of patients being accepted for therapy (and the types of therapy offered) can be compared across different ethnic groups to check whether unintended bias is affecting the consistency of the service offered just as in individual practice (Margison *et al.* 1998, p.88). The likelihood of acceptance, according to social class, offending record, age or gender, is not determined typically by the actual therapeutic model. Usually the decision is based on a complex interplay of factors including the remit of the unit, its fragility or otherwise at the time of referral, and considerations of 'balance' within the group.

An aspect of quality that is even more difficult to conceptualise is the model of 'therapeutic competencies'. In the past, *competence* has often been equated with length of exposure to a defined training programme. In individual therapy there have been attempts to look at particular therapeutic events to assess therapeutic competence; for example, the ability to work with and resolve 'alliance ruptures' (Bennett and Parry 1998). However, this has not dealt with the fundamental problem that our clinical practice is not necessarily built on consistent 'models of task performance'. In the therapeutic community setting, task performance may be specified at least as tightly as for individual practice, but may also be strongly influenced by the current climate of opinion amongst staff members, whether this favours therapeutic optimism or nihilism.

Flexibility of response in clinicians is valued, but this makes it difficult to set minimum standards of clinical performance. In the therapeutic community setting, considerable work is needed on the definition of skills and competencies as in all areas of therapy. But there is an additional dimension: some skills may be required by every staff member, a proportion may only need some. Some skills are distributed among therapists and residents and some skills may be more prevalent in the resident group.

The usual 'skills model' is put under considerable conceptual strain when considering the therapeutic community as a whole. Some key skills among individual therapists have a clear counterpart in the community, such as ability to empathise or confront; ability to contain projections without retaliation and ability to understand and interpret re-enactments in the community. Despite the similarity, the location of the 'skill' is quite different and the usual model of skill acquisition and maintenance is of only marginal relevance.

Similarly, *consistency* is important to those who use psychotherapy services, but the level at which such consistency is conceptualised will be different in the therapeutic community setting. Some aspects are directly comparable to individual practice such as decisions about allocation to treatment, whereas others are less clearly relevant as the therapeutic community is also the residents' home at least on a temporary basis.

Outcomes benchmarking is an approach to quality control that has found increasing favour in recent years (Barkham *et al.* in press). It is a model that is highly relevant to the therapeutic community setting. Benchmarking involves the routine use of one or more outcome measures, ideally repeated on several occasions during treatment. There are simple methods for assessing and comparing change across settings, such as reliable and clinically significant change or RCSC (Evans, Margison and Barkham 1998; Jacobson and Truax 1991). Benchmarks are a way of standardising expected outcomes against large normative populations (in this context drawn perhaps from all therapeutic communities accepting comparable patients).

There are two distinct aspects that need to be considered in developing useful benchmarking for psychological treatments: (1) the individual level, and (2) the service level. The first aspect involves standardising outcome data against which change for a particular individual can be judged. Change for an individual can be referenced against other individuals with similar socio-demographic information, diagnosis and initial severity if the normative data set is sufficiently large.

Such aggregation moves the focus to the second aspect of benchmarking, which applies at a service level. A service will compare its effectiveness with other similar services. Similarity involves comparison of the service structure and function, but services also need to be able to consider their case mix. This means that information that might predict outcome, such as relapse history, severity or comorbidity, needs to be taken into account in any comparison between services. Such comparisons can, given an appropriate organisational framework, lead to improved practice and patient safety (Nolan 2000). To avoid ambiguity the term 'service profiling' is sometimes used rather than 'benchmarking' for the assessment of difference at intake, keeping the term benchmarking primarily for referencing the extent of clinical change. Some examples of comparisons across therapeutic community services are discussed by Lees in Chapter 4 and Davies and Menzies in Chapter 16.

Self-reflexive practice?

A quite different concept of quality for a service is that it can demonstrate that the whole service and the individual members of the team have a capacity to reflect critically on their own practice. The ability to reflect on one's own contribution, particularly where treatments are failing, is one of the hallmarks of skilful practice. In psychodynamically orientated therapeutic communities this may be understood within the frameworks of countertransference and projective identification. Self-reflexive practice is a particular strength of a well-functioning therapeutic community where regular supervision, aftergroups and team awareness meetings allow for this process. In cognitive-behavioural and cognitive-analytic models similar issues may be understood within a framework of re-enactment, and perpetuation of dysfunctional belief systems. In systemic therapy, self-reflexive practice includes the idea that the therapists themselves are part of the broader system, and models of concurrent ('live') supervision are practical manifestations of the commitment to self-reflexive practice.

Practice research networks

One way of bridging the gap between practitioner and researcher has been advocated by Parry (1996, p.443). She suggests that clinicians and service users should be seen as at least stakeholders in research effort, and preferably should be directly involved. More recently this concept has been developed into the idea of practice research networks (PRNs) (Audin *et al.* 2001) to harness the clinical knowledge of practitioners with the methodological expertise of researchers to formulate researchable and clinically relevant questions.

An example of a PRN has been functioning in the north of England as a branch of the Society for Psychotherapy Research. The involvement of clinicians has allowed a clearer formulation of standardised measures that might ultimately be used across the region to aid comparability. The assessment tools have benefited at the same time from the input of expert researchers who can identify pitfalls that might otherwise make the measurements invalid or at least cumbersome to collate.

The advantages of PRNs have been summarised as shown below (Audin *et al.* 2001):

- PRN practitioners collect standardised data for every patient, thus assuring a comprehensive data set for each service and the network as a whole. Participating services can therefore accurately profile their work and record their effectiveness.

- The PRN sets standards and establishes benchmarks to promote service development and effectiveness. The collaborative nature of the group and the large, anonymised data sets available will facilitate this process.

- The PRN methodology (with practitioners providing routine audit information) allows patient-collected data to be focused specifically on clinical issues.

- Because the PRN instrumentation can be agreed upon, and even developed by the practitioners themselves, the data collected are meaningful and highly relevant to current practice. The brevity of the tools also facilitates their routine use in the busy service settings.

- Ideally all data processing, analysis and reporting is provided by a central support centre; therefore, PRN practitioners are able to focus on their clinical duties. Regular feedback of data encourages and facilitates the use of data for service development.

- The multi-site nature of a PRN creates economies of scale that reduces the cost to practitioners (Audin *et al.* 2001).

In practice, all of the therapeutic communities in the UK could be considered as a single PRN, although there is perhaps a logic to keeping concept therapeutic communities separate as their methods of working are so different.

Research in the NHS

The structure for research and development in the NHS in the UK is undergoing a radical review. The proposed arrangements will separate formal partnerships with major funding bodies (such as the Medical Research Council) under the 'Support for Science' programme from NHS 'Priorities and Needs' (devised by the NHS in response to ministerial priorities and research needs identified by systematic review) (Department of Health 2000). One effect of such a re-alignment of funding should be to prioritise areas highlighted in the National Service Frameworks. Priorities for research and development were incorporated in the Strategic Review of Research and Development in Mental Health (Department of Health 2002). The priorities stated emphasise external validity. They include effectiveness research, cost-effectiveness research, user involvement and assessment of ease of engagement. This research will take place in a context of prior work establishing efficacy in high quality, well-designed trials with good internal validity.

There are guidelines available on how to conduct clinical trials with good standards of clinical practice (Department of Health 1999c). All of the above information and regular updates are available from www.doh.gov.uk/ research.

Concurrently there is a programme to improve the governance of research itself (Department of Health 2001). This goes beyond the clinical impact of the research on participants to examine the ethical and probity issues involved in managing substantial research portfolios in the NHS. The first baseline assessment of research governance was completed in spring 2001.

Conclusion: Requirements for evidence-based practice and practice-based evidence

Good research and practice depends on three inter-linked requirements.

The first requirement is for *critical questions* to be posed, which are clinically and methodologically meaningful. Simply showing that there is a detectable but clinically marginal difference between treatments A and B in a large tightly controlled comparative treatment trial is of very little value to the practitioner. In this context, a *critical question* is one that could affect clinical practice. Even when such studies have been carried out, it is difficult to change routine practice, but currently there is a 'research/practice divide', which prevents dissemination of good practice based on research findings, and equally prevents research being informed by questions arising within a critical, self-reflexive practice setting.

The second requirement is to have a *system to measure change* during and following therapy that feels clinically appropriate and also fulfils fundamental criteria for replicability, validity, reliability and fidelity. Such systems are typically modelled on individual therapy practice, and do not necessarily generalise to other settings such as couples, families, groups and therapeutic communities.

Finally, the practice of good evidence-based psychotherapy needs an *infrastructure*. This includes facilities and support to carry out focused literature reviews and critical appraisal. Also, clinicians need an infrastructure for collating and analysing outcome reports on individual patients in a systematic way. This leads to a more reflective practice with the ability to monitor change and identify early in the therapy those cases that are going to go 'off track'. Once 'high risk' cases have been identified they can be prioritised within clinical audit and in clinical supervision. Again, the infrastructure is typically modelled on individual practice and specific attention is needed to providing an appropriate audit and review model for use in groups and communities.

For therapeutic communities, all of the above general points hold, although the implementation is likely to be more complex in a multi-level setting such as a group, and even more so in a therapeutic community setting. The main difficulties in implementing the desirable level of self-reflexive practice, audit and research are mostly pragmatic and related to the multiple levels of analysis possible in a therapeutic community. The general principles of combining evidence-based practice with practice-based evidence are at least as relevant in this setting as in individual therapy.

CHAPTER 4

Practice Evaluation
of Therapeutic Communities

Jan Lees

Introduction

Audit, clinical governance, quality assurance and quality standards and monitoring, and research for evidence-based practice, are current British obsessions. This is particularly true within the National Health Service (NHS), but also applies to social services, and is reflected in regulations for the private sector. In Chapter 3, Margison gives an overview of all these activities, and the links between them, within the context of the NHS in Britain. In this chapter, I want to describe how therapeutic communities in the UK, particularly through the strategies and interventions of the national Association of Therapeutic Communities (ATC), have been developing and expanding both practice in, and links between, research, audit, clinical governance and quality standards, assurance and monitoring, within the national community of therapeutic communities.

Research, audit, clinical governance and quality assurance in relation to therapeutic communities

How do all these activities relate to therapeutic communities? It is important to say here that I am mainly referring to democratic therapeutic communities, based on the models of Tom Main at Cassel Hospital and Maxwell Jones at Henderson Hospital, rather than concept-based therapeutic communities, based on the work of Chuck Dederich, and now a global network of programmes for substance abusers. However, both these therapeutic community treatment models are struggling with similar issues – providing an evidence base for their practice, monitoring of quality standards and accreditation for their treatment programmes.

A fundamental tenet of therapeutic community practice has always been the 'total culture of enquiry' as propounded by Tom Main (1989). Although he was talking more about clinical practice, in terms of unconscious processes within groups and the community as a whole, and about the tensions and role difficulties in a total social system, therapeutic community practitioners always operate with the assumption that everything we do should be available for scrutiny, assessment and evaluation, and for change, if this seems appropriate. Therefore, audit cycles, quality standards monitoring, clinical governance and research are exactly reflected in a culture of enquiry, which are all in turn examples of reflexive practice.

What is it that therapeutic community workers are trying to do, by utilising audit, quality standards monitoring and assurance, clinical governance and research? Overall, therapeutic community practitioners want to both maintain and improve good quality treatments and services for clients. To do this, therapeutic community practitioners need effective ways of informing and improving practice; of making therapeutic community treatment more effective and of making it fit better with client need. Therapeutic community workers also need to provide a fundamental understanding of what therapeutic communities are all about, and how they work – and therefore how they can be replicated.

In addition, therapeutic community workers need to meet the British government requirements of 'evidence-based practice' to ensure continued funding. They also need to provide information about cost effectiveness for those purchasing therapeutic community services so as to ensure therapeutic communities' continued survival and expansion as a treatment of choice (Lees 1999). The British government's emphasis on evidence-based practice has led to more outcome research and evaluations of the effectiveness of therapeutic community treatment. This research, in turn, has had positive effects on the provision of therapeutic community treatment.

Evidence-based practice

For some time in Britain there were criticisms levelled at therapeutic communities. These were based on allegations that there was no research evidence base for the effectiveness of therapeutic community treatment, that therapeutic community treatment was expensive and that buying therapeutic community services could therefore not be justified without an evidence base. This led to some NHS mental health trusts deciding that they would no longer purchase therapeutic community services for their patients. The Department of Health then commissioned a systematic international literature review of all the existing research evidence about therapeutic community treatment for people with personality disorders. This review, which included a meta-analysis of 29 studies, which in turn included eight randomised controlled trials (RCTs), concluded that there was already existing evidence for the effectiveness of therapeutic communities in treating people with personality disorder. Clinical changes in both symptomatology and behaviour in desired directions were also documented in the literature. As a result, NHS trusts have now decided to continue purchasing therapeutic community services (Lees *et al.* 1999; see also Chapter 2).

Another response to the British government's emphasis on evidence-based practice has been for clinicians also to argue for practice-based evidence. This, in turn, is partly in response to the British medical profession's obsession with the RCT, which is difficult to implement for therapeutic communities, but also because of clinical discontent with research, which is not grounded in the real world of clinical practice. It is a reworking of Seligman's arguments about the better suitability of *efficacy* studies, as epitomised by the RCT, or *effectiveness* studies of what actuallly happens to patients under real treatment conditions in the field for psychotherapy research in general. Seligman argues that some treatments are too cumbersome for the efficacy study paradigm, and particularly long-term therapies, especially if there is no fixed duration; where the therapy is self-correcting (which is, of course, a major facet of therapeutic community treatment); where patients have multiple problems or psychiatric diagnoses; and where improvement is concerned with the general functioning of patients, as well as improvements in disorders, or specific presenting symptoms (Seligman 1995). Obviously all of these provisos pertain to the therapeutic community and related research.

Association of Therapeutic Communities/National Lottery Charities Board Therapeutic Community Research Project – A comparative evaluation of therapeutic community effectiveness for people with personality disorders

For this reason, in 1999 and following on from the above systematic literature review, the ATC applied to the National Lottery Charities Board (NLCB) for funding, which it was granted (grant number RB219244), for a naturalistic, comparative, cross-institutional study 'in the field' of therapeutic communities for people with personality disorders (Association of Therapeutic Communities 1999). This study is looking at 21 therapeutic communities in England and Scotland. Some of these therapeutic communities are residential, some are day units; some are in secure environments, some are not; some are in the NHS, some are in the prison service, and some are in the private and voluntary sector. All bar two are democratic therapeutic communities; the other two are concept-based therapeutic communities, of which one is secure and one is in the community. One unit combines a therapeutic community approach with dialectical behaviour therapy, which will provide an interesting comparison, as these are two of the main treatments for personality disorder with an evidence base, but they are often contrasted as competing treatments.

Lees *et al.* have argued that RCTs for therapeutic communities present difficulties, including issues around treatment complexity, treatment dosage and treatment integrity, population selection, dropouts, effects decay and diagnostic shift, and that RCTs in this field have proved impractical (Lees, Manning and Rawlings 1999, p.7 and pp.99–105; see also Chapter 6). Lees *et al.* suggest that cross-institutional and comparative designs provide a methodological alternative for evaluating the effectiveness of therapeutic communities, and this is what is being utilised in the ATC/NLCB Therapeutic Communities Research Project. The cross-institutional design can be both interpretative and exploratory and can also include survey investigation in the design, both to facilitate exploration and to provide a basis for interpretation. It emphasises naturalistic observation of phenomena in the field, and takes natural variations in the field as the basis for the statistical modelling of the interaction of the variations of the treatment components and process with outcome change. However, Lees *et al.* also point out that such an evaluation depends crucially on a clear understanding of what the therapeutic community is; the setting, whether secure or non-secure, in which it is delivered; and at which client groups it is aimed; as well as clear, objective outcome measures (Lees *et al.* 1999).

The ATC/NLCB study is both multi-dimensional and multi-level, with a specific model for managing the different levels of data collected. Moos (1974a, 1997) has developed a multi-dimensional design for treatment settings such as therapeutic communities, based on structural equations and path analytical statistical modelling.

This involves studying natural variations in both process and outcome over a sample of treatment environments, and using the resulting variation in key variables to build a path-analytic causal model of the interaction between the constituent parts of the process, and hence their direct or indirect effects on the outcome of treatment (Moos 1974a, 1997; Cronkite and Moos 1978), as shown in Figure 4.1. Manning and Lees (1985) and Manning (1989) have used this methodology to design a comparative study, and report a cross-institutional design looking at six therapeutic communities in Australia. This study showed that this methodology can capture the subtle variations in programme processes and relate these to outcome. This demonstrated good outcomes, and using structural equations to model the variations in treatment components, they were able to account for 58 per cent of the outcome variance from in-treatment variables (Manning 1989). There are, as yet, no other published attempts to use this design to evaluate therapeutic communities (Lees *et al.* 1999). In addition there are few existing studies of therapeutic communities that deal with more than one community (Bloor, McKeganey and Fonkert 1988; Lees *et al.* 1999).

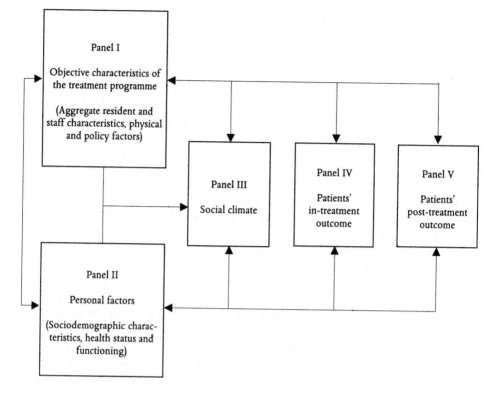

Figure 4.1 A model of personal, programme and outcome variables
Source: Adapted from Moos 1997, p.3; Moos and Lemke 1996, p.2

Research targets

These cross-institutional, comparative designs can be equally descriptive, interpretative and evaluative, and use both qualitative and quantitative measures. The
ATC/NLCB study encompasses all these. The study intends to:

1. describe and measure the populations of the therapeutic communities
    involved, in terms of their background characteristics and their
    symptoms and behaviours at admission;

2. compare the population characteristics of the different sub-groups of
    therapeutic communities in the sample (e.g. non-secure/secure;
    residential/day);

3. describe and measure the characteristics of the treatment
    environments of the therapeutic communities;

4.   attempt to identify the core elements of the therapeutic community, and the treatment process, in this sample of communities;

5.   particularly measure and discuss the profiles, or social climates, of these communities and compare them to typical therapeutic community profiles;

6.   examine how these treatment elements and their inter-relationships with the physical and programme context vary between the sub-groups of the sample;

7.   measure changes in symptoms and behaviours over time in treatment and, for some of the population sample, after discharge;

8.   last, attempt to identify how the population characteristics at intake, and the various elements of the treatment environment and process, are related to good outcome for members.

In addition, and in order to refine a detailed understanding of the treatment elements and related treatment processes, a qualitative analysis of three therapeutic communities, one drawn from each of the main types of therapeutic community in the sample (NHS non-secure; prison service secure; and special hospital secure), has been undertaken simultaneously with the collection of the quantitative data. This qualitative research has involved a mixture of interviews and participant observation of the communities in action. A major focus of these qualitative studies has been on the way in which therapeutic community client members and staff make their way through the therapeutic community in the manner of an informal 'career', and the different kinds of social reality constructed by staff and client community members.

Measures used

The measures being used in the ATC/NLCB research project are related to the causal model illustrated in Figure 4.1 and data are being collected at a number of levels, as shown in Figure 4.2.

Supra-therapeutic community level

1.   A postal questionnaire about the policy environment of the therapeutic community is being sent to each therapeutic community's line managers.

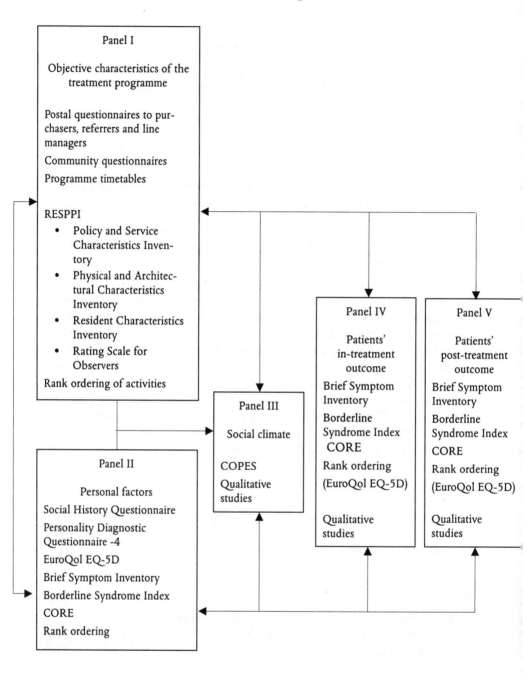

Figure 4.2: Measures related to Figure 4.1
Source: Adapted from Moos 1997, p.3; Moos and Lemke 1996, p.2

2.   A postal questionnaire about knowledge of the therapeutic community, and reasons for referring to it, is being sent to all the major referral agents for each therapeutic community.

3.   A postal questionnaire about the reasons for purchasing the services of the therapeutic community, and their satisfaction about the services brought, is being sent to each therapeutic community's purchasers.

Level of the therapeutic community

1.   A programme timetable, detailing all the unit's activities.

2.   A community questionnaire relating to the history of the unit and its costs.

3.   The Residential Substance Abuse and Psychiatric Programmes Inventory (RESPPI) (Timko 1994). This is an adapted form of the Multiphasic Environmental Assessment Procedure (MEAP), devised by Moos, for the collection of data to use with his path-analytic model for assessing the effectiveness of treatment environments in relation to outcome (Moos and Lemke 1996). This has been adapted for use in British therapeutic communities. RESPPI includes:

   • Physical and Architectural Characteristics Inventory (PACI)

   • Policy and Service Characteristics Inventory (PASCI)

   • Resident (Client Member) Characteristics Inventory (RESCI)

   • Rating Scale for Observers (RSO)

   +

   • COPES (Community Oriented Programs Environment Scale – an adapted form of the Ward Atmosphere Scale, devised by Moos to measure the social climate of psychiatric treatment environments (Moos 1997)). This has been completed at 6-monthly intervals during an 18-month data collection period.

Staff

1.   Rank ordering of community activities.

Client community members

1. Social History Questionnaire – administered at admission or first test administration only.

2. Personality Diagnostic Questionnaire – IV (Hyler *et al.* 1987) – administered once on admission, or first test administration only – for diagnostic and characterisation purposes.

3. EuroQol 5-D (Brooks 1996) – administered three times – on admission, or first test administration; on discharge and at the end of the data collection period – for comparative purposes, for general health care status, with other psychiatric populations across Europe and for outcome evaluation of treatment.

4. Brief Symptom Inventory (Derogatis 1993) – for symptom characterisation, and comparison with US psychiatric populations and change over time.

5. Borderline Syndrome Index (Conte *et al.* 1980) – for symptom characterisation and change over time.

6. CORE (Clinical Outcome in Routine Evaluation) (CORE System Group 1998) – for symptom characterisation and change over time.

7. Rank ordering of helpfulness of unit activities.

    (Points 4–7 above are the measures of change over time in treatment and were administered at admission/baseline; three-monthly during treatment; discharge; and three-monthly post-discharge until the end of the 18-month data collection period.)

8. Re-conviction and re-admission data from central records.

9. Follow-up of dropouts from treatment.

This study will provide extensive descriptive and comparative as well as outcome data about a range of therapeutic community provision and treatment for a range of people with personality disorders. The results of this study should begin to be available from late 2003.

Current issues in relation to research, audit, clinical governance and quality standards in therapeutic communities

Audit, clinical governance and quality standards monitoring are often seen as clinical issues. Therefore, the expectation tends to be that these are done by clinicians, who, in turn, can be nurses, doctors, social workers, psychologists etc. Research, however, has often been seen as somehow separate from these – something done by people with expertise and experience, often from outside – and research has sometimes been seen as imposed from outside the community. There has also been a great deal of controversy about what constitutes audit and what constitutes research, with the argument that audit is the assessment of the quality of care or treatment provided to patients, while research will be based upon the testing of an hypothesis, and the gathering and analysis of data, which is then evaluated in the light of the original hypothesis. However, the boundaries are very blurred. According to Devlin (1993), audit and quality assurance are aimed primarily at improving practice, whereas research seeks new knowledge and therapies. Audit is then used to ensure that any new knowledge is applied correctly in the clinical setting.

Here, Devlin is referring only to prospective innovative research, and therapeutic communities are also concerned with retrospective and evaluative research – does what therapeutic communities do now work, rather than what better treatment can be found and tested for the future?

Armstrong, Calnan and Grace (1990, p.6) have argued that 'Research is occasionally taken to imply purely a difference in scope of enquiry, rather than type of enquiry when compared with audit'. They also quote an editorial from the *Journal of the Royal College of General Practitioners*, which suggested that:

> Research provides information which has relevance and value beyond the particular circumstances of the study. In contrast, audit aims to provide precise information in a particular setting which enables rational policy decisions to be made. (Armstrong, Calnan and Grace 1990, p.6)

What I think we need to do is to break down these definitional barriers. It seems to me that, at some levels, audit, quality standards monitoring, clinical governance and research are all trying to do the same thing. They are all part of reflexive practice and the culture of enquiry. They are all aimed at establishing good practice, evaluating it, and continually trying to improve it.

Therapeutic communities in Britain have been in existence for over 50 years, and although they have always been involved in reflexive practice, their conventional research tradition has not been as great as might have been expected. Although research was an important part of the early therapeutic community innovations, the early therapeutic communities tended to prefer descriptive, qualitative and participant observation types of research, as these were seen as more in keeping with the philosophy and practice of the therapeutic community (see also Chapter 1).

Therapeutic communities were more suspicious of quantitative research, which was felt to reduce people to numbers, and this was seen as antipathetic to the therapeutic community culture and ethos. Therapeutic community members were particularly unhappy about the ethics of research techniques, such as random allocation (for RCTs) or control groups, because these involve withholding treatment from people who are in recognised need of the treatment and are extremely vulnerable, particularly to suicide, but which also run counter to therapeutic community practices, such as voluntarism and the principle of choice, and to selection processes.

Therapeutic communities were also quite hostile to research that was seen as an imposition from outside, and to researchers from outside the therapeutic community. In fact, therapeutic communities are often suspicious of *anything* seen as imposed from outside, or over-bureaucratic, etc. It was often felt that researchers had to be *in* the therapeutic community, doing the clinical work, in order really to grasp and to understand the nature of the work. This meant that there was little quantitative or evaluative research undertaken on therapeutic communities in Britain until the 1970s, when alliances with medicine and psychotherapy were becoming more important (Lees 1999).

The attitude of therapeutic communities in Britain to research has changed significantly since the early 1990s, but there has also been a revived interest in the treatment methods of the therapeutic community, within both the NHS and the prison service in Britain. As a result, there has been a concurrent increase in both the quantity and quality of therapeutic community research work in Britain, with more sophisticated research designs and methodologies, and a better understanding of the complexity of the issues involved (Lees 1999).

Indeed, there is much more of an acceptance now amongst therapeutic community workers, whatever their core discipline, that they have to be involved in audit, research, clinical governance and the monitoring of quality standards in some way and as part of their therapeutic community practice. For example, one NHS mental health trust is proposing that all its staff should be involved in research in some way, that their staff should be either research active or research aware and able to implement research findings in their practice. The implication of this is that it is no longer acceptable to say you are not interested in research, do not understand it or are not involved in it.

Practice-based evidence

While hostility to research may be less among therapeutic community staff nowadays, attitudes in other areas have not entirely changed. For example, there was considerable hostility in Britain to the development of audit standards for therapeutic communities, the development and implementation of the Kennard–Lees Audit Checklist (Kennard and Lees 2001) and to the development of quality standards for therapeutic communities (these will be discussed in more detail later). While there was recognition in the therapeutic community field of the need for, and value of, accreditation, how this was to be done became a really contentious issue.

In Britain, the pros and cons of having accreditation standards for therapeutic communities has been debated for a number of years. The debate has centred around the tension between external – managerial and public – pressures for conformity and accountability, in the form of acceptable standards of practice, and the professional concerns of therapeutic community members about clinical autonomy, as well as their scepticism about the possibility of setting standards for something as complex and fluid as a therapeutic community. Therapeutic community practitioners felt that it would be impossible to prescribe or manualise the therapeutic events and experiences in a therapeutic community in a way that meaningfully reflects the work. In this respect, the therapeutic community is seen as different from other therapeutic techniques that follow an explicit predictable sequence, such as those based on the principles of cognitive behavioural therapy or dialectical behavioural therapy. Some of the concerns were about the potential for ossifying the notion of the therapeutic community, destroying its creativity and reflexivity, failing to capture the essence of something that should be continually changing, and about the inability of quality standards and quality standards monitoring to reflect in any way the mechanisms of a 'culture of enquiry'.

The Kennard–Lees Audit Checklist

The Kennard–Lees Audit Checklist (KLAC) attempted to incorporate the issues discussed above in its audit criteria. David Kennard and I attempted to grasp the nettle of developing a 'checklist' of standards that can be used to accredit a therapeutic community, which are concrete enough to be objectively assessed as present to a greater or lesser degree, but which at the same time reflect the daily living learning experience, and reflexivity, of a therapeutic community in a way that practitioners will recognise as a true picture of what they do or try to do. Therefore, in developing the checklist, David Kennard and I were guided by the view that therapeutic community principles should inform all aspects of the administration and practice of a therapeutic community and its treatment programme. We also felt that these principles should inform and influence the process of audit as well. These principles include:

- a culture of enquiry
- shared decision-making
- everything in the community being available for scrutiny, and feedback, and to influence and change, as part of the therapeutic process

- the work of treatment being done through the medium of relationships

- members being encouraged to develop positive transference, or attachment, to the community as a whole

- in relation to therapeutic communities for offenders, the principle of the community creating the space for offence-paralleling behaviour and its exploration to occur (the development of the KLAC was initially commissioned by HM Prison Service) (Kennard and Lees 2001).

The KLAC is a checklist of standards for democratic therapeutic community delivery. There are 58 items, organised under eight headings, relating to the various aspects of therapeutic community functioning:

- Culture of enquiry

- Treatment programme structure

- Treatment process and community living

- Responsibility and decision-making

- Staff team dynamics and relationships

- Boundaries and containment

- Physical resources

- Staff resources (Kennard and Lees 2001, pp.148–51).

The Community of Communities project

At the same time, the Community of Communities project described below has similarly tried to encapsulate the 'therapeutic community ethos' in its provisions for standards monitoring and accreditation. In Britain, great store has been set by therapies that can be manualised, and then outcomes evaluated against the manual. Therapeutic communities have always found the notion of manualised therapies antipathetic, but have recognised the need for standard setting and quality standards monitoring, with a view to continually improving practice. The ATC decided to grasp this nettle, but to address it in a way that is consistent with therapeutic community principles and practice. The ATC set up a working group to try and develop generic quality standards for all therapeutic communities, by expanding and developing the KLAC. These standards were then piloted with a number of therapeutic communities, and refined in the light of this experience.

The ATC then applied to the Community Fund (formerly the National Lottery Charities Board) to fund a programme of peer reviews of therapeutic communities and their current practice against these standards. The Community Fund agreed to fund this process for three years. This peer review process has been called the Community of Communities. The reviews work on an annual cycle of identifying standards, agreeing these in consultation with member communities (of the Community of Communities), and using these to collect information. The reviews aim to encourage staff and client members to share good practice, help them identify areas for improvement and work towards addressing these in action plans. The information collection stage is split into two parts – a self-review and an external peer review. The peer review has been designed to allow both the reviewed community and members from a peer community to share good practice. Information collected in these reviews will help identify areas for improvement and subsequent work.

The Community of Communities Service Standards for Therapeutic Communities developed and expanded the KLAC under eight new headings:

- Environment and facilities
- Staff resources
- Access, admission and discharge
- Care, treatment and the therapeutic environment
- Information, consent and confidentiality
- Rights, safeguards, boundaries and containment
- Organisation, policy and procedures
- External relations.

The Community of Communities project has gone some way to alleviating the anxiety about therapeutic communities providing adequate evidence of audit and quality standards monitoring, and is a step towards providing therapeutic community accreditation.

Conclusions

In the past, therapeutic communities have tended to see the processes of audit, quality standards and research as bureaucratic, cumbersome and stifling creativity and spontaneity. It can also be argued that the government's regulatory frameworks can be seen as a bureaucratic defence against risk and trust in its workers. It is true that audit, quality standards monitoring, clinical governance and research do take time, and can sometimes feel uninspiring compared to clinical work. However, we are all committed to good-quality practice with our clients and to improving this care and our practice, and it is clear that these processes all facilitate this. It is also clear that providing evidence of good quality care, through quality standards monitoring and accreditation, and evidence of effectiveness, through research, are politically very important and essential to our continued survival as a treatment of choice for our clients. Recent innovations in these areas have shown that attitudes to these tasks can change for therapeutic community members, as evidenced by the fact that many therapeutic communities are embracing the Community of Communities project with enthusiasm, finding it an opportunity to examine their own practice, and to learn from the practice in other therapeutic communities – maintaining the culture of enquiry!

CHAPTER 5

The Research Context for Therapeutic Communities in the USA

George De Leon

Addiction and psychiatric therapeutic communities

In its contemporary form, two major variants of the therapeutic community have emerged. One, in social psychiatry, consists of innovative units and wards designed for the psychological treatment and management of socially deviant psychiatric patients within (and outside) mental hospital settings. The other form therapeutic communities has taken is as community-based residential treatment programmes for addicts and alcoholics.

The differences as well as the similarities between the two main variants of the therapeutic community are discussed in the literature (Jones 1986; Kennard 1983; Sugarman 1986). Jones (1986), for example, broadly summarised major similarities and differences between what he termed as the democratic (or the 'old therapeutic community') and programmatic therapeutic communities (the 'new therapeutic communities'). Both aim to achieve an integrated family identity but with considerable differences in the quality of feelings. Both care about staff and clients, although differences exist as to the interpersonal intimacy between staff and clients. Both are grounded in a similar personality-based view of the disorder as compulsive behaviour in the context of stunted and immature psychosocial development. However, there is considerable difference in how the community is used as a treatment agent. Other specific differences are noted in the organisational structure, the form of group process and the dynamics of change (see De Leon 2000, Chapter 2).[1]

In North America the early differences between two main variants of the therapeutic community have receded. Development of a new generic therapeutic community in the USA has emerged from its various adaptations for special populations and settings and from its modifications of practices. To some extent these changes reflect a 'blend of the two forms' as speculated by Jones (1986). There is a broader focus on psychological and personality problems, a staff composition involving significant proportions of mental health and human services professionals along with non-traditional recovered professionals, moderation of encounter or confrontation and inclusion of a variety of interventions.

The research context for addiction therapeutic communities

A critical distinction of the addiction therapeutic community is the extent to which it has been researched and evaluated. This distinction largely reflects the social, political and scientific *context* of substance abuse treatment in the USA. 'Context' refers to the 'climate' or array of issues that influence public response and funding for drug treatment and research. Typical influences are the status of the substance abuse problems (i.e. changing drug patterns, their prevalence and pervasiveness); the population targets of drug use (e.g. adolescents, the homeless, the mentally ill); the crime correlates of drug use (i.e. safety and costs); health risks (e.g. TB, HIV/AIDS, Hepatitis C and other liver diseases); health costs (private, public costs treatment) and social costs (welfare, workfare, taxes).

'Context' also refers to influences emerging from the evolution of the treatment approach and the therapeutic community research knowledge base itself. For example, in responding to socio-political influences therapeutic communities have modified and adapted the model and method to treat the special populations and problems. Correspondingly, the implementation and evaluation of these modified models have also influenced priorities for funding a research agenda.

In a certain sense, the social context issues for therapeutic community research have remained unchanged in the four decades since the therapeutic community appeared as a major treatment approach. Persistent questions have centred on the comparative and cost effectiveness of residential therapeutic community treatment. Although answered across the years, these questions are continually re-addressed for changing populations of drug users and in changing socio-economic climates.

Both the constant and changing contextual issues have generated a scientific knowledge base that influences the current and future climate of therapeutic community research in the USA. In this chapter I will briefly trace the development of this knowledge base, its related contextual issues and some practical applications.

The main lines of therapeutic community research in the USA are organised into two phases, the early (circa 1973–89) and current (1990 to the present). The key findings and conclusions from the studies in each phase are summarised from a variety of reviews in the literature (e.g. Anglin and Hser 1990; De Leon 1985;

Gerstein and Harwood 1990; Hubbard *et al.* 1989; Simpson 1997; Simpson and Sells 1982; Tims, De Leon and Jainchill 1994; Tims and Ludford 1984). The incremental research in these phases provides the empirical basis for addressing issues in the next phase of therapeutic community research – an agenda for which is outlined in the last section of the chapter.

Research: Phase I (1970–89)

Context and issues

Beginning in the 1960s, the heroin epidemic and its crime consequences launched an expansion of drug treatment resources and research activities. These initiatives continued during the 1970s and 1980s during which drug use became 'enculturated' – marked by the widening cafeteria of drugs of abuse, the decreasing age of first use of any drug and the pervasiveness of use across all levels of the society (De Leon 1994c).

Therapeutic communities had emerged as *alternatives* to conventional medical and mental health treatments for the opioid abuser but their doors were open to alcoholics and other substance abusers. The therapeutic community perspective of the disorder, the client and recovery differed from other major treatment modalities (see De Leon 2000, Part 2). The residents in therapeutic communities were usually the most severe substance abusers with wide-ranging personality problems and social deviancy in addition to their drug use. Thus treatment focused upon the whole person and changing lifestyle and identity rather than simply achieving abstinence. These broad goals could only be achieved through an intensive, 24-hour-a-day, 7-day-a-week treatment in a long-term residential setting.

The therapeutic community approach was not well understood but, more important, it was viewed as expensive, particularly when compared with outpatient counselling and pharmacotherapy such as methadone maintenance. Furthermore, dropout rates were high, suggesting that the broad impact of the therapeutic community was limited when defined in terms of the relatively small number of admissions completing treatment. These issues were fundamental to the survival of the therapeutic community as a *bona fide* health care modality that deserved continued public funding. They framed the key lines of enquiry in Phase I – the description of the social and psychological profiles of therapeutic community admissions, documentation of the effectiveness of therapeutic community treatment and illumination of the phenomenon of retention in treatment.

The research questions were pursued primarily through single programme and multi-programme evaluations funded by the National Institute on Drug Abuse (NIDA) of therapeutic communities involving approximately 5000 adult and adolescent admissions to community-based therapeutic communities. Additionally, secondary analyses were conducted of other data sets, which included over 7000 admissions to therapeutic communities. The main findings and conclusions in each of line inquiry are discussed separately.

Who comes for treatment?

The broad issue underlying this line of enquiry was the validation of the therapeutic community perspective of the disorder and recovery, i.e. that the individuals served required long-term residential treatment. Table 5.1 summarises the main findings from studies describing the social and psychological characteristics of admissions to therapeutic community programmes. These documented that substance abuse among therapeutic community admissions is a disorder of the whole person. In addition to their substance abuse and social deviancy, the drug abusers who enter therapeutic communities reveal a considerable degree of psychological disability, which is further confirmed in the diagnostic studies. Despite the therapeutic communities' policy concerning psychiatric exclusion, the large majority of adult and adolescent admissions meet the criteria for co-existing substance abuse and other psychiatric disorders.

Table 5.1 Profiles of therapeutic community admissions

Socio-demographic profile

Most therapeutic community admissions are males, white and over 21 years of age. They are users of multiple drugs, including marijuana, opiates, alcohol, pills and cocaine/crack. The majority have poor work histories, have engaged in criminal activities and been arrested; and over a third have been incarcerated for drug- and non-drug-related crimes (e.g. De Leon 1984, 1985; Hubbard *et al.* 1984; Simpson and Sells 1982).

The social profiles of admissions to traditional therapeutic community programmes are similar regardless of primary drug preference; and they do not differ significantly from client profiles in therapeutic community facilities established exclusively for certain populations such as adolescents, mothers with their children, ethnic minorities and criminal justice referrals or prison inmates. The profiles of these various populations appear to be more homogeneous than heterogeneous.

Psychological profile

Most therapeutic community admissions mirror the features of both psychiatric and criminal populations. The character disorder characteristics and poor self-concept of delinquent and repeated offenders are present, along with the dysphoria, depression, anxiety and confused thinking of emotionally unstable or psychiatric populations.

Psychiatric diagnoses

Over 70 per cent of admission samples meet DSM criteria for Axis I and Axis II psychiatric disorders in addition to substance abuse or dependence. The most frequent non-drug diagnoses are depression, phobias, generalised anxiety, psychosexual dysfunction and antisocial personality. Comparable percentages of dual disorder are obtained among adolescent admissions to therapeutic communities. Trends indicate that the psychological profile of substance abusers admitted to therapeutic communities has been worsening over the years (De Leon 1989, 1991; Jainchill, De Leon and Pinkham 1986).

Are therapeutic communities effective?

The unique recovery goals of the therapeutic community are changing lifestyles and identities. Thus it was essential to document the effectiveness of the long-term residential therapeutic community particularly as compared to other treatment modalities. A particular issue was the clarification of outcomes among those who do not complete treatment, as dropout occurs in the majority of admissions. Table 5.2 summarises the key findings from these outcome studies. Long-term residential therapeutic communities are effective in reducing drug abuse and antisocial behaviour, and improving psychological status in a considerable number of substance abusers, particularly opioid abusers. The extent of social and psychological improvement is directly related to retention in treatment.

Table 5.2 Post-treatment outcomes for admissions to residential therapeutic communities

Outcomes

Significant improvements occur on separate behavioural outcome variables (e.g. drug use, criminality and employment) and on composite indices of these variables for measuring individual status or success. Maximum to moderately favourable outcomes (based on indices of opioid, non-opioid and alcohol use; arrest rates; re-treatment and employment) occur for more than half of the sample of completed clients and dropouts (De Leon 1984; Hubbard *et al.* 1989; Simpson and Sells 1982).

In the studies that investigated psychological outcomes (e.g. depression, anxiety, self-concept), results uniformly showed significant improvement at follow-up (e.g. Biase, Sullivan and Wheeler 1986; De Leon 1984; Holland 1983). A direct relationship has been demonstrated between post-treatment behavioural success (i.e. reduced drug use and criminality) and psychological adjustment (De Leon 1984; De Leon and Jainchill 1981–82).

Predictors of outcomes

There is a consistent positive relationship between time spent in residential treatment and post-treatment outcome status (e.g. De Leon 1984; Hubbard *et al.* 1989; Kooyman 1993; Simpson 1979). For example, long-term therapeutic community success rates (based on composite indices of no drug use and no criminality) at two-year post-treatment approximate 90 per cent, 50 per cent and 25 per cent, respectively, for graduates/completers and dropouts who remain more than and less than one year in residential treatment: improvement rates over pre-treatment status approximate 100 per cent, 70 per cent, and 40 per cent respectively (De Leon, Wexler and Jainchill 1982).

Client-related factors are small predictors of outcomes at follow-up. The most consistent are baseline frequency of the behavioural outcomes, severity of criminality and psychopathology, which are correlated with poorer outcomes. Demography and social background are the least consistent predictors.

What is known about retention in therapeutic community treatment?

Length of stay in treatment is the largest and most consistent predictor of positive post-treatment outcomes. However, most therapeutic community admissions leave long-term treatment prematurely. Thus, understanding retention was and remains crucial for improving the impact and cost benefit of therapeutic community treatment. Studies have focused upon four areas: retention rates, the temporal pattern of dropout, client predictors of dropout and initial attempts to enhance early retention in treatment. The main findings in each area are summarised in Table 5.3. While a legitimate concern, retention should not be confused with treatment effectiveness. Therapeutic communities are effective for those who remain long enough for treatment influences to occur. Obviously, a critical issue for therapeutic communities is maximising holding power to benefit more clients.

Table 5.3 Retention in therapeutic communities

Temporal pattern of retention

In long-term residential therapeutic communities, completion rates average 10–20 per cent of all admissions. One-year retention rates range from 15–30 per cent. However, more recent trends suggest gradual increases in 12-month retention compared to the period before 1980. Although overall levels of retention vary, the temporal pattern of dropout is uniform across therapeutic community programmes (and other modalities). Dropout is highest in the first 30 days of admission, but declines sharply thereafter. Generally, the probability of continuing in treatment increases with time in the programme itself (De Leon 1991; De Leon and Schwartz 1984).

Predictors of dropout

There are no reliable client characteristics that predict retention, with the exception of severe criminality and/or severe psychopathology, which are correlated with earlier dropout. Studies point to the importance of dynamic factors in predicting retention in treatment, such as perceived legal pressure, motivation and readiness for treatment (e.g. Condelli and De Leon 1993; De Leon 1988, De Leon *et al.* 1994; Hubbard *et al.* 1989; Simpson and Joe 1993).

Enhancing retention in therapeutic communities

Some experimental attempts to enhance retention in therapeutic communities have utilised supportive individual counselling, improved orientation to treatment by experienced staff (De Leon *et al.* 2000) and family alliance strategies to reduce early dropout (e.g. De Leon 1988, 1991). Other efforts include providing special facilities and programming for mothers and children (Hughes *et al.* 1995; Stevens, Arbiter and Glider 1989; Stevens and Glider 1994) and curriculum-based relapse prevention methods (Lewis *et al.* 1993) to sustain retention throughout residential treatment. Though results are promising, these efforts require replication in multiple sites.

Some practices and policy applications influenced by Phase I research

Overall, the Phase I research confirmed that therapeutic communities were serving the most difficult substance abusers. Moreover, findings consistently supported the validity of the therapeutic community perspective on addiction and recovery: substance abuse is a disorder of the whole person; and long-term treatment is needed to achieve the therapeutic community recovery goals of changing lifestyles.

The Phase I research also had practical applications that contributed to a changing context in several ways. For example, therapeutic communities now *focus on retention*. Staff no longer 'blame the client' for early dropout, recognising that motivational/readiness factors should be assessed and enhanced as part of the treatment plan. Though not rigorously surveyed, many therapeutic communities incorporate activities as interventions to enhance early retention, e.g. family involvement, individual counselling, senior staff seminars and medications. Therapeutic communities also *focus on assessment*. Admission practices address client suitability for the therapeutic community as well as risk for early dropout and, increasingly more programmes monitor on a continuous basis progress and motivational changes. Although the basic therapeutic community elements define the treatment approach in different settings, there is an increased awareness of the importance of client-treatment matching. Multi-setting therapeutic community agencies attempt to assess which clients are appropriate for long- and shorter-term residential treatment as well as for therapeutic-community-oriented day care and outpatient treatment.

Therapeutic communities *display receptivity to research*. More therapeutic community agencies participate in research studies and attempt to establish programme-based evaluation capability. Emphasis is placed upon cross-fertilisation of research and therapeutic community clinical practice as illustrated in several publications (Millstein 1994; Tims, De Leon and Jainchill 1994).

An indirect effect of Phase I research has been *increased affirmation and morale*. Research has confirmed the perspective of the therapeutic community and its clinical views with respect to outcomes and retention. This has generally strengthened perceptions of the credibility of the therapeutic community approach. As a result, therapeutic community clinical staff and programme management articulate with confidence what they do and how well therapeutic communities work.

Finally, the empirical knowledge base developed in the Phase I studies surfaced two related issues that contributed to the scientific and policy context in subsequent phases. First, *effectiveness studies*, those conducted on therapeutic community treatment as it is practised in the field, established the benefits of therapeutic community treatment prior to *efficacy studies*, those conducted in controlled conditions. The evidence from the field studies was and remains compelling (in the numbers of clients studied and the replication of findings across years, samples and investigative teams). Indeed, the field studies have provided the main empirical justification for continued federal funding for drug treatment expansion and for treatment services research.

Second, the difficulty in implementing controlled studies or randomised clinical trials in field situations is well known (e.g. De Leon, Inciardi and Martin

1995). This issue has underscored the need for new research strategies to further illuminate treatment effectiveness. Some examples of these, which have been pursued in Phase II, are discussed below.

Phase II (1990–2000)

Context and issues

Phase II witnessed a considerable increase in federal support for therapeutic community research. This reflects the scientific gains in Phase I but also the persistence of the drug problem and the evolution of the therapeutic community itself. The fact that drug *treatment* works does not necessarily solve society's drug *problem*. Substance abuse and related problems remain pervasive in terms of the diversity of populations and drugs of abuse. In response to this, therapeutic communities have moved into mainstream medical, mental health and human services. Moreover, the Phase I knowledge base established the credibility of the therapeutic community approach as well as therapeutic community research. A prominent symbol of this contextual change is the NIDA-funded Center for Therapeutic Community Research (CTCR) at National Development and Research Institutes, Inc. (NDRI).

Therapeutic communities have modified their practices and adapted the approach for special populations, settings and funding requirements. Illustrations of these modifications and adaptations are described elsewhere (De Leon 1997, 2000, Chapter 25). The evolution of the therapeutic community resurfaced basic policy issues such as the feasibility, effectiveness and cost benefits of its various adaptations. In particular, managed care pressures to reduce the cost of treatment have challenged the necessity for long-term residential treatment. However, a second issue that emerged from the adaptations and modifications of the therapeutic community concerned the *fidelity* of the approach itself. The wide diversity of therapeutic community-oriented programmes has raised a variety of theoretical and quality assurance questions.

These issues associated with the diversity of clients served and the fidelity of the therapeutic community adaptations have directed two main lines of inquiry in Phase II – to document the effectiveness of standard therapeutic communities as well as modified therapeutic communities for special populations and to undertake studies clarifying the essential elements of the therapeutic community approach. Federal funding encouraging research on these questions included support for studies conducted at CTCR as well as large-scale multi-modality national surveys such as the National Treatment Improvement Evaluation Study (NTIES) and the Drug Abuse Treatment Outcome Study (DATOS). The findings and conclusions for the main Phase II questions are separately discussed.

Are contemporary therapeutic communities effective and cost-effective for treating the current diversity of substance abusers?

Studies addressed the profiles of admissions to both standard and modified therapeutic communities. These focused upon psychiatric comorbidity, retention characteristics, short- and long-term outcomes and cost analyses. Key populations studied were mentally ill chemical abusers (MICAs), adolescents, homeless, criminal justice clients and mothers with children, as well as methadone-maintained clients. Data collection involved several thousand admissions to the standard therapeutic community programmes in other federally funded studies and over 3300 admissions to 14 modified therapeutic community programmes in CTCR studies. Table 5.4 summarises the findings and conclusions as to the admission profiles and the effectiveness of standard and modified therapeutic communities.

Table 5.4 Profiles of admissions and effectiveness of standard and modified therapeutic communities

Standard therapeutic communities

The national, multi-modality survey studies uniformly showed that community-based standard therapeutic community residential programmes were serving the most severe substance abusers compared to other treatment modalities (Simpson *et al.* 1999). The profiles of admissions indicate that contemporary therapeutic communities are serving individuals who reveal a considerable degree of social and psychological dysfunction in addition to their substance abuse.

Long-term residential programmes obtain positive outcomes in drug use, criminality, employment and psychological adjustment that are comparable or superior to the other modalities treating less severe substance abusers (National Treatment Improvement Evaluation Study (NTIES) 1996; Simpson and Curry 1997). And, cost benefits for long-term residential treatment exceeded those of other treatment modalities, particularly benefits associated with reduction in crime (Center for Substance Abuse Treatment (CSAT), National Evaluation Data Services 1999; Flynn *et al.* 1999).

Planned duration of residential treatment is generally shorter than in earlier years. However, outcomes are still favourable among the clients who complete or stay longer in treatment (Simpson and Curry 1997). Differential effects of longer- and shorter-planned durations of residential stay remain to be clarified, however, in studies that match clients to appropriate planned durations.

Modified therapeutic communities

Drug use and criminality declined along with improvements in employment and psychological status. Again, improvements were correlated with length of stay in treatment (De Leon, Sacks *et al.* 2000; Inciardi *et al.* 1997; Jainchill, Hawke and De Leon 2000; Martin *et al.* 1999; Wexler *et al.* 1999). Aftercare, services beyond primary treatment in the residential therapeutic community, is a critical component of stable outcomes. Thus, regardless of the planned duration of primary treatment, individuals must continue in the treatment process for some undetermined time beyond the residential phase.

Aftercare models must be *integrated* with the primary treatment model in terms of philosophy, methods and relationships to provide effective continuity of care. Controlled studies in progress assess therapeutic-community-oriented *vs* non-therapeutic-community-oriented aftercare models on samples leaving therapeutic community-oriented primary treatment.

Fiscal studies indicate that therapeutic-community-oriented programmes reveal favourable cost benefit gains, particularly in reduction of expenditures associated with criminal activity in mental health services (e.g. French *et al.* 1999; McGeary *et al.* 2000).

The weight of the evidence from the Phase II studies indicates that current standard and modified therapeutic communities provide effective treatment for the current generation of substance abusers who reveal a wide range of social and psychological problems. Based upon its unique self-help perspective, therapeutic communities provide an extremely favourable cost-benefit alternative to traditional institution-based treatments in mental health, hospital, correctional and community-based settings.

What is the therapeutic community treatment approach and why does it work?

Therapeutic communities are complex programmes that are considered difficult and costly to implement relative to other treatment modalities. Specification of the 'active ingredients' of the method and understanding the treatment process is critical to substantiate the validity of the therapeutic community approach, to justify its costs, and to improve the approach itself through research and training.

Studies clarifying the treatment approach were mainly conducted by CTCR at NDRI. These focused upon elaborating the theory and method of the therapeutic community approach; developing instruments for assessing client motivation and readiness for treatment and clinical progress; defining and validating the essential elements of the therapeutic community model; identifying therapeutic community treatment environments that relate to risk for client dropout and providing a conceptual formulation of the treatment process. Data were collected on over 2900 clients in over 12 therapeutic community treatment programmes. Secondary analyses utilised data on an additional 4000 clients in some 30 programmes. Table 5.5 summarises the main findings and conclusions form these studies.

Table 5.5 Clarifying the therapeutic community approach: Findings and conclusions

Programme diversity

Empirical studies have identified the essential elements of the therapeutic community programme model. Therapeutic community programmes have been differentiated in terms of standard and modified types and with respect to environmental factors that relate to dropout (e.g. Melnick and De Leon 1999; Melnick *et al.* 2001a; Jainchill, Yagelka and Messina submitted).

Motivation

The role of motivational and readiness factors in entry and retention in therapeutic community treatment has been assessed (e.g. De Leon, Melnick and Hawke 2000; Simpson and Joe 1993) and initial studies have measured these factors in the treatment process in the therapeutic community (Melnick *et al.* 2001b; Simpson *et al.* 1997).

Clinical assessment

An array of related instruments has been developed to measure client progress in the therapeutic community assessed by the clients, staff and peers (e.g. *Communications* 2000; Kressel *et al.* 2000; Kressel, Rubin *et al.* submitted).

Theoretical framework

Research has contributed to the development of a comprehensive *theoretical framework* of the therapeutic community approach. This framework is utilised to guide clinical practice, programme planning, treatment improvement as well as empirical studies of treatment process and client–treatment matching (De Leon 2000).

Practice and policy applications influenced by Phase II research

Phase II research documented the fact that current standard therapeutic communities are serving the most serious substance abusers. More important, it provided evidence for the feasibility and effectiveness of implementing modified therapeutic community programmes into various institutional settings (mental hospitals, homeless shelters, prisons and methadone clinics). These scientific gains have advanced initiatives to extend modified therapeutic community programmes further into mainstream human services. The most impressive of these advances is the expansion of therapeutic community-oriented programmes in the correctional system and, to a lesser extent, into community residences for the mentally ill and homeless shelter settings.

The clarification of the treatment model, the elaboration of the theoretical framework of the treatment approach, and the supporting research facilitated significant initiatives to improve therapeutic community treatment through *quality assurance* and *training*. National standards for prison-based and community-based therapeutic community treatment have been developed and promulgated. Efforts are underway to establish a process for programme accreditation and staff training based upon these standards and grounded in theory (e.g. Talboy 1998). The training model consists of a uniform *curriculum* including theoretical concepts and clinical practices and an appropriate *format* including didactic and experiential components (*Communications* 1999).

Finally, despite differences in populations, drugs of preference, programme modifications adaptations and fiscal climates, the Phase II research essentially replicated the basic findings in Phase I. The empirical 'lawfulness' of findings across some 30 years of research, even in the absence of conventional controlled designs, has firmly established validity of the therapeutic community approach and, as discussed below, changed the research agenda.

The current phase: A new research agenda

Context and issues

The evolution of the scientific knowledge base through Phases I and II has gradually shifted the research question from *whether* therapeutic communities work to *how* they work. To a considerable extent, this shift reflects both policy and scientific issues. Therapeutic communities 'work' for serious substance abusers, for special populations and in various settings. The weight of the outcome research accumulated over 30 years has established the field effectiveness of the therapeutic community as a *global* approach. However, research must isolate the components of the approach that are critical to its effectiveness in order to establish the therapeutic community as an 'evidenced-based' treatment.

Identifying the 'active treatment ingredients' of the therapeutic community approach remains a compelling question for funding policy as well as science. Reducing the costs of treatment by limiting its planned duration, for example, can be rationally implemented only if the necessary and sufficient therapeutic community interventions are known. More generally, support for therapeutic community research itself by providers, consumers and the public depends upon whether they perceive science as useful in improving treatment.

These contextual issues shape the agenda for the current phase of research. Several lines of inquiry can be subsumed under the broad theme of advancing therapeutic community treatment. The key question and suggested research for each is illustrated briefly in Table 5.6.

Table 5.6 The current phase of therapeutic community research: Several lines of inquiry

How can therapeutic community research be translated into practice?

The value of therapeutic community research for practice depends upon its *utilisation* by the treatment agencies. Thus, training and other technology transfer strategies must be innovated and evaluated to facilitate the use by therapeutic community agencies of existing research-based knowledge. Similarly, models for implementing programme-based research capability must be innovated and evaluated. Studies are needed of the organisational dynamics that foster integration of research into practice at the programme level.

How can service delivery be improved within therapeutic communities?

Therapeutic community agencies are complex organisations whose various components must be integrated to advance and maximise the delivery of treatment. Thus research is needed to clarify: the organisational readiness of therapeutic community agencies to accept and implement change in practices and programming; and organisational integration as to mission, philosophy, perspective and method.

How do therapeutic community programmes integrate into larger systems of service delivery?

Therapeutic community agencies are part of larger systems of service delivery, such as criminal justice, mental health, shelters and schools. Their continued effectiveness depends upon how well they integrate into the broader health care and human services systems. Studies must clarify the impact of the therapeutic community on larger systems and reciprocally the impact of those systems on the therapeutic community. Specifically, evaluations must clarify how therapeutic community programming, research and evaluation activities influence change in larger systems such as prisons, shelters, mental hospitals and alternative schools.

How can the therapeutic community remain cost-effective and retain the integrity of its approach?

Therapeutic communities are treating a diversity of clients with a wide range of problems. Their unique recovery goals of changing lifestyles and identities cannot be achieved realistically under funding pressures to reduce both time and intensify of treatment. The discrepancies between the clinical realities and funding demands can be further reconciled in part through theoretically grounded *econometric* research.

Additionally, research must clarify the effectiveness of short-term therapeutic community treatment, develop and evaluate strategies to *match* client with treatment setting and planned duration. Studies are needed that illuminate the actual cost savings *associated* with treatment intensity (planned duration) and treatment setting (residential, institutional, or non-residential).

The challenge of the treatment process

To a considerable extent the pursuit of the current research agenda is contingent upon the scientific elaboration of the 'black box' of treatment process in the therapeutic community. If links cannot be established explicitly between programme interventions, the course of client change and eventual outcomes, the effectiveness of any therapeutic community-orientated model remains unclear, much less proven.

Similarly, understanding the treatment process is critical to retain the integrity of the therapeutic community approach in its various adaptations. Training curricula to upgrade clinical practices and programme standards to maintain quality assurance must be grounded in the essential elements of the approach. Although theoretically formulated, the 'essentiality' of these elements requires empirical validation through studies of the treatment process.

Thus, illuminating the process of change is crucial to prove as well as improve the efficacy of the therapeutic community treatment itself. However, the global psychosocial ecology of the therapeutic community, the holistic nature of the disorder and the dynamic properties of recovery make describing, much less understanding, the therapeutic community process a formidable challenge. This last section briefly outlines issues and suggested directions for researching treatment process in therapeutic communities.

The research in Phase II has initiated a scientific effort to understand treatment process in therapeutic communities. As described earlier, a theoretical framework of the therapeutic community perspective, model and method and a conceptual formulation of the treatment process were provided. An array of process-related instruments have been developed assessing the essential elements of the therapeutic community model, the programme environment, client motivational factors and individual progress in treatment. Nevertheless, research designs and investigational strategies that are grounded in therapeutic community theory are needed to clarify the complexity of the treatment process itself.

According to therapeutic community theory the treatment process is the dynamic relationship between the community as a context of multiple interventions, planned and unplanned, which are interrelated to effect multi-dimensional change in the individual (see De Leon 2000, Chapter 24). This formulation strains the use of conventional designs that attempt to isolate an 'active ingredient' of the process (e.g. the encounter groups) while controlling for all other ingredients (e.g. community meetings, peer interactions). Moreover, such 'component strategies' usually perturb the fabric of the treatment itself by altering the planned programme of activities. This latter problem has contributed to agency and staff resistance to process research, which is perceived as intrusive and disruptive.

The theoretical framework of the therapeutic community suggests the use of 'global research strategies', which aim to capture the *interrelated impact* of various essential elements (i.e. interventions) of the therapeutic community on individual progress during treatment. These strategies incorporate qualitative and quantitative techniques utilising participant observer, staff and peer and client measurements to assess the process *as it unfolds*. Causal models can depict complex, reciprocal interactions among multiple components, e.g. how participation in the group interrelates with informal peer conversations to produce a desired change in attitude or behaviour. Initial attempts at modelling the process are contained in the literature (e.g. De Leon 2000; Kressel, Palij *et al.* manuscript in submission; Nielsen and Scarpitti 1997; Simpson *et al.* 1997).

Global strategies, however, do not provide direct tests of the 'essentiality' of certain elements in the sense of isolating the necessity, or sufficiency, of particular treatment components. Thus, combinations of global and component research strategies are needed to illuminate the process as well as improve the treatment approach (see examples in Table 5.7).

Table 5.7 Strategies for studying the therapeutic community treatment approach

Comparing treatment models

In reality not all therapeutic communities retain all of the elements that are theoretically considered essential. For example, field studies of treatment type, modified *vs* traditional therapeutic community (e.g. Melnick *et al.* 2001a; Melnick and De Leon 1999) and treatment environments of the therapeutic community (e.g. Jainchill, Yagelka and Messina submitted) attest to the variants in the model. Evaluating the comparative effectiveness of these models provides information as to the active treatment elements that are constant across programmes.

Enhancing treatment components

This variant of the conventional 'component strategy' focuses upon enhancing the magnitude of various therapeutic community interventions ('ingredients') to assess their contribution to the process. It introduces modifications into the treatment that are *theoretically consistent* with the approach. An example is the special use of upper staff ('senior professors') in the first days of admissions to improve retention in treatment (e.g. De Leon, Hawke *et al.* 2000).

Maximising treatment fidelity

This strategy focuses upon the entire treatment protocol rather than identifying specific relationships among the essential elements of the process. However, the validity of the process is demonstrated by *maximising the fidelity* of the treatment approach. Fidelity involves training and monitoring the implementation of the therapeutic community approach in accordance with its theory. The research hypothesis is that maximising overall fidelity *improves* treatment (less dropout, more favourable outcomes) and *reduces the time in treatment* needed for improved outcomes.

Stage-specific process and efficacy

In this strategy the process in the therapeutic community can be studied in terms of its theoretically prescribed phases or stages of treatment. The assumption underlying this strategy is that the efficacy of each stage leads to the long-term treatment goals. Studies can document and assess stage-specific process and efficacy in terms of completion of stage goals. Utilising some of the above strategies, studies can improve or maximise stage outcomes such as induction or orientation to assure retention in treatment and readiness for the entry into the stage of primary treatment.

Beyond appropriate innovative design strategies, however, may be the need to re-conceptualise the global nature of the therapeutic community and the process of change in ways similar to that of families (or villages). For example, some of the 'essential elements' of the 'effective family' are commonly recognised (e.g. structural intactness, positive parental and/or sibling role models, explicit behavioural expectations, social values, open communication, demonstrable expressions of love and acceptance). Presumably, it is the aggregate ('gestalt') of essential elements that facilitates positive psychosocial development among the different children in the family.

Thus, isolating the separate contribution of each element to family effectiveness appears less explanatory or practically useful than assuring that all, or some, threshold level of elements are sufficiently present and active.

From the above family analogy surfaces the complex issue of individual differences in the therapeutic community treatment process. The therapeutic community is a unique social and psychological approach in which the aggregate of essential elements is summarised in the phrase 'community as method'. Individuals change through their participation in all of the community activities (e.g. groups, meetings, work) and roles (e.g. relationships, job functions, group leaders, peer facilitators, role models). Interrelated behaviours, attitudes, experiences, and perceptions gradually evolve into lifestyle and identity change as individuals fully immerse themselves in the community and internalise its teachings (De Leon 2000, Chapter 24).

The term 'threshold' refers to the minimum *density* of essential elements, as well as the *time* of exposure to these elements, which is needed to maximise the community impact. In the therapeutic community the thresholds for community impact on the change process may vary across individuals and sub-groups. Some clients require continuous exposure to all of the essential elements theoretically defined in the long-term traditional therapeutic community. Others may require fewer elements for shorter periods of time. Even among severe substance abusers, who are the clients that long-term therapeutic communities primarily serve, individuals differ in their threshold for community impact. These differences reflect their social and psychological characteristics, e.g. habilitation, psychiatric disturbance and readiness to change, as well as suitability to communal living.

These complexities underscore the need for useful strategies that *match* clients with the therapeutic community model (modified/traditional with respect to essential elements), the duration of treatment (short term/long term), and the setting (residential/non-residential), as well as for studies of individual differences within a particular model. More broadly, the issue of individual differences and thresholds for community impact highlight the need for creative paradigms for researching the therapeutic community process itself. These must be guided by the proposition that the integrity of the community as context and method must be retained to produce individual change.

CHAPTER 6

The Gold Standard

What are RCTs and Where Did They Come From?

Nick Manning

The randomised controlled trial (RCT) evolved in the inter-war years in Britain under the leadership of the Medical Research Council. It aimed to identify the fairest and most reliable way of judging the efficacy of different medical interventions. Similar developments occurred throughout Europe and the USA at that time. The RCT has become the 'gold standard' for the experimental evaluation of medical and social interventions. One reason for this is that under the right experimental circumstances it is the most powerful method we have for irrefutably demonstrating the cause–effect link between some kind of treatment and the effects of that treatment on the subject receiving it. The search for such evidence is a central strategy for a scientific philosophy known as positivism, typically associated with twentieth-century pure science. From this point of view science progresses from the slow accumulation of evidence acquired ideally through controlled experimentation. However, it turns out that many medical and social interventions cannot be undertaken under the 'right experimental circumstances', and hence cannot draw upon the support of an RCT to demonstrate their efficacy.

The RCT involves the experimental allocation of patients to one of several kinds of treatment, or no treatment, to determine, by comparing the results for each group, which patients do better. Within this simple idea there are buried a number of assumptions which we will examine in this chapter, so that we can identify the relevance of the RCT to therapeutic community practice.

What is an RCT?

The classic description of the RCT is often traced back to a paper published in 1948 that contained a particularly clear exposition of the process involved:

> Determination of whether a patient would be treated by streptomycin and bed-rest (S case) or by bed-rest alone (C case) was made by reference to a statistical series based on random sampling numbers drawn up for each sex at each centre by Professor Bradford Hill; the details of the series were unknown to any of the investigators or to the co-ordinator and were contained in a set of sealed envelopes, each bearing on the outside only the name of the hospital and a number. After acceptance of a patient by the panel, and before admission to the streptomycin centre, the appropriate numbered envelope was opened at the central office; the card inside told if the patient was to be an S or a C case, and this information was then given to the medical officer of the centre. (Research Council Streptomycin in Tuberculosis Trials Committee 1948, 769–82)

Before this time, the idea of comparing different types of treatment was not new – indeed such comparisons had been suggested many hundreds of years ago. Even the idea of random allocation had been suggested in 1662 by van Helmont when

> he challenged the academics of the day to compare their treatments based on theory with his based on experience. 'Let us take out of the hospitals, out of the Camps, or from elsewhere, 200, or 500 poor People, that have Fevers, Pleurisies, etc. Let us divide them into half, let us cast lots, that one half of them may fall to my share, and the other to yours… We shall see how many funerals both of us shall have. But let the reward of the contention or wager, be 300 florins, deposited on both sides.' (Doll 1998, 1217–20)

However, there were likely to be several sources of error with such systems. Doctors who had always been used to making decisions as to the best form of treatment for their patients were highly likely to allocate patients to the different groups influenced by a more or less conscious appraisal as to the likely benefits in their view of the results of the treatment. This is a source of bias termed 'selection' bias, as it may result in the selection of patients for each group that is systematic and might influence the results. In other words, the groups would not be comparing 'like with like'. A second source of error was also likely to result from those observers recording the progress of the patients in the different groups who knew which treatment each group was getting. For example, they might inadvertently be more likely to judge those patients getting a well-known treatment as benefiting, simply because they knew that this group was being treated; and similarly they might be less likely to observe improvement in those patients that they knew to be receiving no treatment at all. This is termed 'observer bias'. There may be many other sources of known and unknown bias, often of a random nature.

The solution to such biases was to separate the selection and observation from the clinicians by controlling the allocation of patients through the use of random numbers, and by eliminating any prior knowledge about the patients from those conducting the assessment of the response of patients to their treatment. These strict controls over an experimental process, however, carry with them a number of complications and difficulties that we will explore in more detail, as they have a particular bearing on therapeutic community practice.

What is a trial?

The trial actually involves treating or not treating a group of patients, assessing their responses to treatment over time, and then comparing the average response by the two (or more) groups – technically a comparison of the 'group means'. The notion of treatment itself is not simple. Where a single dimension of treatment is involved, for example the administration of a simple, fast-acting drug in varying doses, then the chain of cause and effect is compelling. However, if the treatment is complex or multi-dimensional, and cumulative over time, such as a psychological or social intervention (and typical of therapeutic community treatment), then the nature of the active ingredient will be difficult to specify with any certainty. Nevertheless, where the change in the mean of the treated group is more than we would reasonably expect by chance, and statistically different from the mean change observed in the non-treated group, then we can infer that the known difference between the groups (that is the treatment) has had an effect. We must note here that the group mean can include those patients who respond strongly, those who respond weakly, and those who have had a negative reaction. We cannot say that for any individual patient we know what change the specific treatment has effected – merely that for the group as a whole. To generalise from the group to the individual, which is known as the 'ecological fallacy', is of course often a step that is made in practice since practitioners are responsible for devising treatments for individual patients for whom they are responsible.

Why control?

Why should we have control or comparison groups? An alternative, for example, might be to try one treatment for a while for each patient, and if it seems unsatisfactory, then to try another one, and so on. Indeed, this pattern may well be a reality for much minor primary care treatment. But how will we know which of the interventions really worked? There may be a delayed reaction from one, which appears to take effect at the time an alternative treatment is applied. There may be coincident impacts from other experiences that the patient has, notwithstanding their current treatment; for example, changes in employment or family circumstances. A slightly more sophisticated approach might be to take a cohort of patients and to subject the whole group to the treatment, assessing before and after the treatment whether there was any improvement. However, we now know that many patients spontaneously improve over time with no treatment at all, and we would not know if this had happened in this case. By using a control or comparison group, we can assume that the impact of any other treatments or extraneous factors is equally likely to have occurred in both groups, if they are big enough, so that such effects can be discounted.

Why randomise?

We have already pointed out that the way patients might be assigned to comparison groups, and the way in which they might be observed, are potential sources of 'selection' or 'observer' bias, respectively. There are other possible sources of bias, some of which we might guess at; for example, the interaction of age, race or gender with selection, treatment or observation. But there may also be unknown biases which we cannot identify, or might not have the resources to identify. These biases can also be assumed to be equally spread between control and treatment groups by the process of random assignment, so that we can be confident that where there are systematic and measurable differences between the groups, these will not have arisen by chance; or at least that we can set a threshold level of chance errors, above which we are confident that the effects we observe are very unlikely to have happened by chance. The logic of this process of randomising errors, so that any real effects shine through, is really very strong.

Fool's gold – Why the RCT is less than perfect

Despite those advantages that flow from the experimental comparison of treatment and control groups in RCTs, there has been a growing critical literature about the limitations of the use of RCTs in practice. We have alluded to some of these already, and many of them are germane to therapeutic community practice. There are a number of problems. First is the precision with which the treatment is developed and applied. Where an RCT is being used in a complex social situation, such as a therapeutic community, knowing exactly what the treatment 'mix' and 'dose' is can be difficult to specify reliably. It is difficult to standardise therapeutic community treatment, which is cyclical and changes in response to the dynamics of the system itself and the mix of individuals within the system. Yet without this, we can never take the further step of being able to take positive results away from the 'laboratory' and spread them into routine practice. The use of RCTs to evaluate social interventions such as crime reduction strategies (Pawson and Tilley 1997) or active employment interventions (Stafford 2002), have been criticised on these grounds. These authors have noted that correctives, such as taking the context of the treatment into account (i.e. 'real-world' proofing), or more careful control over elements of the intervention, are rarely successful. However, they are concerned to rebuff a conclusion that dominated criminological research for many years, after an influential paper (Martinson 1974) argued on the basis of evidence from poor study designs that 'nothing works'.

A second set of problems is the recruitment of patients into the trial. For those chosen, it is often difficult to disguise the fact that the treatment is novel, which is especially the case for therapeutic communities. This 'novelty', recognised many years ago in different ways as the 'Hawthorne' effect, and the placebo effect, whereby anything new tends to create a positive reaction, can generate responses that are difficult to replicate in the control group, and thereby eliminate. An additional problem for therapeutic communities is the 'volunteer' effect – patients have to want to take on a long and challenging treatment; and even when they do, existing community members (rather than researchers) normally have to vote them into the community. A further issue is the ethical difficulty of excluding some patients from a potentially positive treatment. While there may be ways round this, such as the counter-argument that it is unethical to offer treatments that are 'not proven', nevertheless committed practitioners themselves may be strongly motivated to break with the strict protocol of an RCT where they are uncomfortable about these issues. Moreover, there have also been problems over the leakage of both ideas and members between the study groups (Clarke and Cornish 1972), when the groups are necessarily in close proximity. A final problem for complex and lengthy interventions, such as therapeutic communities, is the early dropout of patients from the programme, artificially concentrating those who respond well into the later stages of treatment. Attempts to follow up and monitor those who have left have proved almost impossible without extensive resources.

A third problem area concerns the measures of treatment effect. Many trials suffer from a surfeit of measures, such that inevitably some of them will show positive results by chance, and there is a strong temptation to report those as positive results – in fact a 'type 1' error (Campbell and Machin 1999, p.124). This means that a false positive result has been reported. A variation on this problem is that there is a temptation to measure what can be measured, rather than what theory suggests we should measure. For example, the complex intra-psychic changes – such as 'integration' or reductions in splitting – that are assumed to happen as a product of successful therapeutic community treatment are difficult to measure empirically. In addition, where treatments are being compared, more easily measurable outcomes might give preference to, or be more compatible with, one type of treatment than the other. A further problem is that the active ingredients in the trial (for example, the specific elements of a therapeutic community programme) may not themselves be independent of each other – large groups, small groups and the general culture of the therapeutic community may all be mutually interdependent in their operations and effectiveness. In the same way, whether one person is doing well can affect whether his/her peers do well or not, so that the treatment cannot strictly be considered equal or independent across all cases.

Finally, the mechanics of randomisation and control reveal further difficulties. We have already mentioned the ecological fallacy, in which group averages are generalised to each and every individual within the group as an individual response. This is a major problem in the way of drawing clinical conclusions by generalising from the group means or averages in the trial to the individual cases. It is a commonplace observation in human service interventions such as psychotherapy, that some clients respond very well, but others less so and there are some who will react negatively. While the overall average may indicate success, as Paul (1967) observed, we need to know who does well with which specific treatments under what circumstances. These circumstances may involve a complex treatment 'career' in which progress and regress occur in a curvilinear path, including the stabilisation of improvement months or years after formal treatment has finished. When should the effects of treatment be measured, and in so far as these should be some time after the treatment has finished, how are the subjects to be tracked down and evaluated? The problems of long-term follow-up are legion.

These difficulties have been recognised in the research literature and the Medical Research Council (2000) published a report detailing their advice to those who might wish to develop RCTs for 'complex interventions', such as therapeutic communities. In essence the advice is to spend more time carefully adjusting the design to make the 'complex intervention' less complex. In particular there is repeated admonition to use pre-trial research to try to identify, isolate and thereby focus an RCT on the 'active ingredient'. This is difficult for those working in therapeutic communities, where the whole experience, while made up of recognisable parts, is felt to constitute the intervention. Moreover, the advice does not include any alternative approaches, and leaves undiminished the status of the RCT as the pinnacle of evaluative methods. We turn to a discussion of why this is so, and what the alternatives are.

The politics of knowledge

In the light of these difficulties in the face of what appears to be, and in the right circumstances can be, a powerful scientific method, a vigorous debate has developed; particularly from among those who find themselves excluded from the certainties that flow from experimental results. Mills argued (1970) that there seemed to be a trade-off between those results which were undoubtedly true, but which were answering relatively trivial questions in the controlled experimental situation; and those fundamental questions about what worked in practice in the messy reality of real-world practice, but under circumstances that were difficult to replicate under experimental conditions. This is the well-known distinction between the concepts of treatment efficacy (how a treatment fares in an RCT) *versus* treatment effectiveness (in real service settings).

Although the idea of RCTs was established in the 1940s, the widespread application of RCTs to many, indeed in principle all, medical treatments did not take off as an idea until a widely remarked essay by Cochrane in 1972 made this suggestion. Subsequently, the development of 'evidence-based medicine' came to be widely accepted in the 1990s, with the name of Cochrane enshrined in the national programme for the accumulation of such trials over the whole range of medical activity. This suggests that there are other reasons for the way in which such methods spread than the mere demonstration of their efficacy.

There are two distinct issues that stand out. The first concerns the nature of medical knowledge, from diagnosis to treatment. How does it develop? Under what circumstances, and through what actions does this knowledge come to stabilise sufficiently for new and costly service developments to be undertaken? These are questions of both medical science and medical technology. The second issue centres on government action. Who sets the priorities for government intervention? How are perceived public concerns used to justify new policies, and how are the relevant professional groups involved and persuaded to support and deliver new services?

These two issues, about knowledge and government action, can be theorised and tackled helpfully through 'actor–network theory' (ANT) – a framework that has been developed by social scientists who study science and technology (Law and Hassard 1999). This raises the question of how the development of RCTs has been performed or sustained, and what the heterogeneous elements, human and non-human, are that have been brought together into the evidence-based medicine movement. A particular focus would be the key elements that are sedimented or crystallised repositories of meaning and action, on the basis of which various interests and elements are translated into a coherent strategy for action; for example, the nature of randomness, the controls exercised over the samples and the generalisation of experimental trials to wider populations, which we will discuss further below.

We have already referred to Professor Bradford Hill and Professor Archie Cochrane as two key actors in the development of RCTs. Without their persistent argument within the professional world for this way of evaluating evidence, the RCT would have taken even longer to spread than it has. The more recent development of evidence-based medicine is often described as a (social) movement (Greenhalgh 1998); yet this is the very antithesis of rational, scientifically based action. Why should an argument about scientific proof come to be promulgated by a method more typically associated with a religious sect?

ANT examines the way in which people act on their interests and the processes by which they bring elements of the material world together in pursuit of a strategy or goal. In other words, the focus is on the process involved, rather than the starting points. In particular this includes the notion of the way in which material, technical or information systems are constituted out of the embedded labour or social relations from previous rounds of scientific or technological development (we are all familiar with the qwerty layout of the keyboard as the embedded solution to the separation of mechanical keys on the early typewriter). In the field of psychotherapy research, an example of this might the use of standard assessment techniques, whereby a patient can come to be classified in terms of his/her assessed disorder – for example a personality disorder as defined in DSM-IV (see Manning 2000 for discussion).

Originating in France, ANT has been presented as a sociology of 'translation', in which the key focus is on the way in which social action and material and technical elements are brought together, or translated, into a coherent network out of which certain achievements are attained. In particular, *all* elements are seen as capable of 'action', not merely the human actors in the network: thus in two well-known studies, scallops, in relation to French fishermen and restaurants (Callon 1986), and boats, in relation to Portuguese maritime exploration (Law 1987), are as important as the human actors in the story. In therapeutic communities the large group has come to be seen in much the same way, as an actor in its own right.

There are a number of other key aspects of ANT – itself now the condensed repository of 20 years of social science development, or 'translation' (Law 1992). First is the principle of heterogeneity. This asserts that any elements, human, animal or technical, can be enrolled or translated into the network, without any prior assumptions as to which are the significant actors at any one point – this is be revealed in empirical observation and analysis. In this case, a technical method for allocating patients to control and treatment groups, so that any unforeseen errors are eliminated and different treatment effects truly can be assigned to the treatments involved – that is, the RCT – has come to be a major actor in its own right in conferring legitimacy and significance on particular types of medical intervention. Second is the idea of action at a distance, through which networks can be seen to extend across space and time. The telephone or the scientific paper are good examples of such effects. Clearly this is not a unique aspect of the RCT, but it is important when considering the way in which journal editors select scientific papers. RCTs are much easier to publish than other kinds of evaluation.

A third aspect is the related observation that past networks in which actors have brought together, or translated, a network into the achievement of some strategy, can get simplified or 'punctualised' into a shorthand, taken for granted and often forgotten package or routine; such as the Microsoft machine code embedded into much of the software we use today. The combination of a group of

RCTs on a particular treatment in the form of a 'meta-analysis' is a recent development of evidence-based medicine, in which a statistical summary of RCTs attempts to capture the 'true' underlying effect that is common to them all. In other words, the RCT findings themselves have been fixed as a kind of taken-for-granted summary of past scientific study. While there are careful procedures for checking the quality of the RCTs that are included in such work, the effect is to amplify the power of such previous studies. This has not been undertaken in an equivalent form for qualitative case studies, for example; and in a sense places non-RCT methodologies at a disadvantage when arguing for the effectiveness of particular types of treatment intervention. Nevertheless, an example of such a meta-analysis for therapeutic communities can be seen in Lees, Manning and Rawlings (1999), and is summarised in Chapter 2 where Figure 2.1 illustrates this effect in the government's official hierarchy of acceptable types of evidence for medical treatments, as outlined in the *National Service Framework for Mental Health* (NHS Executive 1996).

Fourth, and bringing these ideas together, there is the idea of strategies and centres (even 'machines') of translation, through which networks are rendered capable of having effects. These effects include the exercise of power and the creation of social structures – themselves highly complex and durable punctualised networks. In the UK, the 'Cochrane collection' is exactly this kind of machine. It is a national repository of RCTs and meta-analyses that have been screened as to their quality, and which are publicly acknowledged as the best kind of RCT-based evidence about treatments. This has quickly acquired such authority that evidence that does not achieve this approval has far less social, professional and political power.

These observations about the way in which knowledge and scientific evidence are developed and spread do not make any claims about whether these systems 'work' or not. Clearly, where an innovation such as the RCT works effectively, there is a powerful reason for it to be widely adopted. Nevertheless, such a technique can become bound up with questions of power and preference, so that at the very least those techniques that are simple and reproducible in the laboratory may come to displace or crowd better alternatives which cannot muster the symbolic ammunition to back their claims to effectiveness. The therapeutic community may be in this position.

Alternatives

What are the alternatives to RCTs? RCTs involve giving treatment, measuring the patient's response in comparison to non-treated subjects and controlling errors through randomisation. In each of these areas there are possible alternatives. If randomisation is difficult to set up and carry through, it may still be possible to achieve an approximate equalisation of bias occurring in both groups by other means. For example, where ethical objections are made, treatment can be offered but delayed for the control group, or an alternative treatment can be offered. A similar effect can occur where there is excess referral for treatment, and a waiting list develops of untreated patients which can act as a control group – quite a common experience in the NHS. A less satisfactory approach might be to offer several treatments sequentially, but in a different order for members of the comparison groups – for example, outpatient support, then therapeutic community treatment, then drug therapy and so on. A further variation on randomisation is to randomise between groups of patients rather than individuals, which is known as a 'cluster RCT'. For example, we could introduce different elements of a regime in different therapeutic communities experimentally over the course of a year to see what effects this might have on outcome. The recent growth in a small number of therapeutic communities of the development of pre-admission support groups, or post-treatment outreach support groups, might make such a design possible by randomly recruiting different therapeutic communities to develop such a service.

Where it is not possible to set up an experimental treatment regime, naturally occurring variations in 'real-world' treatment can be modelled using path analysis or structural equation modelling (for an example applied to therapeutic communities see Manning 1989, Chapter 5). Basically this involves measuring the treatment experiences of patients going through a range of existing regular treatments, and using the natural variations in types of patients, types and lengths of treatments and treatment outcomes to provide data that can be modelled in accordance with a strictly pre-defined set of predictions, to identify which factors are associated with good outcomes. To allow for the measurement of a useful range of variables, however, this design calls for quite large samples, which may not be available if the treatment is new or controversial.

Small samples may force a rather different approach to the search for causal links between treatment and outcome, namely the inclusion or indeed sole reliance on qualitative approaches discussed in outline in Chapter 1. This might involve the active interviewing of patients and staff about their experiences in a therapeutic community, but with a fairly loose design that enables those interviewed to express their views in their own terms. Their responses can be subsequently coded for repeated patterns that seem to indicate where treatment works well. For example, the notion that insight is helpful to psychological change can be captured retrospectively in interviews. A less active strategy would be to observe treatment experiences, for example in group psychotherapy, or in the daily life of the therapeutic community, and to try to identify those that subsequently appeared to lead to good outcomes (Murphy *et al.* 1998).

Conclusions

Knowledge is not neutral. It is a socially created and socially shared resource, which has time and time again proved to have limited shelf life in science. In the case of therapeutic communities there has been some uncertainty about what we now know about its effectiveness, and how this might be improved. The RCT is for many observers of medical and social practice a powerful method of developing a strongly legitimate means for gathering evidence which carries extensive social power.

However, the RCT as practised is not an appropriate gold standard solution for all problems. It certainly cannot be the required standard for an assessment of the therapeutic community movement, or a single local therapeutic community. While it could answer some questions about therapeutic communities, there would be massive problems and large costs. This is not to say that RCTs should not be done where appropriate.

Other approaches may be needed first though, and continued monitoring of therapeutic communities through a variety of assessment methods will be necessary not only to replace RCTs if cost or feasibility rules them out, but also to check whether RCT results are sustainable and generalisable.

CHAPTER 7

Characteristics of Effective Treatment Environments

A Process-Outcome Model for Research on Therapeutic Communities[2]

Rudolf H. Moos

Three assumptions guide our approach to understanding therapeutic communities and their outcomes. First, in order to examine the influence of therapeutic communities on patients' adaptation, we need to measure key aspects of the treatment process and environment. Because the main therapeutic ingredient of therapeutic communities is thought to be 'community as method' (De Leon 1997; Kennard 1998), it is important to assess systematically variations in the organisation and implementation of therapeutic communities. Accordingly, we describe some measures that enable us to identify specific aspects of therapeutic communities and to examine their influence on patients' in-programme and community adaptation.

Our second assumption is that, although therapeutic communities are increasingly diverse, a common conceptual framework can be used to evaluate them, and that doing so has several advantages. We set out a framework that enables us to identify similar processes in different types of therapeutic community, compare therapeutic communities on how well they are implemented and contrast therapeutic communities in different contexts, such as those that are hospital- or community-based.

Our third assumption is that more emphasis should be placed on examining the effectiveness of matching specific types of patients to varying treatment programmes. We need to focus particularly on how different types of therapeutic community vary in their impact on patients who differ in their level of impairment and the chronicity and severity of their disorders.

Conceptual model

The conceptual model shown in Figure 7.1 follows these guidelines and provides a framework for examining therapeutic communities and how they and their patients mutually influence each other. In this model, the connection between the objective characteristics of the programme (panel I), patients' personal characteristics (panel II), and patients' adaptation in the outside community (panel V), is mediated by the programme social climate (panel III) and by patients' in-programme outcomes (panel IV). The model specifies the domains of variables that should be included in an integrated evaluation.

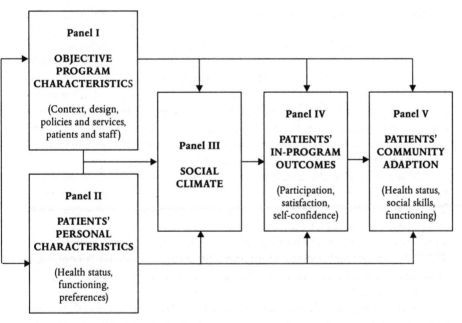

Figure 7.1 A model of the relationship between program and personal characteristics and patients' outcomes

The objective characteristics of the programme (panel I) include the programme's institutional context, physical design, policies and services, and the aggregate characteristics of the patients and staff (the suprapersonal environment). These four sets of programme factors combine to influence the quality of the programme cultural or social climate (panel III). The social climate is part of the therapeutic community environment, but we place it in a separate panel to highlight its special status. The social climate is in part an outgrowth of objective programme characteristics and also mediates their impact on patients' functioning. In addition, social climate can be assessed at both the programme and the individual level.

Personal factors (panel II) encompass an individual's sociodemographic characteristics and such personal resources as health and cognitive status, and chronicity and severity of mental and functional impairment. They also include an individual's preferences and expectations for specific characteristics of therapeutic communities, such as the level of participation and structure.

Both programme and personal factors affect patients' in-programme outcomes, such as their interpersonal behaviour, participation, satisfaction and self-confidence (panel IV). In turn, in-programme outcomes influence such indices of community adaptation as patients' health status, social and work skills and psychosocial functioning (panel V). For example, community meetings, peer counselling groups and policies that enhance patients' decision-making (panel I) may contribute to a cohesive and self-directed social climate (panel III). In such a setting, a new patient may be more likely to develop supportive relationships with other patients and be active in a counselling group (panel IV) and, ultimately, to show better community adaptation (panel V).

The model depicts the ongoing interplay between individuals and the therapeutic community environment. Patients who voice a preference for more self-direction in their daily activities may help initiate more flexible policies (a change in the programme). Patients who participate more actively in community meetings or in-programme work may experience improved self-confidence (a change in the personal system). More generally, individual outcomes contribute to defining the characteristics of the programme; for example, when the in-programme behavioural outcomes for all patients in a therapeutic community are considered together, they constitute one aspect of the suprapersonal environment.

Measuring the treatment environment

When my colleagues and I began our research on therapeutic communities, prior programme evaluations and clinical experience convinced us of the need to develop procedures to characterise systematically treatment environments. Naturalistic descriptions and empirical studies of psychiatric programmes supported the belief that the treatment milieu (the community) was a key factor in contributing to patients' outcomes. Accordingly, we developed the Ward Atmosphere Scale (WAS) and the Community-Oriented Programs Environment Scale (COPES) to measure the social climate of hospital-based and community-based programmes, respectively.

Table 7.1 WAS and COPES subscale and dimension descriptions	
	Relationship dimensions
1. Involvement	how active and energetic patients are in the programme
2. Support	how much patients help and support each other and how supportive the staff are towards patients
3. Spontaneity	how much the programme encourages the open expression of feelings by patients and staff
	Personal growth dimensions
4. Autonomy	how self-sufficient and independent patients are in making decisions and how much they are encouraged to take leadership in the programme
5. Practical orientation	the extent to which patients learn social and work skills and are prepared for discharge from the programme
6. Personal problem orientation	the extent to which patients seek to understand their feelings and personal problems
7. Anger and aggression	how much patients argue with other patients and with staff, become openly angry and display other aggressive behaviour
	System maintenance dimensions
8. Order and organisation	how important order and organisation are in the programme
9. Programme clarity	the extent to which patients know what to expect in their day-to-day routine and the explicitness of programme rules and procedures
10. Staff control	the extent to which the staff use measures to keep patients under effective controls

Each of these scales is composed of ten subscales that measure the actual or the preferred treatment environment. These ten subscales assess three underlying sets of dimensions: relationship dimensions, personal growth dimensions, and system maintenance dimensions (Table 7.1). The relationship and system maintenance dimensions primarily reflect the internal functioning of the programme, whereas the personal growth dimensions reflect the main areas in which staff members hold performance expectations for patients.

The rationale and steps involved in the development of the WAS and COPES, and normative and psychometric characteristics of the scales, are described elsewhere (Moos 1996a; 1996b). In brief, the WAS and COPES norms are based on a total of over 350 programmes, including programmes in the UK. The WAS and COPES profiles are quite stable over four- to six-month and 12-month intervals, but they also are sensitive to changes such as those that may occur during a programme reorganisation. The subscale intercorrelations average between .25 and .30, indicating that they measure distinct though somewhat related aspects of treatment environments.

We developed Ideal Forms of the WAS and COPES to enable patients and staff to describe their ideas about an optimal treatment programme. We wanted to identify areas in which patients and staff have similar or different goals and to find out how much staff members' goals vary from programme to programme. We also wanted to compare actual and preferred programmes and to give patients and staff an opportunity to identify areas they wanted to change.

Assessing programme implementation

To find out how well a therapeutic community is implemented, an evaluator must measure the actual programme against a standard of what the programme should be. Sechrest and his colleagues (1979) identified three sources of information that can be used to define a standard for programme implementation: normative data on conditions in other programmes, specifications of an ideal programme, and theoretical analyses or expert judgement. Some programmes may be well implemented with respect to all three of these criteria but, more commonly, a programme may meet or exceed normative standards but not yet be optimal in terms of its patients' or staff members' desires.

Normative classic and concept-based therapeutic communities

To develop normative standards by which to assess programme implementation, we conducted empirical cluster analyses of patients' perceptions of hospital-based and community-based treatment programmes. These analyses identified six main types of treatment programmes, one of which we conceptualised as a classic therapeutic community type. A second type, which we originally labelled as relationship-oriented, exemplifies the 'concept-based' therapeutic community model (Moos 1997).

The classic therapeutic communities are well above average on the relationship and personal growth dimensions, but low on the system maintenance dimensions (Figure 7.2). Patients are active and involved in the programme and are encouraged to discuss their personal problems and express their feelings freely, to be independent and to learn social and work skills. However, the programmes lack structure, primarily because of staff members' efforts to enhance patients' independence and freedom.

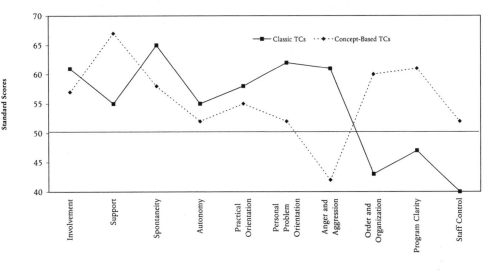

Figure 7.2 Patients' perceptions of the social climate in classic and concept-based therapeutic communities

The newer 'concept-based' therapeutic communities, which tend to exemplify the Synanon, Phoenix House, Day Top, or Second Genesis models, typically develop a more structured and directive milieu (Figure 7.2). These programmes emphasise supportive and open relationships in the context of clear expectations and a well-organised setting. According to patients' perceptions, these programmes have somewhat fewer performance expectations than classic therapeutic communities; they are comparable on autonomy and practical orientation but are much lower on personal problem orientation and discourage the open expression of anger. These profiles provide a standard against which to measure how well a new therapeutic community is implemented (for examples, see Bell 1983; Manning 1989; Trauer, Bouras and Watson 1987; Verhaest, Pierloot and Janssens 1982).

Preferences and theoretical analyses

A more individualised method for generating an implementation standard is to identify an ideal form of the intervention. As noted earlier, the Ideal Forms of the WAS and the COPES ask patients and staff to specify their preferences about the treatment milieu. This information enables an evaluator to compare actual and preferred treatment milieus, provide feedback to patients and staff about the discrepancies and initiate steps to improve the programme.

Following the Kingsley Hall model (Laing 1971), Mosher and colleagues (Mosher 1991; Wendt *et al.* 1983) developed Soteria House, a group home for acute schizophrenic patients rooted in the tradition of intensive interpersonal intervention, the concepts of moral treatment and crisis theory. Residents and staff saw Soteria as highly supportive and expressive and as oriented toward autonomy, self-understanding and the open expression of anger. Consistent with a classic therapeutic community, Soteria was well below average on all three of the system maintenance dimensions. These patterns, which remained stable over a four-year interval, were very close to patients' and staff members' ideals, indicating that the programme was well implemented with respect to both normative and preference criteria.

Alternatively, evaluators can conduct a conceptual analysis to see how well a programme is implemented in line with a particular theory, such as the precepts of moral treatment. In this vein, Appelbaum and Munich (1986) described the transformation of two psychotherapy-based units for schizophrenic patients and patients with severe character disorders into a rehabilitation programme based in part on moral treatment ideals. The psychotherapy model emphasised understanding patients' psychodynamics, discussing staff members' feelings in team meetings and employing an egalitarian decision-making process. To implement the rehabilitation model, decision-making power was redistributed such that patients and staff worked jointly to design treatment plans. While some staff resisted the redefinition of roles, positive results included more supportive relationships among patients, greater patient autonomy, increased patient participation in therapeutic activities and more emphasis on the restoration and development of patients' social and vocational skills.

The value of implementation assessments

Implementation assessments are of considerable practical value. They enable evaluators to find out whether programmes with contrasting professed treatment goals actually develop distinctive treatment environments consistent with these goals. They can also identify programmes that are well implemented according to staff but not according to patients.

Another important application is to help programme managers decide whether to establish and maintain a therapeutic community in a specific context, such as an acute psychiatric admissions unit or a medically oriented hospital setting. In fact, implementation assessments have shown that therapeutic communities can function in these contexts, but that they tend to be less supportive and more structured than typical classic therapeutic communities (Pullen 1982; Squier 1994; Steiner, Haldipur and Stack 1982). In addition, due to their complex social system, dependence on a stable staff group and need for relative administrative autonomy, it may be difficult to maintain well-implemented hospital-based therapeutic communities over the long term (Friis *et al.* 1982).

Finally, implementation assessments can indicate how well concept-based or classic therapeutic communities can be developed in previously untried venues, such as a maximum security forensic hospital (Caplan 1993), a jail (Glider *et al.* 1997) or a non-residential day hospital programme. In this vein, Comstock and colleagues (1985) organised an intensive outpatient programme with a range of skills training and educational activities and therapy groups that emphasised open communication and self-understanding. The programme emphasised the relationship dimensions and personal problem orientation, and there was relatively little focus on organisation, clarity or staff control. A decline in patients' health care costs after they participated in the programme suggested that a non-residential classic therapeutic community may be an effective treatment modality (for descriptions of other non-residential therapeutic communities, see Bucardo *et al.* 1997; Stevens, Chong and Erickson 1997).

To benefit from implementation checks, therapeutic communities need to incorporate ongoing formative evaluation and obtain regular feedback about the treatment milieu. These procedures encourage staff involvement in programme planning and design, make staff more aware of the treatment climate and how it influences patients, identifies problematic aspects of the programme, help patients and staff understand that they can alter the programme and institute specific changes to do so, and enhance motivation to plan longer-term process and outcome evaluations.

Determinants of treatment climate

Therapeutic communities vary widely in the quality of patient and staff relationships; the emphasis on personal growth dimensions, such as autonomy and practical orientation; and the level of organisation and control. This finding raises an important question: why do therapeutic communities develop in such disparate ways? What leads to an emphasis on support, or on autonomy, or on organisation and control?

To address this issue, we expanded the conceptual framework shown in Figure 7.1 to focus more specifically on the connections between panels I and III in the model. As shown in Figure 7.3, the model posits that the institutional context (factors such as ownership, size and staffing) and physical, policy and aggregate patient and staff characteristics can influence directly or indirectly the treatment climate. The impact of these four sets of programme factors stems in part from the social climate they help to promote. In turn, the social climate can mediate or alter the influence of these four domains on patients' and staff members' morale and well-being.

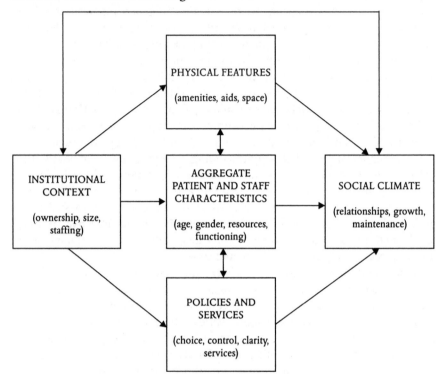

Figure 7.3 Determinants of social climate in psychiatric and substance abuse treatment programs

To examine the model empirically, we developed the Residential Substance Abuse and Psychiatric Programs Inventory (RESPPI) (Timko 1995, 1996), which assesses the four sets of determinants of the treatment climate. One part of the RESPPI, the Physical and Architectural Characteristics Inventory, measures physical features that add convenience, aid recreation and provide support for patients and space for patient and staff functions. A second part, the Policy and Service Characteristics Inventory, taps requirements for patients' functioning (expectations for functioning, acceptance of problem behaviour), policies that reflect the balance between individual freedom and institutional structure (policy choice, resident control, policy clarity provision for privacy) and the provision of services and activities. Another part of the RESPPI, the Resident and Staff Characteristics Inventory, assesses residents' demographic characteristics, functioning and activity involvement, and the resources available from staff in terms of experience, training and diversity.

We used these procedures to examine the determinants of treatment climate in a set of more than 90 hospital and community treatment programmes (Timko and Moos 1998). With respect to institutional context, non-profit programmes and smaller and better staffed programmes were more supportive and well organised and had more emphasis on autonomy and practical and personal problem orientation. More physical amenities and space also contributed to a supportive and self-directed programme, as did more resident control and clearer policies. More health and treatment services were associated with more emphasis on residents' skills development and self-understanding.

The aggregate characteristics of the residents and staff in a programme were also associated with the treatment environment. When residents had more social resources and staff were more experienced and effective, programmes tended to be more supportive and self-directed and more likely to emphasise self-understanding. In contrast, programmes with more mentally impaired residents tended to be less supportive and self-directed and less focused on practical and personal problem orientation. Overall, the institutional context and physical, policy and suprapersonal factors have mutually reinforcing influences on the type of social climate that emerges in a programme (Moos 1997; Moos and Lemke 1994).

Treatment climate and treatment outcome

We turn now to examine the associations between the treatment environment and treatment outcome; that is, the connections between variables in panel III and panels IV and V in the conceptual model shown in Figure 7.1.

In-programme outcomes

Prior studies have identified some general relationships between aspects of the treatment environment and patients' in-programme outcomes (Moos 1997). Most broadly, patients in supportive programmes that emphasise self-direction, the development of work and social skills and self-understanding tend to develop more positive interpersonal relationships, to report that treatment enhances their self-confidence and to be more satisfied with treatment. Patients in well-organised and clear programmes that play down staff control also do better on these in-programme outcomes.

The associations between the treatment environment and patients' coping behaviour are more focused. Specific aspects of the programme are linked to patients' initiatives in consonant areas. Programme involvement promotes patients' affiliation; personal problem orientation facilitates patients' self-revelation; a focus on anger enhances patients' expression of anger. High staff control makes it more likely that patients will passively follow staff directives; it is also associated with low patient morale and self-confidence, less affiliation and open discussion of personal problems and less liking for staff members.

These aspects of the treatment environment are also linked to patients' dropout rates and engagement in treatment. Programmes that lack focus on the relationship and system maintenance areas have high dropout rates; patients who report less emphasis in these areas are more likely to leave treatment prematurely. Engagement in treatment seems to be more dependent on an emphasis on patients' personal growth, especially autonomy and self-understanding. Overall, these findings show that a supportive, well organised treatment environment that is somewhat self-directed and sets moderate to strong performance expectations contributes to patients' better in-programme outcomes.

Adaptation in the community

In general, aspects of the treatment environment that are associated with better in-programme outcomes are also linked to better psychosocial functioning and integration in the community. Cohesive programmes that are relatively well organised and emphasise the personal growth dimensions, especially autonomy and practical and personal problem orientation, tend to mitigate patients' symptoms and contribute to their psychosocial functioning and self-care and community living skills. Programmes that keep patients out of hospital focus on the personal growth areas, especially independence, self-understanding and skills development, as well as on maintaining supportive relationships and a moderate level of structure (Moos 1997).

Some research has identified an association between patients' perceptions of a treatment programme and their adaptation in the community. Specifically, patients who appraise a programme more positively, which may reflect the formation of a therapeutic alliance and better integration into treatment, seem to derive more benefit from it. As a case in point, we found that patients who appraised their treatment environment more positively consumed less alcohol and had fewer physical symptoms and less depression ten years later (Finney and Moos 1992). Although the precise mechanisms remain to be determined, patients' perceptions of a treatment programme may provide important information about their integration into the programme and long-term post-treatment adaptation.

Patient–programme congruence

The findings just described identify general associations between treatment environments and patients' outcomes. However, some models of person–environment matching suggest that functionally competent individuals are better able to adapt to environmental demands than are individuals with impaired functioning. Accordingly, a self-directed social climate that has high performance expectations and relatively little structure should have the most benefit for functionally able patients.

In contrast, functional and mental impairments set limits on more disturbed patients' adjustment and behaviour. Patients with acute schizophrenic disorders often find interpersonal stimulation disturbing; cognitively impaired patients may find it hard to cope with a strong emphasis on self-direction and skills development. Programmes that require patients to structure their own daily activities also may be too demanding for some individuals. As patients' cognitive and psychosocial skills improve, they should be able to cope with a more demanding and somewhat less structured setting.

Our reviews of studies in this area show that performance expectations and programme structure do seem to affect patients differently, depending on their level of impairment (Moos 1997; Timko, Moos and Finney 2000). More intact patients react more positively in moderately structured programmes that have more emphasis on self-direction, skills development and self-understanding, whereas more disturbed patients prefer more structure and less emphasis on performance, especially self-disclosure. Patients who are functionally intact but have problems controlling their impulses, such as many patients with personality and substance use disorders, also are likely to experience better in-programme outcomes in highly structured settings.

Future directions

Currently, there is a resurgence of interest in therapeutic communities, which are developing in increasingly diverse contexts and encompassing a diverse group of specialised patient populations (Campling and Haigh 1999; De Leon 1997). To promote the continued growth and effectiveness of therapeutic communities, researchers need to pursue a number of issues, three of which we consider here.

Theory-based treatment evaluation

Although clinicians have employed modern therapeutic community-based treatment modalities for almost 60 years, we know very little about how and why therapeutic community treatment does or does not work. We assume that active participation in a therapeutic community initiates a maturational process that promotes specific proximal changes (such as an enhanced sense of personal responsibility and self-confidence), which, in turn, are associated with longer-term ultimate outcomes (such as abstinence from substance abuse, cessation of criminal behaviour and gainful employment). Much has been written about the underlying theory of how these change processes work, but they have rarely been examined empirically.

By measuring specific indices of therapeutic community processes and services, and by linking these indices to patients' proximal and ultimate outcomes, researchers can make a contribution towards theory-based therapeutic community programming. Following these ideas, Morgenstern and colleagues (1996) assessed proximal outcomes that many theorists believe may mediate ultimate outcomes of 12-step substance abuse treatment. Commitment to a goal of abstinence and to avoiding high-risk situations was linked to the ultimate outcome of abstinence from substance use. However, several other proximal outcomes, such as acknowledging powerlessness over the abused substance and belief in a higher power, were not associated with later abstinence. Findings such as these show how a theory-driven evaluation can identify proximal changes that may mediate treatment outcome (for an extension of these ideas to cognitive-behavioural treatment, see Finney *et al.* 1998).

Evaluations of therapeutic communities are most useful when embedded in a theoretical context – when an evaluation tries to explain or generate additional knowledge about treatment processes and their connections to in-programme and longer-term outcomes. Because this approach embeds an evaluation in a theory of the treatment process and of the patients' disorder, it is more likely to identify sources of treatment failure and decay in treatment gains and to help formulate ways to improve treatment.

The role of staff and the therapeutic community as a workplace

A therapeutic community is not only a treatment setting for patients; it is also a workplace for staff. To develop an effective treatment setting, the work climate in a therapeutic community should enable staff to fulfil their enhanced role as both caretakers and participants. In this respect, Kennard (1998) has focused on the experience of working in a therapeutic community and provided some guidelines for staff behaviour, and Pullen (1999) has emphasised the role of the therapeutic community in promoting self-discovery among staff members as well as among patients.

More broadly, characteristics of the health care workplace, such as involvement, task orientation and clarity, have been associated with staff members' satisfaction and performance (Moos and Schaefer 1987) and the treatment milieu (O'Driscoll and Evans 1988). In a study of substance abuse programmes, Moos and Moos (1998) found that staff in a supportive and goal-directed workplace were more likely to create a supportive and goal-directed treatment environment. Patients in such a milieu participated in more treatment services, were more involved in self-help groups, were more satisfied with the programme and improved more during treatment.

These findings imply that work and treatment climates may mutually reinforce each other and that both can have consequences for staff members as well as for patients. Where relationships are supportive and the workplace is organised flexibly, staff members experience higher morale, perform better and are more likely to create a supportive and self-directed treatment environment. More research should focus on the staff community and how it affects the social climate in a therapeutic community and staff and patient outcomes.

Therapeutic communities and individuals' broader life contexts

We have formulated an expanded evaluation paradigm that conceptualises patients' functioning and well-being as affected not only by treatment but also by ongoing life context and personal factors (Moos, Finney and Cronkite 1990). This paradigm explicitly considers factors outside treatment and how they influence treatment entry, treatment experiences and treatment outcome. It highlights the complexity of the treatment and rehabilitation process and places a therapeutic community in context as one among many sets of factors that influence outcome. In this respect, evaluations of therapeutic communities need to consider the role of continuing care and participation in self-help groups, as well as the influence of family and work settings, on long-term treatment outcome (De Leon 1997; Moos *et al.* 1999).

Along with an emphasis on theory-based evaluation and the role of therapeutic community staff, the use of an expanded evaluation paradigm that considers life context factors outside treatment affords the opportunity for greater insight into the mechanisms through which therapeutic communities exert their effects, better understanding of other factors that contribute to recovery and relapse, and an enriched database with which to develop more effective therapeutic communities oriented towards patients' normal life situations. Evaluation research directed toward these issues should benefit patients and staff and the therapeutic community movement in the effort to develop more humane and potent therapeutic programmes.

CHAPTER 8

Using Qualitative Research Methods in Therapeutic Communities

Barbara Rawlings

Briefly stated, field research is the systematic study of ordinary events and activities in the settings in which they occur. A primary goal of field research is *to understand what these activities and events mean to those who engage in them.* To gain this understanding, field researchers collect data by interacting with and observing people during the course of their daily lives, usually in some self-contained setting such as a workplace... (Bailey 1996, p.1 – emphasis added)

'Field research' is a term taken from anthropology. It denotes the work of entering and exploring 'the field' of other people's culture and activity, describing it, analysing it and rendering it reportable and understandable to larger audiences. In this chapter 'the field' is the therapeutic community. I will describe the kinds of methods that field researchers use to gather and think about information – qualitative methods – and suggest how these can be used both by outsiders and insiders to pursue research questions.

What are qualitative methods?

The term covers a range of techniques and analytic procedures (Bailey 1996; Bell 1993; Burgess 1984; Gilbert 1993; Hammersley and Atkinson 1995). Data are often collected through interviews and/or observation, but studies can use other methods. Traditionally researchers have supplemented interviews and observations with examinations of existing documents or by asking subjects to keep diaries, which record their views of events and their thoughts and feelings. More recently, researchers have used tape recorders, not just to record interviews, but also to record 'naturally occurring activities' such as meetings or therapy groups, and have used these to examine how the talk leads from one topic to another. Occasionally videotape is used, so that the relationship between visual cues and speech activities can be explored. Recently, too, researchers have begun to use focus groups, which are a specialised form of group interview and which encourage people to talk between themselves so that the researcher can listen in.

Qualitative methods tend to be flexible. To a greater or lesser extent (depending on how the research is being carried out) the task is one of exploration and discovery. This means that it is generally seen as constraining to have too clear an idea of what the findings might contain. Although the researcher may have a topic (e.g. 'How do the night staff operate?' or 'How do new admissions affect the resident group?') the amount and variety of data that can be collected, which will have some bearing on these questions, can be staggering. Once the research is underway, the original questions may be replaced with questions that seem stronger and more firmly rooted in the actual practice of the people being observed, and so the data collection can become more focused as the researcher becomes more confident about what is important in the area under scrutiny. (This is very different from a strictly quantitative approach, which would require a preliminary hypothesis and a series of formal questions with pre-coded answers. Quantitative research relies on all subjects being asked the same questions in the same way so that researchers can be confident that the answers can be meaningfully grouped and compared.)

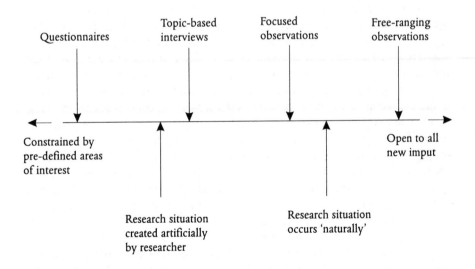

Figure 8.1 Range of qualitative approaches

It is useful to think of the qualitative approach as offering different degrees of flexibility (see Figure 8.1). Here, some of the different ways of collecting data have been ranged along a continuum, which depicts a range of flexibility, from 'constrained' on the left to 'open' on the right. This is only part of a much longer theoretical continuum. Other research methods will provide much more constraint than interviews and even the most open-minded of researchers will be constrained by the sheer impossibility of recording every single event observed.

According to the diagram, questionnaires offer the least flexible approach to research. Qualitative questionnaires consist of a list of questions which are open-ended, and which encourage the respondents to reply in their own words, rather than just to say 'yes' or 'no' or to tick a pre-coded answer. Questionnaires can take a long time to go through, and can produce some very authentic data, but they lack the flexibility of other methods since the questions have been pre-designed and are unlikely to be changed during the course of the study.

Topic-based interviews offer rather more flexibility, since the researcher goes into the interview with a list of things he/she wants to cover, rather than a specified set of questions. This means that the interview can feel much more like a conversation, since the researcher, in covering the topics, can change the order and ask extra questions as appropriate. The researcher can perhaps become more involved in the work of eliciting information as anyone might do when someone is telling them about their life or work. There is more flexibility here, since questions are not pre-designed, and new topics can be added to the list and others dropped depending on who is being interviewed or what seems to the researcher to be important.

Over to the right-hand side of the continuum in Figure 8.1 are observational methods in which the researcher takes on the less obtrusive role of spectator. Observations may be focused on a particular topic from the beginning of the study (e.g. 'How do staff and residents talk about residents' therapeutic progress?'). Or they may be free ranging, with no particular focus, which gives the researcher a chance to become familiar with activities by simply experiencing whatever is going on. Using a free-range approach, a researcher may collect data on anything that is said or done, without any conscious attempt to concentrate on particular topics. As time goes on, however, and certain issues begin to look more promising or important, these observations may become more focused, and move a little to the left on the continuum. Thus observational methods offer great flexibility and allow the focus of the research to become gradually attuned to the culture and topics under observation, rather than setting out from the start with an idea of what the end product will comprise.

There are other differences between the right- and left-hand side of the diagram which need explaining here. These are to do with the amount of control the researcher has over the content and the types of data that can be collected. In questionnaire research the control of what is to be talked about is firmly in the hands of the researcher, since the questions have been pre-designed, and this puts a boundary around what will count as an answer. In topic-based research, the researcher has slightly less control, since up to a point respondents can be allowed to take over the task of selecting topics and talk about what *they* feel is relevant. This means that each interview may be very different from the others. The order of topics may differ, the time and attention given to topics may differ and new topics may be introduced which are not addressed by other respondents. Nevertheless, the researcher still remains in control. It is generally up to the researcher to decide how and when the interview begins, when it is finished and when to stop talking about one topic and move onto the next. Moreover, the researcher has created the situation: if the researcher were not there, the interview would not be happening. The researcher who uses observational methods however has no special control over what is said and done, and would not want to have. He/she is not there to elicit particular data but to see what happens, whatever that is.

The status of interview data is different from that of observational data. Interview data are given to the researcher second-hand and the interviewer must rely on what the subject says for information. Observational data, however, are collected directly, first-hand. Inevitably, interview data are selected and formulated for the researcher by the respondent, whose relationship to 'what actually happened' is going to be a function of the story-telling activity and guided by story-telling considerations such as what the respondent thinks the researcher is interested in, how the respondent wants to come across and to whom the respondent thinks the researcher is going to report.

This is not to say that interview data are second-rate compared to observations of naturally occurring situations. Often interviews are the only means available to collect information, and much good qualitative research uses questionnaire and topic-based interviews. These do provide an opportunity for respondents to talk in their own words, and can thus open up hitherto unsuspected areas of thinking or concern. Where researchers are already fairly knowledgeable about a topic area and want to collect the views of a number of people, they can be very useful. Indeed, if the researcher wants to know what someone thinks privately about an issue, it would be difficult to manage this without some kind of one-to-one conversation. Interviews are also very useful in settings like therapeutic communities for ascertaining and exploring organisational history or for looking at a range of different perspectives on the same topic. For example, supposing the study were to look at the relationships between different professional groups on the staff, it would be worth interviewing a number of long-standing staff members to see how they viewed relationships with other staff, and how they described and explained the historical development of any relationship difficulties.

Observation in therapeutic communities may often be more accurately called 'participant observation', since researchers rarely sit entirely on the sidelines and may be actively involved in discussions or in therapeutic activities. This is particularly true for staff members or residents who conduct a piece of research, since they will be embedded firmly in the life of the community before the study begins and will almost certainly remain embedded throughout. But is also true for outsider researchers since, simply by being allowed to observe and agreeing to follow the community's rules on confidentiality and disclosure of information, they become, even if only marginally, part of the community (see Morant and Warren this book). If the researcher's aim is to become immersed in the culture of the organisation (and often a qualitative researcher will aim for this in order to understand better what is going on) then a powerful way to achieve immersion and test understanding is to attempt to participate in the 'real action' of meetings and other activities. The temporary humiliation of making a mistake and having it pointed out is nothing compared to the insight that can be achieved from such an experience. Participant observation offers the researcher the opportunity to 'learn by doing' as well as to learn by watching and can be very informative.[3]

On the diagram, other methods could be placed. For example, 'naturally occurring documents', such as minutes of meetings, clinical files and handover reports, which are written for the purposes of the organisation and not primarily for the researcher, would go towards the right. Tape recordings of interviews would go towards the left, but tape recordings of meetings, which are happening anyway, would go to the right. Focus groups, which are set up artificially by researchers in order to investigate a particular topic, would go towards the left.

A qualitative research project may use a combination of the methods outlined above. Observations and interviews are often used together, since once the researcher has identified, through observation, which topics to pursue, interviews offer a reasonably quick and efficient way of gaining a lot of focused information. Moreover, interviews offer the chance to get individual views on events. While observations of community meetings will be helpful for seeing how staff and residents work together in public, interviews with individual residents may then throw light on, for example, what 'really goes on' when the staff are not present.

A qualitative approach may be used on its own, or in conjunction with quantitative methods (Bryman 1988). Often a qualitative study involving, say, some observation and some wide-ranging interviews with key people, may be conducted at the beginning of a quantitative study, so that the researchers can feel confident that respondents will understand the questions and that the questions asked are the right ones. Additionally, a quantitative project may pose questions which can only be answered through a subsequent period of qualitative study. For example, suppose a researcher wanted to evaluate the success of a therapeutic community treatment programme. The project might begin with discussions with a range of people such as staff, residents, referrers and associated managers or professionals, to ascertain what they mean by the term 'successful treatment'. This information could be used to create standard research forms to be completed before, during and after treatment, and which ascertain the extent to which residents fulfil these criteria of success when they leave or perhaps a year or two after they leave. These forms can then be completed for every resident who joins the therapeutic community for a set period of time, and later analysed statistically to show the level of success in treatment overall. This analysis may show that certain types of resident seem to have been less successful than others, or that a longer stay is more likely to produce change than a shorter one. But while the statistical findings may be able to state that positive change is related to the length of time in treatment, or that the community is better at treating certain types of patients, they will not be able to say why this is. Thus a further study would be required, this time more in-depth and qualitative, to try to answer these questions. The structure of the project would thus be sequential: qualitative followed by quantitative followed by qualitative – a sort of methodological sandwich. Alternatively, a qualitative study may be designed to incorporate some quantitative enquiry, or designed to run alongside a statistical project to provide a more detailed and rich description of the topics under investigation than could be gained otherwise (Gunn *et al.* 1978).

Problems

One of the biggest problems with qualitative research is achieving and maintaining distance. In order to carry out a good quality study, the research needs to get close enough to the views and feelings of the people being studied to understand what it would be like to be in their shoes, and to see things from their point of view. For the outside researcher, this means that the task involves almost becoming a member of the group, but always knowing that he/she is not really a member of the group. It is an emotional balancing act, and during the data collection stage, the researcher needs an outsider to talk to, just to remind him/herself of his/her true mission in the community. For the insider who is doing a research project – the staff member or resident – the need for outside help is even greater, since most of the time he/she is a genuine member of the community and completely caught up in the need for action rather than reflection. It is very easy for staff members to make assumptions about what is the best way of doing something, or to interpret behaviour in clinical ways, because this is what they are trained and paid to do, and because this is what matters in the therapeutic community. But a researcher needs to be able to stand back from this and see behaviour through a different lens. For example, one of the questions in which a clinically immersed member of staff might be interested would be whether or not a resident is working (i.e. actively and genuinely engaging in therapeutic activities at work). An 'over- involved' piece of research might get caught up in the debate and look at the arguments for and against, weigh these up in the light of what is known about the resident, come up with an answer and propose this answer as being 'better' or 'more complete' than the decision of the staff. A less involved analysis might look at the arguments for and against and examine how they are proposed, and how different pieces of information get brought in to sway the argument one way or another. Instead of coming up with a better answer to the practical question 'Is this resident working?', the report would show how the staff use their knowledge of the resident, their knowledge of therapeutic theory and their debating skills to come up with their own answer. The report is thus not in competition with staff activity, but descriptive of it (and in its own way can be of practical benefit to the therapeutic community by providing a 'window' on events and practices).

It is through descriptive work like this that the body of published knowledge we have about therapeutic community process has been built up. In the next section I want to look at some of these studies and describe how they were carried out.

Robert Rapoport: Community as Doctor

From 1953 to 1957 Robert Rapoport, an American anthropologist, carried out a participant observation study of the Social Rehabilitation Unit at Belmont (now Henderson) Hospital. He spent the first year of his stay familiarising himself with the structure and functioning of the unit, and getting to know the people. Rapoport was a stranger to therapeutic communities and essentially worked as an anthropologist might do when studying a primitive culture. This involved listening, watching, learning the language, learning the ways people explained and described things to each other, studying relationships and networks and becoming accustomed to the patterns of activity which made up the daily life of the community. Because he was a researcher and was prepared to join in with social activities – Manning (1997) recalls him playing the clarinet with the music group – he was able to get to know residents on a more informal basis than members of staff could do. He tried to view the staff as objectively as possible, preferring to record and study their beliefs and opinions rather than accept them as valid interpretations of reality. Not surprisingly perhaps, this anthropological distance created a tension between Rapoport and the medical director at the time, Maxwell Jones (Manning and Rapoport 1976). In the refusal to 'buy into' the clinical interpretive framework, and to pursue instead a descriptive and analytic agenda, researchers always run the risk of upsetting the people being studied, who may feel unjustly criticised or let down by such treatment. Maxwell Jones wrote later, 'For me to discover the discrepancy between what I thought I was doing as a leader, and what trained observers saw me doing was frequently a painful – but almost invariably a rich – learning experience' (Jones 1968).

Published in 1960, Rapoport's book *Community as Doctor* has become a classic text providing, on the basis of his anthropological observations, the now almost ubiquitous concept of the 'four pillars' of therapeutic communities: democratisation, permissiveness, reality confrontation and communalism. This provides an example of how research observations can be fed back into the community, and indeed into therapeutic community culture in general, and themselves used as yardsticks for assessing the integrity of therapeutic community work.[4] For example, Eric Cullen's paper 'Can a Prison be a Therapeutic Community?' examines HMP Grendon in the light of these four pillars, and shows how they need to be modified to deal with the issues of prison security (Cullen 1997).

Bloor, McKegaldy and Fonkert: One Foot in Eden

During the 1970s and 1980s several researchers carried out qualitative studies of therapeutic communities (Fonkert 1978; McKeganey 1982; Rawlings 1980), focusing especially on how the largely democratic organising principles and procedures were employed to provide therapeutic treatment. These studies provided information in the form of lengthy individual case studies with in-depth descriptions of local organisation and practices. Bloor, McKeganey and Fonkert (1988) noted that this detailed qualitative work was often criticised on the grounds that it usually focused on just one or two institutions and did not offer any real comparative information. In response, they produced *One Foot in Eden*, a comparative study of eight therapeutic communities based on their own qualitative research studies. They noted that there were many different kinds of institutions with claims to the title of therapeutic community, which differed radically in their staffing, clientele, social organisation and approaches. Between them they had studied communities for adolescents, drug users, children with physical and learning disabilities and adults with neuroses and personality disorders. The communities were located in hospitals, community settings, day treatment centres and spiritual communities. The authors had all studied them using primarily participant observation techniques, recording their observations as field notes and attempting to focus on the clients as much as on the staff. In one case the researcher had carried out his fieldwork in the role of a resident, and he had written his report from that point of view. Through a series of *ad hoc* processes, the eight studies were put together according to a series of themes, which looked at how each one dealt with issues of reality confrontation, resident progress, resistance to therapy and the external environment. This was not an easy task, since each study had originally been written as a unique case study, embedded in its own categories and descriptive structure, and had not been written with this later comparative exercise in mind. Nevertheless, the book stands as the only example of qualitative comparison for therapeutic community research. Indeed, there is very little comparative work done at all in therapeutic communities, qualitative or otherwise, and very little such ambitious qualitative comparison done in any other ethnographic field.

The appendix to the book provides an account of the research methods employed, and examines how the social roles the researchers took on impacted upon their data, and at the effect of their own beliefs and behaviour on their field relationships. They ponder, for example, what the effect was of them all being white males in their twenties and thirties. How had this affected the quality of their relationships with different members of staff and different types of resident? What had the different community members thought of them, and how had it affected their stay? And how had their own views and assumptions about community members affected the choices they made about whom to talk to, what to do and what to take note of? The debate demonstrates how closely the qualitative researcher is tied into the life of the organisation he/she is studying. They write:

> Self-evidently we did not go native, though there were occasions when writing our fieldnotes seemed a tiresome irrelevance. Rereading our fieldnotes we actually encounter something of a puzzle. Our notes sometimes reveal such a degree of engagement with the events in the community that it is rather difficult to explain how we summoned or retained the necessary reflectivity to write them down at all. (Bloor *et al.* 1988, p.219)

Practitioners' accounts

One reason for outlining qualitative approaches to research in this book is because they may help people who are already members of therapeutic communities to carry out their own research projects. Indeed, there is a tradition of 'practitioner accounts' in the world of therapeutic communities (Almond 1974; Flynn 1993; Irwin 1995; Jansen 1980; Jones 1982; Schoenberg 1972; Whiteley and Collis 1987), which describe and explain therapeutic community philosophy and activity. Flynn (1993) and Irwin (1995) provide detailed descriptions of cooking and baking groups, and the interactions and events that make them therapeutic as well as working activities.

Practitioners, though, provide a different view of therapeutic communities, which is inevitably a 'clinically interested' view. Practitioners have joined the community for reasons other than research. Their work is to provide a treatment for others, and they judge themselves and are judged by how well they do this. Often they are trained or become trained in particular psychodynamic theories and interactional skills, which shape their professional viewpoint and expertise. It would be very difficult for someone in this position to stand back and analyse therapeutic community activity from a distance (even supposing they wanted to) as if that activity was 'anthropologically strange'. The researcher, however, has a different training and a different reference group, and however immersed in the culture he/she may become at times, the possibility of standing back and achieving a distance from the views and urgencies of a clinical perspective is always present. The researcher is judged not on clinical performance, but on descriptive acuteness.

In general, practitioner accounts are a continuation of debates about treatment. Practitioner descriptions add to the general stock of practical knowledge about what treatment is available, how (in the practitioner's opinion) it works, when (in the practitioner's experience) it works, why it works and when it hasn't worked. Others can agree or disagree, or alter their own practice on the basis of what they have read. These are people in the field, doing roughly the same sort of work, talking to and learning from each other. The qualitative researcher does not so much contribute to the debate as examine it as a whole and produce a description, which outlines the kinds of things people say, the kinds of problems they come up against and the kinds of ways they try to solve the problems.5 (Such an enterprise may well be seen to be of practical value to the therapeutic community, who may incorporate the research findings into their own debates, but this is different from the report having been written *as part of* those debates.)

Despite the differences between the practitioner's enterprise and that of the researcher, the methods that can be used to collect and analyse data can be identical. Recently, indeed, due to changes in training curricula, clinical professionals have adopted qualitative research methods in order to pursue academic and practical investigations into aspects of clinical work. Thus, an understanding of observation methods, semi-structured interviewing, questionnaire design and the analysis of diaries and documents has started to become part of the clinician's toolkit, and practitioners are becoming more skilled at pulling together a wider range of information about topics, and at applying more rigorous analytic techniques to it.

Summary

In this chapter I have outlined a range of qualitative research methods and discussed how these can be used in the therapeutic community. I have examined different methods in terms of their flexibility and the extent to which they intrude into the 'natural' life of the setting under review. I have also discussed some of the problems that researchers meet, in particular the need to become both immersed in the field and distant from it. I ended the paper with a consideration of some of the particular problems of practitioners who engage in research and a discussion of the different interests of practitioners and outside researchers.

CHAPTER 9

Outsiders on the Inside

Researchers in Therapeutic Communities

Nicola Morant and Fiona Warren

Introduction

The role and position of the researcher in a therapeutic community are unique, both in relation to other community members and in comparison to researchers based within other health service settings. The aim of this chapter is to present some reflections on the positioning of research and researchers within a therapeutic community, based upon our own experiences as therapeutic community researchers. In focusing on these issues, we will not be addressing questions about what form of research is most appropriate for therapeutic communities but, rather, the processes and functions of research at interpersonal, organisational and socio-political levels. We argue that the unique roles and positions of therapeutic community researchers are associated with key features of the therapeutic environment. In particular we identify the 'culture of enquiry' and associated high levels of reflexivity,[6] and the close integration of researchers, staff and clients/residents[7] that characterise therapeutic communities. In order simultaneously to conform to the collective ethos of the community and to maintain a stance that allows the conduct of high-quality research, the researcher may take up a position that we describe as an 'outsider on the inside'. The dynamics of interactions and relationships with staff and clients therefore become much more important than for researchers in more traditional mental health settings. We point out how these can impact upon the quality of therapeutic community research via, for example, their influence on study response rates. The researcher's role, as neither clinical staff team member nor client, can contribute to the life of the community in other ways; for example, in offering an alternative perspective on issues with which the community is struggling. In the final section of the chapter we offer some pragmatic suggestions for how researchers can negotiate the interfaces between research and clinical agendas and between independence from and integration within the organisation.

The context of therapeutic community research

As far as research is about contributing to knowledge and understanding, there are some basic assumptions about the nature of the research process to be addressed before we proceed further. Social scientists argue that scientific knowledge construction is a social process, which both shapes and is shaped by socio-political agendas and ideologies, and is set within specific historical and cultural contexts (Knorr-Cetina and Mulkay 1983; Merton 1973). We find this standpoint useful. It allows us to highlight and become aware of the impact of both micro-social processes (those within the specific therapeutic community environment) and broader macro-social processes such as the various agendas (political, financial and so on) that characterise contemporary mental health services. It also reminds us that the production of knowledge and research output is not as separate from the people and institutions that generate it as we often assume. Product and producer are always linked. Given this, it may be helpful at this point for us to state our own positions and reference points. The arguments we put forward represent some reflections on our own experiences of being researchers in a specific therapeutic community, Henderson Hospital. Each of us comes to this from a particular perspective, with a background in psychology, a discipline that provides a rigorous training in (primarily quantitative) research methods, and in which the individual is usually taken as the unit of analysis. The first author (NM) is a social psychologist with experience of conducting research in other mental health settings. The second author (FW) is a research psychologist with extensive experience of research at Henderson Hospital.

So what are the key characteristics of the therapeutic community environment that may constrain the researchers or shape the research process? First, a defining feature of a therapeutic community is a 'culture of enquiry' (Main 1983). This constitutes a collective belief in the value of continual reflection on interpersonal dynamics and processes as a central therapeutic tool that helps ensure the quality and effectiveness of clinical work. The centrality of this collective self-reflection to therapeutic community working contrasts with many traditional mental health environments where there may be insufficient time, resources or motivation to enter into such a reflexive process. Historically, the 'culture of enquiry' ethos has been significant in ensuring that research activity has been central to therapeutic communities, rather than merely a periphery activity grafted on at a later date (Manning 1976). One of the most famous texts on the therapeutic community approach was written using ethnographic methods at Henderson Hospital in which researchers spent long periods of time participating in all the activities of the community (Rapoport 1960). From these very early days, a tradition of the tolerance of such research activities was cultivated. However, it is only in the last five years that there has been a resurgence of external interest in therapeutic community research. We discuss some of the implications of this for researchers in therapeutic communities below.

Second, a fundamental principle of the therapeutic community is 'democratisation' (Rapoport 1960). Within a context in which the contribution of all community members is assumed to be valued equally, researchers tend to be much more integrated into the daily workings of the clinical environment than in most mental health settings. This poses a considerable challenge to the principles of objectivity and independence that are the cornerstones of the scientific research paradigm. We will return to this complex issue and its implications for the position of the therapeutic community researcher in the following section.

As well as the micro-social features of the therapeutic community, we should also be aware of the broader context in which therapeutic community research takes place, and consider how this may impact upon the research process. Therapeutic communities have an increasingly high profile in contemporary mental health policy and research, largely as they have been endorsed as one of the few treatments successful for people with personality disorders (Dolan, Warren and Norton 1997; Lees, Manning and Rawlings 1999; Reed 1994). With the rise of 'evidence-based medicine' (Sackett et al. 1996) and a growing concern (at least within the British context) with the cost of health care, research has become an increasingly politicised tool, used to support arguments for or against the funding of particular treatment approaches. In summarising some of the research issues for contemporary therapeutic communities, Lees (1999) emphasises that the current political climate necessitates research activity. She suggests three broad purposes of therapeutic community research: informing and improving clinical practice, improving understanding of how therapeutic communities work and meeting the requirements of evidence-based practice. This summary reflects the emphasis in today's health services on *evaluative*, as opposed to *theoretical* research. It also highlights how, despite claims to independence and objectivity of specific research studies, the determination of broader research agendas is not an entirely neutral process.

Roles and relationships within and beyond the therapeutic community

The unusual position of the researcher in a therapeutic community has the potential to bring both advantages and difficulties to the research process and to the individual researcher's personal experience of this. We have argued in general terms that the therapeutic community provides a highly unusual context to the research process, and that these contextual factors may shape the research and its findings. In this section we focus more specifically on how these processes of influence may operate. We begin by considering the roles and relationships that a researcher may be involved in within the therapeutic community. We then turn our attention to the roles a researcher may take up in relation to individuals and organisations external to the therapeutic community.

The researcher within the therapeutic community

Objectivity, neutrality and the possibility of collecting and analysing data in a bias-free way are the cornerstones of the scientific paradigm to which the majority of researchers subscribe.[8] The example of a researcher asked to evaluate the clinical effectiveness of a treatment programme – a common task for researchers in mental health – serves to illustrate these criteria. In designing and conducting the research, the researcher should be able to put aside his/her personal opinions about the programme and to disregard the agendas of clinicians providing the service (who obviously believe in the treatment philosophy and may have a strong desire to see research support for their views). Once the data are collected, the researcher must approach their analysis in a value-neutral way, prepared to accept the findings of statistical analysis regardless of whether they support or refute prior preconceptions or hoped-for outcomes. These are standards against which the academic community purports to evaluate research and which provide the basis of its acceptance or rejection of research findings.

This independence and division of clinical and research activity is operationalised in most health care institutions through researchers inhabiting a separate physical space and interacting with clinicians and clients only as much as their specific research tasks require. Compared to this, the researcher in a therapeutic community setting occupies a more integrated position. He/she is much more a member of the 'family', attending meetings, sharing office space with clinical staff, joining in community activities and often taking some part in clinical work. This reflects the therapeutic community ideology that sees all members of the community as equally valued (regardless of their specific role), as well as the importance placed on community and collective responsibility. Along with this, it is recognised that a vital aspect of doing therapeutic community research is an in-depth understanding of the principles, practice and daily dynamics of the therapeutic community. This understanding feeds into all stages of the research process, from being able to identify relevant research questions to designing methods of data collection that are practicably viable within the therapeutic community environment.

However, the researcher is not a community member in the same way as other members. He/she may not be a clinician and so may not participate in the life of the community in the same way as other members. For example, at Henderson Hospital researchers only attend some of the community meetings, and do not vote on decisions taken there. This creates an ambiguous position for the researcher of being neither truly 'in' nor truly 'out'. The researcher's position can be described as an 'outsider on the inside'. Similar issues are discussed by Grove (1984) in relation to participant observation studies, but we would argue that the dilemma of 'positioning' is central to the working life of all therapeutic community researchers, regardless of the paradigm within which they are working. The challenge, then, for the therapeutic community researcher is how to combine the status of quasi-integral community member with an independent stance in the design and conduct of research. The researcher's day-to-day work within the therapeutic community involves grappling with this paradox: how to conduct oneself so as to achieve a balance between respecting and participating in the therapeutic community ethos and maintaining the principles of a research method.

This ambiguous position as invisible community members may stimulate questions amongst staff and residents about the researcher's role. Questions such as 'Who is that person?'; 'What does he/she do?'; 'What is "research"?'. Particular dynamics and relationships with staff and resident groups may be likely to develop as a function of this unique positioning. Kennard (1979) notes that although therapeutic community staff and residents have a variety of attitudes towards research, they commonly view it as:

1.   a process that will eventually tell us whether or not therapeutic communities work;

2.   something that cannot tell us anything useful as there are too many factors involved; or

3.   an ethically unacceptable, impersonal and mechanical way of approaching people.

These views may reflect, at least in part, genuine ignorance and misunderstandings about the nature and function of research. Researchers can respond by attempting to explain the nature of their work, the reasons for conducting research and the realistic outcomes and uses of research projects. Informal contact with staff and residents or more formal occasions such as staff meetings or community groups can be used to do this. This can serve a useful function in disseminating understanding of research amongst staff and residents.

Beyond this, however, the commonly held views noted by Kennard may reflect more psychodynamic issues raised by the positioning of researchers in relation to other therapeutic community members. Faced with the inherently uncertain and difficult nature of therapeutic community work, staff may have collective fantasies about the power of research to produce neat and definitive solutions about clinical work. Or they may feel threatened by the evaluative nature of research which, they consider, involves making judgements about their clinical competence. Given the highly structured nature of clinical work in therapeutic communities, clinical staff may feel jealous or resentful of researchers who have more autonomy and apparent freedom than they may. In addition, the researcher may often be considered a 'senior' member of the staff team, attending management and organisational strategy meetings. The therapeutic community culture of self-reflection is a powerful tool should such situations arise, enabling the staff team and the community as a whole to recognise and ward off the potentially harmful effects of these dynamics.

On a more positive note, the positioning of the researcher within the staff team can serve some useful functions. In the intense dynamics of a therapeutic community, the researcher's position as someone who is simultaneously integrated into the community and separate from many of its key therapeutic activities can provide a third perspective to complement those of clinical staff and residents. While the researcher is a member of the staff team, his/her distance from the daily struggles of clinical work can often provide a different way of seeing an issue or a pragmatic problem with which the staff team is struggling. Valuing difference and the alternative viewpoints this can bring is inherent to the therapeutic community ideology, and the specific positioning of the researcher has potential to enrich the life of the therapeutic community in this way.

Another potentially positive effect of the researcher's integrated position within the community is in enhancing the involvement of clinicians in research. In the daily clinical programme, clinical staff may have very little time to think about and conduct research. Yet professional training and professional bodies are increasingly expecting their members to have one eye on research and/or audit as part of their daily work. The researcher in a therapeutic community can, and arguably should, have within his/her remit the role of encouraging clinicians to become involved in research. This could take place via the development of a regular 'research clinic' in which the researcher could advise on realistic and methodologically sound research. Clinicians have often had only basic teaching on the principles of research methodologies and this could enhance their professional development. Such collaborations ensure that research questions and design are informed by clinical issues and remain clinically relevant. At Henderson, for example, a monthly research meeting held at the academic base of St George's Hospital Medical School provides supervision of ongoing research projects in the therapeutic community.

The researcher's relationship with residents within a therapeutic community also has important implications for the research process. Part of the reason that research is at least partially integrated into the life of the community at Henderson Hospital is motivated by an ethical obligation to keep residents informed about how the information they provide is used. There are likely to be very real anxieties and concerns among residents about the purpose of research data, much of which centres around extremely personal topics. In addition, a therapeutic community is designed to empower residents and it is a duty of the research effort not to undermine this. Therefore, refusal to participate in a study and other concerns about research must be respected. It may be difficult, for example, for residents to distinguish between evaluation of a treatment programme and evaluation of the people participating in that programme. It is crucial that researchers have opportunities – either formal or informal – to clarify this distinction as part of the daily life of the therapeutic community. As far as possible – excepting the need to respect personal confidentiality, which we discuss in more detail later in this chapter – the research process should be transparent and accountable to the whole community. This can have positive effects on the research process in terms of improving response rates and anticipating any likely support needs during or after data collection. Given that therapeutic communities are usually fairly small, low response rates can be especially problematic in leading to such small numbers as to negate statistical analysis or necessitate extended periods of data collection. Collaboration between researchers and the whole (both resident and staff) community in design of the practical implementation of a research methodology can reduce the risks of low response and/or causing distress. A regular meeting where research issues are discussed forms a liaison link between the community and the research staff at Henderson, for example.

However, it is not simply the *number* of research participants that may be affected by relationships between researchers and residents, but also the *nature* of this participation. The psychodynamic issues that emerge in relationships between residents and researchers may reflect broader ways that residents relate to staff and people they perceive to be in positions of authority. For example, new residents may want to be 'model patients', agreeing unconditionally to requests to participate in research. Some residents may use the research process as an opportunity to act out or cause disruption in order to gain attention. Thus there may be significant differences between those who participate and those who choose not to participate in research. Finally, there are complex issues around responding to questions about feelings and psychological states during a period of intense psychotherapy. In some cases there may be a pull towards over-emphasising problems and difficulties, perhaps associated with a fantasy that this will elicit special treatment or concern from the staff team. In other cases, or at other points in therapy, residents may under-emphasise their problems to researchers as a way of stating their independence, protecting themselves or hiding their vulnerabilities. In addition to robust research methods and, where necessary, large sample sizes, the clarity of the researcher's role and his/her position in relation to the community will help to ameliorate these effects. Of course, this must include clear communication about the confidentiality of research data.

These examples serve to highlight that the skills required to conduct therapeutic community research are much broader than those associated directly and solely with the research process. The therapeutic community researcher needs to construct a position as part of the community, forming relationships with staff and residents that extend beyond the interactions required for the tasks of research, while simultaneously retaining an ability to conform as much as possible to the principles of sound research. Negotiating and maintaining this interface between research and clinical practice is not easy, and the struggle to achieve it is one that characterises the daily lives of therapeutic community researchers. However, in all the examples we have given, the awareness of interpersonal and intergroup dynamics is a key skill. Reflexivity has the potential to enable the development of relationships within the community that are beneficial to the research process, to the working experiences of the researcher, and to the life of the community.

Beyond the therapeutic community

We turn now to the researcher's relationships with outside organisations, considering these in relation to our earlier point that macro-social processes can shape the production of research. Within the National Health Service (NHS) context in Britain this can include the dynamics of the internal market, financial and political factors. For example, at the time of writing the British government is concerned with the social risks associated with people with a diagnosis of 'dangerous personality disorder', and is keen to commission research into treatment strategies, including therapeutic community treatments for this group. Recognition of these external agendas plays an important role in strategic decision-making about research. For example, research that assesses cost-effectiveness may be more influential among purchasers, managers and budget holders than, for example, studies of clinical processes. It can also be used to ward off closure threats (Dolan and Norton 1998). However, researchers must also be vigilant that political agendas do not over-ride obligations to remain true to their data and to the rigours of sound methodology. The selection of research questions should not be made solely in response to political demand. Previous research, scientific rigour and methodological appropriateness are the primary considerations in such decisions. It would be easy, for example, for therapeutic communities to respond to the demands of those who equate evidence-based medicine with randomised controlled trials (RCTs) of efficacy by conducting a hurriedly, poorly planned trial. On the other hand, many authors have highlighted caveats in the application of RCT designs in therapeutic community settings (for example, Dolan and Coid 1993; Manning, Chapter 6 of this volume). These include the ethical issues associated with random allocation to treatment or no-treatment conditions, and the interdependence of residents' experiences that challenges the assumption of independence of cases. Finally, the current dynamics of the internal market have the potential to encourage an environment that inhibits collaboration between therapeutic communities. This may be detrimental to the potential for comparative research across various therapeutic community environments, a need that has been recently recognised by Lees *et al.* (1999).

The researcher may be required to play strategic roles in developing external relationships with funders, purchasers and academic and practitioner communities. While there is nothing particularly unusual about this, these relationships may be shaped by the marginalised position that therapeutic communities have tended to occupy within the arena of mental health care. Manning (1979) argues that the traditional therapeutic community interest in research can provide a 'cultural bridge' between therapeutic communities and the more mainstream professional establishment that holds the balance of power in distribution of resources and shaping of the cultural landscape in the world of mental health. In this sense, researchers may find themselves acting as ambassadors for therapeutic communities in their interactions with fellow researchers and academics. Yet again this raises the potential for tensions between independence and involvement. However, the researcher's membership of an external research community can encourage the therapeutic community to look 'out' as well as 'in' and facilitate its ability to function within the broader social environment.

The researcher's external roles may also have implications within the therapeutic community, and it is in this sense that the distinction between 'internal' and 'external' roles and relationships that we have made in this section becomes blurred. The rising profile of research in the political/economic arena of the NHS can have knock on effects in the local clinical environment with, at worst, the potential to generate rivalries, competition and antagonism between researchers and clinicians. In effect, external politics and power relations can become mirrored in the internal politics and power struggles within clinical teams and between individuals within the therapeutic community staff team. The increasing role of researchers in long-term planning, funding and organisational decision-making may be perceived by clinicians as usurping their established power base. A sensitive and open staff team will recognise the possibility of these tensions between clinicians and researchers, and attempt to work through them. Both researchers and employing institutions should be aware of the potential for these difficulties and tread carefully in the development of roles within the community.

Surfing the interfaces

Having sketched out what we consider to be some of the key characteristics of the researcher's role both within and beyond the therapeutic community, we move in this section towards some suggested responses to the issues we have raised. These derive from our own experiences and, as such, are not an exhaustive list but a reflection of some of the strategies we have found useful in enhancing the quality of both therapeutic community research and our experiences of daily working life. As the title of this section suggests, we are concerned primarily with how the researcher can successfully negotiate the interfaces that challenge therapeutic community research. To reiterate, research work in therapeutic communities straddles at least two interfaces: between research and clinical agendas, and between positions of integration and independence in relation to the community.

The issue of confidentiality best illustrates the difficult ethical and methodological dilemmas presented by blurring the agendas of research and clinical work. Different therapeutic communities manage research and clinical confidentiality in different ways. At Henderson, clinical confidentiality applies to the community. In other words, nothing within the community is confidential from other members of the community (except physical medical information) but all is confidential from the outside world. The exception to this is information provided as part of research. In this sense, the research process is breaking one of the fundamental rules of therapeutic community working that there should be free and open channels of communication, and that no individual withholds clinically relevant information about another community member. Nevertheless, research confidentiality is deemed necessary for several reasons: to enhance the validity of research data (residents may withhold information or self-censor unless they feel confident that expression of views about experiences in the community will not have repercussions), because results are disseminated to an external audience, and because of the need to maintain research independence. However, where research concerns issues such as self-harm or sexual abuse, there is obviously the potential for difficulties. If a resident tells a researcher in confidence that they are feeling suicidal, what should be done? In our own research we have used a guiding rule of maintaining confidentiality for all research material except in cases where withholding information from the wider clinical staff team could put the individual at serious risk. This policy has emerged through discussion with the whole community. We consider it vital that *before* researchers embark on therapeutic community research they think carefully about confidentiality, and engage in thorough discussion with therapeutic community staff, external academics and the whole community where appropriate. It is also important to ensure that all new members of the therapeutic community are aware of these policies, and that they are consistently implemented throughout the lifetime of the project.

In addition, the researcher's ambiguous position – as an 'outsider on the inside' – also raises issues to be discussed and resolved. Integration of the researcher into the daily life of the community brings with it exposure to the emotional intensity of the clinical work. Researchers without prior clinical training may be ill-prepared for this, and the offer of support or supervision for the emotional content of the research role should be considered by the team. Yet, as the one member of the team with a research role, the researcher may feel isolated from a peer group with similar training and focus. There are many potential dangers of failing to monitor and consider this aspect of the researcher's position. These can include the following: the researcher becoming over-invested in the therapeutic process in a way that compromises research 'independence' and the ability to make judgements driven by research rather than clinical needs; lack of immediate access to peer group supervision for the minutiae of methodology and data analysis; narrow thinking about the research potential of the situation; and demoralisation as a result of working in an environment in which research issues are generally less urgent than clinical business. In order to avoid these pitfalls we suggest that researchers should establish some 'thinking space' for themselves away from the clinical unit. This may be formalised via an attachment to an appropriate academic department, providing an opportunity for links with a research peer group and enabling the researcher to maintain a focus on the research task and the integrity of the research method. Just as clinicians need time to reflect on their practice, researchers may benefit from study leave or the opportunity to work in a physically different location at times in order to maintain the independent stance required for research. As with any research post, attending conferences provides an opportunity not only to disseminate and receive feedback on research findings, but also to interact with researchers in other domains and to share and compare working practices and experiences.

Having argued for a degree of separation, we also consider it important that both researchers and the institution should recognise the value of maintaining good relationships within the community. Poor internal relationships in the context of a therapeutic situation that promotes empowerment are likely to lead to poor response rates or poor-quality responses, greater likelihood of response biases and other subversions of the research effort. Respect for the community shown by open communication, consistency of agreed policies around issues, such as confidentiality and sufficient integration to allow discussion of any issues raised by research, can all contribute to good-quality relationships without entailing compromises of research method or independence. Of course, this needs to be achieved while retaining time for data collection, analysis and dissemination. The design of a researcher's role should take account of this need for balance in expenditure of time and energies. Finally, researchers should aim to maintain self-reflection and sensitivity regarding how their roles and relationships with outside organisations may impact upon dynamics within the community.

Conclusions

It is important to recognise that the role of a researcher in a therapeutic community is particular, to be reflective about this and to recognise both the opportunities and the dangers this affords. The researcher occupies a particular position that is not quite 'in' the therapeutic community. There are several reasons for this: being driven by the principles of research rather than a clinical view; having a 'special' role and a different purpose from the majority of the staff team and the rest of the community; and needing to follow different rules from other members at times; for example, in managing the confidentiality of research material. In this respect researchers sometimes appear mysterious and may be regarded with mistrust by other community members.

On the other hand, neither is the researcher an 'outsider'. He/she is usually based on the community site and integrated into staff meetings and some community meetings; he/she fulfils some roles as a community member, such as contributing to staff business meetings and to external training and dissemination events. We have argued that this position can afford benefits to the success and quality of research and to therapeutic communities in other ways. However, there is a danger that those truly on the 'outside' might perceive this positioning as a blurring of the clinical and research agendas, and that this may lead them to question the independence of therapeutic community research. We have highlighted some of the ways in which the research process can be respected, whilst simultaneously contributing to the life of the institution in ways that do not compromise methodological rigour. Collective awareness of the complex issues involved can facilitate the reflexive exploitation of the researcher's unique role and combination of skills and, it is to be hoped, help us guard against unintended consequences or misuse of research results.

CHAPTER 10

The Psychodynamics of Being a Researcher in a Therapeutic Community

Living the Borderline Experience

Diana Menzies and Jan Lees

Introduction

There is an argument that researchers who are employed by a therapeutic community are too involved in the system to be unbiased. Their salary depends on the unit surviving and, most probably, they believe in the principles that govern the workings of a therapeutic community, which is why they have found employment there. This is similar to the allegiance effect that has been found in other forms of psychotherapy research whereby there is an association between the researcher's allegiance to a particular form of therapy and outcome of treatments compared (e.g. Luborsky *et al.* 1999). However, the idea that a researcher can *not* become involved while researching a therapeutic community is counter to experience, whoever his/her employers might be. It is this tenet that we would like to explore in this chapter.

We will discuss how researchers become involved in the psychodynamic life of the therapeutic community, first in relation to the conscious and unconscious (countertransference) issues on the part of the researchers. We will then look at the conscious and unconscious (transference) issues on the part of those being researched. Relevant to both groups are the desire to form relationships and the implications of the researcher being a part of the group matrix, as an 'outsider on the inside' (see Chapter 9), but also being on the margins of the inside of the community – in 'borderland' (Lawson 2000, p.4). We will also consider the, sometimes unclear, boundary between researcher and clinician and the power differential between researcher and researched.

Context

The authors' experiences come from working in therapeutic communities, most recently Francis Dixon Lodge and Henderson Hospital, where the residents have histories of trauma, abuse, deprivation or neglect in childhood and whose diagnosis as adults includes personality disorder. This is relevant to the content of this chapter as the particular psychopathology of the residents shapes the dynamics at play in the community, operating not only between residents but also between residents and staff, and between different staff members, including researchers. The personality organisation of the residents in Francis Dixon Lodge and Henderson Hospital is borderline, as described by Kernberg (1976). This means that they tend to cope with feelings of overwhelming anxiety by unconsciously separating people and situations in their minds into 'good' and 'bad' (splitting), by projecting intolerable feelings or parts of themselves into others and by inducing the recipients to identify with these projections and act accordingly (projective identification). Thus certain staff members and other residents will be seen as all good and others as bad. They also bring with them templates of past relationships upon which they base their expectations of future relationships. For example, a child who has grown up in an abusive household will have internalised this abused/abuser relationship as a template. As an adult, he/she will unconsciously re-enact this, sometimes playing the role of abuser to him/herself through various forms of self-harm or harm to others, and sometimes drawing others in to play the role of abuser to him/herself. The unconscious pull to become part of this re-enactment may be strong, hooking into the recipient's own internal dynamics, such that the early family scene may be re-created in the community. The internal dynamics of the staff must be considered too, as we all bring with us our own templates for relationships based on past experiences. Thus we may be susceptible to being drawn into playing particular roles in response to communications received from residents. Personal reflection and supervision are important necessities both to prevent the community from becoming as destructive as the original experience, and to learn from what is being communicated.

With this in mind, researchers at both Henderson Hospital and Francis Dixon Lodge are included in the morning handover meeting, after-groups, staff meetings and business and team awareness meetings, so that they are aware of, and can talk about, current dynamics relevant to the community. If involved in face-to-face contact with the residents, they also attend clinical supervision.

The researcher's influence

The observer effect

Whether the subject is quantum physics or social science it is now well recognised that the act of researching necessarily affects the subject being researched, a concept known as 'reactivity' or 'the observer effect'. In research where there is an interpersonal element, it is not only the act of researching but also the researcher him/herself that affects the results. This is more pronounced in qualitative research such as interviews or focus groups, where the attitudes and personality of the interviewer shape what informants will say (McLeod 1996), but is relevant also to research in which the presence of the researcher is less overt, as in quantitative research. For example, the *act* of asking client members of a therapeutic community to complete a questionnaire will in itself bring about a change in the client members, whether in thoughts or feelings, and colour the structure of the treatment programme. Will this affect whether, and how, the questionnaire will be completed? If the research involves interviewing client members in an otherwise all group-based treatment programme, the structure itself is radically altered. Add on the *person* of the researcher and more questions, feelings, ideas and fantasies, conscious and unconscious, on the part of both researched and researcher will come into play. A researcher coming from 'outside' may have different fantasies associated with him/her but will have them none the less.

We would argue then that the researcher in the therapeutic community will become 'involved', or a participant, in the system, like it or not. This involvement is likely to be different depending on the relationship between the researcher and the therapeutic community, including whether the researcher is part of the therapeutic community staff. What would seem to be important is an awareness of how this involvement affects the research process. Morant and Warren address both the practical reasons for the researcher being on the therapeutic community staff, as well as some of the resultant dynamics, in Chapter 9 of this volume. It is sometimes assumed that a researcher who is 'external' to the staff team will be more independent and less involved in such dynamics. We would argue, however, that this is not necessarily the case. The reality is that every researcher works within a particular context that can affect the research process. As much as there can be loyalties to the model by those employed by the therapeutic community there can be biases against, caused by political, financial, cultural or personal reasons. The unorthodox, and sometimes seemingly privileged, status of the therapeutic community can cause envy and rivalry, which can just as easily lead to non-neutrality on the part of the researcher. The allegiance effect is not biased in whom it affects.

Being part of the staff team

Having the researcher as part of the staff team goes some way towards establishing the collaborative relationship between researcher and clinician that is necessary for an awareness of the dynamics which could be influencing the research process. By attending some community meetings, being involved in handover and other staff meetings, and attending in-service training sessions, or theoretical seminars for new staff (as happens at Francis Dixon Lodge and Henderson Hospital), the researcher gains a good understanding of the principles underlying therapeutic communities. This is recommended so that one knows which research questions are relevant and how best to ask them within this particular setting. For example, will the client members be approached about the research individually or in a group? Will they complete the questionnaire individually or in a group? If the latter, will it interfere with something else that would have been going on? If so, how might this impact on the research and their therapy? These questions can be discussed in the community meeting with client members and staff, in line with the therapeutic community model, which may help counter the notion of research as alien to the rest of the programme. Seeing the researcher as part of the staff team and valued by them may increase client members' willingness to participate in the research, as well as contributing to the development of what has been called a 'research alliance' (Grafanaki 1996). This sort of participation by the researcher in the therapeutic community is methodologically congruent with the therapeutic community philosophy. One of the earliest research projects in a therapeutic community was that undertaken by Rapoport on the Social Rehabilitation Unit at Belmont, later to become Henderson Hospital, in the 1950s (Rapoport 1960). As an anthropologist he recognised the necessity of becoming involved in what he was studying and took several years to study the community. His research was observational and descriptive and involved his team sitting in on groups and questioning residents and staff on what they thought was important in creating the therapeutic milieu. This level of involvement is near one end of a spectrum, the level being determined by whether the research methodology is, for example, through participant observation, interviews, focus groups or purely questionnaires.

Living on the margins of the therapeutic community

Unless the researcher is employed with a dual role (discussed below), he/she does not have any clinical input to the client members which, along with the separate role of the researcher, tends to place him/her on the margins of the community. To the inside world of the therapeutic community the researcher may appear an outsider but to the outside world he/she appears an insider. As for anyone living on the margins of a society, this position can be an uncomfortable one. It is here that powerful unconscious emotions can be stirred up on the part of both the researcher and the researched. To the person on the outside, therapeutic communities often present as somewhat idealised, self-contained units, which engender much curiosity and a pull to belong. Looking in at the strong bonds created by the sharing of a belief in the model, of intimacies in therapy and of communal activities between staff and client members can engender strong feelings of envy in the outsider. This may be added to by the clinical staff feeling that the clinical work is the 'real' work, leaving the researcher feeling like an intruder and guilty for not contributing to this.

For those on the periphery who feel neither fully on the inside nor on the outside, the wish to belong may be powerfully experienced. When this is frustrated, as is experienced frequently by individuals joining the community, and more so as a part-time member or one on the margins, strong feelings of rejection, envy, rage and resentment can be stirred up. The strength of these feelings suggests the evocation of similar emotions from past early experiences. In the group analytic literature, the group has often been seen as representing the mother or the family. To be denied access to these leads to anxiety, rage and despair, followed by withdrawal and rejection when denial of access is prolonged with no opportunity for working through of these feelings (Bowlby 1973). It is not uncommon to see staff who are working on the margins of the therapeutic community (not only researchers) drawn into the dynamic of wanting to belong through more involvement and then withdrawing when this is denied, of feeling rejected and then wanting to reject. Add to this the tendency to swing between idealising the therapeutic community (usually when away from it and talking about it to others) and denigrating it (when your research item has been left off the agenda yet again) plus feelings of anxiety and apprehension, confusion and a feeling of never getting it right, and the experience of living on the margin can begin to sound like the diagnostic criteria of the borderline personality.

We should not be surprised by this, as these feelings are not only responses of the researcher to the ordinary frustrations and anxieties of their work, or indeed the evocation of earlier experiences in the researcher's life. They are also feelings and experiences that have been projected into them by the client members in an unconscious attempt to resolve their distress. These feelings are therefore important communications about the internal worlds of the client members. To be useful to the client member, however, and to free up the researcher, it is necessary to have a forum to make sense of what is going on. For example, is the researcher's current anxiety to do with the actual research or is it something that has been projected into him/her by a particular client member or the group as a whole? This is not easy to disentangle, even among qualified clinicians; which points to a need for a suitable space to reflect on what is going on. If the researcher has been in a clinical meeting where research was being discussed then this space may be in the after-group. If not, a separate supervision group will be needed, either with the clinicians or in a separate space with someone able to help reflect on the dynamics.

The researcher as an individual

As Bowlby (1988) describes in his theory on attachment, there is a basic need in every individual to form relationships with others; we all need to belong. But the researcher as an individual, with his/her own particular psychological make-up, is also important. What draws someone to work in a therapeutic community? Is there a particular desire to belong to a community? If this were too strong, then the feelings evoked by being on the periphery could be overwhelming and interfere with the research and the health of the researcher. From experience, these feelings are more likely to be felt in the few months after starting the job and to diminish once the worker on the periphery has established his/her own place. Although little could be found in the literature concerning factors that draw people to work specifically in therapeutic communities, there is some evidence that particular types are drawn to both work and reside in a therapeutic community. Wesby et al. (1995) discovered that there was a greater percentage of introverts and intuitives amongst client members and staff than would be expected of the general population. This does not necessarily help us, however, in determining how someone is going to be affected by the dynamics of working in a therapeutic community.

There are studies relating to psychotherapists and psychologists working in other occupational settings. A study by Murphy and Halgin (1995) compared psychologists who had chosen a clinical career with social psychologists whose career was in research and teaching. The latter had significantly less experience of personal problems and troubled families than the clinical psychologists, whose motivation for their career choice was partly influenced by a desire to resolve personal problems. There was no difference between the two groups on professional altruism, although therapists more often referred to a desire to help individuals whereas social psychologists referred to a desire to change society. These differences might not be seen, however, if clinicians and researchers working in a therapeutic community were compared, due to its particular social and therapeutic context. Indeed, as Morant and Warren discuss in Chapter 9, there is less split between the roles/work of researchers and clinicians in therapeutic communities than in more traditional mental health environments. Suffice it to say that a certain degree of emotional robustness is required of both clinician and researcher working in this setting. At the same time, therapeutic community researchers have chosen a different career path from other academic researchers, who may feel more comfortable working with objective facts and with ideas, rather than with the sorts of emotions and the lack of certainty involved in working in therapeutic communities. Certainly, the characteristics and motivations of therapeutic community researchers offer an interesting and potentially fruitful area of study.

The researcher as interviewer

If the research involves interviews, it may be that this is the only dyadic situation in an otherwise group-orientated programme. This may raise issues for the re-searched and the clinical staff (who may feel resentment or envy), as well as the re-searcher. Research interviews may involve inquiring about personal experiences which are painful for the researched, leaving them with disturbing feelings which could be acted out. It has been noted in the general psychotherapy/counselling literature with regard to qualitative research how blurred the boundary can be between this and clinical work. Even with self-report questionnaires, material may be divulged to the researcher that is not known by the clinical team; this may pose them with ethical and moral dilemmas. For example, as a researcher one may feel that one needs to offer complete confidentiality to those one is interviewing, in relation to the information one receives, in the hope that one will be given more privileged information. However, privileged communications run counter to therapeutic community and practice. In addition, the interviewee may tell the researcher he/she is at risk – for example, that he/she is self-harming or intends to self harm – and this may not be known to the clinical team. Holding this infor-mation is usually neither appropriate nor safe for the researcher, or for the client member.

In some therapeutic communities the researcher also has a clinical role, or a clinician may take on some research. This is potentially more confusing for the re-searched (e.g. is he/she interested in me or the research?) and can cause conflicts within the researcher. Lanza and Satz (1995) describe the tensions felt in carrying this dual role in an outpatient setting, for example, when a 'good candidate' was assigned to a control group, and make recommendations on how to protect the research from bias.

The influence of the researched

Researcher as receptacle

We have discussed issues relating to the person of the researcher and his/her position in the community, which make the probability of him/her remaining 'uninvolved' unlikely. Another powerful influence on this is the form that the researcher takes in the minds of those being researched. This will be both at an individual and group level. It may be most intensely felt when the researcher represents something for the group. For example, the position of the researcher on the margins of the therapeutic community may resonate with feelings of alienation and marginalisation frequently experienced by people with mental health problems within their own families and within society. These feelings may be experienced at an unconscious level but, due to their painful nature, be projected onto the researcher in an attempt to be rid of them. How much more bearable to see someone else as the outsider than oneself. Non-research staff, whether they are also being researched or not, may also resonate with these feelings considering the marginalised position which therapeutic communities often inhabit in relation to general psychiatry, in which case the researcher may be scapegoated by this process of projective identification. Clinicians may also feel jealous of researchers for not being involved in the difficult clinical work, and seemingly having an easier time. These processes may be more easily disentangled when the researcher is part of, and the research owned by, the staff team.

The researcher may also be a convenient receptacle for feelings, thoughts and fantasies which are not felt to be safely placed with the clinical staff, who in turn may be relieved by this displacement. Being in the community only part-time the researcher may represent the absences and abandonment felt by client members when clinical staff go home at the end of the day or week, or are working elsewhere. He/she may become incorporated into the paranoid fantasies of those being researched. If the researcher is usually silent in the community meeting other than on research issues, he/she may be seen as a voyeur, a silent useless mother or sibling who didn't speak up for them or a powerful authority figure whose non-intervention meant that childhood abuse continued. Indeed, if material has been divulged to the researcher and not to the clinical staff, secrets being shared but withheld from the rest of the 'family' may be re-enacted. If perceived as the outsider on the inside, the researcher may symbolise the outside world which has let a participant down, the system which does not care; or, if the participant is doing the research task for fear of saying no or because of a need to please, then it may feel as though a past abusive relationship is being re-enacted with the researcher.

Projections onto the researcher are not only, or always, negative and, in accordance with the tendency to idealise and denigrate brought about by the primitive need to keep good and bad separate, projections may swing from positive to negative. The researcher may be seen as the expert or as holding special knowledge about a resident. This may be expressed by long messages written to the researcher on the forms, in the wish for a special relationship, for someone who will be a saviour or rescuer. The age, gender and ethnicity of the researchers may also feed into this, particularly if individual interviews are conducted. Sexuality, hard enough to talk about in the group at the best of times, may get split off into unspoken yearnings for that which is unobtainable. On the other hand it may be that a question asked by the researcher will act as a catalyst in the gaining of insight, the researcher becoming an alchemist in the process of therapy.

Potential therapeutic community researchers, reading the above, may feel daunted by the process of research in a therapeutic community where hidden obstacles can snare the process at any stage. With many of the dynamics unconscious and potentially only coming to light if acted out, one may be put off from even starting. However, our aim is to forewarn the researcher that there *will* be psychodynamic processes, which will tangle up the research process, and to then look at how these may be anticipated, minimised (but not cancelled out completely) and managed.

Most important is that the research is owned by the staff team. Frequent and regular contact with the researcher is important and allows two-way communication. With the researcher as part of the team, clinical staff can be involved in discussions on how best to bring in research issues. They will also be alert to dynamics which may interfere with the research through the continual process of enquiry in the community, and be available to talk these through with the researcher, either in the after-group of a clinical meeting, in supervision or in a separate space if required. Thought should be given to the wording of letters regarding the research and a space for the researched to ask questions or give feedback about the process. External researchers will need either to meet with the staff team at regular intervals or to have a respected and/or influential member of the staff team 'carrying' the research on the inside. In Chapter 13, in their report of a prospective controlled study at the Cassel Hospital, Chiesa, Fonagy and Holmes describe how their research project came to the brink of collapse and that important mitigating factors were that the principal investigator had been on the staff team for some time, and that the hospital director was favourably disposed towards the project.

An example of when the dynamics were openly expressed during research occurred when the residents in one therapeutic community had been asked to complete some self-report questionnaires, which they had done together in a community meeting. It was the first time most of the residents had taken part in any research in the therapeutic community, there having been several months since the last project had finished. Research had been lost from the culture. The researcher was still quite new to the therapeutic community, and this was the first time he had approached residents for their help. The photocopier had broken down that morning so the information he had prepared to distribute to the residents about the research, along with the questionnaires, was not available. Instead, he told them about the project and gave them the written information later. There had been no signs of concern from the residents when completing the questionnaires and so he was surprised to hear from the clinical staff during the week that there had been a backlash after the written information had been distributed. One resident in particular said she felt tricked into completing the questionnaires. She had understood that the research was for internal use only but the written information had said it would be used, in an anonymised form, in a wider context. She and others were concerned that they would be recognised from the demographic details they had given. Strong feelings were expressed to the researcher in the next community meeting, and he felt anxious and largely unsupported by the clinical staff. Over the next few days the situation escalated, with the resident expressing intimidating thoughts towards staff. It became evident that the researcher had become equated with a terrifying persecutor in the resident's internal world, fear and revenge lying behind the resident's fantasies. The anxiety and fear spread to the group as a whole, with Bion's basic assumption of fight or flight being prominent. However, due to the researcher's weekly presence in one of the community meetings and at staff meetings, and the continued addressing of the issue by other staff in his absence, there was an opportunity for repair and resolution to occur. In retrospect, it was realised that the importance of the long gap since the last research project had not been appreciated. So, although the staff were used to research being part of the experience of the therapeutic community, this was not so for the residents and thus, the community as a whole. The importance of proper preparation and provision of information for the residents, on an ongoing basis, was also evident.

Dynamics of power

Last, we would like to consider whether the power dynamic between the researcher and the client members in therapeutic communities is different to that between the client members and the rest of the staff. The nature of the democratic therapeutic community is to try and reduce the power differential by flattening the usual client member/staff and staff/staff hierarchy. Thus, by their involvement in running the community, in selecting client members for the therapeutic community and in each others' therapy, the client members gain a sense of empowerment and self-worth which has often been lacking in their lives. In keeping with this, staff always keep the community informed of their forthcoming absences and general whereabouts. This is not always as possible for the researcher, who is so part-time in the community. This may lead to the paradox of the researcher seeming to be more powerful to the client members because of his/her relative independence but feeling less powerful in him/herself because of his/her position on the margin.

Although the client members are informed that the research forms are anonymous, and some feel depersonalised or devalued by being 'only a number', they also paradoxically worry about confidentiality when giving personal information. They may feel the researcher has power over them by (supposedly) knowing this information which, unlike clinical information, may not be shared with the rest of the community. In addition, if the client members have not been involved in designing the research project, it may be hard for them to own it and feel instead that it is something being put upon them, even if they choose to consent to it. And, because of their past abusive relationships, it is possible that they may feel they have been coerced into participating in the research even if they do consent.

At Francis Dixon Lodge, research issues are raised and discussed regularly in community meetings, and results fed back in the same forum. Although the researcher here is part-time, some of the clinical staff – nurse therapists – are also involved in some of the research projects, which provides for continuity in the researcher's absence but also enables research to be kept on the agenda. There are also *ad hoc* meetings between staff, including the researcher, and residents to discuss possible or ongoing research projects and research issues. At Henderson Hospital, a researcher and a clinical staff member have a brief weekly meeting with two resident representatives and any others who wish to attend to discuss any research ideas and issues. At less frequent intervals, a longer meeting is nego-tiated in one of the community project slots, to inform of new projects and to feed back results in a general way.

The interest this sort of feedback engenders, in both Francis Dixon Lodge and Henderson Hospital, varies among the residents. Some do not want to know anything (devolving all their power), while others wish to then go and read up all the previous research done at Francis Dixon Lodge, Henderson Hospital or on therapeutic communities in general; again, this exemplifies the polarisations which characterise the borderline personality. Although the latter response may be part of a healthy wish to be informed, it may also represent a dynamic of needing to be in control. Exploration of this issue has been felt by some residents as (and it could be) staff wishing to maintain power through knowledge, or as a patronising concern for their welfare (Will they be able to understand the termi-nology and technicalities? Will they misinterpret the findings? Will they be offended by seeing their predecessors described as psychopaths and themselves as severely personality disordered?). However, such meetings have also been the source of resident-led research, one of the aims of the current government, and very much in keeping with therapeutic community ideology, it is a step towards redressing the unequal power dynamic which has often existed between those being researched and the researchers.

Not always does the power differential seem to be against the client members. Temple *et al.* (1996) found that some patients in an outpatient setting thought that the researchers were assessing the work of the therapists, whose job they believed to be dependent on positive results. This has implications for whether the questions are answered honestly, and puts those researched in what may feel like a powerful position. Those angry at the community, for example, for being discharged, may covertly express their hostility through their responses to ques-tionnaires or by not participating. Menzies *et al.* (in press) found that more negative results were reported to a psychotherapist by a group member after he left an outpatient group in which he had felt hostile towards his group therapists than he reported to an independent researcher, showing that the answers given may bear on feelings towards therapy or therapist. Answers given may also depend upon whether the participant thinks the researcher may be able to influence them getting further therapy, emphasising the need for researchers to make it clear to the researched about the division between the roles of researcher and clinician.

Finally, it would be an interesting project in itself to explore the feelings and thoughts that client members have towards the researcher, comparing a setting where the researcher is employed as one of the staff team with one where he/she is not. Although such a project would tap into the conscious rather than unconscious experiences, it could nonetheless provide some interesting findings.

Conclusion

Through the above exploration of some of the psychodynamics of being a researcher in a therapeutic community, it is evident that this position can be as tricky to navigate – maybe more – as any other on the staff team. We have argued that it is impossible *not* to become involved in the therapeutic community process while being a researcher, however little contact there is and, indeed, to be a participant is in keeping with the therapeutic community model. The involvement we describe is brought about by conscious and unconscious dynamics, which inevitably affect everyone involved and shape the research. This is counter to the position held by positivist researchers that research is objective and neutral. We would argue that it is the researcher's responsibility to consider the factors that will influence the research and its findings and to put in place measures that will minimise these, while acknowledging that obliterating them altogether is not possible. Having the researcher on the staff team allows for the collective anticipation and exploration of interfering psychodynamics, helped by the experience of the clinicians. The research can then also be owned by the whole team; without this the project is likely to flounder. We have acknowledged the difficult and often isolated position occupied by the researcher on the margin of the community, even if he/she is part of the staff team, and how the psychodynamics incumbent on this position can make one feel as if one is living the borderline experience.

SECTION III

Research Findings

CHAPTER 11

What Makes a Therapeutic Community?

A Comparative Study of Ideal Values

Fiona Dunstan and Sarah Birch

In recent years the National Health Service (NHS) has experienced a great deal of structural and organisational change. During the 1970s and 1980s rapid advances in medical science, combined with heightened expectations and an increasing demand for medical treatment, raised serious concerns about the feasibility of providing unlimited access to health care (free at the point of delivery) in the way that had been envisaged by the pioneers of the NHS in 1946 (Timmins 2001). In an attempt to bring health service spending under control, successive governments have implemented a series of reforms that have had profound ethical and moral implications. The introduction of the internal market in 1992 forced clinicians to re-examine the empirical bases of their therapeutic interventions and evidenced-based practice is now high on the agenda.

As might be expected, mental health services have not been immune to this shift in emphasis and although, in some areas, research into the clinical effectiveness of psychological therapy is still in its infancy (Parry and Richardson 1996), there is now a great deal of evidence which demonstrates the efficacy of the therapeutic community model of treatment. For example, following their meta-analysis of therapeutic community outcome studies commissioned by the High Security Psychiatric Services Commissioning Board, Lees and her colleagues concluded that 'There is accumulating evidence [...] of the effectiveness and particular suitability of the therapeutic community model of treatment of personality disorder, and particularly severe personality disorder' (Lees, Manning and Rawlings 1999, p.8). Such evidence has been crucial in supporting appeals for additional funding for this client group and, subsequently, two new national centres (at Birmingham and Crewe), specialising in the therapeutic community approach to the treatment of individuals with severe personality disorder, opened.

However, it is not always clear from the literature precisely what the term 'therapeutic community' means, as different settings, often with very different treatment regimes, call themselves therapeutic communities (Whiteley and Gordon 1979). In addition, evidence for the efficacy for the treatment is often sought before the details of it are elucidated (Imber 1992). The study described in this chapter was an attempt by the authors to examine the ideal values and practices of six different therapeutic communities. The results of the research will be discussed below, as will the methodological issues associated with multi-centre research of this kind. We realise that elements of our analysis will be subjective but believe that this does not necessarily detract from the validity of our findings, providing that we make our stance explicit. It is important to own one's perspective so that readers can consider alternative ways of understanding the data from different perspectives. With this in mind, to ground the analysis, we have provided a brief account of our research stance and our experiences in the communities, which we believe also may have had an impact on the results of the study.

Previous research

Clark (1965) drew a distinction between the 'TC proper' and the 'TC approach'. According to Whiteley and Gordon the defining features of a therapeutic community (TC) are that it is 'A specific, specialised treatment process utilising the psychological and sociological phenomena inherent in the large, circumscribed and residential group' (Whiteley and Gordon 1979, p.105). However, many non-residential units also call themselves therapeutic communities, as do those which offer individual treatment in addition to group work and it may be that a 'family resemblance' (cf. Rosch 1973) might be a more useful conceptualisation. This pragmatic approach has been adopted by the Association of Therapeutic Communities (ATC), but it is clear that within the association there are very real differences between groups, not only in the way clinicians work but also in patients' levels of functioning. These differences make direct comparisons between communities more difficult but it may be that some core values can be identified.

Rapoport (1960), in his pioneering study of Henderson Hospital, identified four themes which he felt characterised the philosophy of the unit: 'communalism', 'democratisation', 'reality confrontation' and 'permissiveness'. He developed a questionnaire designed to measure the extent to which these themes are manifested within staff and patient values. In the 1970s Manning re-administered this questionnaire along with an exercise asking respondents to rate the community activities in order of importance. He found that the endorse-ment of the four themes by community members had increased, but he concluded that there was a lack of congruence between ideology and practice since socio-therapeutic aspects were under rated while more formal psychotherapy aspects were highly valued (Manning 1976).

However, in recent years clinicians have questioned the validity of Rapoport's concepts for the modern therapeutic community. Haigh (1996) has suggested that containment is a key feature of the current approach and it may be that different themes predominate in different settings. Rapoport (1960) himself wrote that the therapeutic community is 'based on convictions as yet untested by thorough-going evaluative procedures' (p.51) and it could be argued that this continues to be true (Birch, Dunstan and Warren 1999).

Over the years a number of studies have examined the similarities and differ-ences between therapeutic communities. Price and Moos (1975) used the Ward Atmosphere Scale (Moos 1980) to study the culture of 144 different treatment programmes. From the pattern of scores they identified 19 therapeutic communi-ties, which 'strikingly resemble[d] the type of milieu therapy described by Jones (1952)' (Price and Moos 1975, p.184) in that the balance of power resided largely within the resident/patient group. Another study by Crockett and his col-leagues (1978) surveyed the organisational culture of 20 British therapeutic com-munities. Their results showed that although all of the communities were struc-tured around such cardinal therapeutic community features as the daily community meeting and small group activities, the percentage of time devoted to groups varied significantly from community to community. This seemed to be related directly to the similarity of the community to the ideal therapeutic community model.

Whiteley and Collis (1987) attempted to explore the curative factors that might be occurring within the different groups using Yalom's group factors (Yalom 1975), which Bloch et al. (1979) also used to study the therapeutic process. They found certain curative factors such as learning from interpersonal actions to be prominent. They also found that as the length of time within a community increases the curative factors reported change from those expected from regressed patients (such as acceptance), to the more sophisticated (such as self-understanding).

Following a number of internal and external changes at Henderson Hospital, Suddards and Wilks (1996) conducted a piece of exploratory research to determine whether the culture, as described by Rapoport (1960) in his anthropo-logical study of the hospital *Community as Doctor*, had been affected. From their clinical practice, they generated a list of 44 statements that they believed repre-sented important aspects of the therapeutic community approach to treatment and using this as an audit tool they demonstrated that although the culture had been affected, Rapoport's four themes continued to guide contemporary clinical practice.

In summary, there appears to be a lack of consensus over what qualifies as a therapeutic community. Furthermore, within each variation there are different explanations for what might constitute the main curative factors, and there may be some disparity between therapeutic community ideology and practice. The aim of the project described below was to examine therapeutic mechanisms and evaluate current practice in terms of the ideal values held by staff and residents in therapeutic communities. A questionnaire was used which contained the items from Rapoport's original study, in addition to the questions piloted by Suddards and Wilks in the spring of 1996. An important event section was also included to examine therapeutic factors (cf. Bloch *et al.* 1979). In essence this project attempted to amalgamate two strands of research: that of Rapoport (1960) and Manning (1976, 1989) into therapeutic community ideology and practice, and a therapeutic factors study conducted at the Henderson Hospital by Whiteley and Collis (1987) in the late 1980s.

In keeping with Main's 'culture of enquiry' (1946), as we approached the new millennium, it seemed appropriate to re-evaluate current therapeutic community practice and determine whether there was any difference between communities in their perceptions of ideal values. The identification of therapeutic ingredients would enable aspects of the approach to be more widely generalisable and more easily evaluated.

Method

Research stance

Both researchers had a background in academic (rather than clinical) psychology and both had recently joined the research team at Henderson Hospital when the project was carried out. The project was supported by the whole community (staff and residents). The write-up of the results was submitted to the University of Surrey by one of the researchers (FD), in partial fulfilment of a BSc (Hons) degree in psychology, and the first section of the results have previously been published as a journal article (Birch *et al.* 1999).

Instrument

The 58 items in the questionnaire were derived from two sources: a 14-item questionnaire developed by Rapoport (1960) to examine his four tenets; and statements from the pilot questionnaire used by Suddards and Wilks (1996). Rapoport's scale included such items as: 'Patients should take responsibility for their own treatment and play an active part in the treatment of others' (democratisation) (p.55) and 'While a patient is outside the community s/he should try to forget about his/her problems as much as possible' (reality confrontation p.63). Suddards and Wilks' (1996, p.14) new questions included 'It is very important that individuals can learn by making mistakes' (permissiveness); and 'Cleaning should be a shared activity, done by both staff and residents' (communalism). For a more detailed exposition of this section of the instrument used in the study see Birch et al. (1999).

The second section asked participants to consider which groups they felt were most important and to rank them in order of importance from one to ten (one being the most important, ten being the least important). Because different communities offered different groups it was not possible to adhere to the format used initially by Rapoport (1960) and subsequently by Manning (1989).

The third section of the questionnaire was qualitative and followed Whiteley and Collis' (1986) study in that it asked respondents to describe the most important treatment event during the last week for themselves or someone else. Bloch et al.'s (1979) method for the study of therapeutic factors was used to categorise these descriptions. They were derived from the group factors developed by Yalom (1975). These were: catharsis; self-disclosure; learning from interpersonal actions; universality; acceptance; altruism; guidance; self-understanding; vicarious learning and instillation of hope.

Samples

A meeting of the ATC research group was used as a forum to explain the project and to recruit communities for the pilot study. Data were collected from 263 individuals (152 patients/inmates and 111 members of staff) in the six therapeutic communities that are listed below. The patient/inmate participants evidenced a range of emotional and/or psychiatric disorders including personality disorders (American Psychiatric Association 1994); serious disturbance in emotional and/or social functioning; depression and somatisation of symptoms. All of the patients/inmates and members of the clinical staff (including prison officers in Grendon Underwood)[10] who were present on the study days were eligible for inclusion.

This study collected data from six therapeutic communities:

HENDERSON HOSPITAL

Resident group: 24 adult patients were eligible for inclusion in the study. Everyone who was approached agreed to participate (14 females and 10 males). Approximately 40 per cent of patients admitted to the unit have forensic histories (Dolan and Coid 1993a). All treatment at the hospital is group-based.

Staff group: 20 members of a multi-disciplinary staff team agreed to participate in the study (14 females and six males).

CASSEL HOSPITAL

Patient group: 40 patients were invited to participate in the study. Nine patients (eight females and one male) agreed to complete the questionnaire. The hospital specialises in the treatment of adolescents, single adults and whole families with severe emotional difficulties and problems (Griffiths 1995). Treatment is conducted in individual psychotherapy sessions and in groups.

Staff group: 24 members of a multi-disciplinary staff team agreed to participate in the study (14 females and ten males).

INGREBOURNE CENTRE

Client group: 45 patients were eligible for inclusion in the study. Twenty agreed to participate (12 females and eight males). Subjects were members of a mixed community (residential and non-residential), which specialises in the treatment of personality disorders (American Psychiatric Association 1994). All treatment at the centre is group-based.

Staff group: 12 members of a multi-disciplinary staff team agreed to participate in the study (six males and six females).

HM PRISON GRENDON UNDERWOOD

Inmate group: 220 male inmates were eligible for inclusion in the study, 77 agreed to participate (age range 21 to 60 years). Grendon prison is a high-security unit with five separate therapeutic community wings. Medical referrals include diagnoses of psychopathy and antisocial personality disorder (American Psychiatric Association 1994). The main categories of offences were: violence (murder, manslaughter and grievous bodily harm), sex (rape, indecent assault and incest), dishonesty and arson (Cullen 1994). All therapy is group-based.

Staff group: 36 members of a multi-disciplinary team agreed to participate in the study.

WINTERBOURNE THERAPEUTIC COMMUNITY

Patient group: 12 patients were invited to participate in the study and seven of them agreed to complete the questionnaire. This is a day centre for 12 adults with personality disorder, where all treatment is group-based.

Staff group: seven members of staff agreed to participate in the study.

COMMUNITÀ RAYMOND GLEDHILL IN ROME, ITALY

Patient group: 15 patients were eligible for inclusion in the study and 12 agreed to participate. This is a therapeutic community for adults with a range of mental health problems who can stay for up to three years. All treatment is group-based.

Staff group: All 12 members of staff agreed to participate in the study.

These communities all differ in various ways including type and number of clients, structure of service provision and therapeutic programme, number of staff and their respective disciplines and location, but they all ascribe to the 'family resemblance' model (Rosch 1973) of the therapeutic community adopted by the ATC.

The questionnaire was administered to the staff and residents of the six communities. The nature and aims of the study were outlined to each group by two researchers in a meeting of the whole community,[11] and an option was given to complete the forms in a group session although this was only taken up at Henderson Hospital.

Translation of the questionnaire into Italian for Communità Raymond Gledhill

The questionnaire was translated into Italian by a senior staff member working in Communità Raymond Gledhill and, to ensure that the translation was accurate, the questionnaire was then 'back translated' into English by another researcher (who was not familiar with the study). Following this procedure, only minor amendments were required before it was administered to community members in the therapeutic community in Rome.

Procedure

The study was explained to each community in a large group session and a vote (for or against participation) was taken in the meeting. Residents/inmates and staff were told that the survey was being conducted to assess the views of community members on the operation of the therapeutic community model. In each case subjects gave informed consent and the project was given approval by the appropriate institutional or ethics committee for the region. Participation in the study was voluntary and the limits of confidentiality were discussed with each participant, in line with the BPS *Code of Conduct* (British Psychological Society 2001). Community members were also assured that their participation in the study would not affect their treatment in any way. All of the residents/inmates and staff members who were present in each of the communities on the study days were eligible to join the project.

The method of administration varied slightly from site to site for pragmatic reasons. The intention had been to standardise the procedure by administering all of the questionnaires in group sessions. Unfortunately, this was possible only at Henderson owing to timetable constraints in the other communities. So, in all the other communities participants filled in the questionnaires individually and returned the forms to a central collection point.

Data analysis

The data were coded and analysed using the Statistical Package for the Social Sciences (SPSS Version 6). Multi-variate data analysis consisted of a principle factor Analysis (PFA). Coakes and Steed (2001) write that 'Factor analysis is a data reduction technique used to reduce a large number of variables to a smaller set of underlying factors that summarise the essential information contained in the variables… [F]actor analysis is [often] used as an exploratory technique when the researcher wishes to summarise the structure of a set of variables' (p.155). This means that PFA can be used to look for coherent patterns in the data, such as a pattern in the way that questions on a questionnaire are answered. This statistical technique is frequently used to examine whether a questionnaire is measuring what it was designed to measure, such as Rapoport's four themes. The question-naire used here would be thought to demonstrate evidence of validity if the answers could be statistically grouped according to the four themes. There is of course a circularity here, as it is possible that it is the themes which lack validity rather than the questionnaire itself (Thompson and Daniel 1996).

Results

Examination of the evidence for Rapoport's four themes

Since the aim of the study was to identify the main themes underlying contempo-rary therapeutic community practice, an exploratory PFA was performed on the questionnaire data. The responses of both the staff and resident groups (in all six of the communities) were pooled to provide a large enough sample for multi-variate analysis, and the different sections of the questionnaire were examined both separately and together.

The results did not support the four dimensions originally proposed by Rapoport. Nor did they provide evidence of a new thematic structure. The analysis using Rapoport's items extracted two factors, which largely conformed to a simple structure; however, only 34 per cent of the total variance was accounted for. The factor structure of this analysis can be seen in Table 11.1.

			Table 11.1 Rapoport's questionnaire			
Question	Factor I	Factor II	Question	Factor I	Factor II
2	0.11	0.58	30	0.75	-0.14
6	0.62	-0.05	35	0.30	0.45
10	0.48	0.08	40	-0.24	0.60
13	0.68	-0.11	44	-0.05	0.37
16	0.28	0.49	50	0.54	-0.34
19	-0.01	0.58	53	0.48	0.22
27	-0.23	0.38	58	0.51	0.07

The coefficients relating to each factor are highlighted for clarity. It can be seen from the table that only 14 questions from a total of 58 could be grouped in relation to a coherent factor. One of the factors that emerged consisted largely of items relating to confrontation and permissiveness, while the other seemed to relate more to democracy and communalism. However, this interpretation is problematic given the number of questions which did not fall into a recognisable pattern (hence the lack of variance in the results accounted for).

When all the items were combined (i.e. Rapoport's original statements and those generated by Suddards and Wilks) and the analysis was repeated there was no discernible pattern in the way the items loaded onto the emergent factors, which made it difficult to interpret them in any meaningful way. For a more extensive presentation of the results of Part One of the questionnaire, see Birch *et al.* (1999).

The most important group

Unfortunately, it was not possible to make any direct statistical comparisons between the sites in this area. Although the timetables of all of the communities studied were structured around such cardinal therapeutic community features as the daily community meeting and small-group therapy, the variation (between communities) of the ancillary groups was considerable and this makes it virtually impossible to employ a ranking system in a useful way. However, it is interesting to consider that at Henderson Hospital the general consensus across staff and residents was that the community meeting and the small groups were the most useful. Notably, when the answers from staff and residents were examined separately it could be seen that staff valued the community meeting most highly while residents favoured the small groups. In the other communities it was usually the smaller groups, such as psychodrama and art therapy, that were valued above community meetings.

Most important therapeutic event

The third section of the questionnaire revealed a variety of Bloch et al.'s (1979) therapeutic factors, which corresponded to those found by Whiteley and Collis (1987). The 'most important treatment events' were classified by two researchers and reliability was measured in terms of percentage agreement (82 per cent overall).

In total, 149 people of the whole sample of 263 completed this section of the questionnaire. The distribution of therapeutic factors coded from these responses can be viewed in Figure 11.1. The most frequently occurring factor was learning from interpersonal actions, followed by self-understanding and vicarious learning.

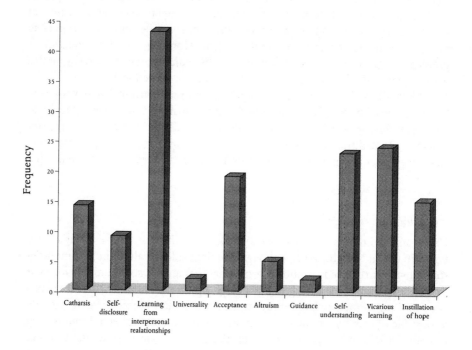

Figure 11.1 Frequency of therapeutic factors in six therapeutic communities

Of this sample, the greatest number was written by inmates at HMP Grendon. However, chi-square analysis revealed a non-significant difference between the answers given by each site, as coded using Bloch *et al.*'s (1979) therapeutic factors.

Of the 149 people who responded, 89 of these were patients or inmates. Chi-square analysis did not reveal a significant difference between the factors of these samples.

Finally, chi-square analysis did not reveal a significant difference in factor type according to length of stay in the community.[12]

Examples of each factor were as follows:

CATHARSIS

'Being able to tell a member of staff that I had felt upset by them. This was said in a community meeting. I felt more relaxed after speaking my feelings and I feel I now trust the staff more.'

SELF-DISCLOSURE

'When I first came here I didn't know what my feelings were and I learnt to draw [in art therapy] my thoughts which were my feelings and then I managed to open up in group meetings and develop more in my small group. Eventually I started to understand my cycle of offending and my addiction to drugs...and how it started in childhood – feeling hurt, resentful and suppressing it and then not being able to cope with it and resorting to crime and drugs to make me feel happy as it was easier than talking about it.'

LEARNING FROM INTERPERSONAL RELATIONSHIPS

'Someone admitted he had told lies about a violent fantasy – said he had made it up to gain attention...it confirmed my belief that his story was a fantasy and maybe now a fresh start can be made to help this person to face reality and be honest with his group members. It was important for me, as I do not like this person. My patience appears to have deserted me. I am trying to identify reasons for my reactions and I am happy that I am at present in control of these feelings and that I am not reacting by using violence and do not wish to harm him. I find that I am still finding the will to try and help this man and therefore still learn to help myself with my own problems.'

UNIVERSALITY

'I am the youngest member of the group which in a lot of ways is good because I pick up a lot from the older members. For example, a few days ago I was very worried about my life and where it's going. I got very down because I don't want to fail in life. I took this worry to the group who in turn gave me some useful advice. I felt a lot better afterwards. The good thing about the feedback is that there's always someone who has been where I am now.'

ACCEPTANCE

'One of the group members had behaved in an improper manner. When his behaviour was pointed out to him he reacted with anger and this carried on throughout the week, denying what he had done at first and demanding an apology and later on admitting it but still holding grudges towards the rest of the group. It's been a strain on us all throughout the week. My reaction was at first that I wanted to help him, then anger and resentment towards him because of the untruths to becoming confused and not knowing what to do. I think this was important because it tested the group in all sorts of ways and it certainly tested me. But most important was how the group pulled together and supported one another and despite personal feelings gave everything we could to support him.'

ALTRUISM

'A resident discharged herself. Residents, staff and myself helped her in a discharge group with planning, support and to make sure that she was safe when she left the unit. The next day I travelled with her to where she was staying. This was a long journey and I had to return back the same day. The journey took 13 hours; it was tiring, stressful and quite hard work. I was reassured to know that I had done everything I could to support her.'

VICARIOUS LEARNING

'The entertainment rep stole money from the community. He refused to admit it when it was blatantly obvious that it was him. I was so annoyed that he had stolen from me but I also felt like a hypocrite because I have been a thief for most of my life and I had no feelings for my victims up until that point. For the very first time I could actually relate and feel how (or some of how) my victims felt. This was a great learning process for me. It has gone a long way in helping to stop committing crime and creating victims.'

GUIDANCE

'A new staff member had arrived and two boys (both of the same age but one had been a resident longer) became rude, verbally abusive, then went on to become boisterous, noisy and threatening. The established patient was told [by the community] that he should manage better and help the newer one. Both boys apologised to the new staff member.'

INSTILLATION OF HOPE

'A member talked of her experience of the support call network and how her contact with others is much fuller now. This sort of individual feedback about change and growth, in the context of the whole group, has a really holding effect and instils hope and a sense of safety in the whole community.'

SELF-UNDERSTANDING

'I sat for a few weeks with a problem about a group member being hit by another resident. I found it very hard to speak about the issue but in the end I did confront it. It left me feeling guilty because I had broken one of my codes. But the reason I felt the way I did about this issue was because it related to my own crime. I had made my victim feel helpless and now I felt helpless to stop one person hitting another. The humiliation I felt was the same as my victim's. That's why I could not speak about the issue.'

The experience of doing multi-site research

In line with Goffman's (1961) social anthropological approach, Rapoport (1960) believed that carrying out research in a therapeutic community necessitates a familiarisation with the environment so that results can be meaningfully interpreted. In the case of multi-centre research, this task is more complicated. Each therapeutic community has its own vagaries and identity, and reaching an understanding of those which are not purely superficial takes time. It also requires therapeutic community members to allow you to experience their therapeutic community in a genuine way, and this may not always be the case for a multitude of reasons. Qualitative research often emphasises the interaction between the researcher and the research, in producing the results (Smith 1995) through a 'sustained engagement' between the two.

An alternative, more 'scientific' standpoint would hold that familiarisation with the environment is not only unnecessary but undesirable, as it may subjectify the research and therefore render it invalid. Proponents of this perspective would argue that it is possible to avoid the so-called 'Hawthorne Effect' (Roethlisberger and Dickson 1939) and to measure objectively and accurately the qualities of an environment in a way which allows standardised results for the purposes of comparison.

Both perspectives have value, and both could be seen as germane to therapeutic community research. In this case, however, it was felt that an awareness of what it is like to be in each therapeutic community would be useful in understanding the data collected. In addition, the development of a relationship with therapeutic community members meant that they were willing to impart personal information, which we feel has enriched our results. Each therapeutic community had a different atmosphere that seemed to derive from more than obvious structural differences such as a residential or non-residential settings. As researchers we were welcomed into each community in a variety of different ways. Some residents or inmates challenged the rationale behind our research and wanted to know in detail what we would do with the information we received. This made it necessary for the researchers to be accountable for the work they were doing, one of the benefits which Punch (1998) emphasises in his discussion of the pros and cons of field research. It was also in keeping with therapeutic community philosophy to enable the research to be part of the 'culture of enquiry' (Main 1983). Some were keen to talk about their experiences, and wanted to hear more about the other therapeutic communities we had visited. In some places we were asked to join in everyday activities such as cooking and cleaning, while in others we remained in more of an observer position. All these differences felt comfortable within their own context, and allowed us to understand what made each therapeutic community unique. They also enabled us to experience a range of researcher positions from which different levels of information could be gathered. On the whole it was a rewarding experience, giving the exploration of therapeutic community values personal meaning.

Discussion

The factor analysis performed on the items of the original questionnaire did not support the four constructs proposed by Rapoport (1960). This result could be interpreted in one of two ways, as discussed in detail by Birch *et al.* (1999). First, is it possible that the four themes proposed by Rapoport may not reflect current therapeutic community values. However, since there is no record of any psychometric evaluation of the original questionnaire data, it is not possible to compare these results with Rapoport's, who did find evidence to support his four themes. A second interpretation could therefore be that the questionnaire itself lacks validity, a possibility which is enhanced by the addition of the new questions from Suddard and Wilks' more recent study in 1996. Birch *et al.* (1999) conclude that the four themes may still be applicable as a general framework for examining therapeutic communities, within which more specific ideas and practices are constantly changing.

Had it been possible to run separate analyses on each of the samples, different factor structures might have emerged for each community. Unfortunately, the sample sizes in this study were too small to permit this. Hammond (1995) points out that correlation coefficients tend to be less reliable when estimated from small samples (fewer than 200), and he suggests that there should be at least four times as many subjects as variables. It may be that some form of cluster analysis could be used to investigate the underlying structure of the six samples. It was, however, beyond the scope of the study to investigate this option.

Whiteley and Collis (1987) pointed out several paradoxes in Rapoport's findings using his four themes. He found that although each theme was espoused by staff members at Henderson Hospital, the importance placed on them by residents changed over time and adherence to these themes as therapeutic community values did not correspond to the success of their treatment. For example, residents who believed less strongly in the importance of democracy and communalism were able to establish a closer relationship with staff members and responded better to treatment. Similarly, permissiveness was found to be less helpful as it did not reflect the realities of life outside the hospital, and therefore an adherence to this value meant that people were less prepared for discharge.

Whiteley and Collis (1987) inferred from these paradoxes that the themes might be more usefully encompassed within therapeutic factors such as those developed by Bloch *et al.* (1979). Catharsis and self-disclosure could both be seen as demonstrating permissive characteristics, while democracy enables altruism to occur. Confrontation includes learning from interpersonal actions and vicarious learning, and communalism arises through such factors as universality. Whiteley and Collis (1987) measured these themes at Henderson Hospital and they found that as the length of time within a community increases, curative factors change from those expected from more regressed patients (such as acceptance) to the more sophisticated (such as self-understanding). They found learning from interpersonal actions was the most common factor, followed by acceptance and self-understanding. A further interesting finding was that most of the therapeutic events occurred outside the formal psychotherapy groups.

However, the limited findings concerning the most important group showed some evidence that participants felt the smaller psychotherapy groups were the most valuable. This is consistent with Manning's findings that both staff and residents placed the most importance on small groups, and that residents ranked the community meeting only fourth (1976, 1989). He concluded that this demonstrated a lack of congruence between therapeutic community ideology and practice, and the philosophy behind therapeutic communities suggests that it is the community experience as a whole that works to effect therapeutic change. An alternative interpretation might be that the community provides a container for more intense therapeutic interaction within it. Such interaction could take the form of both small therapy groups and events occurring during the course of each community day.

Following on from this hypothesis, the therapeutic factors found in this study correspond to the pattern found by Whiteley and Collis (1987), in that learning from interpersonal actions was also the most common therapeutic factor, while self-understanding also featured prominently. Perhaps it is unsurprising that learning from interacting with others should be one of the most therapeutic aspects of a clinical setting where the community itself is thought to be imbued with therapeutic qualities. Whiteley and Collis (1987) write of the containing function of the community whereby new ways of interacting with others are possible, and where feedback will be given about how that new behaviour was construed. This is in fact more than reminiscent of Rapoport's reality confrontation. Perhaps Whiteley and Collis (1987) were right in their hypothesis that the four tenets outlined in *Community as Doctor* (1960) could be encompassed within Bloch *et al.*'s (1979) therapeutic factors.

Unlike in previous findings, there was no significant difference in the type of factors identified according to the length of time a person had been a member of the community. It is possible that moves towards preparing people for treatment within a therapeutic community has meant that they are more fully aware of what the nature of the work might be. In addition, any differences found between these results and former research might be due to the fact that this is a multi-centre study where differences between communities could cancel out trends in the overall sample.

Conclusions

It is difficult to draw generalisable conclusions from the study. However, the evidence suggests that different clinical populations (i.e. those in secure and non-secure settings; day-care and residential settings) may espouse very different ideal values and may find different elements therapeutic, so that to try and draw meaningful comparisons between groups is unhelpful. It may be that as clinicians and researchers we have to accept that there are certain things that cannot be categorised and measured in a 'scientific' way – at the present time, as critics of psychometrics such as Kline (1998) would suggest. This is not to say that it will never be so; simply that, given the present state of our knowledge and the crudity of our research tools, we do not, currently, have the means to accomplish the task. Clarke and Cornish (1972) write that the comparative evaluation of institutions is complex, and the task is made even more difficult in this instance by the divisions and disagreements among theorists about what constitutes an 'authentic' therapeutic community. For, while it may be easy to expound on the central theoretical tenets of Rapoport's (1960) original model, it is more difficult to accommodate all of the recent clinical variations within a single framework.

In addition, more subjective qualitative techniques such as that used in the third section of our questionnaire can add an interesting and useful perspective to clinical research. Rather than confine the responses of participants within a pre-set framework of a forced-choice questionnaire, the therapeutic events section provided a space for respondents to structure their own response. This meant that our analysis was grounded in the data (Henwood and Pidgeon 1992), therefore enabling patients/inmates to retain their voice in line with therapeutic community philosophy. Further exploration of the data may allow the emergence of other relevant concepts, in the same way that grounded theory allows the space for new ideas to arise (Strauss and Corbin 1990).

Postscript

A colleague, on being asked to describe therapeutic community practice, replied: 'Therapeutic community practice is what you are doing when you say you are working in a therapeutic community'. And it may be. After all, there's many a true word…

CHAPTER 12

Researching Concept-Based Therapeutic Communities

Susan Eley, Rowdy Yates and Jane Wilson

Introduction

This chapter reports on the activities of the Scotland-based research team within the Improving Psychiatric Treatment in Residential Programmes for Emerging Dependency Groups (IPTRP) project, a three-year multi-site programme co-ordinated by the Department of Social Psychiatry at Maastricht University and funded by the Science Directorate General of the European Commission in response to the Biomedicine and Health, Fourth Framework programme in the area of research on methods of evaluation of the effectiveness of prevention strategies.

The study brought together a total of nine universities or research centres from the participating EC countries and 33 residential treatment services. In addition, one further research centre and two residential treatment centres in Norway joined the initiative as non-EC (third-country) partners (see Table 12.1).

The main aims of this chapter are to outline our approach to researching therapeutic communities and to describe some findings from our research into the psychosocial impact of childhood trauma in therapeutic community clients. Finally, we draw some brief conclusions from our experience in order to make recommendations for future research by independent researchers.

Table 12.1 Number of researched therapeutic
communities by country

Country	Number of therapeutic communities	Research participants
Belgium	5	127
France	5	72
Germany	1	61
Greece	4	205
Italy	5	112
The Netherlands	1	100
Norway	2	102
Scotland	3	134
Spain	1	30
Sweden	4	85
Total	31	1028

Therapeutic communities in the UK context

Our research involved a prospective study of consecutive adult admissions to three therapeutic communities (TCs) in Scotland (Table 12.1). George De Leon (1994a) writes of the therapeutic community:

> The TC can be distinguished from other major drug treatment models in two fundamental ways. First, the TC offers a systematic treatment approach that is guided by an explicit perspective on the drug use disorder, the prison, recovery and right living. Second, the primary therapist and teacher in the TC is the community itself, which consists of the social environment, peers and staff members who, as role models of successful personal change, serve as guides in the recovery process. Thus, the community is both the context in which change occurs and the method for facilitating change. (p.18)

Within the IPTRP project, the European therapeutic communities were diverse in nature. The Scottish therapeutic communities shared the common characteristics of having:

- professionalism as a basis
- partnerships with external professionals
- democratic principles
- an openness to research innovation and change to practice.

As such, the three therapeutic communities in Scotland that participated in the emerging dependency groups research were examples of 'new' therapeutic communities. The 'new' therapeutic communities have been recently described as involving some of the aspects of the more 'traditional' American therapeutic communities such as employing ex-addict staff and using self-help groups while adopting basic principles of European social psychiatry and social work practices by incorporating harm reduction into their treatment protocols (Kaplan *et al.* 1999).

Within the UK, the history of the therapeutic community movement can be traced through three distinct (though often interlocking and complementary) threads. Early experiments in the use of therapeutic community principles in the UK were heavily influenced by the work of pioneers in the field of treatment of maladjusted children, including Aichorn, Steiner and Pestalozzi. These key figures had in turn been influenced by the early psychoanalytic work of Freud, Moreno, Adler and Jung (Bloor, McKeganey and Fonkert 1988; Pines 1999). The Little Commonwealth, established by the charismatic and eccentric Homer Lane (Bridgeland 1971) could arguably be described as the forerunner of all the subsequent therapeutic community experiments; particularly those with delinquent children and adolescents (Wills 1967) and finds its echo in the present day work of the Camphill Communities.

While most of these early experiments (the Little Commonwealth, the Hawkspur Camp experiment, Norman Glaister's Order of Woodcraft Chivalry etc.) could be characterised as community-based (often rural) initiatives, the second thread to the therapeutic community movement saw many of their self-governance principles transferred into a psychiatric inpatient setting (Kennard 1983).

In 1946, Tom Main set out the basic principles of what was to become known as the 'democratic' therapeutic community in *The Bulletin of the Menninger Clinic* (Main 1946). This new work had been influenced, not only by the earlier work with adolescents, but also by the development of psychoanalytic practice at Cassel Hospital and the Tavistock Clinic and by the work of Bion and others with traumatised ex-servicemen (Pines 1999).

The third and final thread of the therapeutic community phenomenon in the UK is specific to the treatment of drug dependents. The 'concept-based' therapeutic communities which began to be established in the USA in the 1960s were largely based on the innovative work of Dederich in California, where his

Synanon Community had been established in Santa Monica as an offshoot of the local Alcoholics Anonymous group (Rawlings and Yates 2001). The apparent successes of these therapeutic communities coming at a time when British policy was focused on containment rather than treatment inspired a number of British psychiatrists (many of whom had been involved in the democratic therapeutic community movement) to import the model into the UK (Kooyman 1992).

While these three models are quite distinctive in their character and approach, they do share a common belief in the use of the therapeutic encounter, where the community itself becomes the instrument of change. Self-governance/regulation, indeed self-help, is central to the approach of all three types of therapeutic community, while in the concept-based therapeutic communities, the encounter is formalised in a confrontational group (Bratter *et al.* 1985, p.461); the encounter process, with its emphasis on community-negotiated rewards and punishments, its insistence on openness and honesty and its reliance on the collective will, is fundamental to the movement as a whole.

Thus, research within the setting of a therapeutic community is presented with a number of particular challenges, the most important of which is integration into the process of change itself. Since all inputs and interventions are regarded as integral to the growth and evolution of the community and of the individuals within it, data collection cannot remain a 'clean' entity but will be subsumed into a melange of influences.

The research encounter

In direct contrast to the purpose of encounter groups, as part of the therapeutic process, the researcher aims to seek explanation or comprehension. The Scottish research team, led by one of the authors (JW) into the three therapeutic communities who collaborated and participated in the research, adopted a qualitative participatory research approach. The team acknowledged that research could integrate into professional encounters with the residents and facilitate treatment through a feedback loop being in place.

Gaining access to a therapeutic community, as an independent researcher, can be a dilemma. Broekaert and colleagues (1999) noted that

> those whose work was characterised by their enthusiasm and by the extent of their personal input, felt ill at ease when faced with research which used surveys based on classic medical terminology. (p.22)

In the Scottish study, we found that the researcher became involved not just in data collection and the supervision of data collection by therapeutic community staff, but also in the delivery of staff training, the design of programme changes and even the running of groups with residents.

Any research team (whether in partnership or independent) should be mindful of the potential for conflict if there is inadequate discussion of the aims, objectives and needs of the research project and the aims, objectives and needs of the therapeutic community approach. Lack of communication can spell early termination of a research project. From our experience in Scotland, we would argue that the research encounter can be part of the therapeutic process rather than being at odds with it. Scientific rigour does not need to ride roughshod over the principles and approach of a therapeutic community. In this case, the clinical (and research) tools were added to the residents' records and so offered 'added value' to the work of the therapeutic community.

A therapeutic encounter and a research-orientated encounter share many aspects in common, although some principal differences do exist (see Table 12.2). We believe that therapeutic communities which indicate an openness to research innovation could form mutually beneficial partnerships with independent research centres who could become focal points for expertise in researching therapeutic communities.

Researching childhood trauma in Scottish therapeutic community residents

Public awareness and concern about the nature and extent of childhood sexual abuse (CSA) has grown dramatically over the past 20 years. Hearing the voices of survivors who disclose their experiences draws multi-agency attention (and, one hopes, intervention) to the horrendous life histories of many individuals in society.

Initially, attention was concentrated on children who had been abused or who were currently in abusive situations. More recently, the legacy of abuse and its potentially damaging effects on adults has become the focus of inquiry. While very early studies on CSA suggested that little or no long-term harm resulted from such experiences (Bender and Blau 1937), the accumulation of empirical evidence over the last decade leaves little doubt that child molestation is extremely likely to have adverse effects on adult survivors (Briere and Zaidi 1989; Finkelhor et al. 1990; Sanders and Giolas 1991).

Substance misuse is consistently noted as a possible outcome and as a group, substance misusers report significantly higher rates of CSA than has been found in the general population. The relationship between substance misuse and a history of childhood trauma has been established in countless studies (Boyd et al. 1998; Jarvis and Copeland 1997; Najavits, Weiss and Shaw 1997; Porter 1993; Rosenhow, Corbett and Devine 1988; Simpson et al. 1994; Yandow 1989). Prevalence rates currently range from between 57 and 90 per cent for women and 37 and 42 per cent for men. However, the vast majority of these studies have been carried out in the USA and little or no work has been undertaken in Scotland or Europe.

Table 12.2 Principal differences between a therapeutic encounter and a research-orientated encounter

	Therapeutic encounter	*Research encounter**
Individual with problematic drug and/or alcohol use	The client	The participant
Relationship between the individual in the therapeutic community and the interviewer	Interactive and designed to facilitate disclosure as part of treatment	Interactive and designed to initiate disclosure at the participant's will under ethical procedures**
Data collection tools	Designed from experience with population groups to gather information meaningful to treatment of the client within the therapeutic community	Replicable, standardised tools designed from large-scale studies with target population to collect appropriate data on groups to test hypotheses
Scale	Focus on each client during their treatment	Focus on many participants as part of a study group
Nature of data	Qualitative	Qualitative approach but with quantifiable data

* It is assumed that the research encounter would be a qualitative interview as opposed to a survey methods approach.

** All research conducted by staff and students at the Department of Applied Social Science, University of Stirling is subjected to scrutiny by an ethics committee. Research practices, particularly in research with groups vulnerable to exploitation, follow the current professional guidelines of the British Sociological Association. Some researchers may follow the guidelines of the British Psychological Society as appropriate to their professional background. It was clearly stated to the participants in the therapeutic communities that non-participation or withdrawal from the study at any time would not compromise their treatment within the therapeutic community.

Within the IPTRP multi-site research programme, we were able to add to our understanding of childhood trauma in Scottish therapeutic community residents. Two of the authors (JW and RY) developed a childhood trauma initiative. Our early research studies, using retrospective methods, looked at the prevalence of the histories of CSA amongst drug users presenting for treatment and the experiences of CSA survivors in accessing services and of the staff in providing them (Scottish Drugs Training Project 1998).

In our early research, a series of interviews were conducted with CSA survivors who had experienced drug/alcohol problems in adult life; this included a questionnaire-based survey conducted with workers in drug projects throughout Scotland and a focus group study set up to explore the experience and survivor issues in their agencies. Forty-seven addiction services in Scotland participated in this third phase of the research. Although no quantitative data was available and few agencies kept detailed statistics in respect of this area of their work, contributions from focus group members made it clear that prevalence levels – among both men and women – were likely to be at least as high in Scotland as had been indicated in American studies. However, this retrospective study could only provide a 'snapshot' of the current situation in Scotland. In our recent larger-scale prospective study within the IPTRP Phase 3 initiative, we were able to broaden the scope of this earlier study to examine childhood trauma in its widest sense and to estimate both prevalence and implications for treatment. Advantages and disadvantages of retrospective and prospective methods are described in Table 12.3.

Similarities between the therapeutic encounter and the research-orientated encounter have already been alluded to in this chapter. In our earlier research studies, participants vividly described types of disclosure and behaviours which strongly suggest that disassociation (a defensive disruption in the normally occurring connections among feelings, thoughts, behaviours and memories) was commonly employed and that many of these clients were exhibiting post-traumatic distress. This 'snapshot' study was innovative within the European field of childhood trauma and substance use but was limited by the lack of a conceptual framework within which to understand childhood trauma and its possible outcomes. At the time, this presented a tangible dilemma for clinical professionals, researchers and clients. In the earlier research study, many participants reported feeling overwhelmed and confused by what appeared to be an array of bizarre and severe psychological and behavioural problems. The SDTP served as a focal point of expertise in this area, providing training to ensure that staff in this field can understand and assess the relationship between childhood trauma, post-traumatic stress disorder and other psychiatric symptoms which may present alongside drug or alcohol misuse.

One of the main differences between a therapeutic encounter and a research encounter is the use of replicable standardised tools (see Table 12.2). In our recent

Table 12.3 Advantages and disadvantages of using retrospective and prospective research methods in drugs-orientated research

	Advantages	*Disadvantages*
Retrospective methods	Quick	Relies on memory
(Often cross-sectional)	Cheap	Investigator bias possible
	Provides a 'snapshot'	Recall may be demanding for participants
		Possible inaccuracy
		Time-consuming
		Requires literacy
Prospective methods	Accuracy	May affect participants in therapeutic community treatment
(Sometimes cross-sectional but often longitudinal)	Little reliance on memory	Requires a co-operative partnership between participants and researcher
	Repeated measures could be taken	Time-consuming
		Requires literacy

study of 134 residents across three Scottish therapeutic communities, we used, among other standardised instruments, the European Addiction Severity Index (EuropASI) and the Childhood Trauma Questionnaire (CTQ).

The EuropASI (Kokkevi and Hartgers 1995) is the European adaptation of the fifth edition of the Addiction Severity Index (McLellan *et al*. 1980, 1992). It is a relatively brief, semi-structured interview, which offers a multi-dimensional profile of the client by covering six main problem areas (medical, employment, alcohol and drugs, legal, family/social and psychiatric) most often associated with substance abuse. Scoring is based on two indices for each dimension: the interviewer's severity rating and the composite scores. The interviewer's severity ratings are developed via a two-step method. First, the interviewer indicates on a nine-point scale a preliminary rating of the severity of each dimension, using only the objective data solicited in each of the problem areas and the present need for additional treatment. Second, the client's subjective assessment of the severity of each dimension and the need for additional treatment, using a five-point scale, is considered and the interviewer may adjust the final severity rating. Composite scores, which range from 0 to 1, are arithmetically based indicators of current (30-day) problem severity. Computation of these scores follows a strategy similar to that used in the American ASI (Koeter and Hartgers 1997).

The EuropASI allows social data, highly relevant for treatment, to be collected for every research participant (and self-reported information on their kin and non-kin networks) in the therapeutic communities. Although the EuropASI asks about abuse, simple knowledge that abuse has occurred does not allow for detailed diagnosis as to the specific nature of the client's traumatic experiences and the implications for treatment.

To address this within the Scottish approach to the European multi-site IPTRP project, the research team was anxious to build upon the understanding of childhood trauma in individuals with problematic drug and/or alcohol use. We encouraged the Scottish therapeutic communities participating in the research to include a further research instrument that could assess trauma as well as psychopathology.

Within the therapeutic communities, several instruments were piloted but they proved to be either too intrusive, too narrow in scope or too time-consuming to administer. In addition, many of the instruments had not been adequately tested for validity and reliability. We eventually decided to use the Childhood Trauma Questionnaire (CTQ) developed by Dr David Bernstein (1994) in New York. It met all our requirements for inclusion in the study and had been tested extensively, demonstrating strong validity and reliability ratings.

The CTQ (Bernstein et al. 1994) is a brief, non-intrusive retrospective measure of child abuse and neglect. It consists of a self-report screening questionnaire, which is administered easily across different settings and takes approximately ten minutes to complete. Early methods of assessment described trauma in global undifferentiated terms using broad categories. Most studies explored only one or two forms of trauma; primarily sexual and physical abuse. Until recently, little research had been done on the impact of emotional abuse and neglect.

However, the life histories of many addicts depict multiple types of neglect and abuse experience in childhood. We felt that the combination and degree of different forms of maltreatment required a multi-dimensional assessment to analyse accurately their impact and relationship to alter psychopathology. The CTQ covers multiple areas of maltreatment (physical abuse and neglect, sexual abuse and emotional abuse and neglect) using a dimensional system, which is quite specific and measures maltreatment by intensity. The version of the CTQ instrument used in our recent study consists of 53 statements, which clients rate on a five-point scale ranging from 1 (never true) to 5 (very often true).

From our experience, we would recommend the instrument as valuable for both clinical and research purposes. With it, staff can easily create trauma profiles of clients presenting for treatment. This provides clinical identification of those clients with maltreatment histories who are at particularly high risk of relapse and who may need more intensive and focused interventions. It becomes a way for screening people early on in their treatment and identifying those who are likely to have multiple or severe problems. It also promotes early intervention and prevention work, which could help to minimise later psychopathology. Such interventions could be very valuable for work with young populations of substance misusers who are survivors.

As a research tool, the CTQ is very useful for doing structural equation modelling and cluster analysis; it can model experiences and create a quantitative picture of maltreatment profiles for large groups of people, defining patterns of maltreatment that occur in different groups. Cluster analysis enables us to compare clusters in terms of their clinical characteristics, psychiatric diagnosis and trauma profiles.

Studies have indicted that self-reports on the CTQ are highly stable over time (Bernstein *et al.* 1994), show convergent and discriminant validity with other trauma measures (Bernstein *et al.* 1994; Fink *et al.* 1995), and tend to be corroborated when independent evidence is available (Bernstein *et al.* 1997).

The final section of the chapter will present some findings from our research with three therapeutic communities in Scotland using the two standardised tools mentioned above: the EuropASI and the CTQ.

BIOMED II Project: The psychosocial impact of childhood trauma on therapeutic community clients in Scotland

Participants in the study were male and female clients consecutively admitted to three residential treatment units across Scotland during the period from June 1997 until October 1998 and who gave informed consent to participate in the study. Inclusion criteria were that participants should be aged between 16 and 60 and with a fully detoxified status.

The standardised assessment battery, including the CTQ, were administered in the third to fourth week of treatment when clients participating in the study had achieved a fully detoxified status. The CTQ was the only self-administered instrument. In order to overcome any literacy problems, clients were given the choice to complete the questionnaire on their own or have the interviewer conduct the assessment.

Interviewers were selected from the staff team at each of the research sites and trained in the administration of all instruments used in this study. These trained interviewers piloted each of the instruments in the three months prior to implementation of the research assessment procedures.

Complete and usable CTQ and EuropASI tools were elicited from 91 research participants (60 males and 31 females). Table 12.4 summarises the background characteristics of the study group. The study group was all aged between 16 and 44 years old and reported mainly living in a large city. Only a small proportion of the group had a valid driving licence. Nearly three-quarters of the group had been mainly unemployed over the previous three years.

Clinical assessment of the study group from the EuropASI across the six domains (medical, employment, alcohol, drugs, legal, family/social and psychological) highlighted the different needs of the male and female populations in the present study. Compared to male drug users in this study, female drug users in treatment services were assessed as having a greater need for interventions concerning the legal, family and social, and psychological areas of their life (Figure 12.1).

The level of childhood maltreatment varied significantly by gender ($p < 0.001$) (Figure 12.2). Compared to men, over half the female population under study reported the high trauma level, where a high score is undesirable.

Among the male drug users in Scottish treatment services, previous lifetime history of suicide attempts was associated with severity of childhood trauma as measured by the CTQ ($p = 0.017$). Among the female drug users, previous lifetime history of anxiety ($p = 0.003$) and prescribed psychiatric medicine ($p = 0.025$) were more prevalent in those with a high trauma (Table 12.5).

Table 12.4 Background characteristics of the research participants in three Scottish therapeutic communities (n=91)*

	Males		Females		Total	
	n	%	n	%	n	%
Age (in years)						
16–24	21	35.0	16	53.3	37	41.1
25–34	32	53.3	12	40.0	44	48.9
35–44	7	11.1	2	6.7	9	10.0
Current residence						
Large city (>100,000)	51	86.4	24	80.0	75	84.3
Medium (10–100,000)	3	5.1	5	16.7	8	9.0
Small (rural) (<10,000)	5	8.5	1	3.3	6	6.7
Valid driving licence						
Yes	11	18.6	4	13.3	15	16.9
Usual employment pattern in past three years						
Full-time	7	11.9	5	16.7	12	13.5
Part-time (regular hrs)	6	10.2	2	6.7	8	9.0
Part-time (irregular hrs)	0	0	4	13.3	4	4.5
Unemployed	45	76.3	19	63.3	64	71.9
In controlled environment	1	1.7	0	0	1	1.1
Residence in last month						
Home	44	74.6	22	75.9	66	75.0
Prison	6	10.2	3	10.3	9	10.2
Alcohol/drug treatment	4	6.8	2	6.9	6	6.8
Medical treatment	3	5.1	2	6.9	5	5.7
Psychiatric treatment	1	1.7	0	0	1	1.1

* For some of the background variables n<91 if participants declined to disclose personal information.

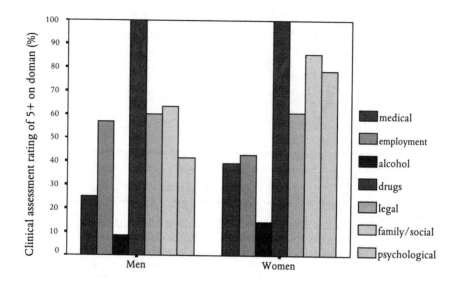

Figure 12.1 Addiction severity by gender

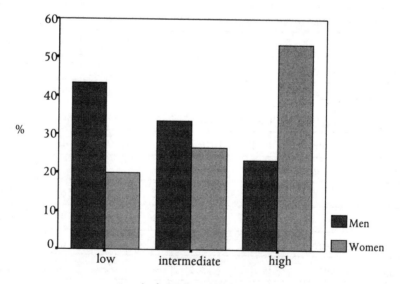

Level of childhood maltreatment

Figure 12.2 Level of childhood maltreatment by gender

Table 12.5 Reported psychiatric symptoms (recent and lifetime) by level of maltreatment identified by the Childhood Trauma Questionnaire

	Level of maltreatment (CTQ)						
	Low		Intermediate		High		Chi-square
	n	%	n	%	n	%	p value
Prescribed psychiatric medication							
In past 30 days	3	9.4	2	7.4	6	20.7	0.259
In lifetime	7	21.9	6	22.2	18	62.1	0.001
Suicidal ideation							
In past 30 days	5	15.6	5	18.5	13	44.8	0.033
In lifetime	11	34.4	13	48.1	22	75.9	0.005
Suicide attempts							
In past 30 days	0	0	1	3.8	4	14.3	0.054
In lifetime	9	28.1	10	38.5	20	69.0	0.004

Table 12.5 highlights the association between lifetime psychiatric symptoms and severity of childhood trauma for men and women combined: prescribed psychiatric medicine ($p=0.001$); suicidal ideation ($p=0.006$) and suicide attempts ($p=0.002$).

Summarising childhood trauma histories in this population, it is interesting to examine the five domains of childhood trauma. There is little difference between men and women in terms of emotional and physical neglect; the entire study group has heightened scores within this domain. However, women have significantly higher scores (which are undesirable on this scale) for emotional abuse, physical abuse and sexual abuse (Table 12.6).

Table 12.6 Comparisons between male and female users
undergoing treatment across the domains of the
Childhood Trauma Questionnaire (n=90)

	Males (n=60)		Females (n=30)		Chi-square p value
	Mean	SD	Mean	SD	
Emotional abuse	28.8	12.1	37.9	14.2	0.002
Physical abuse	13.8	7.9	17.7	9.8	0.045
Sexual abuse	8.8	4.0	17.0	10.2	0.001
Emotional neglect	38.9	14.3	42.4	17.8	0.314
Physical neglect	15.0	5.6	16.6	7.3	0.253

The results of this study confirm the relationship between child maltreatment and substance misuse. Child abuse and neglect predicted a range of symptoms of psychological distress for both men and women in this sample. This issue has considerable implications for policy, planning and resource allocation, which will have an impact on education, prevention and treatment in both the addiction and the mental health fields.

We need to continue to refine our assessment procedures if we wish to provide more focused and appropriate interventions and improve service provision for this population.

Implications for relapse prevention in therapeutic communities

The crucial significance of this research for therapeutic communities is its significance for the prediction and pre-emption of relapse. Relapse prevention accounts for a major area of work in the addiction field. Yet one of the greatest unacknowledged contributors to relapse may be the failure to identify and treat underlying childhood trauma issues.

However, much of the work undertaken in treatment services on relapse assumes a cognitive recognition of 'situational cues' (Marlatt and Gordon 1985), which can be predicted and prepared for and for which alternative strategies can be adopted. A major feature of post-traumatic stress disorder is the intrusion of unbidden memories and feelings; that is unpredictable 'internally generated' stimuli.

When substance use is reduced or stopped altogether, painful memories and feelings associated with the original trauma may surface. The pain and anxiety that emerges might be overwhelming and clients may fall back on old behaviours that temporarily provide relief but create even worse problems in the future. All too often, symptoms associated with the trauma may be overlooked, seen as a secondary issue to be addressed at a later time, or misconstrued as a result of the addictive process.

Furthermore, current models of relapse prevention, which focus primarily on thought processes and behaviours, might be less effective for addictive survivors. In relapse prevention work, clients are encouraged to identify high-risk situations, examine and alter both cognitive and behavioural responses and develop a new repertoire of coping strategies. Unless these clients are able to develop coping strategies to deal with fragmented and volatile emotional states, which act as internal triggers, they remain highly vulnerable to relapse.

Many clinicians who work with both CSA and addictions have argued that if the emerging symptoms of abuse are not recognised and treated appropriately, the risk of relapse is greatly increased.

As Young (1990) states

> current theories of relapse prevention have not addressed the high potential for relapse associated with internally generated phenomena, such as the effects of early childhood sexual abuse...many of the relapses that may appear to be stimulus contingent, as current theory proposes, may in fact turn out to be internally generated. (p.249)

There is much we have yet to learn about trauma and its effects. However, we do know the extent to which the childhood of many addicts is characterised by considerable trauma and loss. Researching therapeutic communities, with the new advances in accessible validated clinical instruments suitable for research, allows both researchers and practitioners to gain a firmer handle on the nature, extent and severity of trauma experiences. They anchor presenting symptoms in a context, which offers a new window through which to view pathology.

Conclusions

There are three main conclusions – or rather, recommendations – from our experiences of researching therapeutic communities.

First, we encourage the adoption and maintenance of standardised clinical assessment tools such as the EuropASI and the CTQ in therapeutic communities. While these tools hold their own as part of treatment protocols, they also offer the 'added value' of being research-friendly, validated instruments. The EuropASI has been used now in a variety of different treatment populations including prisons, community settings and other European therapeutic communities and across countries and cultures, not least within the ten partner countries in the IPTRP project (Belgium, France, Germany, Greece, Italy, the Netherlands, Norway, Scotland, Spain and Sweden).

Second, we recommend that the application of research tools in treatment settings, such as therapeutic communities, requires clinical professionals with experience of drug and alcohol treatment services and with research training. The CTQ and the EuropASI are not 'straight off the shelf options' and require accredited training to administer the tools.

Third, we conclude that researching in the 'new' therapeutic communities, from our Scottish experience, can serve as a mutually beneficial testing ground for hypotheses and serve as an appropriate feedback loop for improvements to drug and alcohol treatment services. In the bigger picture, such studies can and should influence national public policy affecting the treatment of adults with problematic drug and alcohol use.

In this chapter, we have offered a flavour of the activities of the Scottish research team, as part of the IPTRP project, in researching therapeutic communities. Finally, we would warn against simple extrapolation of the findings in this Scottish study. Whilst we believe that we have uncovered important new information regarding the profile of young men and women entering residential treatment for substance misuse, this level of trauma experience may not be present in the wider substance-misusing community. Certainly, there is evidence elsewhere that it is the most damaged, most severely dependent individuals who are treated on a residential or inpatient basis.

CHAPTER 13

An Experimental Study of Treatment Outcome

The Cassel–North Devon Personality Disorder Project

Marco Chiesa, Peter Fonagy and Jeremy Holmes

In this chapter we give a description of a prospective controlled study, which started in 1993 at the Cassel Hospital and is now in the final stages. An historical account, including social and political factors which led to the development of a new clinical programme, will be discussed and the methodological requirement for a comparative study will also be outlined. Results to date and their possible implications will be briefly presented.

Background to the study

Despite innovative clinical developments, since its foundation in 1919 the Cassel traditionally employed a long-term hospital-based approach to the treatment of mental health disorders presented by adults, adolescents and families (Denford 1986; Kennedy, Tischler and Haymans 1986; Main 1989). After a thorough and accurate assessment procedure with regard to suitability, which involved a full psychiatric, psychodynamic and psychosocial appraisal, patients were placed on an often lengthy waiting list. Admission was expected to last for an average of 16 months, but no less than one year, during which time patients were treated in individual and group psychotherapy, and were exposed to a structured and intense programme of sociotherapy in the therapeutic community setting, based on the principles of psychosocial nursing (Barnes 1968; Chapman 1984). At the end of their stay no aftercare was planned, and patients were discharged back to their own communities.

The philosophy underlying this one-stage approach was based on the assumption that such an abrupt severance from hospital treatment was a necessary experience to tackle patients' dysfunctional dependence on health services and to promote independent functioning. Indeed, further contacts with the hospital were actively discouraged and not even a clinical follow-up session was offered at any time after discharge. In the early 1980s patients were offered a three- to six-month reassessment following discharge to appraise the extent of the gains achieved during their stay at the hospital. Although several patients were improved on clinical grounds, most found the abrupt termination of treatment rather traumatic, and many experienced difficulties in the transition between hospital life and re-integration to community life. A sizeable minority did not cope well in social and interpersonal functioning and showed clear signs of symptom distress, while a few had to be readmitted to hospital.

Evidence from several studies has shown that personality disorder in general, and borderline conditions in particular, need long-term treatment for a more favourable outcome, and patients with these disorders were found to be highly sensitive to experiences of separation (Gunderson 1985; Kernberg 1984). Therefore, the need for aftercare provision for these patients became an important consideration. In addition, the need for a lengthy hospital stay for all patients was questioned. It became obvious that if an outpatient follow-up programme had been available some patients may have been able to be discharged earlier. The way treatment was organised seemed to affect the length of stay. Although the Cassel Hospital programme was geared towards ego-enhancing activities, confrontation and clarification of acting out and disruptive behaviour, to reduce the likelihood of regressive pulls (Griffiths and Leach 1998), inevitably the full immersion in a year-long hospital treatment often created formidable difficulties for the smooth re-adaptation to societal life. Many patients needed support and ongoing psychosocial work to master the transition from hospital to community life.

In addition, the wider psychiatric culture had developed and was now fervently embracing new concepts that had led to a dramatic shift from hospital-based to community-based strategies for the treatment and management of mental disorders. This development was leaving psychotherapy hospitals and therapeutic communities more isolated within their psychiatry base, as they were seen as swimming against the tide (Schimmel 1997). A further major threat came in the early 1990s from the reorganisation of the British National Health Service (NHS) that led to the development of an internal market through the division between purchasers and providers of mental health services. Within the new system cost became an increasingly important factor as health authorities struggled to buy health care within a limited budget.

Within this changed cultural and organisational context, expensive long-term psychosocial hospital treatment of personality disorder seemed, to some, an increasingly dispensable luxury. Already in the USA, traditional institutions such as Chestnut Lodge, the Menninger Clinic and the Borderline Unit at Cornell University were experiencing severe difficulties in maintaining and justifying long-term hospital stay for their patients and, due to third-party pressures, they were compelled either to close or to make substantial changes to their clinical programmes. In the absence of clear evidence-based guidelines, referrals to the adult unit of the Cassel Hospital steadily declined from 126 in 1992 to 52 in 1998 (Chiesa and Iacoponi 1998). In several instances health authorities refused funding for referred patients, and the overall process for extra-contractual referrals and funding became littered with difficulties. Pressures on clinicians to refer to local resources rather than to specialist services became an increasing trend.

Due to the convergence of the above-mentioned clinical and political factors the time seemed ripe for new service developments at the Cassel. A modified programme for adult patients, which included a combination of hospital-based and community-based strategies, was discussed and outlined in a protocol. The expected hospital stay was to be reduced by half (to six months), but would be followed by outpatient treatment consisting of 12- to 18-month twice-weekly group analysis with concurrent outreach psychosocial nursing for the first six months. The hospital executive and the whole hospital staff discussed at length the proposal, and eventually it was agreed that the new programme would be introduced at the beginning of 1993, when a small outreach team was formed (Chiesa 1997; Pringle and Chiesa 2001).

It also became clear that both the traditional hospital-based and the newly introduced mixed programmes needed empirical evaluation as to their relative effectiveness. Although a retrospective study was carried out in the early 1980s (Denford et al. 1983; Rosser et al. 1987), methodological considerations (small and selected sample, diagnosis and pre-treatment assessments made retrospectively, lack of comparison group, failure to include dropouts) noticeably limited claims regarding treatment effectiveness. A new research protocol for a controlled prospective study was drafted, with a view to implementing it in coincidence with the launching of the new clinical programme at the beginning of 1993. The Cassel research team forged a rapport of collaboration with the psychoanalysis unit at University College London, the academic Department of Psychiatry at Charing Cross Hospital, the Centre for the Economic Study of Mental Health at the Institute of Psychiatry and the psychiatric services within North Devon Healthcare NHS Trust.

Research culture and therapeutic community

At the outset, the introduction of the combined hospital and community-based programme (step-down model, or SDM) and of the research project created a mixture of apprehension, anxiety, fear and hostility in the hospital. Several members of staff felt that two different programmes within the same unit might not be compatible as they could create difficulties in running the therapeutic community regime and stimulate competition and envy among patients. In addition it was felt that, although the SDM might make sense on clinical grounds for some, it was still an unknown quantity and many believed that patients might suffer by being prevented from benefiting from a fuller experience in the inpatient setting. It was also feared that there might be a negative impact on patients from the research programme, regarding potential splits between the clinical and research teams. Patients could be distracted away from the therapeutic programme or become disturbed as a consequence of the application of structured and semi-structured interviews, which delve into past painful experiences of neglect and abuse. These reservations and other events threatened the survival of both the new clinical programme and the research project. As anxiety and ambivalence grew within the hospital, patients who refused to be part of the SDM were re-allocated to the hospital-based programme and refused participation in the research. A growing overt and covert hostility expressed by influential sub-groups of patients and staff brought the research to the brink of failure. A series of meetings among senior staff and letters and informal talks from the Mental Health Trust Headquarters and the Charing Cross and Westminster Medical School (now Imperial College) helped to address some of the problems and restored a sense of purpose within the therapeutic community concerning the new developments. Gradually the situation improved, the potential value of the new programme was understood and a more tolerant attitude towards research became established.

The serious difficulties of carrying out a major research project within the Cassel therapeutic community illustrates the importance of establishing a research culture within the institution. This can only be achieved through a painful but necessary process of working through the issues, dynamics and transferences that the research endeavour, new to the institution, evokes. The creation of a relatively separate research team, and the introduction of practices and interactions necessary for the research to take place, are at first experienced as alien and threatening to the established practices and dominant institutional culture. The multi-faceted activities of the research team and, indeed, the values and ideas inherent in evaluative projects, become equated with an external, foreign object that could disrupt and threaten the clinically-based, familiar philosophy upon which the therapeutic community programme is based. As such it evokes primitive transferences characterised by a mixture of suspicion and persecution that in turn mobilise hostility and attempts to extrude the alien and threatening entity. Indeed, in our experience, beyond the initial verbal conscious agreement, powerful underlying forces, often expressed in a passive–aggressive fashion, were directed against the running of the project. An additional element was that the research ran simultaneously with the introduction of a newly introduced clinical programme, which in itself was a source of major anxieties, perceived as a threat to established practices.

Important mitigating factors were that the principal investigator (MC) had been a member of staff for several years and that the hospital director was favourably disposed towards the project. The presence of an internal key figure representing the research may in the end outweigh the operation of primitive reactions, transferences and projections. It is unlikely that the study would have succeeded if the main thrust of the research had come from the outside. Professionals operating inside the institution can more easily maintain a constant dialogue and open channels of communication within the institution, and hence have more opportunities to work through conflicts and difficulties.

There is no doubt that the climate following the internal market reform of the NHS that threatened the survival of many specialist institutions, and the increased emphasis on evidence-based medicine to justify practices, made the adoption of outcome research at the Cassel Hospital a fundamental milestone. Staff gradually understood the key function of research work as a means, not only of survival, but also for constructive and creative development of therapeutic community practices. Hence a true research culture began to grow across the disciplines within the institution. One of the results has been that the patients' group, on the whole, has fully accepted voluntary and informed participation in research, which many report as beneficial to focusing and complementing their treatment.

The project

The protocol concerned the comparison between three conditions: two specialist treatment programmes and one control sample. One group included patients treated for a year in the inpatient psychosocial therapy programme of the Cassel Hospital with no subsequent outpatient treatment (the hospital-based model or HBM). The second group comprised patients who were offered six months' inpatient psychosocial treatment at the Cassel Hospital, followed by 18 months' outpatient group dynamic psychotherapy and six months of concurrent outreach nursing in the community, both under the auspices of the Cassel Hospital (the step-down model or SDM). The third group comprised of personality disorder patients who were not exposed to psychosocial treatment, but were receiving 'standard care' from their local general psychiatric services (best available treatment) within North Devon Healthcare NHS Trust (the North Devon Personality Disorder Group or NDPDG).

Entry criteria in to the three samples included a good command of English, an IQ equivalent of at least 90 and an Axis-II (American Psychiatric Association 1994) diagnosis of personality disorder. Patients with a previous diagnosis of schizophrenia or delusional (paranoid) disorder, those who had been inpatients at another hospital continuously for two years or more, those who showed evidence of organic brain damage and those currently involved in criminal proceedings for violent crimes were excluded from the study sample. All patients admitted to the Cassel between 1993 and 1997 were allocated to the two treatment conditions according to criteria of geographical accessibility. For logistical reasons patients residing within the Greater London area (GLA) and able to attend outpatient treatment were allocated to the SDM, while patients residing outside the GLA were allocated to the HBM (Chiesa and Fonagy 2000). Although both treatment programmes contain similar features, mainly in the inpatient stage, the presence in one group of a lengthy outreach treatment maximises the likelihood of differences emerging. In addition, the HBM contains an inpatient stay which is twice the length of that in the SDM and involves a 40 per cent greater input in terms of costs.

In the North Devon arm of the study patients with a clinical diagnosis of personality disorder were screened through the Personality Disorder Questionnaire (PDQ-IV) (Hyler 1994) and then placed on the North Devon Personality Disorder case register (Holmes et al. 2001). These subjects were invited to participate in the research project. Those who consented were matched with the Cassel groups on Axis I and II (American Psychiatric Association 1994) diagnoses, age, gender and socio-economic status, and were interviewed and subjected to the same assessment procedures as the treatment groups. The North Devon group would meaningfully reflect the outcome of non-specialist treatments within the NHS at this time.

The choice of measures used in the study (Table 13.1) was the result of several considerations. First, obtaining a comprehensive demographic, diagnostic and clinical characterisation of the sample would enable identification of the type of patients treated by the Cassel and to compare the three sub-samples to exclude sampling bias. Second, it allowed an evaluation of outcome that included several key dimensions of functioning (symptom distress, social adaptation and global assessment of mental health), scored from three main vantage points (self-rated, rater-based and clinician-based). Third, the use of mainstream standardised instruments means a greater chance for the results of the study being accepted by the general psychiatric world, hence increased influence on policy makers; in addition, it allows comparisons across different studies. The use of such measures within a therapeutic community may at first seem alien to the philosophy of treatment but in reality they are not hostile to the aims of treatment. A reduction of symptom distress, an improved social adaptation and a global improvement of mental health, as well as a decrease of acting-out behaviour, are among the indicators that therapeutic community treatment has been successful.

The problem of psychiatric diagnosis within therapeutic community treatment is controversial since it goes against a destigmatising culture in which individuals are valued for their own separate identity and often-idiosyncratic problems, rather than being diagnostically labelled. The use in the study of operationalised diagnostic criteria was aimed at the systematic identification of the different psychiatric syndromes and complex personality difficulties present at admission. In addition, a clear diagnostic presentation of the sample may give indications about prognosis and suitability for therapeutic community treatment, and employ a common language with general psychiatry. On the other hand, the DSM-III-R classification is limited by the categorical approach to diagnosis, which does not take account of differences in severity within the same category.

Table 13.1 List of control and outcome measures used in the study

Measure	Frequency of application
'Structured Clinical Interview' for the DSM-III-R (SCID-I and SCID-II – Spitzer *et al.* 1990), for Axis-I and -II diagnosis	Intake
Cassel Baseline Interview, for demographic and clinical description of samples	Intake
National Adult Reading Test, to assess IQ equivalents	Intake
The Symptom Check List – 90-R (Derogatis 1983)	Intake, 6, 12, 24 months
Social Adjustment Scale (Weissman 1975)	Intake, 6, 12, 24 months
The Global Assessment Scale (Endicott *et al.* 1976)	Intake, 6, 12, 24 months
Community Adjustment Questionnaire, rates parasuicidal behaviour, self-mutilation, inpatient episodes etc.	Intake, 12, 24 months
The Adult Attachment Interview (George, Kaplan and Main 1985)	Intake, 24 months
Client Service Receipt Interview (Beecham and Knapp 1992)	Intake, 6, 12, 24 months

High comorbidity rates further complicate the assessment of personality disorder pathology. For Axis II disorders there is no agreed method to rate severity of personality disorder. One approach is to rank the diagnosis hierarchically according to a clustering definition: Cluster A (schizotypal, schizoid, paranoid) the most severe, Cluster B (borderline, antisocial, histrionic, narcissistic) the middle range of severity, Cluster C (dependent, avoidant, obsessive-compulsive) the least severe. A different method used by others is the calculation of a total score computed by summing all criteria met on the specific structured measure employed (Dolan, Evans and Norton 1995). A further approach, given diagnostic criteria are met, is to rate severity according to results from other measures of impairment such as symptom distress or social maladjustment. A comprehensive critique of the shortcomings of currently used operational diagnostic systems is found in Westen and Shedler (1999a, 1999b). They propose an alternative approach that quantifies clinical observation to develop a useful, empirically grounded classification of personality pathology, which leads to the identification of naturally occurring groupings of patients, based on shared psychological features. The proposed method relies on Q-sort descriptions based on an interview that resembles a clinical interview rather than the direct question format used in current Axis II structured interviews. However, for the present study we decided to use a system based on operationalised DSM-III-R criteria, in keeping with most current work in this field.

This is one of the few studies of psychotherapy outcome that has included an economic evaluation of treatment. This will provide crucial insights first about the costs to society of untreated personality disorder, and second about effectiveness in relation to cost. Thus, even if the outcome of the two inpatient treatments do not substantially differ in terms of magnitude of improvement, cost-related issues should yield information of importance from the standpoint of service provision.

A further strength of the project resides in the use of the Adult Attachment Interview (AAI) (George, Kaplan and Main 1985) as a way to assess structural (internal) change. We will compare significant shifts present at 24 months in the five main categories (secure–autonomous, dismissing, preoccupied–entangled, unresolved–disorganised, cannot classify), and key sub-scales (narrative coherence, coherence of thought, metacognitive capacity, passivity of thought, clarity of recall, emotional states, degree to which early unfavourable experiences have been worked through etc.). In addition, the use of the AAI allows for the prediction of the durability of external improvements as shown in the symptomatic and social adaptation domains. In this way, we hope to test the hypothesis that only where structural change has occurred will there be stable external improvements.

In summary, the design included the use of operational diagnostic criteria; a comprehensive demographic, pre-morbid and predictive characterisation of the sample; a multi-dimensional measure of outcome (symptom distress, social adaptation, global assessment of mental health); an intent-to-treat approach; the monitoring of inter-current treatment; the assessment of structural change and economic evaluation. Measures were applied at intake, 6, 12 and 24 months.

Personality disorder features and outcome

The study is now towards its conclusion and in this chapter we shall present data concerning demographic, diagnostic and clinical characteristics of the three samples; and outcome in the dimensions of symptom distress, social adjustment and global psychiatric assessment, and in clinical variables (self-harm and psychiatric admissions).

Out of the 135 patients admitted to the Cassel that constituted the potential study sample, 18 patients refused consent to the study, while 23 withdrew in the very early stages of the project. Four patients belonging to the HBM tragically committed suicide within one year of admission. Of these, two were still in treatment when they took their lives while the other two had already been prematurely discharged from the hospital. Patients were on average in their early thirties, two-thirds female and mostly single, separated or divorced (70%). A difference emerged between the Cassel samples and the North Devon samples with regard to educational status. While 71 per cent of the patients admitted to the Cassel had achieved or were engaged in further education (above GCSE-level), the majority of the North Devon patients were educationally disadvantaged, with only 22 per cent going into further education. Difficult and traumatic backgrounds were commonly found. Experiences of early maternal deprivation and early loss were reported in 45 per cent of the cases, while reported sexual abuse and molestation (45%) and physical abuse by care-givers (40%) were very high. Only 14 per cent were in employment at intake, while 75 per cent had not worked during the previous year.

With regard to psychiatric morbidity, over 50 per cent had engaged in either self-mutilating or parasuicidal behaviour during the previous year, while two-thirds had been admitted at least once for psychiatric treatment. Only 5 per cent had never been prescribed psychotropic medication; the median time on medication in the previous year approached 12 months. Most patients presented comorbidity within and between Axis I and II diagnoses. Current mood disorders (51%) and anxiety disorders (55%) were the most common psychiatric syndromes among the samples. Substance use (17%) and eating disorders (15%) were also well represented. On Axis II, within the Cluster B spectrum, 70 per cent of the patients met criteria for borderline personality disorder (BDP), while 50 per cent met criteria for Cluster A (paranoid, schizoid and schizotypal) personality disorder. Most patients also fell within the Cluster C group, with dependent (55%) and avoidant (36%) the most represented categories. A low prevalence of narcissistic (10%) and antisocial personalities (6%) was found, which emphasises the difference between this group of personality disorder and a forensic sample. On average each patient fulfilled criteria for two current psychiatric diagnoses (Axis I) and 3.5 for personality disorder (Axis II).

The high level of medical and mental health service utilisation made by these patients is borne out by the baseline finding for the previous year. On average they visited general practitioners 13 times a year, attended a casualty department three times and spent 45 days as inpatients in a psychiatric institution.

We found that treatment attrition within 12 weeks from admission was significantly higher in the HBM sample (Chiesa *et al.* 2000), which accounts for the lower-than-expected difference in average hospital stay in the two treatment samples (8.7 months for the HBM and 6.2 for the SDM).

With regard to outcome at 24 months (see Table 13.2) in the three main dimensions of symptom distress (SCL-90), social adjustment (SAS) and global assessment of mental health (GAS), we found that the two Cassel samples improved significantly over time on all three measures. In contrast, patients in the North Devon sample presented only a modest, although statistically significant, improvement on the GAS, but remained unchanged on the SCL-90 and the SAS. A comparison between the two treatment groups at the Cassel showed that the SDM sample had a faster level of improvements in social adaptation and global assessment of mental health, and it scored significantly better on the GAS at 6 and 12 months, and SAS at 12 months. However, there was no significant difference by the 24-month assessment.

Since results based on average scores do not give information concerning within-group variability, we calculated improvement as a categorical entity. This allows the calculation of how many patients have improved, remained unchanged or deteriorated. The first step entails the calculation of 'reliable improvement' in each of the outcome measures, as defined by Jacobson and Truax (1991). This formula takes into account the standard error of measurement, which is a function of the reliability of the instrument. In the dimension of psychiatric morbidity (SCL-90 GSI), over half of the patients in the Cassel treatment groups were found to be reliably improved, compared to 30 per cent of patients in the general psychiatric group. We found that SDM had significantly higher rates of reliable improvement in SAS as compared with the HBM sample (39% *vs* 15%); however, by 24 months we found no difference between the two groups (41% *vs* 40%). Improvement rates in the control group (NDPDG) in SAS were negligible (6%). While 39 per cent of patients in the SDM improved on the GAS, by 12 months only 17 per cent in the HBM did so, and the difference remained significant at 24 months (48% *vs* 22%). GAS reliable improvement in the NDPDG was found in 12 per cent of the sample.

An important finding concerned prediction of short-term outcome (12 months). It was found that patients who met criteria for borderline personality disorder were six times more likely to improve significantly if they were allocated to the SDM than if they were allocated to the hospital-based programme; hence a borderline personality diagnosis and treatment allocation in the SDM predicted positive outcome at 12 months. However, this finding was no longer significant by the 24-month follow-up.

Table 13.2 Outcome scores at 6, 12 and 24 months in the three samples			
Variable	HBM n=46	SDM n=44	NDPDG n=42
SCL-90 GSI* mean (sd)			
Intake	2.07 (.60)	1.86 (.82)	1.87 (.76)
6 months	1.80 (.52)	1.49 (.83)	1.74 (.78)
12 months	1.68 (.63)	1.39 (.91)	1.74 (.79)
24 months	1.63 (.67)	1.22 (.89)	1.77 (.78)
SAS* mean (sd)			
Intake	2.68 (.45)	2.56 (.54)	2.69 (.34)
6 months	2.55 (.34)	2.37 (.47)	2.71 (.39)
12 months	2.46 (.42)	2.17 (.58)	2.72 (.36)
24 months	2.34 (.41)	2.03 (.53)	2.69 (.38)
GAS** mean (sd)			
Intake	45.78 (6.76)	46.70 (6.48)	45.41 (6.84)
6 months	49.16 (7.65)	53.83 (9.43)	46.46 (8.89)
12 months	51.09 (9.66)	58.71 (13.76)	49.22 (8.29)
24 months	54.68 (13.23)	60.73 (14.77)	50.28 (7.83)

* range: 0 (least pathology)–4 (maximum pathology)
** range: 0 (maximum pathology)–100 (least pathology)

A significant reduction in acute psychiatric morbidity was found in the SDM group by 24 months. The percentage of patients who self-harmed was reduced by half, the incidence of attempted suicides fell from 56 per cent to 16 per cent and only one in ten was readmitted to hospital by 24 months. Changes in the same variables were more modest in the other two groups.

Discussion

The results of the study to date show that a specialist inpatient psychosocial approach to personality disorder is significantly more effective over time than standard general psychiatric care in the dimensions of symptom distress, social adaptation and global assessment of outcome. The higher effectiveness rates on these dimensions, compared with those of the control group, confirm the results of previous studies in the UK for similar patient groups (Bateman 1999; Dolan, Warren and Norton 1997). In addition, it lends support to the finding that a general psychiatric approach to the management of personality disorder may provide a degree of containment, and hence prevent deterioration, but has little or no impact on key dimensions of functioning. The implication of these findings is that large amounts of general psychiatric resources devoted to personality disorder may not be justified by the relatively poor results shown, and that spe-cialist facilities dedicated to the treatment of these patients may be a more effective and ultimately cost-effective approach.

The SDM has shown greater effectiveness than the HBM in improving social adaptation at 12 months and in overall improvement of mental health at six and 12 months. In addition, significantly greater reliable improvement rates have been found on the SAS at 12 months and GAS at six and 12 months. The faster improvements in these dimensions and the significant reduction in self-harm and hospital readmission shown by the SDM poses pertinent questions concerning the optimal duration of inpatient stay and, above all, the need for ongoing treatment following discharge from hospital. These results point to the desirabil-ity of a phased approach to inpatient treatment of personality disorder, and in particular for borderline patients who are known to react very badly to abrupt ex-periences of separation and abandonment (Gunderson 1996), as in the case of discharge from an intense and highly emotionally involving period of hospitali-sation at the Cassel. The ongoing outpatient psychosocial programme functions as a crucial container for the patients' intense separation anxieties and as a support for the transition from hospital to external community life. This empirical finding is consistent with a psychotherapeutic approach that emphasises attachment and connection as an adjunct, rather than in opposition, to autonomy and internalisation of the lost object.

Empirical research and therapeutic community treatment in the past have sometimes formed an uneasy partnership, as research methodologies and ways to assess effectiveness were considered rather alien to therapeutic community culture and practices. Much fruitful debate and development has taken place, which has created a new atmosphere of co-operation. Therapeutic community practitioners have come a long way to appreciate that common goals can be forged and that the empirical validation of a clinically proven effective treatment for serious mental conditions such as personality disorder can only be beneficial to the long-term survival of such approaches and help forge vital bridges with general psychiatry. In equal measure, advances in the development of more adequate evaluative instruments, more sensitive to the target population of thera-peutic communities and to the process of the treatment characteristics of such milieux, have contributed to a greater acceptance of research.

CHAPTER 14

Assessing Outcome
at Henderson Hospital
Challenges and Achievements

Kingsley Norton and Fiona Warren

Introduction

There is an increasing expectation for greater service accountability for research evidence on which to make decisions about health care planning. Nationally, mental health care now has 'the same priority as coronary heart disease' (Department of Health 1999a). In parallel, there is an increase in the demand for, and expectations of, the quality of research evidence underlying mental health treatments. The evidence base for a therapeutic community approach to the treatment of personality disorder has been endorsed recently (Reed 1994; Royal College of Psychiatrists 1999). This acknowledgement supports the Department of Health decision to fund the development of the Henderson Hospital service by replicating it in two new areas of the UK (National Specialist Commissioning Advisory Group 1999).

Reviewing the research conducted at Henderson Hospital shows that the evidence for this treatment has accumulated over time. It also shows that methodological approaches to evaluation of this therapeutic community have developed in their sophistication and rigour. However, some of the exacting criteria of evidence-based medicine, in particular the requirement for randomised controlled evidence, continue to present challenges to the evaluation of the therapeutic community model of treatment. In this chapter we review the research that has been conducted at Henderson Hospital since the inception of the treatment model (see Table 14.1) and discuss the methodological issues arising from these studies.

Table 14.1 Outcome studies of Henderson Hospital

Study	n	Follow-up period	Criteria of success	Success rate %	Description of sample
Rapoport (1960)	64	1 year	Improved clinically since admission	41.0	All discharged men
Tuxford (1961)	86	2 years	In employment	55.0	All male probation and Borstal discharges
			No recidivism	61.0	
Taylor (1963)	?	9 months	In employment	60.0	Discharged men
Whiteley (1970)	112	2 years	No recidivism	43.6	Discharged men
			No re-admission	57.5	
			Neither of above	40.0	
Copas and Whiteley (1976)	104	2 years	No recidivism	42.0	Discharged men
	87		No readmission	47.0	Same 104 as above
	104	5 years		33.6	

Study	N	Time	Outcome	%	Sample
Copas et al. (1984)	194	3 years	No re-admission	41.0	Male and female discharges
		5 years		36.0	
	51	3 years	No re-admission	23.0	Non-admitted controls
		5 years		19.0	
Dolan, Evans and Wilson (1992)	62	8 months	Improved psychological functioning on SCL-90	55.0	Male and female discharges
Dolan et al. (1996)	24	1 year	Reduced costs	90.0	Male and female discharges
Dolan et al. (1995)	117	1 year	Service usage	80.0	Male and female referrals
	247 (44 unfunded)		Re-offending and/or re-admission	45.0	Non-admitted referrals
Dolan, Warren and Norton (1997)	70	1 year	Clinically significant change in borderline personality disorder symptomatology	42.9	Male and female discharges
	67			17.9	Male and female non-admitted controls

After Dolan and Coid (1993)

Development of research methodology at Henderson Hospital

Henderson Hospital is fortunate that the evaluation of its treatment approach began very early in its history, with Rapoport's team's landmark anthropological study during the 1950s funded by the Medical Research Council and the Nuffield Foundation (Rapoport 1960). This is fortunate in at least two ways. First, the early introduction of research into the community meant that the institution had some 'research culture', or at least some research reference points, although, in fact, these were not always positive! Second, some continuity of findings can be traced over what is now a long period of time (over 40 years) adding weight to the body of evidence about the value of this therapy in the treatment of personality disordered patients.

Rapoport's study was aimed primarily at describing and uncovering the processes and philosophies underlying what was, at that time, an experimental approach to rehabilitation. However, the final report – *Community as Doctor* – also contained an outcome study (Rapoport 1960). The comprehensive anthropological approach used provided a detailed description of the institution at the time and so allows for some comparisons between the therapeutic 'regime' as it was and as it is now. Although some features of the treatment have changed, many features that may be key characteristics of this community have not. For example, the selection of new residents by current residents remains the same today, although the size of the community has reduced considerably.

The unit was founded in 1947. Rapoport's study took place between 1953 and 1957. Having discovered that doctors gave the most conservative assessments of individuals' improvement, in comparison with patients and other staff, their assessments were used to investigate improvement of patients between admission and discharge. However, the proportion of patients who had improved between admission and one-year follow-up was assessed by the research sociologist and research social worker. Although the assessment measures were not described in detail and the inter-rater reliability is not known, the study showed that 41 per cent of patients were judged improved at one year post-treatment.

In addition, this study found a significant relationship between length of stay and improvement *during* treatment. Eighty-two per cent of patients were judged improved between admission and discharge if they stayed over 201 days in the therapeutic community, in comparison with 19 per cent of those staying less than 30 days. The relationship of length of stay to outcome at *one year post-discharge* was significant (52% of those staying longer than 201 days were judged improved at one year versus 37% of those staying less than 30 days). The study also suggested that improvement is inversely related to severity of disturbance, though the measurement of this was crude. Unsurprisingly, but clinically importantly, the study found significantly more of those who improved between admission and discharge than those who did not improve during treatment to show improvement at one-year follow-up. The study found significantly greater improvement at one-year follow-up in those with strong, versus those with weak, 'ego strength'. Being married and having moderate or milder disturbance were also associated with improvement at follow-up.

Many questions were explored by this study. However, the outcome measures were acknowledged to be crude and poor in terms of reliability. The statistical analyses were not sophisticated (e.g. each of the relationships with outcome were examined separately with no controls for interactions or multiple testing). However, all participants were included in the study, irrespective of their length of stay (the 'dose' of treatment they received).

Rapoport's study was followed closely by Tuxford (1961) who describes a small outcome study of men admitted to the hospital on probation or on licence from Borstal. The length of follow-up was very variable (2–22 months) but responses from probation officers were received for 72 out of 86 of the men. Seven levels of post-treatment adjustment were identified. Seventeen per cent of men were in the poorest category, and the mean length of stay in treatment for that group was four months. Thirteen per cent were in the highest functioning category and the mean length of stay in this group was five-and-a-half months. However, the most successful group, although their length of stay was less than half the maximum possible (the maximum stay was one year, as now), had committed no further crimes since discharge and seven of the nine men in this group had remained out of hospital for over a year. Interestingly, the pre-treatment crime rates are similar for the best and worst outcome groups. As the author admits, it is difficult to draw clear conclusions from this study. It seems unlikely that the additional month in treatment accounted for the differing success rates between these two groups. However, leaving the seven sub-categories of improvement aside, 55 per cent of the men in this study were employed and 61 per cent did not recidivate in the follow-up period.

Whiteley's study of the improvement of discharged men built on Rapoport's and Tuxford's earlier work by using more objective assessments of study partici-pants and a longer follow-up period (Whiteley 1970). The Criminal Records Office and Ministry of Health were used to gather data on convictions and psy-chiatric re-admissions two years post-treatment on a cohort of 122 consecutive male discharges. The study found that the conviction rate reduced from 45.9 per cent before treatment to 35.2 per cent of the sample post-treatment. Fifty-eight per cent of patients were not re-admitted to a psychiatric hospital within two years. Of those with previous convictions, 43.6 per cent had not been re-convicted at two and 40 per cent at three years post-discharge. At two years post-discharge 40 per cent of patients had good outcomes, having been neither re-convicted nor re-admitted to a psychiatric hospital in this time. This binary criterion utilised is simplistic but it is also stringent, given that 70 per cent of the patients had convictions and 54 per cent psychiatric admissions (35% had both) prior to their specialist treatment. Once more, all patients had been included in this study, irrespective of length of stay in treatment. A relationship between length of stay and treatment outcome was again found. Of those who stayed longer than three months, a non-significantly greater proportion were neither re-convicted nor re-admitted within two years than of those who stayed fewer than three months.

This study was validated by a further study investigating the prediction of success following treatment, which found 47 per cent of a second cohort of 87 discharged men to have been neither re-convicted nor re-admitted at two years post-treatment (Copas and Whiteley 1976). This study also increased the follow-up period for the earlier study and found that the success rate was only slightly diminished, to 33.6 per cent, at five years post-treatment.

Up to this point, the study methodologies applied to Henderson Hospital had improved in terms of the measures of success and length of follow-up period. However, all remained limited by a lack of comparison groups, making it difficult to attribute the observed improvement to the treatment rather than other factors, such as the passage of time. The association of improvement with length of stay did support a treatment effect, however.

An improved methodology, incorporating comparison groups, assessed 245 referrals to the hospital, 194 of whom were admitted and 51 not (Copas et al. 1984). This study also improved on previous methods by assessing psychological functioning. Results for the treated group were consistent with previous studies using behavioural functioning. At three years, the success rate was 41 per cent and at five years, 36 per cent. A proportion of the 'untreated' controls were also shown to be successful, but rates were 23 per cent and 19 per cent at three and five years. Once again, length of stay in treatment showed a positive relationship with success rate. The proportion of those patients staying less than one month in treatment who had successful outcomes was found to be similar to the no treatment control group. The proportions of successful patients increase steadily with length of stay until nine months, after which there was no further improvement. Seventy-one per cent of those patients who stayed in treatment for nine months or more were neither re-convicted nor re-admitted at three years post-treatment follow-up. Sixty-five per cent of them remained free of re-convictions and re-admissions at five years post-treatment.

A more detailed investigation of psychological symptom improvement between admission and post-discharge follow-up followed shortly (Dolan et al. 1992). This study, while flawed in a similar way to the earlier outcome studies by the lack of a control group and a short period of follow-up, used more stringent success criteria by incorporating calculation of the clinical significance of change and using a standardised psychological assessment tool. This study showed 55 per cent of 62 patients to have improved reliably and 32 per cent to have improved clinically significantly. There was a less marked, non-significant, trend for improvement related to longer length of stay in treatment.

A marked shift in approach to evaluating the effectiveness of Henderson treatment was prompted by the threat to specialist services by the introduction of the purchaser/provider split and the extra-contractual referral system in 1991 (Dolan *et al.* 1996). The competition between internal considerations and clinical decisions to treat required a change in the evaluation of services. Two papers followed a cohort of admissions comparing costs to health and penal services in the one year prior to, and following, treatment (Menzies, Dolan and Norton 1993; Dolan *et al.* 1996). Given the small sample size and lack of comparison, this study could usefully be replicated because its findings were remarkable (Dolan *et al.* 1996). The methodology has informed larger studies of other thera-peutic communities (see Chapter 16). The service usage in the one year following treatment at Henderson was one-tenth that estimated for the year prior to admission. The study showed that treatment costs could be recouped within two years assuming maintenance of the level of usage in the first year post-treatment. The impact of this research on the service was remarkable given the simplicity of the study in comparison with the accumulating evidence discussed above. An imminent closure of the unit was avoided and time bought, in which Henderson was able to formulate its evidence base and submit for a more secure central funding base for the hospital (which eventually resulted in the development of two replica services).

In the meantime, a large-scale research study was launched in which both psychological symptomatology and service usage were to be assessed. This study represented the largest prospectively studied cohort of personality-disordered patients at the time of its design. The principal paper from this study was also creditable as it assessed outcome in terms of core personality disorder symptoms rather than by proxy measures such as suicidal behaviour, service usage or mood states. This study found highly significantly greater improvement in borderline symptoms in the treated (n=70) than non-treated (n=67) groups. Again, the success rate is consistent with previous studies as 42.9 per cent of the treated group were found to have improved clinically significantly, compared with 17.9 per cent of the non-treated group (Dolan, Warren and Norton 1997).

The use of non-admitted referrals to the service as a comparison group is more appropriate than selecting a group of personality disordered patients from another service since there may, indeed, be some relevance of the 'stage' at which a personality disordered patient is when they are referred to a specialist service. However, it is far from perfect as the reasons for non-admission are also likely to be relevant to prognosis. The funding changes in the NHS identified above provided this study with a sub-group of patients whose reason for non-admission was refusal of funding by the health authority. It could be argued that this is a further improvement on the non-admitted comparison group because the reasons for non-admission may relate less to the clinical characteristics of the patient. In this sub-group, the success rate was 18.2 per cent, very similar to the non-admitted group as a whole. This study also found a highly significant correlation with length of stay in treatment and improvement in borderline symptoms.

The study, however, also suffered from several flaws. Although a comparison group was used, it was selected naturalistically. For the psychological outcomes, the measures were self-report and resulted in a low response rate.

In order to overcome some of the difficulties with collecting self-report data from personality disordered patients, this study also collected service usage information from the referrers and general practitioners (GPs). Dolan reported these outcomes on a truncated sample of the study in which data were obtained from referrers and/or GPs for 119 admitted and 247 non-admitted referrals (Dolan *et al.* 1995). Given the criticisms that can be applied to the use of a naturalistically allocated comparison group, the analysis in this study was applied to the sub-group of non-admitted referrals for whom the reason for non-admission was refusal by their health authority to fund the treatment (n=44). Using the stringent criteria applied by the earlier Whiteley studies of no re-admission or re-conviction, this study showed that 80 per cent of the admissions had not been re-admitted to psychiatric inpatient facilities, had not been re-convicted, or both, compared with 45 per cent of non-funded non-admissions. The details of this study are interesting since they confirm the results of the study of costs conducted on a much smaller sample from this study (n=24) described above. Significantly fewer of the admitted group were found to have had further psychiatric admissions or to have re-offended but there was a non-significantly greater proportion of the admitted group who had been utilising outpatient psychiatric treatment. These results do suggest a lessening in the severity of difficulties, as inpatient treatment is no longer required. However, this is coupled with an increase in the outpatient service usage. One argument which has been advanced to explain these findings is that the specialist input of Henderson Hospital may enable personality disordered patients to make more appropriate use of the services that are available than they were able to prior to specialist treatment.

Once again, the relationship between length of stay and outcome was explored in this study. However, the results do not suggest such a strong relationship between length of stay in treatment and subsequent service usage as was found between length of stay and change in borderline symptoms (Dolan *et al.* 1997). While those who stayed longer than nine months in treatment were less likely than those who stayed fewer than three months to have been admitted as inpatients (16% *vs* 33%, p=0.017) and they were also less likely to have used psychotropic medication (24% *vs* 37%), or offended (7% *vs* 18%), only the difference in psychiatric inpatient service usage reached significance.

This arm of the most recent outcome study improves on some of the methodological difficulties with previous study designs by gaining information on a more 'objective' outcome measure and obtaining information on a larger proportion of the sample than was possible with self-report questionnaires. However, the validity of data collected from professionals about the service usage of their clients is uncertain given the lack of centralised records for health service usage. There is also the difficulty of extrapolating results at one year post-treatment to longer lasting improvements. Further research is currently underway at Henderson, following this cohort of referrals up to ten years post-treatment to explore mortality rates and criminality, using centralised records.

Summary

These evaluations of Henderson Hospital have used a variety of success criteria from clinical assessment through re-conviction and re-admission to core borderline personality disorder symptomatology, encompassing a range of aspects of functioning related to the personality disorder diagnosis. These studies suggest that treatment is successful in between 40 per cent and 60 per cent of residents up to five years post-treatment. There is also some consistency of findings, suggesting a positive association between length of stay in treatment and improvement at follow-up. Cost-offset has also been used as a measure of outcome and suggests a 90 per cent reduction in service usage costs post-treatment.

Those patients who do not improve following receipt of treatment may have simply not changed or, more important, they may have deteriorated. Several of these studies of Henderson Hospital have also assessed no change and deterioration. In Rapoport's early study, 28 per cent of discharged men were judged to be unchanged and 31 per cent to have worsened. In the Tuxford study, 28 per cent of patients were in the poor outcome category and 17 per cent considered treatment failures. Dolan found 6.5 per cent to have deteriorated reliably. One very important outcome in this group of patients is mortality. Deaths of personality disorder patients from unnatural causes exceeds by 3.5 times the expected frequency (Martin *et al.* 1985). Thirty to sixty per cent of completed suicides are estimated to have a personality disorder (Paris *et al.* 1987; Stone *et al.* 1987). Death rates have been reported in several outcome studies of Henderson. Whiteley (1970) found four deaths (3.6%) by three years post-treatment. For two of these the verdict was suicide and two accidental death. Copas *et al.* (1984) found zero deaths at five years post-treatment. Research is currently under way using Office of National Statistics data to establish deaths in the cohort studied by Dolan (1997).

Discussion

The democratic therapeutic community approach used at Henderson Hospital has been endorsed by the Department of Health as one of the treatments of choice for severe personality disorder in the form of funding for service development based on Henderson Hospital. This endorsement follows the recommendation of an expert committee jointly commissioned by the Department of Health and Home Office that reviewed the research on treatments for psychopathic and antisocial personality disorder and concluded that 'more units such as the Henderson Hospital should be developed' (Reed 1994, para. 9.30). The body of research evidence developed over time at Henderson Hospital has directly contributed to the development and expansion of this particular service.

The 'replication' of Henderson has contributed further to the increase in profile of the therapeutic community approach to treatment in general. It has also attracted greater scrutiny to the evidence base, not just for Henderson but also for the democratic therapeutic community approach in general. Indeed, acerbic debate has been prompted in the medical press (Kisley 1999) as the evidence base for policy decisions such as the central purchasing of this service development are questioned. Although there are methodological flaws in all the evaluations of Henderson Hospital, several recent reviews of the literature on outcome studies for treatment of personality disorder demonstrate that the evidence for other treatments also lacks rigour and cogency (Bateman and Fonagy 2000; Dolan and Coid 1993; Roth and Fonagy 1996; Warren *et al.* 2003). In addition, the recent systematic review and meta-analysis (Lees, Manning and Rawlings 1999) produced the highest possible level of evidence for the therapeutic community approach showing a robust-looking odds ratio for the positive effect of treatment. However, even this evidence is unable to obviate the need for further debate in this area.

Henderson Hospital is a small treatment resource that has been extensively researched considering its size. Perhaps being one of the earliest therapeutic communities and attracting curious anthropologists set a precedent for the conduct of research. The medical directors of the hospital over the years were particularly interested in the contribution of research to clinical practice, and the research conducted was of a good standard, evolved over time and has resulted in a cumulative body of evidence for a treatment effect of this approach to personality disorder. The evidence suggests a clinically meaningful treatment effect in 40 per cent of admissions for treatment. Those who stay longer than three months in treatment show some improvement over those who do not receive treatment, and those who stay for over 200 days are more successful still (70% improved) with improvement maintained up to five years post-treatment with only slight deterioration. However, these results clearly show this treatment is not a panacea, as the association with length of stay shows the high dropout rate from the treatment. On the other hand, the study designs and methodological approaches are not without flaws and the evidence base can still be questioned. According to the hierarchy of evidence-based medicine espoused in health services today, the cohort study evidence of the effectiveness for Henderson Hospital remains at level III (a). The most recent study was included in a meta-analysis of therapeutic community treatment for personality disorder (Lees *et al.* 1999) with studies of other communities. Several challenges to the evaluation researcher are presented by Henderson Hospital and its client group, some of which have been overcome, some partially overcome and some not confronted. The most recent study, which was prospective in design, attempted to follow over 600 patients (Dolan, Warren and Norton 1997). Low response rates reduced sample sizes for the self-report data. However, the study incorporated multiple approaches to assessment (self-report assessments were augmented by data supplied by GPs and referrers). The full results of this study thus present a more rounded picture of outcomes in this client group, as a range of psychological measures were used in addition to the Borderline Syndrome Index and data were collected from independent sources on service usage (Conte *et al.* 1980).

Methodologically, the use of randomisation and control groups is problematic. Considerable methodological difficulties exist – for example, with the selection group in which current residents are involved: it can be argued that randomisation after this group would undermine the empowering function of it. Randomisation before this group would entail referrals accepting that, having gone through randomisation, they would then have to undergo the selection process and then still perhaps not receive treatment. In addition, those not chosen by the selection process post-randomisation would continue to be analysed as 'treated' although they never, in fact, received any of the treatment, with the exception of that one meeting. Randomisation at either of these points in any case takes place after some selection has already occurred, i.e. the referring clinician has decided to refer a particular personality disordered patient. The sample could not, then, be a truly random sample of personality disordered patients. There have also been arguments that the status of knowledge about personality disorder treatment makes randomised controlled trials (RCTs) premature (Dolan and Coid 1993a). Selection of an appropriate alternative against which to randomise is also a key concern. Henderson is unusual in offering a residential treatment for a whole year. Similar treatments are not really available unless they are other therapeutic communities, which makes them redundant as control treatments. Randomisation to no treatment or to treatment as usual brings ethical difficulties, given the high risk of this group for suicide or major life-changing activities such as serious criminal offences. These are just some of the considerations that have precluded the use of RCT methods at Henderson thus far.

Although approaches such as cognitive behaviour therapy (CBT) are viewed positively as singular, in spite of being delivered in different settings by different clinicians, therapeutic communities have historically prided themselves on their differences. In the current climate of evidence-based medicine, such resistance to 'oneness' presents a threat to therapeutic communities because a large proportion of the evidence for therapeutic communities in the UK has been collected on so few communities. In addition, other therapies, such as CBT and its variants, are working towards standardisation, through manualisation and fidelity research. The therapeutic community approach does not lend itself easily to a similar development and this presents an additional barrier to research methodology. There is a great need for further research into the effectiveness of the therapeutic community approach and the RCT issue must be confronted and resolved.

With the recent UK government's endorsement of therapeutic community treatment, Henderson Hospital, along with other therapeutic communities within the NHS, finds itself in the mainstream of mental health services. Ongoing research is clearly a requirement, as part of the clinical governance agenda. Henderson and, arguably, other NHS therapeutic communities must strive for the same standards of effectiveness and evidence as other medical specialties and sub-specialties, as ought all mental health therapies.

Within the field of personality disorder there is scope both for further treatment development and also a higher level of proof of treatment effectiveness. The challenge is clearly to achieve the highest possible level of evidence: RCTs and meta-analyses. On the other hand, it is important to avoid the temptation to believe that good-quality evidence is equated with RCTs (Slade and Priebe 2001). It is not likely that RCTs in the field of therapeutic community research will be able to provide all the necessary evidence. To this end there is scope for an imaginative range of both qualitative and quantitative approaches and much merit, subjective and otherwise, to be gained from greater research collaboration between therapeutic communities in the future.

CHAPTER 15

Research on the Norwegian Therapeutic Community Network

Sigmund Karterud, Geir Pedersen and Øyvind Urnes

The Norwegian Network of Psychotherapeutic Day Hospitals is a non-profit organisation that was founded in 1993 (Karterud *et al.* 1998). Currently, the network consists of ten different day hospitals, which are owned by larger university or municipal hospitals. The aim of the network is to provide mutual support for quality assurance, professional development, Internet facilities, research and survival issues. The network has a high prestige in the Norwegian psychiatric community. It is governed by a board consisting of one representative from each unit, the daily co-ordinator and one elected leader (SK) who maintains a connection to the psychiatric research department of Oslo University.

Day hospitals can apply for membership and the criteria are the following:

- A day treatment format, which is mainly based on group therapies.

- A patient population consisting mainly of patients with personality disorders.

- A firm commitment and ability to comply with the basic requirements of membership, which includes a range of diagnostic and evaluatory procedures.

New members pay a starting fee of £4500, which covers a specially designed Windows-based software system, all tests and schemes involved in the system, systems training, a diagnostic training course (SCID-II) (First *et al.* 1995) and a psychometric test course. Other members pay an annual membership fee of £3600, which covers user support, site visits, Internet websites, systems development, comparative data work, research and one annual conference. The network is run by a daily co-ordinator, systems developer and researcher (GP).

The membership criteria do not contain any ideological claims. However, most of the units adhere to therapeutic community and group analytic principles. A large proportion of the staff is trained by the Institute of Group Analysis in Oslo, which runs three block training programmes covering the country as a whole. The theoretical understanding and therapeutic principles in the network are significantly influenced by psychoanalytic self-psychology (Karterud, Urnes and Pedersen 2001).

Most units run a two-phase treatment programme. The initial day treatment phase is usually limited to 18 weeks. The second group psychotherapy outpatient phase is usually limited to 3–4 years. Altogether, the network treats approximately 320 patients a year in the day treatment phase. In addition, the network runs 34 outpatient groups that contain approximately 250 patients. Table 15.1 shows the diagnostic distribution according to Axis II of DSM-IV of the first 1244 patients treated in the network (Karterud *et al.* 2003). Eighty-nine per cent of the patients received one or more (on average 1.6) personality disorder (PD) diagnoses. Avoidant and borderline PD were the most frequent diagnoses.

A typical day treatment programme consists of a combination of some or most of the following group therapies: large group (community meeting); psychodynamic group psychotherapy; art therapy group; body awareness group; exercise group; cognitive group; cognitive-behavioural group for anxiety disorders; cognitive behavioural group for eating disorders; problem solving group; medication group; housekeeping group and expressive group.

All patients are diagnosed and evaluated with different procedures at the following points of time:

1. initial interviews;

2. intake in the day treatment programme;

3. discharge from the day treatment programme;

4. one year follow-up;

5. discharge from outpatient group psychotherapy;

6. five years' follow-up.

The instruments include:

- a sociodemographic form
- a psychiatric history form
- a social support form
- an intimate relationship form
- a satisfaction with life form

Table 15.1 Total and main personality disorder diagnoses in 1244 patients treated in the network 1994–2000

Diagnoses	Total n	Main n (%)
Schizotypal	26	22 (2)
Schizoid	14	9 (1)
Paranoid	162	155 (13)
Antisocial	36	9 (1)
Borderline	356	275 (22)
Narcissistic	26	11 (1)
Histrionic	17	5 (0)
Avoidant	481	253 (20)
Obsessive-compulsive	129	41 (3)
Dependent	179	38 (3)
Not otherwise specified	225	192 (16)
Diagnosis deferred	26	26 (2)
No PD	208	208 (17)
Total	1651	1244 (100)

Mean number of PD given any PD diagnosis: 1.6 (SD=.94).
Source: Karterud et al. 2003

- MINI or SCID-I for symptom diagnoses (Sheehan *et al.* 1994; Spitzer *et al.* 1987)
- SCID-II for personality disorder diagnoses (First *et al.* 1995)
- NEO-PI-R for assessment of personality factors (Costa and McCrae 1992)
- GAF for assessment of global functioning (APA 1994)
- SCL-90R for symptoms (Derogatis 1983)

- a 47-item version of Alden *et al.*'s IIP-C (Alden *et al.* 1990) called Circumplex of Interpersonal Problems (CIP) (Pedersen 2002) for interpersonal problems
- WAS-TP (Pedersen and Karterud in press), a modified version of WAS (Moos 1974b) for perception of treatment programme climate
- a medication form
- a treatment compliance and treatment complication form
- a day treatment and programme evaluation form for patients
- a follow-up form covering psychosocial functioning
- outpatient group climate, and
- an outpatient group evaluation form.

All units are obliged to use these instruments. The local units own their own data, but at regular intervals anonymised data are transferred to one common database for the network as a whole.

Research

Currently we do not conduct any 'traditional' qualitative therapeutic community research. This type of research was done prior to the establishment of the network (Karterud 1989). In the following list we do not include the theoretical work being done either in self-psychology or in group analysis.

Research for system development and system technology

The main motivational force in recruiting so many units and staff in high quality and systematic data-gathering is, according to our view, the experience of high standard clinical benefits from the software system. Large resources are invested in the system to make the different evaluation forms valid and logically consistent and to provide a wide range of easily accessible reports to the clinicians on all topics covered by the forms and the psychological tests. A lot of experimentations have been done on the most useful graphic expositions of SCID profiles, symptom profiles, interpersonal profiles, NEO-PI-R profiles, programme climate profiles, patient satisfaction profiles, various indexes etc. As our common database grows and our knowledge of the psychometric peculiarities for this patient population grows as well, the system becomes updated with respect to the help menus that explain principles of test interpretations.

Part of the system is thus a learning device for the assessment of personality pathology and personality functioning. This highly technical approach has been supplemented by a textbook by the present authors on the nature, diagnoses, evaluation and treatment of patients with personality disorders according to our self-psychological and group analytic approach (Karterud et al. 2001).

Research related to system development has resulted in modified versions of the Ward Atmosphere Scale (Moos 1974b) and the Inventory of Interpersonal Problems (Horowitz et al. 1988). The Ward Atmosphere Scale (WAS) was translated into Norwegian and implemented in the 1970s. However, it reflected an organisation of health care systems and social structures that has become rather distant from that characterising the late 1990s. Using thematic and psychometric analysis as a base, we improved the instrument by increasing internal consistency, sharpening the homogeneity of the scales and shortening the length of the instrument by 50 per cent. Due to differences between the original and revised versions we renamed the new instrument the Ward Atmosphere Scale for Therapeutic Programs (WAS-TP) (Pedersen and Karterud in press).

Increasing concern about the semantic insufficiency in our Norwegian version of the Inventory of Interpersonal Problems – Circumplex (IIP-C) led to a thorough analysis of the properties of this instrument. The analysis disclosed major weaknesses in the instrument's internal consistency and homogeneity, which led to a more extensive reorganisation of the instrument's internal structure. The revision led to an instrument with satisfactory psychometric, as well as thematic, properties with regard to the Interpersonal Circumplex. Due to the rather extensive revision we renamed the revised instrument the Circumplex of Interpersonal Problems (CIP) (Pedersen 2002). As it formed a part of the revision of IIP-C, which was based on a large clinical sample (645 patients), it was desirable to see if there was any support for the revision based on a non-clinical sample (Pedersen 2001). Second, we also wanted an estimate of the 'normal' level of reported interpersonal problems as a reference material. A sample of 169 non-clinical subjects participated in a survey, and they are now our reference group in regard to patients' scores on the revised IIP-C, as well as SCL-90-R, and a self-report quality of life scale.

Reliability research

The above-mentioned research on WAS and IIP-C also involves reliability issues. However, the reliability problems are more urgent when it comes to therapist ratings. We have not yet invented any scientific procedure for testing the reliability of the diagnoses assessed by the clinicians. Still we have to rely on our written instructions, the training courses and a presumably growing competence in diagnostic assessments according to the LEAD principle (Spitzer 1983). LEAD is an abbreviation of Longitudinal Expert All Data and implies a diagnostic procedure which takes into account all possible information/data (including structured interviews) alongside a longitudinal observational approach and consensus among experts.

From a scientific point of view we are somewhat better off concerning ratings of Global Functioning (GAF). In 1998 the network was sponsored by the State Mental Health Agency to develop an Internet-based programme for learning and evaluation of GAF rating competence. We created 25 vignettes, which covered the whole range, from ultimate helplessness and self-destruction to superb functioning, and which also covered the most common psychiatric disorders as etiological agents. Those vignettes were assessed by 19 expert psychiatrists from all over the country. We chose 20 of these vignettes that revealed least variance among the experts and defined the means as our gold standard. We then designed an interactive Internet program, which contained manuals and explanations and a response system based upon means and standard deviations. The State Mental Health Agency decided that from the year 2000 psychiatric professionals would be obliged to rate all patients being treated in mental health institutions (outpatient departments as well) on GAF. The Internet program is the basic source for training and this new obligation spurs the usage of the program. A vast amount of data is accumulated which makes it possible to revise the gold standard according to a national consensus. We are also able to detect rating variances according to sex, age, profession, geographic location etc.

Since we use GAF as a crucial outcome measure in the network, we were interested in assessing the competence and conformity across units in the network. We conducted local courses as well as a formal reliability test across the units. Seven authorised GAF vignettes, taken from the national GAF training programme, were assessed by group consensus of the staff in the eight units. There was no consistent pattern of under- or over-estimation at any unit. Intra-class correlation (ICC, version 1.1) was .96. In a second test 58 therapists throughout the network rated six vignettes individually; ICC (1.1) was .83.

Outcome research

One important motive for joining the network is to have 'twin' units for comparison of treatment results. Previous studies have been done at the Ulleval Day Hospital (Karterud et al. 1992; Wilberg et al. 1998a). Without this, how can one know whether the results are good or bad? Is a 30 per cent dropout rate high or low? Are suicide attempts by 5 per cent of the patients during treatment 'normal'? Is a mean symptom decline of 0.4 points on the general symptom index (GSI) of SCL-90R satisfactory? Are some patients (groups) more satisfied than others? How are such questions related to the severity of psychopathology at the unit? Or to the ward climate?

These topics are dealt with at the annual conferences of the network. Data from the different units are compared and discussed. A large comparative study on 1244 patients treated at eight different treatment units in the network has recently been published (Karterud *et al.* 2003). Outcome (including effect sizes) at discharge and one-year follow-up is calculated for dropouts/completers as well as personality type and type of day hospital. One main finding was that high-intensity units (treatment programmes with approximately 16 hours a week) did not have better results than low-intensity units (approximately 10 treatment hours a week). The low rate of completed suicide (0.1%) and suicide attempts during treatment (3%) is noteworthy when we take into consideration the frequent and dangerous combination of severe personality disorders and clinical depression at admission. Of the total patient population, 39 per cent had performed previous suicide attempts. One follow-up study by Mehlum *et al.* (1991) indicated a low suicide rate (1%) in the 2–4 years after day hospital treatment.

Approximately 60 per cent of the patients receive psychotropic medication during the day treatment programme. Do we know anything about the effects? Friis *et al.* (1999) made a study on the effect of medication on a sample of 102 patients. They studied a particular sub-sample of patients with comorbid Axis I mood disorders. Of these, 62 per cent received antidepressant medication (mostly SSRIs), while 38 per cent did not get any antidepressants in spite of their depression. Rather unexpectedly, the results showed that patients who received antidepressant medication had a poorer symptomatic improvement than those who did not.

Results from the post-discharge group psychotherapy have just been submitted for publication (Wilberg *et al.* submitted). The material was 187 patients with complete data and who had terminated group psychotherapy during the years 1994–99. Average treatment time was two years. The most disturbed patients responded less to treatment, while patients without PD had a very good outcome. There were also important differences between different therapy groups. In conclusion, the following remedies for enhancing treatment effects were suggested:

1. better assessment of suitability;

2. treatment guidelines and quality control of the group therapies;

3. a systematic offer of additional treatment.

As a supplement to this study, we are now performing a qualitative interview study of ten borderline patients who have dropped out of the continuation treatment and their group therapists in order to find out more of the (intersubjective) reasons for premature terminations.

Follow-up studies

Outcome research includes follow-up studies. Follow-up investigations at one and five years after day treatment are part of standard clinical procedures in the network. Follow-up data have also been presented at the annual conferences. Several follow-up studies from the Ullevål Day Hospital have been published (Mehlum *et al.* 1991; Vaglum *et al.* 1993; Wilberg *et al.* 1999a). Briefly, the results indicate that on average patients who complete the treatment programme keep or improve their treatment gain, while patients who terminate prematurely suffer a relapse. The multi-centre study (Karterud *et al.* 2003) included a one-year follow-up of 661 patients. These extended data confirmed the results from the Wilberg study. We have also published a follow-up study of borderline patients being treated by group psychotherapy after discharge compared with borderline patients who did not receive such treatment (Wilberg *et al.* 1998b). The group psychotherapy patients were significantly better off on all crucial variables. The five-year follow-up investigation will be terminated by summer 2003. We expect to have data on approximately 250 patients.

We have also made some studies on the different therapeutic elements of day hospital treatment programmes. Patients (n=319) at the Ullevål Day Hospital rated the art therapy group as significantly more helpful than all other group therapies (Karterud and Pedersen submitted). Inspired by these findings, we have written guidelines for art group therapy as part of a combined treatment programme for patients with personality disorders (Johns and Karterud in press). Another study indicated effect of the cognitive-behavioural group for anxiety disorders on phobic anxiety (measured by SCL-90R) Based on these outcome studies and literature reviews, we have discussed what is the optimal composition of short-term day treatment programmes when approximately ten treatment hours a week seems sufficient (Karterud and Urnes in press).

Basic research

We will now summarise some of the basic research undertaken by the network to try to address dilemmas in the field. Clinical assessment of personality diagnoses is time consuming. Are self-report questionnaires useful instruments for clinical purposes? Wilberg, Dammen and Friis (2000) compared the Personality Diagnostic Questionnaire – 4+ (PDQ-4+) (Hyler 1994) with SCID-II interviews according to the LEAD principle. The results showed that PDQ-4+ was too invalid to be recommended for clinical purposes.

There is a current debate on a categorical versus a dimensional approach to personality disorders. The five-factor model of personality (i.e. neuroticism, extraversion, openness to experience, agreeableness and conscientiousness) provides a dimensional model for assessment of personality disorders. NEO-PI-R is the most popular questionnaire within psychiatry for measurement of the five factors. Wilberg *et al.* (1999b) investigated the discriminatory power of NEO-PI-R on borderline and avoidant personality disorders diagnosed according to DSM-IV. The results showed that NEO-PI-R had a good discriminating ability with respect to borderline and avoidant PD. Avoidant PD seemed to be closer conceptually to variations in personality traits as defined by the five-factor model than borderline PD (BPD).

The Wilberg *et al.* study of NEO-PI-R (1999) questioned the ability of NEO-PI-R to grasp aspects of psychopathology. We have looked at the power of NEO-PI-R to predict dropouts from day hospital treatment. Preliminary results indicate that none of the NEO-PI-R dimensions significantly predict dropouts. The negative results may be due to the use of a small sample. However, the dropout predictive power of NEO-PI-R seems rather low. These data are unpublished.

Which theoretical models of personality disorders fit best with available empirical data? We have looked at material from 930 patients with personality disorders. Among those were 252 diagnosed as BPD. We have investigated the frequency distribution of the BPD criteria among patients without and patients with a BPD diagnosis, the number of different BPD criteria combinations (we found 136 different combinations of 256 theoretical possibilities), the factor structure (one factor solution), item correlations, diagnostic efficiency of each criteria and correlation between number of BPD criteria and severity (Johansen *et al.* submitted). We conclude that the borderline construct fits very well with a prototype category, that the emptiness criteria should be better defined and that the BPD criteria list in DSM-IV should be revised according to new data of diagnostic efficiency. Our results support the view that our concepts of personality disorders (e.g. BPD) do not correspond with distinct categories in the real world, but that our concepts are best understood as ideal types (constructed 'prototypes'), which individuals can be more or less like. Since the 'chronic feeling of emptiness' criterion was the less valid borderline criterion, we plan for a qualitative interview study of borderline patients on the question of perceived emptiness, in order to refine this criterion.

There is a growing interest in attachment theory and personality disorders (Fonagy 1999). Several studies have shown that BPD is associated with unresolved attachment patterns. Other specific personality disorders are not well studied. It is hypothesised that patients with avoidant PD are characterised by a dismissive attachment pattern. It is interesting that in one study this pattern is connected to a good outcome of psychotherapy (Fonagy *et al.* 1996). In an ongoing study at the Ullevål Day Hospital, patients with avoidant and borderline PD are being investigated with the Adult Attachment Interview.

The literature on countertransference is largely anecdotal and theoretical. Since countertransference is such a hot issue in the treatment of personality disorders, we have performed a study where ten therapists filled out a countertransference form for each patient (n=70), early and late in treatment. The design makes it possible to investigate the commonly held hypothesis that borderline patients evoke stronger (and possibly different) countertransference reactions than patients without a personality disorder or with other types of personality disorders, e.g. dependent, avoidant and obsessive-compulsive.

It is a common observation that the coherence of the self is reflected in the body (posture, respiration, muscular tone). However, empirical research is hampered by a lack of valid and reliable instruments. Patients from the network participated in a reliability study of the Comprehensive Body Examination (Friis et al. 1998).

In our opinion, diagnoses are important for clinical and research purposes. But how are they perceived by the patients? Do patients feel stigmatised? Or relieved? Or is it dependent upon how this information is delivered? Patients from the network have participated in a qualitative study on the experiences of being diagnosed as personality-disordered.

Future perspectives

The strength of our approach so far has been the rigorous assessment system being implemented by many co-operating day hospitals, which have yielded a vast amount of data and very large samples. The multi-centre study on 1244 patients (Karterud et al. 2003) and the borderline criteria study on 960 patients (Johansen et al. submitted) are the largest studies ever being published in those fields. However, from a strict scientific point of view, several of our studies have had a sub-optimal exploratory design. As we see it, the network has now been consolidated as a practice research network and we observe a willingness to move further into more experimental research. Thus, we currently plan to do a randomised controlled trial on the continuation group psychotherapy. After day hospital treatment, patients will be randomised to combined group and individual treatment as the experimental condition, or back to a referral agency (treatment as usual) as the control condition. Another issue, which is discussed, is randomisation to 12 or 24 weeks of day hospital treatment in order to investigate the impact of treatment length. Meanwhile, we will continue with basic research. Studies of the validity of the paranoid and the avoidant PD constructs are underway; likewise a study of differences in severity between the PD categories. The category personality disorder NOS is also waiting for researchers, as is the stability over time of personality features according to the five-factor model. By this combination of psychotherapy and basic research, we hope to contribute to more refined combined therapies/therapeutic programmes for patients with different personality structures.

CHAPTER 16

Economic Evaluations in Therapeutic Community Research

Steffan Davies and Diana Menzies

This chapter will outline some of the basics of health economics and briefly review the literature on economic evaluations of psychotherapy. Economic evaluations of therapeutic communities will be covered in more detail, particularly recent cost-offset studies conducted in the UK. Ongoing research and emerging findings will be reviewed and the chapter will conclude with a discussion of some practical issues for conducting research of this kind in a therapeutic community environment.

Therapeutic communities research came of age with the publication of *Therapeutic Community Effectiveness: A Systematic International Review of Therapeutic Community Treatment for People with Personality Disorder and Mentally Disordered Offenders* (Lees, Manning and Rawlings 1999; see Chapter 2). The authors examined 8160 articles on therapeutic communities. They found 113 outcome studies, including 10 randomised controlled trials (RCTs), 10 cross-institutional studies and a further 32 studies using some kind of control group. A meta-analysis of the 29 suitable studies found 'very strong support to the effectiveness of therapeutic community treatment' (p.3). This provided Type I evidence for therapeutic community effectiveness according to the UK National Health Service (NHS) *National Service Framework for Mental Health* (Department of Health 1999a) criteria: at least one good systematic review including at least one RCT.

The review contained some studies with an economic element, i.e. those addressing the costs of treatment and changes in costs. Three more recent studies (Chiesa, Iacopani and Morris 1996; Davies, Campling and Ryan 1999; Menzies, Dolan and Norton 1993) were included in the review. While all studies showed a reduction in service utilisation (and hence NHS costs), as all were uncontrolled they were excluded from the meta-analysis. Economic evaluations, in the context of the wider strong evidence base for therapeutic community treatment, are still in their infancy.

Health economics

Health economics is the study of the relationship between supply and demand in health care. Although the roots of health economics can be traced back at least to the late seventeenth century, modern health economics began in the late 1950s (for general background see Jefferson, Demicheli and Mugford 2000). American economists such as Milton Friedman and Kenneth Arrow began to analyse the application of classic economic theory to health care. This was initially to aid decisions on resource allocation and as a vehicle for social reform. The development of methods of economic evaluation of health care have, in combination with further developments in medical technology and socio-demographic changes, led to a rapidly expanding literature. Economic evaluations are now built into many RCTs and are a crucial factor in converting their results into practice, particularly if differences in the efficacy of drugs or psychotherapies are marginal.

Basic concepts in health economics include effectiveness, efficiency, benefit and costs.

- *Effectiveness* is the ability of a specified intervention to produce the outcome intended.

- *Efficiency* is a measure of the relationship between inputs and outputs. For example, if two procedures were equally effective but one cost half that of the other, the cheaper would be the more efficient.

- *Benefit* is a measure of the good produced by a treatment. Benefits need to be quantifiable to enter into economic analyses. For example, life years gained by performing a procedure would be a benefit. Life years gained could also be weighed against the quality of life in that time.

- *Costs* can be divided into three cost areas:

  - *direct costs* borne by the health care system, community and family in addressing the problem

  - *indirect costs*, which are usually due to lost production but may also be a consequence of, for example, violent crime associated with alcohol

  - *intangible costs*, which are usually of psychological sequelae such as pain or loss of leisure time.

Types of economic evaluation include: cost-of-illness (COI); cost minimisation analysis (CMA); cost effectiveness analysis (CEA); cost utility analysis (CUA) and cost benefit analysis (CBA). These are described briefly below.

Cost-of-illness

COI, also known as burden-of-illness, studies are descriptive studies that aim to itemise, value and sum the costs of a particular problem or condition. The aim of this is to estimate a disorder's economic burden on society. COI studies have traditionally been used to highlight and weight different health or social problems. This allows comparisons to be made between them, thus informing public debate and aiding decision-making. More recently, COI studies have been used by the pharmaceutical industry to establish the size of potential markets and encourage the use of new products. A COI analysis begins with a traditional public health approach. For a defined condition, e.g. a diagnosable illness, occurring in a defined population such as a health service district, specific information is needed. This would include: the incidence (the number of new cases in a given period); the prevalence (the number of people affected by the condition at a point in time); the seriousness, (e.g. mortality, morbidity) and the overall costs. COI studies only take account of the costs of resources expended on the condition; they do not compare alternatives.

Cost-minimisation analysis

Economic evaluation models work by analysing the inputs (resources used) of different interventions and their consequences. In cases where interventions have the same qualitative and quantitative consequences, economic analysis can concentrate on inputs and seek to identify the intervention with the lowest costs. If, for example, this involves comparing two drugs, the analysis is relatively simple. If, however, it involves introducing a new method of providing a service, the ways costs are allocated become much more critical. For example, should the training and equipment costs of setting up a new service be depreciated (paid off) over one or ten years?

Cost-effectiveness analysis

In addition to the input costs of different interventions, CEA also measures the effects. Effect may be on a single dimension such as mortality, or prevention of a case of infection, or it may combine a number of dimensions, such as time to remission of a depressive illness and prevention of relapse. Care must be taken that different interventions do not just shift costs. For example, an intervention leading to earlier discharge from hospital may save NHS costs but increase social services costs. To be feasible effects must be in measurable natural units and interventions compared in terms of cost per unit.

Cost utility analysis

CUA is used to study interventions that produce different consequences, both in terms of quantity and quality of life, which are expressed in utilities. These incorporate length of life and subjective measures of well-being. The best-known measure is probably the quality adjusted life year or QALY. Interventions are then compared in terms of cost per unit utility. The use of utility avoids the difficult issue of determining the costs of benefits. An example could be the provision of a hip replacement: that is not life-saving but improves the quality of life greatly. Palliative surgery for cancer may prolong life for a period but with only a marginal improvement in quality.

Cost benefit analysis

CBA relies on the ability to cost both inputs and consequences. By putting a monetary value on a benefit – for example, time free from symptoms of disease – this allows comparisons with other socially desirable outcomes such as improved education, and hence earning potential, or reduced travelling time due to road improvements. CBA may also be used to cost different interventions producing the same output; for example, treating depression with antidepressants or counselling. Interventions such as prevention programmes have no direct benefit but may save costs in the future. This concept is called *discounting*, where present inputs are measured against future benefits, e.g. the benefit of not developing Hepatitis B after immunisation.

Psychiatric disorders are often difficult to define accurately and tend to run chronic long-term courses, often with fluctuations in severity. They are rarely cured by a short one-off intervention, such as a course of antidepressants or a few sessions of counselling, even though these may produce real short-term benefits. There are often problems in defining treatments received as these may be in a number of modalities: drug treatment, inpatient care, individual and/or group psychological therapies or social support. Interventions may also be difficult to define, e.g. supportive psychotherapy, the effects of a therapeutic milieu. Major psychiatric disorders also affect multiple areas of functioning. For example, a depressed patient who attempts suicide may well have contact with the police, ambulance services, accident and emergency, general medical services, intensive care, psychiatric services, social services and general practice. In addition, the patient may require time off work or lose his/her employment and become reliant on state benefits. Their quality of life will be impaired and this will also affect relatives and carers. Major psychiatric disorders tend to have profound social consequences leading to prolonged hospitalisations and needs for social care, increasing the numbers of possible variables for complete economic evaluation. In addition to the numbers of cost variables to consider, some of the consequences of psychiatric disorders are very difficult to describe in economic terms; for example, the costs ascribed to personal distress or the impact of parental mental illness on children. Psychiatric disorders can also create socially disorganised and unstable lifestyles making tracing research participants and continuing to engage them in research more problematic.

The 'gold standard' of economic evaluations, as with other medical research, is usually regarded as the RCT. Due to the problems in studying psychiatric disorders, particularly personality disorders, RCTs are often impractical and inappropriate (see Chapter 6 for further discussion). Economic evaluations, with their added complexities of multiple cost dimensions, are therefore even more difficult. Economic evaluations in therapeutic community research are often at best only partial evaluations. The most common of these is the cost offset study. This type of study seeks to offset the differences in costs before and after treatment against the costs of treatment leading to an argument that treatment is self-funding over a certain time period. Three of these studies are discussed later.

Economic evaluations of psychotherapy

There is a growing body of evidence for the clinical and economic benefits of psychotherapy, although evidence for specific therapies and conditions is far from comprehensive (see Aveline 2001). Mumford *et al.* (1984) reviewed 58 controlled cost offset studies designed to investigate the effect of psychotherapy on subsequent health care utilisation, mainly general medical and surgical services. They reported an average 73.4 per cent reduction in inpatient usage and a 22.6 per cent reduction in the utilisation of outpatient services. Inpatient charges accounted for 75 per cent of total costs.

Gabbard *et al.* (1997) reviewed all MEDLINE-referenced papers relating to the impact of the effects of psychotherapy on costs of care over a 10-year period (1984–94). Their search identified 41 articles covering 35 studies. This was reduced to 18 by using the following exclusion criteria: absence of a control group; medical rather than psychiatric conditions studied; not including cost data or related measures. The 18 papers covered a variety of therapies: cognitive behavioural therapy; behavioural family interventions; dialectical behavioural therapy; dynamic psychotherapy; family therapy. A variety of disorders were also studied, including schizophrenia; affective disorders; borderline personality disorder; anxiety disorders; substance misuse. The findings of 80 per cent of the randomised and 100 per cent of the non-randomised studies suggested that psychotherapy had a beneficial impact on a variety of costs. The most significant elements of these costs were again inpatient treatment and employment. For the more severe psychiatric conditions (affective disorders, schizophrenia and borderline personality disorder) only four (of 14 studies) included employment as an outcome variable, while 13 included hospitalisation. Hospitalisation was again the most significant element of costs during follow-up.

Economic evaluations of therapeutic communities

The Northfield Experiments, which pioneered the post-war therapeutic community movement proper, were a response to economic adversity, namely the large numbers of psychologically distressed soldiers and inadequate treatment resources in terms of psychiatric and nursing staff. The involvement of 'patients' in their own treatment was a very cost-effective response to the problem. Delivering treatment in groups with patients involved in their own therapy was far more cost effective than individual treatment that was simply not available in sufficient quantity to meet war time demand.

A recent example investigating, indirectly, comparative costs of therapeutic community and standard treatment can be seen in Pullen's (1982) description of Street Ward at Fulbourn Hospital, Cambridge. Fulbourn Hospital had three admission wards, each covering a geographically defined local population. The patient populations and admission and discharge criteria were similar as each ward provided the acute admission service to a catchment area within a demographically similar area. Street Ward was run as a therapeutic community while the other two were conventional psychiatric wards. Street had a shorter mean length of admission at 16.8 days than the other wards at 34.9 and 38.1 days. The shorter mean admissions were not explained by differences in the numbers of admissions or re-admissions.

Rosser et al. (1987) reported the five-year outcomes of an admission cohort to the Cassel, a residential therapeutic community, in 1977–78. Data on service use and costs were collected retrospectively for 28 subjects. These variables were followed up prospectively by interview. The group was mixed diagnostically with a neurotic, a borderline personality disorder and a psychotic group. At five-year follow-up they calculated costs using an 'estimated lifetime profile' giving a mean gain of £42,000 for successes, £26,000 for partial success and a loss of £14,000 for failures. (The mean cost of treatment at the Cassel at the time was £8,000.) The comparability with later studies (below) is limited due to the lack of service utilisation data and the patient group. Diagnostic categories including psychotic illness and chronic alcoholism would be unlikely to be treated in contemporary democratic therapeutic communities. The length of follow-up is far longer than the later studies and relatively complete with at least partial data on 96 per cent of those admitted.

The advent of the internal market reforms of the early 1990s provided the key stimulus to the application of health economics to NHS therapeutic communities. The best-known residential therapeutic communities in the UK, the Cassel and Henderson, were both dependant on referrals from a wide catchment area centring on the Thames regions. Before the internal market reforms, referrals could be made solely on clinical grounds and the costs met by the treating unit and health authority. The internal market created contracts between local purchasers and providers to let resources follow the patients with remuneration linked to treatment of individual patients or local populations. For specialist tertiary services funding was by the extra-contractual referral (ECR) mechanism. In addition to a clinical referral, agreement was needed by the health authority to pay for therapeutic community treatment. The effect of this change was illustrated in 'One year after the NHS Bill: The extra-contractual referral system and Henderson Hospital' (Dolan and Norton 1992) which describes a drop of 25 per cent in initial referrals. Only 36 per cent of ECR requests (outside South West Thames region) in the 1991–92 financial year were approved by 1 May 1992. Many referrals were blocked clearly on financial grounds alone (Dolan, Evans and Norton 1994). This situation led directly to a series of explicit economic evaluations of therapeutic communities in an attempt to justify the funding of therapeutic community treatment (Menzies et al. 1993).

The methodology of the Henderson studies (Dolan, Warren, Menzies and Norton 1996; Menzies et al. 1993), which was replicated, with variations, by later studies (Chiesa et al. 1996; Davies et al. 1999), compared the costs of utilisation of psychiatric services and periods of imprisonment, for one year before and after treatment at Henderson Hospital. The difference between these costs was offset against the cost of treatment at Henderson. Based on the assumption that the pre- and post-treatment costs would remain stable over time, it was calculated that the treatment at Henderson would be self-funding in just over two years.

The Henderson sample consisted of 29 patients resident in 1992. Previous service usage was calculated from case notes and resident questionnaires, and follow-up was by postal questionnaire to residents, general practitioners (GPs) and referrers. Costs were Henderson's contract costs and average psychiatric costs for the Thames regions. Five patients were lost to follow-up, a potential source of bias if patients who did particularly badly (or well) selectively refused to participate.

The Cassel study (Chiesa et al. 1996) examined a much larger range of services and costs: GP; medical and surgical; laboratory investigations; tobacco and alcohol consumption; use of medication; psychotherapy; psychiatric services. However, this study used different pre- and post-treatment groups. Follow-up was by structured interview although there was a 50 per cent dropout rate in the post-treatment group that may have biased the findings. The costs used were the same as for the Henderson study, but no costs were reported for the Cassel treatment.

Francis Dixon Lodge (FDL) is a 16-bed residential therapeutic community. Davies *et al.* (1999) studied a consecutive series of admissions to FDL from 1993 to 1995. Eighty per cent were local, funded by a block contract with the health authority, and 20 per cent were ECRs requiring individual approval by their health authorities. Information was collected directly from referring consultants and GPs but only for psychiatric inpatient admissions in the three years before and one year after treatment at FDL. Follow-up was complete but only 83 per cent of local patients had been discharged for one year at the time of the initial study. There was a significant difference between the local and ECR groups with a higher mean age for the local group (28.1 *vs* 24.5 years) and smaller mean duration of psychiatric admissions over three years before admission (56.3 *vs* 168 days). There were no other significant differences in psychiatric or demographic variables. It was argued that the local patients were likely to be referred earlier in their psychiatric career as there were no financial barriers to referral. The ECR patients were more likely to utilise significant acute resources before referral to FDL, helping referrers to justify purchasing expensive therapeutic community treatment. The cost-offset calculation estimated that treatment at FDL would be paid for in four years for ECR admissions and 7.6 years for local patients. Although treatment costs were higher for the ECR group, the time to fund treatment was shorter as there were greater costs before admission, due to longer admissions, which could be offset against treatment costs. The longer time to fund treatment, in comparison with the two years at the Henderson, was due to a different cost structure. Acute admissions were much cheaper in the Trent region than in the London regions and the costs at FDL were higher partly because it lacked the economies of scale of the larger (29-bed) Henderson. For local patients earlier referral may have prevented the acute costs being incurred in the first place.

Although none of the studies reported significant differences between pre- and post-treatment service utilisation for any of the variables studied, all reported a reduction in both service utilisation and total costs after therapeutic community treatment. This was most dramatic for the reduction in acute psychiatric admissions, the most significant cost element (Figure 16.1). Table 16.1 shows a comparison of these three studies in terms of patient groups, outcomes, length of follow-up, dropout rates, sources of costs and cost savings over one year.

All these studies have a number of weaknesses. None included a control group although, as all were struggling to attract admissions, no active alternative treatment was available and none had access to the substantial research funding necessary to support a controlled trial, this is unsurprising. The range of variables studied to derive costs was limited to aspects of direct costs ranging from inpatient admissions only for FDL, to psychiatric, medical and employment (un-costed) for the Cassel. The pre- and post-admission periods were limited to one year, too short for one to be confident of change in a chronic condition such

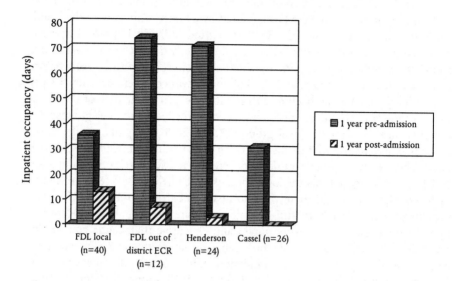

Figure 16.1 Inpatient occupancy pre- and post-therapeutic community treatment
Source: Davies, Campling and Ryan 1999

as personality disorder. It is possible that the year before treatment was particularly bad, precipitating referrals, especially for ECRs. The year after may be atypical with initially good progress that isn't maintained. Longer periods of pre- and post-treatment follow-up are required to substantiate the estimates of time taken to fund treatment.

There is also a question about the generalisability of results from the different studies. The diagnostic make-up of the Henderson and FDL samples is similar, with a majority of patients classified as DSM-III-R borderline (75%) or its ICD-10 equivalent, emotionally unstable personality disorder (87.5%). Diagnostic classifications are not given for the Cassel sample.

The initial Henderson cost-offset studies were very influential (Davies 2001). Not only did they lead to attempts to replicate them but they were also important in influencing purchasers of psychiatric services. This is most obvious in the decision of the National Specialist Commissioning Advisory Group to fund two new units on the Henderson model in Birmingham (Main House) and Crewe (Webb House). The availability of cost-offset data has also been influential in arguing for funding of individual cases.

Recent and ongoing research

Since the initial FDL publication (Davies *et al.* 1999) there has been further follow-up of the FDL cohort. Information on acute psychiatric admissions for three years pre- and post-treatment has been collected for the complete sample (Figure 16.2; Davies and Campling 2003). Mean acute admissions escalated in each year preceding admission for the local and ECR groups. The ECR group had substantial usage in each of the three years before admission, while the local group rose from a low level in the third year before treatment at FDL. Acute admissions decreased year on year in the three years post-admission for the local group. For the ECR group there was a peak in the second year, mainly due to one patient. However, the mean duration of admissions post-treatment was still below that of any pre-admission year. Acute bed occupancy was significantly lower in each year of the three years of follow-up than the year before admission for the whole group ($p<0.005$; $p<0.01$; $p<0.001$) and the local patients ($p<0.01$; $p<0.005$; $p<0.005$). Occupancy over the three years after treatment was lower than for the three years before treatment for the out-of-district patients ($p<.05$) and for the whole sample ($p<0.05$). The difference in the year before treatment and the first ($p=0.09$) and third years ($p=0.07$) after treatment approached significance for the small out-of-district group. These figures add weight to the cost-offset arguments on time to fund. Although the levels of service utilisation are not constant pre- and post-admission, the benefits in reduced admissions are maintained over time.

The study also reported a mortality of 6 per cent from suicide and accidental death within, or just after the end of, the follow-up period. All suicides and accidental deaths occurred in patients with admissions of under 42 days (the mean length of admission was 223 days). This emphasises the high risk of suicide amongst therapeutic community patients with personality disorder, especially those who do not engage successfully with services.

Chiesa *et al.* (2002) have recently completed a prospective study comparing health service utilisation in patients treated at the Cassel Hospital with those treated in a general psychiatric setting in North Devon (GPP). By providing a comparison group in this study it was possible to examine whether or not these changes only occurred in the group offered specialised treatment. There were two forms of specialised treatment, one being a 12-month admission at the Cassel Hospital with no further treatment following discharge (IPP) and the other being a six-month admission at the Cassel Hospital followed by 18 months of outpatient psychosocial treatment (SDP). The latter consists of twice-weekly groups plus outreach psychosocial nursing (see Chapter 13). There were significant differences between the groups with GPP patients being significantly more likely to be married or be separated, widowed or divorced (70% GPP, 36% IPP, 24% SDP). IPP and SDP patients were more likely to have had a college education (76% IPP and SDP, 24% GPP), and were higher consumers of psychotherapy

Table 16.1 Comparison of cost-offset studies from three NHS therapeutic communities			
	Henderson	*Cassel*	*FDL*
Definition of disorder	74% borderline personality disorder	Not defined	87.5% emotionally unstable personality disorder
Outcome	Service utilisation psychiatric and prison	Service utilisation psychiatric and medical	Service utilisation psychiatric inpatient only
Follow-up	1 year follow-up	1 year follow-up	1 year follow-up
Controls	None	None	None
Followed up for 1 year/sample size	24 of 29	26 of 29 26 of 52	47 of 52, 100% those discharged
Costs Therapeutic community	Contract price NHS tariffs Thames regions	No cost for therapeutic community given	Health authority contract prices, Trent region tariffs for ECRs
Other services		Used Henderson figures	
Mean cost of therapeutic community treatment	£25,641	Not given	ECR £34,910 Local £23,769
Cost savings 1 year pre- *vs* post-admission	£12,658	£7423	ECR £8574 Local £3137
Time to fund assuming stable service utilisation	2 years	Not given	ECR 4 years Local 7.6 years

Source: Chiesa et al. 1996; Davies et al. 1999; Dolan et al. 1996

before treatment (and after for IPP). Inpatient psychiatric usage for all groups was remarkably low in comparison with previous studies with annual mean costs between 116 and 208 Euros (£72–£130 at an exchange rate of 1.6 Euros to the pound).

Total service utilisation costs for the year following 'expected' discharge compared to costs for the year before treatment were lower for all groups. Significant reductions were demonstrated for SDP and IPP, with SDP more marked. Casualty department costs were also reduced following the combined specialist programme and general psychiatric treatment, suggesting fewer acts of self-harm and parasuicide; but not following the residential therapeutic community only programme. Reduction in symptomatology was found following treatment in both specialist programmes but not in the general psychiatric treatment sample. There was a significant association between the symptomatic improvement in the two specialist treatment programmes and cost at follow-up, but this association was not found for the GPP group. This is perhaps not surprising, as GPP was more of a maintenance treatment rather than a specialist, intensive intervention. No costs were given for the treatment at the Cassel (IPP and SDP) so no comment can be made on potential cost offsets and time to fund treatment, or comparisons with the costs of GPP. The study supports the increasingly common practice of providing follow-up support to patients after leaving therapeutic community residential programmes.

Finally, as part of the agreement in 1999 to fund two new therapeutic communities based on the Henderson Hospital model by the National Specialist Commissioning Advisory Group, an independent evaluation of the three services has been instigated. The health economic strand of this evaluation will report alongside the clinical progress strand with the aim of evaluating and comparing the costs and effects of treatment across the three sites. Resource use before and after treatment will be measured using a questionnaire designed for this study. Data will be collected for the 12 months before admission and every three months following discharge, whether planned or premature, to a maximum of 24 months after admission. Original referrers and GPs will also be contacted to cross-check service use. Indirect costs such as those from lost employment and care-giver time will be calculated as well as the direct costs of hospital- and community-based services, criminal justice services, specialist accommodation and sheltered employment. In this way the costs per year before, during and after treatment at each of the three democratic therapeutic communities will be calculated and compared, the cost-effectiveness measured and differences between sites and sub-groups explored. At the time of writing this study is still in progress and no results are available yet.

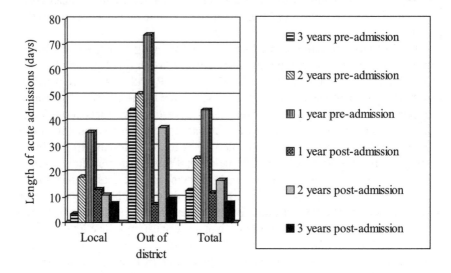

Figure 16.2 Mean length of acute admissions pre- and post-therapeutic community treatment
Source: Davies and Campling 2003

Practicalities of economic evaluation research

As we can see from the earlier discussion of health economic principles, to conduct a proper evaluation would ideally involve a number of elements. A control group or groups would be necessary, ideally a no treatment and a comparison treatment, both randomised. Other elements would be very detailed examination of resource utilisation from which to derive costs including inpatient care, medication, contact with health, social care and criminal justice agencies, benefits, employment and taxation. This type of study would, however, be very costly, create great practical difficulties and as discussed elsewhere (see Chapter 6), may be ethically dubious.

In practice, as with the studies discussed earlier, investigators are likely to undertake smaller studies aimed at evaluating/auditing their own services. This may involve comparing patients' service utilisation pre- and post-treatment or, as the literature expands, in comparison with other published studies. Multi-centre studies would have the advantage of greater numbers and hence statistical power but would also have additional complexities in terms of comparison of treatments offered and patient groups.

The following are some brief notes on issues to consider in designing small-scale outcome studies that include economic elements.

Sample

It is important to define the sample as tightly as possible. This could be as simple as a consecutive list of all admissions between certain dates. Once defined it is important to be rigorous and transparent.

Follow-up

As a counsel of perfection follow-up should be as complete and as long as possible. Missing even a small number of the original sample can bias the results, and this may be a particular problem for therapeutic community research as those with poor outcome are less likely to stay in touch with services and other ex-residents. If information is collected from ex-residents directly by writing to them this is likely to lower the response rate. Administrative follow-up through medical records systems and GPs will be more complete, as in the FDL study, but will confine outcomes to those reliably recorded; with admission and death being most reliable. Conversely, information gained from direct contact may be more complete; particularly for social outcomes such as employment and benefit status. If a patient is registered with a GP tracing is possible through the national registration office in Southport.

Outcomes

As we have seen from this review of the economic impact of therapeutic community treatment, for those with severe disorders inpatient care is the most frequently examined outcome. This is because it is both the most expensive and the easiest to measure. Other elements of care such as day hospital and outpatients' attendances may be significant but are less costly and often less well recorded. As community services become a more significant part of overall care packages, they are likely to represent a greater cost element; and it is hoped that recording of contacts and costs will improve. For offender populations imprisonment and re-conviction are obvious outcomes. Data on these are held centrally by the Home Office and Prison Service. Home Office data on conviction are not wholly accurate, reflecting only convictions not offences, and have a lag of several months before appearing on information systems. Death, whether by suicide or natural causes, is another important outcome which, although having an economic impact, is difficult to quantify. Data on deaths and causes of death are again recorded centrally and are available from the Office for National Statistics.

Recent changes to the way research ethics committees interpret confidentiality and consent are making it increasingly difficult to conduct rigorous follow-up studies. The need to obtain consent from all patients in a follow-up study will lead inevitably to higher dropout rates and potentially biased results. It is probably impossible to repeat the methodology of the FDL study under current (2002) ethics committee regulations (Medical Research Council 2000; NHS Executive Information Policy Unit 2001).

Conclusion

Interest in the economic aspects of therapeutic community effectiveness has been present since the earliest developments in the field. The advent of the internal market stimulated an increased interest in economic evaluation as services sought to justify themselves to purchasers. All these studies, in common with the overwhelming majority of those examining the economic benefits of psychotherapy, reported a reduction in costs following treatment. The situation for NHS therapeutic communities is now healthier than it has been for many years, with a number of new therapeutic communities in existence or being planned. This is due in part to the availability of a politically persuasive evidence-base to support their clinical and economic benefits. Further studies underway, or just reporting, improve on earlier methodologies and provide further support for the economic as well as clinical benefits of therapeutic communities.

CHAPTER 17

Grendon

A Therapeutic Community in Prison

Elaine Genders and Elaine Player

Grendon prison was opened in 1962 as a unique experiment in the psychological treatment of offenders whose mental disorder did not qualify them for transfer to a hospital under the Mental Health Act 1959. Its original purpose was to investigate and provide treatment for those with mental disorders that were thought to be responsive to treatment, assess those whose offences suggested mental morbidity, and to explore ways of dealing with the psychopathic offender (Commissioners of Prisons 1963).

Over the last three decades or so, and in keeping with changes in the general prison population, the criminal profile of inmates at Grendon has shifted away from property offenders serving relatively short terms of imprisonment, toward those serving longer sentences for violent and sexual offences. The renewal of interest in providing treatment opportunities to prisoners that occurred in the prison service during the 1990s has enabled Grendon to appear far less anachronistic than it did at the end of the 1980s when our research was undertaken (Genders and Player 1995). At that time little was known about the Grendon regime, which was variously perceived as the jewel in the prison service's crown or as a relic of a penological era when rehabilitation was thought to be a realistic objective of imprisonment and when notions of individual pathology were held to be at the root of offending behaviour. Our own criminological education led us to assume a degree of scepticism about the relevance of a therapeutic prison and to anticipate that a major function of our research would be to reveal Grendon's primary purpose and 'hidden agenda' of penal control. In the event, this was not substantiated. Although the control functions of the therapeutic community were prevalent their significance was not reducible to a simple conflict between custody and treatment. Neither could the therapeutic programme be distilled into a positivistic caricature that defined offenders as individually flawed and denied the structural causes of criminality.

The important issue to emerge was not that custody and treatment were antithetical, but how they could be accommodated within a single institution. The study ultimately became less concerned with whether therapy could be used to exert control and more concerned to discover how such control differed from that enforced in other prisons and what purposes it served. Consequently, our research focused on how therapy was negotiated in a penal setting and how the resultant therapeutic process gave rise to specific patterns of change among its participants.

The design of the study called for a methodology capable of not only recording the prevalence of certain practices and beliefs but also uncovering the organisation and pattern of social processes. For this reason a varied set of methods was employed, including the analysis of official records, semi-structured interviews, self-completion questionnaires and, most important, long periods of observational work that extended over two years of fieldwork in the prison. In this chapter we propose to summarise some of the main findings that emerged in relation to three broad areas of interest. First, the ways in which the institutional partnership between the prison and the therapeutic community, two highly incongruous cohabitees, was accomplished. Second, the pattern of individual therapeutic development and its collective institutional representation as a staged therapeutic career. And finally, the ways in which men who were transferred to other prisons to complete their sentences adapted to the change, and whether there was any evidence of a therapeutic effect in their methods of adjustment.

The cohabitation of the prison and the therapeutic community

It is now well understood that establishing a therapeutic community within a custodial setting requires certain modifications to the traditional prison culture. Prisons exist to contain those assigned to them by the courts and to do so under conditions conducive to the maintenance of good order and control. They tend to be socially divided and hierarchically organised societies, producing a 'them and us' social structure in which the staff monopolise the legitimate power. Regulation is typically imposed by means of a system of explicit and non-negotiable rules which seeks to bring about conditioned obedience, by coercion if necessary. As such, the prison operates to de-personalise the individual and seeks to inhibit the expression of personal choice. In contrast, within the therapeutic community attendance is voluntary and the primary objective is treatment, the very enactment of which may require the expression of symptomatic attitudes and behaviours that could well threaten order and question discipline. Unlike the prison, the therapeutic community aspires to encourage the development of personal identity and to facilitate its expression; and it is organised to minimise social divisions and to enfranchise all members in the democratic exercise of power. Within this structural context, regulation is achieved by means of a process that permits negotiation: rules are made by the community and may therefore be changed by the community. In this way, compliance is fostered by a commitment to the rules, facilitating the development of a system of internalised norms rather than a system of externalised rules.

The successful operation of a prison therapeutic community depends upon the extent to which the dual requirements of treatment and control can be met to the satisfaction of all concerned. While Grendon can be conceived as incorporating two institutions – the prison and the therapeutic community – its primary identity is that of a prison and, as such, it is subject to the same formal rules as the rest of the prison system. Consequently, whatever level of co-operation the prison extends to the therapeutic community, it must reserve the right to step in and seize control whenever the security and discipline of the establishment are perceived to be under threat. So within each of the wing communities, the staff teams retain the ultimate authority to make or revoke decisions in the name of the prison. Hence, the level of co-operation between the two institutions essentially refers to the degree of tolerance which the prison is able to extend to the therapeutic community while protecting its primary concern for the security of the establishment and the maintenance of its internal discipline and order. Our research suggests that such co-operation is made possible by the fact that both the prison and the therapeutic community are designed to regulate deviant behaviour; and both are concerned to maintain conformity in order to preserve the interests of their respective organisations – albeit that there are differences in the precise nature of the conformity required and the means by which this is achieved.

Interviews conducted with a sample of 102 residents undergoing therapy revealed five mutually dependent characteristics as elemental in the creation and maintenance of the therapeutic environment at Grendon. First, the development of mutually supportive relationships between residents and the expectation that everyone will contribute to the life and well-being of the community. Second, the free-flow of communication between residents and staff which fosters the recognition that everyone has an interest in safeguarding the health of the community and furthering therapeutic objectives. Third, the general atmosphere of safety fostered by the 'no violence' rule, which encourages individual expression by minimising the fear of physical retribution. Fourth, the permission and encouragement that is extended to residents to enable them to confront and find solutions to the problems which underpin their current predicaments. And finally, there is the sense of privilege which is associated with admission to Grendon and which is facilitated by the shared knowledge that the rest of the prison system is organised along very different lines.

Ultimately, though, the success of the venture hinges upon the degree to which officers and inmates are able to modify their traditional prison roles, in order to break down the social divide between the 'keepers' and the 'kept', and to facilitate co-operative relationships and alternative working practices. Every resident in Grendon's therapeutic communities has encountered the culture of a conventional prison with its customary hierarchy, which places men convicted of certain elitist offences at the top of the pecking order, and those convicted of sexual and violent offences against women and children at the bottom. And they are familiar with the code of conduct that demands loyalty and solidarity amongst prisoners and condemns any fraternisation with the staff, who tend to be seen as members of an opposing force. Within the therapeutic community, this culture must be dismantled and replaced with one that accommodates the possibility of therapeutic relationships: where status is accorded on the basis of therapeutic progress and all members of the community, both staff and inmates, are viewed as full and equal participants in the therapeutic endeavour.

Parallel changes are required among the staff. There must be a flattening of the formal hierarchy and the bridging of the usual divide between civilian and uniformed groups found in most conventional prisons. Instead, what is needed is an emphasis upon multi-disciplinary democratic teamwork, where everyone participates as a full and equal member of the staff group in the process of decision-making. Considerable emphasis is placed upon close working relationships between prisoners and prison staff in which inmates are treated as individuals and are accorded equal status irrespective of their crimes and personalities. Hence, the uniformed officers must act as guides, arbiters and protectors to men towards whom they may feel great antipathy. They must also learn to extend a high level of tolerance towards behaviour which their formal training in prison discipline requires them to define as insubordination. In essence, officers are expected to exercise control through therapeutic means and to interpret deviant behaviour as the manifestation of a man's problems and thus as material for discussion rather than as an offence requiring a formal hearing.

Therapeutic development

There is little doubt that, as prisons go, the regime at Grendon provides a humane environment for both residents and staff. But in order to confirm Grendon's identity as a *therapeutic* prison, it must be established that the regime engages residents in a therapeutic process and is not simply providing a benign asylum. Therefore, we asked two questions: first, is it possible to identify changes in the men's attitudes, beliefs and behaviour during therapy; and second, do these changes constitute part of a graduated process, whereby specific and related stages of development are achieved within certain periods of time?

When interviewed, almost all the men reported significant changes in both their attitudes and conduct, which they attributed to the therapeutic regime. Most typically, they said that by talking about themselves and listening to, and identifying with, the experiences of others, they had gained a greater understanding of themselves and of their problems. About a third also claimed to have gained in self-confidence and similar proportions said that they had become more skilled at communicating and socialising with others, felt less isolated and alienated from the rest of the world and had a better understanding of, and empathy with, other people and their problems. Moreover, about four out of ten men felt that the benefits they had accrued from therapy were reflected in demonstrable changes in their behaviour.

Because we wanted to see whether these changes were being achieved as part of a *staged* therapeutic process, we divided the sample of 102 residents into three groups: those who had been at Grendon for less than six months; those who had been there between six and 12 months; and those who had stayed for 12 months or longer.[13] We then compared these groups in relation to three specific areas of change: modifications in their adherence to traditional prison culture; developments in their perceptions of their problems; and changes in their assessments of the benefits they had derived from therapy.

The resultant pattern indicated that the first six months at Grendon might be characterised as a settling-in period, in which traditional prison culture is deconstructed. During this time residents reassess their problems and undergo a process of acclimatisation to the therapeutic community, which enables them to experience a sense of acceptance, belonging and social integration. The end of 12 months appears to secure a process of re-socialisation, in which the men review their social skills and revise the ways in which they interact with others. Such reformulation seemed to facilitate a greater degree of satisfaction in their relationships with others and particularly with those in authority. After the first year there is a consolidation of achievements and a furtherance of the intellectual component of therapy. In this period a higher proportion of residents than in any earlier period said that they had gained confidence and trust in staff, had moved towards a greater acceptance and exercise of social responsibility and had developed insight into the related nature and underlying causes of their own problems.

However, any evaluation of an individual's trajectory through this process must be based on an assessment of change that is related to his particular problems. Consequently, we constructed a five-stage career model to provide a framework within which to evaluate, more objectively, each man's progress in therapy. The first stage is that of *recognition*: the man has to recognise that he has problems and be able to define at least some of their constituent elements. The second stage is concerned with *motivation*, when, having recognised that he has a problem, the individual has to demonstrate a desire to seek a solution and to change. The third stage registers the genesis of *understanding*, which, in effect, marks the beginning of therapeutic activity. It is during this period that the man will acquire some appreciation of how his problems have arisen and how they are interconnected and relate to other aspects of his life. The fourth stage represents the point of *insight*, when the individual will achieve some understanding of the things he must change in order to resolve his problems. Finally, there is the *testing* stage, during which the man has to test out in practice at least some of the new and alternative ways of coping.

We interviewed 69 men shortly before their departure from Grendon, pending either their release or their retransfer to other prisons. Their responses indicated that progression through all five stages of the career was highly correlated with the length of time they had spent in therapy. There appeared to be a critical period at or after 18 months, when the majority of men had successfully progressed through all stages. Significantly, only 19 per cent of the men who were leaving after less than 12 months in therapy reached this final stage; in comparison with 33 per cent of those who were leaving after a period of between 12 and 18 months and a notable 88 per cent of those who were going after 18 months or more.

It might be possible to use the career model as a predictive instrument to identify specific types of individuals who might be expected to progress further in therapy than others and, conversely, those who might be expected to make very little progress. However, in this respect it must be remembered that therapy takes place within a social context. Thus, the ability of an individual to remain in therapy for the requisite time and to make progress within the therapeutic process might indicate his greater amenability to this type of intervention. Alternatively, it may simply reflect the operation of social processes within the institution and the capacity of the community to tolerate the expression of his deviance.

Therapeutic adjustments after transfer

At the time of our research most men who were received into Grendon were not released directly into the community but were transferred to another prison to complete their sentence. This raised questions about the ways in which these men adjusted to life back in the mainstream of the prison system. In particular, whether their experience at Grendon led to a more positive process of adjustment that was beneficial to both the individual prisoner and the prison to which he was sent. We contacted and interviewed a total of 40 ex-Grendonians in 12 different establishments. Some of these men had participated in the study at Grendon but some had no prior experience of the research. The sample was heavily weighted towards prisoners serving long sentences, particularly lifers, largely because this phase of the study was conducted towards the end of the fieldwork period and the long-termers were the most likely to be remaining in the system. Half of the sample had spent at least a year at Grendon and almost a third of them had remained for 18 months or longer. They had been back in the system for varying periods of time, ranging from two months to five years, although half the men had been transferred from Grendon more than 12 months previously.

Although there was widespread agreement amongst the inmates that therapy at Grendon had been a positive and beneficial experience for them, most said that they had encountered certain difficulties in readjusting to a conventional prison environment. These problems fell into one of three broad categories. First, there were difficulties associated with getting used to new routines and practices, particularly in local prisons where there tended to be severe restrictions upon their freedom of movement and limited opportunities for varied activities. The second type of difficulty was linked to the men's psychological adaptations to their sentence. For example, many of the men had spent much of their time in Grendon focusing on events – past, present and future – outside the prison walls; and returning to a conventional prison, where such opportunities were rare, served to emphasise their confinement and exacerbated their sense of frustration. However, the difficulties that were most commonly expressed fell within the third category and concerned the adjustments the men had to make in order to compromise with the demands of a conventional prison culture. Inmates found that they had to come to terms with the fact that the rest of the prison system did not run as a therapeutic community. Those men who previously had a high profile as a disruptive prisoner experienced special difficulties in confronting their old image due to the expectations of prison staff and other prisoners. Prison officers were said to be perpetually suspicious and to assume that the men were simply manipulating the system for their own devious ends, whereas other prisoners attempted to involve them in disruptive activities or accused them of having been brainwashed.

Inmates who had previously been on Rule 43 for their own protection also experienced particular problems of adjustment. For most of these men, returning to the conventional prison system had meant a return to the fear of intimidation, the threat of violence and the monotonous reality of social isolation. Their time at Grendon had been a period in which they had been treated as individuals, rather than perpetrators of a particular crime, and one in which they had been permitted the freedom of personal expression and the opportunity to participate as equal members of a community. Back in the system they were again at the bottom of the inmate pecking order, dispossessed of any right to express themselves or to lay claim to any identity beyond that which was ascribed to them by virtue of their criminality.

Aside from the *difficulties* the men experienced in adjusting to life in the mainstream of the prison system, there were evident *costs* that were attached to some ex-Grendonians after their transfer. For many inmates the process of therapy had been a painful experience, in which defences that had taken a lifetime to erect were dismantled within months. For those who had embarked upon a therapeutic career but who had, for whatever reason, left Grendon prematurely, there was a discomfiting sense of non-completion. They spoke of feeling ill-equipped to deal with the half-emptied contents of Pandora's box. One man described it as:

> like going to have your appendix out and they cut you open, take out your appendix, and send you home without stitching you up again. You look at the hole and you wonder what the hell you are going to do with it.

Men who had been transferred back to their originating establishment because they were assessed as unsuitable for therapy at Grendon were particularly likely to feel that their excursion had been a costly one. At the very least their expectations had been raised and disappointed. They often returned frustrated, angry and with an overriding sense of failure. Regardless of how persistently the staff explained that the assessment process was designed to evaluate whether Grendon could provide a suitable medium for dealing with their problems, and was not a means of judging whether they were 'good enough' for Grendon, inmates staunchly perceived the experience in terms of personal success or failure. Some of the men, who were transferred back because therapy at Grendon was not suitable for them, were also informed that they could benefit from some other kind of specialist programme, such as an educational or training scheme, or, in some cases, a more intensive one-to-one psychotherapeutic intervention. Rather than sweetening the bitter pill of failure this tended only to heighten the men's frustration since, in their not unreasonable view, the likelihood of them ever gaining this help was extremely remote.

Despite the difficulties and costs encountered by men who had been transferred back to conventional prisons, most of the inmates followed up in the mainstream system felt that their time at Grendon had made it easier, rather than more difficult, for them to complete their sentence. This was particularly evident among those who had stayed at Grendon for 18 months or longer. The main ways in which Grendon was said to have eased their time was by increasing their social skills and enabling them to gain insight into their own behaviour and their interactions with others. In consequence, many inmates said that they no longer felt driven to maintain an image that ensured they would fit in with the dominant culture, and that they were more able to identify and avoid those situations that compounded their difficulties of surviving in the prison environment. Men who had previously represented a problem for prison discipline were most likely to claim that their period in therapy had changed their behaviour in prison. This underlines the importance of the therapeutic regime at Grendon as a resource not only for prisoners but also for the prison system.

There are two specific areas to which much effort and energy were devoted at Grendon and which could be expected to have some consequences for the management of prisoners transferred back into the system. The first of these broadly concerned the dismantling of traditional prison culture, and the second focused upon the need for individuals to develop non-violent strategies for dealing with difficult and potentially disruptive situations.

The dismantling of prison culture was evident in the increased levels of tolerance extended to men convicted of crimes that, in other establishments, would destine them to segregation under Rule 43. Among the ex-Grendonians followed up in the system it was clear that the increased levels of tolerance initiated in the therapeutic communities were largely maintained after the men were transferred back into the system. Inmates who had previously harassed and even assaulted men on Rule 43 said that their change of behaviour had been due entirely to the effects of their time at Grendon. They attributed it to the insight they had gained into the problems which men on Rule 43 faced and, through the empathetic process of therapy, to having acquired an ability to reflect upon their own reactions, rather than making a knee-jerk response.

Changes to the relationships between prisoners and prison officers provides another example of the ways in which traditional prison culture was undermined by the Grendon experience. As we discussed earlier, breaking down the barriers that traditionally exist between prisoners and prison officers is at the heart of much of what goes on at Grendon. Although the relationships the men enjoyed with officers in the therapeutic communities were rarely rediscovered with staff elsewhere, half of the men followed up after transfer were able to identify ways in which their relationships with prison officers had become less hostile as a result of their time at Grendon. All of the men who claimed to have altered their behaviour to prison officers claimed that two factors were responsible for the change. The first was that prison officers at Grendon, by adopting a less authoritarian and more caring approach, had broken down their prejudices and destroyed the stereotype that dominated the folklore of prison culture. The second was that changes in their own attitudes towards the resolution of difficult situations had led to fewer inflammable situations arising.

Some of the most common and potentially most threatening problems to prison management arise from inter-personal disputes between inmates or between inmates and staff. Three-quarters of the men who had previously presented problems for prison discipline said that following their experience at Grendon they had either avoided all arguments with other inmates or had resolved them in ways that were less violent and aggressive. Although disputes with prison staff were still relatively prevalent amongst the inmates with long disciplinary records, half of these men maintained that they had resolved their differences in new and socially acceptable ways. This self-reported data was supported by a review of the inmates' disciplinary records. Although the scale of the follow-up study precluded a detailed review of disciplinary offending, there was some statistical evidence, supported by qualitative data, which showed that men who had previously represented a disciplinary problem were significantly less likely to be placed on report after their period at Grendon. Again, the men who had stayed at Grendon for 18 months or longer were the most likely to lay claim to these positive changes of behaviour.

Conclusion

The resurgence of interest in developing programmes for offenders, both in prison and as part of community sentences, has resulted in the creation of more therapeutic communities within the criminal justice system. Most significantly, a new privately owned prison, HMP Dovegate, has opened and is providing 'a second Grendon' to accommodate prisoners in the north of the country. Evaluations of programme effectiveness are now central to these enterprises. Our research was not designed as an evaluative study, although it did attempt to assess Grendon's success in relation to the *facilitation of therapeutic work* within the wing communities, the *completion of treatment* within the structure of the therapeutic career and the *re-integration* of ex-Grendonians back into the mainstream prison system. At the time of our research we concluded that the therapeutic work in the communities at Grendon was not directed *primarily* to the prevention of crime. This may have been offered as a legitimate ambition, or as a justification for its existence, but the principal undertaking of therapy was to facilitate and promote the welfare of each individual. The assessment of programme achievements and the development of what is described as 'evidence-based practice' is to be welcomed – if only that it might act as a countervailing force against populist manipulation of criminal justice policy. The danger, however, is that success or failure will be determined by the reduction of recidivism. While this must be a worthwhile goal it should not be pursued to the exclusion of other therapeutic achievements.

The therapeutic communities at Grendon undoubtedly encourage lawful, non-violent, conciliatory and, above all, *individual* resolutions that may assist an individual in developing a less criminogenic lifestyle. But in the absence of any throughcare linked to the Grendon experience, therapeutic achievements are likely to be weakened. Most important, it should be remembered that work in the therapeutic communities does not address or challenge the *collective* problems that are endemic in the socio-economic structures from which most prisoners are drawn. For these reasons the evaluation of recidivism should not be given undue weight in assessing Grendon's therapeutic achievements, or indeed the effectiveness of any prison therapeutic community. Results from the Grendon Reconviction Study are to be welcomed but they should not eclipse the significance of the humanitarian role that Grendon plays (Marshall 1997). The men who go to Grendon are typically in a state of distress and the therapeutic communities work to restore that person and to relieve their pain. This is the essence of its rehabilitative task.

CHAPTER 18

Leaving the Therapeutic Community

Nicola Morant

Introduction

The process of leaving a therapeutic community is an integral part of therapeutic community treatment, based on an assumption that detachment from treatment is equally as important as the earlier processes of attachment and engagement in therapy. Anticipating and managing painful feelings associated with separation, detachment and transition are often key areas of therapeutic community work (Norton 1992; Wilson 1985). Leaving a therapeutic community involves the negotiation of psychological and social boundaries between 'inside' and 'outside' (Foster 1979). Particularly for those who have attended a residential therapeutic community, this is a major transition requiring adaptation to the norms of a different social context, coping with the loss of psychological bonds formed within the therapeutic community, and dealing with practical issues associated with housing, money and organising daily activities. Yet perhaps because of the therapeutic community focus on dynamics *within* the community, there has been less research and clinical interest in what happens *after* clients leave the community. Follow-up research has tended to focus on relatively specific treatment-outcome variables measured quantitatively, and our understanding of what this transition *feels like* for clients themselves is relatively small. Better awareness of these processes could have benefits for clinical work, and could usefully inform the development of integrated services for clients who may have long-term support needs.

This chapter reports on a study that uses semi-structured interviews to access the views and experiences of a cohort of ex-residents of Henderson Hospital, a therapeutic community in Surrey, UK, that offers residential treatment for people with moderate to severe personality disorders for up to one year (Dolan 1997; Chapter 14 of this volume). Therapeutic communities vary in the processes and structures they set up surrounding leaving. Those in place at Henderson at the

time this research was carried out involved a structured programme of psychotherapy groups designed to help residents prepare for leaving both psychologically and practically (Norton 1999). Until 1996 Henderson Hospital offered no
formal aftercare facilities. However, in November 1996 an innovative new outpatient service attached to the therapeutic community – Henderson Outreach
Service Team (HOST) – was established. This research was carried out as part of a
multi-method clinical audit project evaluating the development and success of
this new service (Morant et al. 1999; Morant and King 2003). Fifteen service
users were interviewed twice, once within three months of leaving the therapeutic community and again six months later. Three areas of clients' experiences
were explored: the process of leaving a therapeutic community; adaptation to independent living; and access to and experiences of local support services.

Why research service users?

Historically, the views of people who use mental health services have tended to be
ignored by those involved in research and service development. This serves to
perpetuate the common assumption that mental health problems necessarily
render a person's views and experiences unreliable or invalid. In contrast, the
therapeutic community model emphasises democratic and communal decision-making and responsibilities, and flattened hierarchies within and between
staff and patient groups. Compared to most traditional mental health services,
this treatment philosophy encourages high levels of service user involvement and
genuine user empowerment. The translation of these principles into therapeutic
community research/audit produces a commitment to including and valuing the
voice of service users; for example, as evidence on the quality or appropriateness
of service delivery, treatment outcomes or therapeutic processes. While this was
once a marginalised and unusual position, the last five years have seen a growing
recognition among researchers, policy makers and providers of (mental) health
services of the importance of including and valuing the views of service users.
This shift is taking place in clinical audit (Kelson 1996; Rigge 1994), service development and monitoring (Beethforth, Conlan and Graley 1994; Ramon 2000;
Rose et al. 1998) and research (Faulkner 1997; Rose 1996).

   Compared to service providers, the recipients of services may have very
different (but equally valid) perceptions of the value of a particular treatment, or
may vary in the importance they attribute to various aspects of the service. In
relation to psychodynamic treatments in particular, Macran et al. (1999) argue
that their inherently collaborative and interpersonal nature suggests an evaluative
approach that recognises the perspectives of both client and therapist. As well as
the message of respect and inclusion that research/audit activity on service users'
views can engender, the tangible benefits of user involvement can include
improvements in the sensitivity of services to genuine need, increased public

accountability of service developments, increased treatment compliance and reduced dropout rates.

Why a qualitative approach?

> The structured nature of many patient satisfaction surveys may fail to reveal why people behave in a certain way and how they would like services improved... Qualitative surveys enable purchasers and providers to find out about services from the users' point of view and may make the participant feel more actively involved. Most importantly, qualitative research enables the users to set the agenda. (Kelson 1996, p.102)

Many writers have pointed out the limitations of accessing service users' views using exclusively structured and quantitative methods. For example, Goodwin *et al.* (1999) argue that structured questionnaires are insensitive. A study by Greenwood *et al.* (1999), comparing a structured patient satisfaction questionnaire with a semi-structured interview, confirms that there are problems with structured methods and suggests that qualitative methods may be more successful in capturing the complexities and breadth of the concept of patient satisfaction. Jeffery, Burrows and West (1997) argue that attempting to access service users' views via structured, fixed-format 'satisfaction' questionnaires only serves to limit users' expression. Structured questions are likely to reflect researchers' rather than users' agendas, and as such may serve to maintain the traditional power imbalance between professionals and service users.

The argument for open-ended methods is particularly strong in relation to psychodynamic forms of treatment such as those that occur in a therapeutic community environment. Therapeutic community work is fundamentally hermeneutic – it aims to enable clients to understand and bring about change in their psychic and relational worlds. However, meanings and subjectivities are not readily quantifiable and do not lend themselves to precise measurement. It is extremely difficult to capture the complexities of human experience with which psychotherapies grapple using an exclusively quantitative approach. Broekaert *et al.* (1999) have called for more qualitative and phenomenological research methods as ways of capturing the dynamic growth of whole persons that characterises therapeutic community work. Qualitative and inductive methods can be used to explore broad processes of change during and following psychotherapeutic treatments, and can complement usefully the specificity of quantitative methods.

Use of qualitative methods is not without problems, however. The analysis of qualitative data is complex and requires both specialist training and time. Despite the common misperception that 'anything goes' in qualitative analysis, there are requirements to implement certain methodological processes in order to ensure the validity of qualitative analysis (Elliott, Fischer and Rennie 1999). Goodwin *et al.* (1999) warn that even qualitative interviews may be coloured by power relations between interviewer and interviewee, and that the researcher's existing views may influence the analysis of data. Despite these caveats, they argue that qualitative methods are superior to their quantitative counterparts in accessing users' views. This increasing recognition of the value of researching service users' views qualitatively mirrors a greater acceptance in recent years of qualitative methods in (mental) health research more generally (Buston *et al.* 1998; Murphy *et al.* 1998).

The study: Aims, design and methods

The study aimed to investigate three specific questions from the perspective of service users:

- How did residents experience Henderson Hospital treatment and, in particular, how did they experience the process of leaving Henderson?

- What are the experiences of ex-Henderson residents in the months following their discharge and how do these change over time?

- What are ex-residents' service needs and expectations? How do these compare to their experiences of services they are currently receiving?

Design and respondents

The project used semi-structured interviews with a cohort of Henderson leavers and adopted a longitudinal design. Participants were interviewed twice, once soon after leaving Henderson and again six months later. A longitudinal design makes it possible to investigate ex-residents' service needs and experience as they change over time.

The interview sample consisted of 15 ex-Henderson residents with the following inclusion criteria:

- discharge from the therapeutic community to the local catchment area covered by Henderson's outpatient service (HOST) and

- residential treatment at Henderson Hospital for at least one month.

People who stayed at Henderson for less than one month were excluded on the basis that they were unlikely to have successfully engaged with treatment or to have planned a programme of post-discharge support and treatment. A sample size of 15 was decided upon, as it was hoped that this would allow the project to investigate a variety of service user perspectives within a reasonably representative cross-section of therapeutic community leavers (although this is ultimately contingent on participation rates – see below). First interviews were conducted between one and three months of leaving the therapeutic community. The second interview was conducted as near as possible to six months after the first interview.

Interviews

Semi-structured interviews included a set of open-ended questions corresponding to the three areas of investigation outlined above. For all topics, general questions were combined with more specific probes. For example, a general question on how respondents felt they had been coping since leaving the therapeutic community was followed by probes on specific areas of life including practical issues, daily activities and psychological issues. All questions were covered with all interview respondents, although not necessarily in the same order. The second interview covered many of the same issues as the first interview so as to allow comparisons over time. On average, first interviews lasted between 45 minutes and one hour, and second interviews lasted between 30 and 45 minutes. For the purposes of analysis, interviews were tape-recorded with respondents' permission. Interviewees were provided with a copy of their interview transcript if they wished.

Data analysis

Interview data were subjected to thematic content analysis. This was done manually and involved successive readings of the interview text with the aim of exploring and comparing themes within and between interview transcripts. Initially a detailed reading of the data was conducted, in which broad themes were noted. The data were then divided into smaller units of meaning, which varied in size from a sentence to a paragraph of text, and these were subjected to more fine-grained analysis. The analytic strategy was both inductive and deductive. Thus, analysis aimed to provide answers to the questions listed above, but was also data-driven to the extent that it allowed themes and responses that had not been anticipated to emerge in the final analysis. The analytic strategy adhered to the ideal of maintaining a steady and explicit dialogue between ideas and evidence (Strauss and Corbin 1994), and paid attention to both qualitative and quantitative aspects of the data (i.e. both what was said and the frequency of themes across interview respondents). However, frequency was not taken to be the only indicator of significance – comments that challenged a trend or presented a different experience or viewpoint from that of other respondents were considered to be equally as informative as themes expressed by a large proportion of respondents. The reporting of results below includes illustrative extracts from interview transcripts. The presentation of findings aims to give readers a flavour of the broad themes that emerged, but for reasons of space omits some of the detail captured by this study.

Findings

Interview respondents

Study participants were recruited over a 14-month period from April 1997 to June 1998. During this time a total of 71 patients were discharged from Henderson Hospital, of whom 34 were ineligible for the study either because they were not resident in the local area or because they had stayed at the therapeutic community less than one month. Thirty-seven people remained eligible for the study, of whom 22 (60%) indicated that they were willing to participate. Of these 22 potential participants, three were subsequently re-admitted to hospital and so were unable to participate, two dropped out of the study before the first interview, and two did not attend interview appointments. Fifteen people were interviewed at Time 1 (one to three months after discharge), and nine of these were interviewed again at Time 2 (six months later). Six participants were not included in the second phase of the study either because they were uncontactable (n=3), or because they failed to attend interview appointments at least twice (n=3). Already, these figures give an indication of the problems often manifested by this group of people with personality disorder diagnoses: frequent relapses and hospital admissions, treatment dropout, unpredictability and transient lifestyles are not only the problems targeted by clinical work, but are characteristics that hamper the research process.

The final sample of respondents (12 women and three men) included slightly more women than the baseline ratio of 2:1 women: men for all admissions during the study period. Those who were interviewed also stayed at the therapeutic community slightly longer on average than people who were eligible but declined to participate in the study (45.4 weeks compared to 33.2 weeks). This compares to an average length of stay of 24.1 weeks for all admissions during the study period. Eleven of the interview respondents had completed a full 52 weeks in treatment (the maximum and recommended period) and had left the therapeutic community in a planned way. Of the four other respondents who left earlier, one discharge was planned and the remaining three were unplanned.[14]

Themes at first interview

THE LEAVING PROCESS

Looking back on their experiences of therapeutic community treatment, all respondents considered it to have been a valuable experience; although one person had both positive and negative views and several respondents had found the experience very challenging. The fact that the treatment programme encourages people to express difficult feelings and to explore the impact of past experiences on their behavioural and inter-personal patterns was highlighted as a particularly beneficial (but often difficult) aspect. Similarly, the unanimously expressed view by all 15 respondents was that the process of leaving had been extremely difficult. Leaving was described variously as 'horrific', 'heart-wrenching', 'exciting but scary', 'extremely traumatic' and 'gut-wrenching, really painful'. In this respect there were no differences between the views of residents who had planned their discharge and those whose leaving was unplanned.

The psychological and practical work involved in leaving a therapeutic community is incorporated into the treatment programme at Henderson Hospital in the form of two regular groups. Residents are encouraged to join a twice-weekly 'leavers' group' for three months prior to leaving. This small psychotherapy group is designed to help those approaching the end of treatment explore feelings such as anxiety, fear and loneliness associated with imminent discharge and transition (Parker 1989). In addition, a 'welfare group' with a more sociotherapeutic orientation is designed as a forum in which residents plan the practicalities of their discharge, including liaising with outside housing, social services and mental health agencies, while collectively reflecting on the feelings aroused by these processes (Esterhuyzen and Winterbotham 1998).

In discussions of how the leaving process is dealt with at Henderson, more positive comments are made about the leavers' group than the welfare group. Thirteen respondents had attended the leavers' group, of whom ten had found this group beneficial or very beneficial. The leavers' group was usually described as a useful forum in which to exchange, express and share similar feelings with other residents who are coming up to leaving. Views of the welfare group were more mixed, and the expression of both positive and negative views was the norm. Criticisms, although not universal, tended to focus on the unstructured and resident-led nature of this group. Although respondents understood that this is congruent with the general ethos of therapeutic community treatment, many of them would have preferred a more didactic approach from staff running the group. Some respondents felt frustrated by the extra time and effort they perceived were added by staff's deliberately non-directive stance. For example:

> Welfare group was a good group. It was quite a painful group as well 'cos you know you are coming up to leaving, but I found the group very useful. It's very frustrating though, welfare, because sometimes whichever staff would be in there, they just wouldn't help and would get you to do it yourself... Even to get them to write a letter was like a battle and then the amount of time you would have to go through talking about why you wanted a letter written, it was like you could have moved on to something else. I think it had its positives and negatives... I can understand where they're coming from about needing to help

yourself and get the information yourself but it's going overboard when at least they could help you rather than just leave you with it. (Interviewee 8)

An issue raised by several respondents in relation to leaving Henderson is the disparity between the therapeutic community culture and that of other services and professionals. Whereas the therapeutic community encourages service users to take responsibility for ensuring that their needs are met, in other services users are expected to take a much more passive and dependent role.

> I think what makes it worse is the contrast between the way the Henderson tries to work and the way things work on the outside. That I found a major obstacle…it's very frustrating because it's like, you can feel the intentions are there most of the time, but it just doesn't match, it doesn't correspond with the way people work on the outside. So we've got a social worker in the welfare group whose main job is to enable myself and others to become our own social workers. When you leave, when you're in the leaving process, you become a client again, people want to speak to your social worker which again leaves you in a very peculiar situation which is frustrating for everyone… It does seem like the Henderson, when you leave, is this little glass house of idealistic thinking and you do need to bridge it a bit more effectively in my experience. (Interviewee 1)

Another aspect of leaving that many respondents found difficult is the contrast between the 24-hour structure of a residential therapeutic community and returning to independent living in which there may be little or no external structure and/or regular contact with others.

> I think there's like a really big gap, you know. Up until the time you go you still have groups and you still have your structure… You get home and when you wake up the next morning there's no 9.15 [community meeting], there's no people and the difference is just gigantic. There's no sort of intermediate…it's like from one extreme to another, which I think for any person in that situation, I think they'd find it incredibly difficult. (Interviewee 10)

EXPERIENCES SINCE LEAVING THE THERAPEUTIC COMMUNITY

The process of adapting to independent living in the months following discharge is also experienced as very difficult, with a commonly reported pattern being a sequence of 'highs and lows'. One respondent describes the period since leaving as a 'rollercoaster'. Immediately following discharge, positive feelings, optimism and excitement are common. However, these are soon replaced by more negative experiences. These typically consist of a combination of various difficulties including psychological problems (depression and anxiety); feelings of isolation, loneliness and lack of structure; a return to previous dysfunctional behaviour patterns; strained relationships with friends and family; and difficulties in managing practical issues associated with housing, social services or contact with mental health services. The following interview extract describes these patterns well:

> When I left I thought I'm going to be really upset and sad and all the rest, and my first couple of days I was. I was swearing at everyone on the day I left and then I was really upset and then, even before I got home, I was really happy. I was crying and I was happy and then for my first couple of days I was really quite high. It was excellent and I was thinking 'what's this problem of leaving, it's fine'. And then after that I started going down. And then I've had loads of going really, really low and then going a bit high and then going really low. (Interviewee 12)

A 'post-therapeutic community dip' appears to be the norm, and is reported in some form by all respondents at first interview. Respondents report having felt suicidal (n=3), having abused alcohol and/or drugs (n=3), feelings of depression (n=3), self-harming (n=2) and having had impulses to self-harm (n=2). One person had been admitted to a psychiatric inpatient facility for a short time since leaving. Practicalities, particularly around housing, and the fact that important others may not understand the therapeutic community experience, are sources of additional difficulty. Nevertheless, when asked how the period since leaving compared to how they were before admission, all respondents gave at least partially positive responses. While some thought they were clearly coping better or able to live a more normal life, others described this as an ongoing process. A common theme was slipping back into old patterns, but having more insight into feelings and behaviour patterns as a result of therapeutic community treatment. However, this is often experienced as a double-edged sword.

> It became very difficult: you tend to go into your old patterns, almost immediately. I did and started drinking too much, taking drugs again and just sort of went downhill. But what I think was different though, was that you could see what you were doing, you could sort of say, 'Oh, this is what I'm doing again, this is my old pattern'. So it...it gave me the strength to sort of look at it objectively and think, you know 'this is wrong, this is what I've done before, this is bad news'. I think it takes about three months really for you to get your head round some things and to put things in practice... You come out and all the people from your family and friends they don't know...can't understand what's gone on in there...they've got no idea. (Interviewee 9)

> Sometimes I think I'm coping worse because I'm more aware of how I'm feeling and before I didn't really have a clue, I was just not feeling anything. I do find it makes it worse. (Interviewee 8)

SERVICES NEEDS AND EXPERIENCES

The extract below illustrates a commonly expressed need for continuing support after therapeutic community treatment:

> I think that I need to continue what I started at the Henderson, 'cos there's no way that you can go through the whole of your life in one year, or the aspects of your life that you feel were the traumatic episodes that you need to move on from. I think you make a huge start on things at Henderson, but I do think that you're left in the air with lots of thoughts and feelings, and need a way of speaking to somebody where it's on a regular basis and not something that's intermittent or not supported. (Interviewee 2)

The nature and amount of support and treatment that respondents received from local mental health services appears to be very variable. At the time of the first interview (1–3 months after leaving the therapeutic community), all except two respondents had had some contact with other mental health services that included regular contact with one professional. The majority (n=10) had had contact with two or more mental health services or professionals. The most common professional contact was a community psychiatric nurse, or CPN (n=5) or a key worker (n=4), but regular contact with psychiatrists, clinical psychologists and psychotherapists was also reported. Other support services included activities and groups at a local resource centre or mental health day unit (n=5), and access to a 24-hour telephone crisis line (n=2). One person reported a comprehensive network of support that included attending a resource centre five times a week, seeing a psychologist weekly, a housing support worker and a 24-hour crisis line. These disparities may reflect both variations in ex-residents' support needs and geographical variations in local mental health services (and in particular their attitude to providing services for people with personality disorders).

Although respondents describe many of these facilities as useful or supportive, dissatisfaction is common. A common complaint is that community mental health services are too 'psychiatric' for ex-therapeutic community residents who do not share the problems of severe mental illness experienced by the majority of users of these services. Neither are local services able to provide the intensive psychotherapeutic forms of treatment that characterise therapeutic community treatment. Talking about her experiences of a mental health day centre, one responds commented:

> I feel a bit resentful that they're not like being at the Henderson... I get quite angry when I go to the art group because I can concentrate, I can motivate myself and I can focus on something. And the idea of those groups is that — that's the idea of the groups. But I can do that... I don't mix very well when I'm there because I don't want to get used to it, because I don't want to be pulled down by the type of people that go there. Now that sounds really disrespectful of those people but I am not on medication and these people are

heavily medicated... I think accessing the psychiatric services as minimally as possible is meeting my needs actually. (Interviewee 2)

In the first few months since discharge, 13 out of 15 respondents had had some contact with HOST, the newly established therapeutic community outpatient service. Against a background of other services that are experienced as less appropriate to their needs, ex-therapeutic community residents value this form of aftercare. There is shared understanding between them and HOST clinicians (whom they usually know from the therapeutic community) about their problems and the issues they have covered in therapeutic community treatment:

It's someone from the Henderson really, 'cos it's so different from any conventional psychiatric service, it's so special really. (Interviewee 7)

On the other hand, the sense that this post-discharge input from HOST is insufficient was common. This may reflect both a sense of loss of the therapeutic community culture and structure, and also the fact that at the time, limited resources enabled HOST to provide only intermittent support to Henderson leavers. Shaw (1999, p.162) points out that expressions of service satisfaction should be understood with respect to 'contextualised aspirations and expectations'. Therefore, interviewees were asked what, for them, would constitute an 'ideal world' in terms of post-residential therapeutic community service provision. Suggestions included more support with practical issues, for example in the transition to independent living, more appropriate housing provision, and a regular forum in which to meet and share experiences with other people who have recently left the therapeutic community.

Themes at second interview

Many of the themes that emerged from initial interviews were repeated in second interviews. In particular, the continuing nature of psychological and practical problems, and discrepancies between ex-therapeutic community residents' support needs and the style of services offered by local mental health facilities, remained constant themes. However, some new themes and variations were also detected.

Changes over time

Leaving the therapeutic community is experienced as a process that takes several months. Becoming aware of what you have learned during treatment, processing the therapeutic community experience (including exposure to the feelings and experiences of others), and developing a new equilibrium were generally experienced as long-term processes that could take several months.

It does take three, four, five months to see perhaps what you have learnt…
You're not just taking away your feelings when you leave the Henderson,
you're taking away so much of other people's stuff and it's…that's very difficult as well, trying to deal with it…all the things you've seen and it weighs
quite heavy on your mind sometimes. But yeah…you do, you know, you do
learn to cope a bit better and you do tend to see it more after six months. So it's
a difficult period the first six months. Just going in loopholes, you know, just
going up and down, up and down. And I think the more you try, I think the
more and more steady you get – hopefully, that's what I'm looking for: a more
consistent way of life. (Interviewee 9)

All nine of the people interviewed at Time 2 described the time since first
interview in both positive and negative terms. Similar to interviews at Time 1, a
series of 'ups and downs' was commonly reported. However, of those who were
able clearly to identify a change, only one respondent considered herself to be
worse than at the time of the first interview, compared to four people who
described general improvements in the previous six months. The gradual
building up of a structure to daily life and a network of resources were cited as
factors that helped in making these improvements. In addition, some respondents
had been able to resume activities that they had been too unwell to do since prior
to their admission to the therapeutic community. One person was attending
college, one was working part-time and a third was planning to start a college
course. As part of this sense of progression and separation, several respondents
talked about how their relationships with other ex-therapeutic community
residents had changed. Whereas this had been an important source of support in
the initial post-discharge period, some respondents felt a need to move on, or
found the need to provide continual support to others difficult:

Interviewer: How important is the ex-Henderson residents' community to you?

Interviewee 3: It was important, but it's becoming less and less so… It's okay
when you first leave to actually have a network of support, but I think the
longer you're out of there the more you want to put wedges between you and
dear old Henderson. Because it's very easy to get dragged down by somebody
that's down, who's having a bad time, decides they're going to take an
overdose or try to hang themselves and that. You just get tired of them. You get
tired of running around after people.

Despite reported improvements, severe psychological disturbance was still in
evidence at Time 2. Of the nine people interviewed, three had been admitted to
an inpatient psychiatric facility in the past six months (one three times), and a
further two reported at least one episode of self-harm and sporadic alcohol abuse.
Asked which specific areas of life they were finding most difficult at the time,
social interaction and personal relationships were the most commonly identified
areas (n=4). Other reported difficulties were loneliness, motivation, difficulties

with mental health professionals, and the slow pace of change. As at Time 1, housing continued to be a significant practical difficulty, with four respondents having moved house since the first interview. The following comment reveals a perceived unmet need, but also demonstrates how the leaving process can be problematic because it requires the therapeutic community culture to interface with its broader social environment:

> I do feel that there needs to be more help with housing. I mean it's all very well to empower people to look for housing but there comes a point, really, when professionals can pull more strings. So many people around you end up in unsuitable housing that I think there should be better liaison by the housing officer in the Henderson, just to find appropriate housing for people. Maybe even an affiliation with certain housing associations who are familiar with the way Henderson works and the needs of people from Henderson. (Interviewee 14)

Contact with services

Seven of the nine people interviewed at Time 2 were receiving aftercare support/treatment with HOST. In addition, of the six respondents who declined to be interviewed for a second time, clinical notes showed that all but two had some contact with this service. Experiences of this treatment provision (usually in the form of weekly group psychotherapy) were generally positive. Again continuities with the therapeutic community treatment programme, and being able to continue psychological work begun there were identified as beneficial aspects of this therapeutic community-linked service:

> I suppose it takes the edge off all that alienation that you have leaving Henderson and nobody having a clue where you're coming from. I don't just mean professionally – people don't have a clue. I mean personal life as well, you know your friends have no idea what you've been through, it's such a unique experience. I don't know, it's like being in a war or something [laughs]... Everybody I've spoken to has found it absolutely vital really, because it's very holding, but also that issues still come up. It's like opening a Pandora's box really, I think, going into therapy. You can't...go back into denial in the same way. And the reality is that you are more aware of your own dysfunction or of your own struggling or you need somewhere to go with that and it's very reassuring, I suppose to go to Outreach because you know they're already in that mode of thought... It's a continuation like I said – you learnt X at Henderson and you go outside and everybody else is offering you Y, and Outreach is the only place that is still offering you X. They're still sticking by the rules of being honest, exploring therapeutic relationships, sticking with difficult feelings. Trying to stay medication free in so much as you're not masking your feelings but rather trying to deal with them. Because that seems to be one of *the* major

differences in terms of other services that are offered. They still seem to be very much based on 'how can we take these feelings away from you'. You know like my GP is wanting to put me on antidepressants and stuff. (Interviewee 14)

Positive comments about the therapeutic community-linked service were interspersed with some more negative comments. These revolved primarily around difficulties of establishing trust in an outpatient group psychotherapy setting (n=2), and the fact that HOST treatment is usually limited to up to one year following discharge from the therapeutic community (n=2).

All nine respondents were in contact with other mental health services at Time 2, although again, variations in the amount and type of input were apparent. The profile of these services was similar to at Time 1 and typically included regular contact with an identified individual (key worker or CPN). All but one of the respondents attended some form of day centre for between one and five days a week, where they typically participated in at least one group activity and/or saw a key worker. Although many positive comments were made about these facilities in terms of the structure and contact with other people they provide, their inappropriateness to the treatment needs of ex-therapeutic community residents remained a common theme. Two respondents had dropped out of day centre facilities because they did not feel that their needs were being met.

Discussion and evaluation

Analysis of interview data suggests that people leaving residential therapeutic community treatment can find the transition to independent living extremely difficult and often experience serious psychological and practical difficulties in the following months. Ex-therapeutic community residents with a personality disorder diagnosis have multiple and long-term support needs that fluctuate over time. They are particularly vulnerable to relapse during the weeks following discharge, when their need for a structured and consistent form of support can be acute. Interviews highlight how continuities between the residential therapeutic community and its outpatient service are valued. In contrast, the different treatment ethos and client group of some community mental health services is experienced as inappropriate by many ex-therapeutic community residents.

As aids to evaluating the validity and generalisability of qualitative research, Elliott, Fischer and Rennie (1999) recommend 'situating the sample' and 'owning one's own perspective'. The findings reported here represent common themes expressed by a sample of 15 ex-residents of Henderson Hospital, a residential therapeutic community specialising in treatment for people with a diagnosis of personality disorder. These specific characteristics must be taken into account in judging the generalisability of findings to other therapeutic community contexts. In addition, because this study was conducted as part of an evaluation of a new therapeutic community-related outpatient service (HOST), it only considered a sub-sample of ex-therapeutic community residents, namely those discharged to the local area.[15] People whose normal place of residence is further afield may face other difficulties in leaving, including less contact with ex-therapeutic community peers, no access to the therapeutic community out-patient service, and local service providers who are less aware of the specific nature of therapeutic community treatment. People who stayed at the therapeutic community less than one month were also excluded. Again this group's experience of leaving may be very different. One might predict that such a short stay may be indicative of problems of attachment within the therapeutic community and so leaving, for them, may be characterised less by difficulties of detachment. This is an area in which future research might be beneficial, especially as less is known about clients who choose not to use services than about those who do (Morton 1995). Finally, it should be remembered that research participants are a self-selecting sample. In this study, participants stayed at the therapeutic community longer on average than non-participants. We could also speculate that participation may be motivated by a desire to please or to extend contact with the therapeutic community. Respondents may form a more idealised group of 'good residents' than those who chose not to participate in the study.

The particular social and interactive context in which data were collected and analysed may also shape the findings. One possible dynamic that may have coloured the interview interaction is that, despite attempts to clarify the differentiation between clinical and research agendas, respondents may be tempted to over-estimate their service needs to an interviewer known to be associated with service providers. Interviews were designed and analysed to provide findings relevant to the evaluation of a specific service, by a researcher who was professionally located as a member of the therapeutic community. Although the notion of research objectivity is inappropriate to qualitative research (Banister et al. 1994), it is important for the researcher to maintain reflexive awareness of these 'positioning' factors and provide a transparent account of them for the reader (Henwood and Pidgeon 1992).

Despite these inevitable caveats, there are many potential benefits to this kind of qualitative research. Research in which the perspective of service users is the central focus can provide useful information for service providers preparing residents for discharge from a therapeutic community. There has been very little qualitative research to date on service users' lives following therapeutic community treatment. Respondents' experiences of a clash of cultures and service ethos between the therapeutic community and other mental health services are relevant to attempts to improve the interface between therapeutic communities and other local services. The longitudinal design of this study has provided information not only on the immediate post-discharge period but also on more long-term needs and experiences. This is potentially useful to the development of therapeutic community aftercare services which, in this study, are valued by clients for providing continuity of therapeutic work. Such studies also serve to remind researchers and clinicians that therapeutic communities operate within a social milieu that poses particular challenges to clients moving between the therapeutic community and the 'outside' world. Many of the experiences reported by ex-therapeutic community residents highlight the relationship between internal, psychic realities and external, material realities, and remind us of the need to consider this interface in clinical work.

Stages Used in a CRD Systematic Review

Report Number 4 (CRD 1996) lays out a number of stages for the conducting of the review. Phase 0 (CRD 1996, pp.1–4) describes the identification and assessment of the need for a review and the process by which the work is assigned to the reviewers. This is to ensure that the review is relevant to the NHS and elsewhere (in this case the authors were not involved in this stage of the process, but it meant that there was not an extant relevant review, or one currently already in progress).

Phase 1 (CRD 1996, pp.5–10) and Phase 2 (CRD 1996, pp.13–16) describe the planning that should take place before the review is started. Phase 1 involves assessing the volume of literature, i.e. primary research in the field; through database searches and citations; assessing study designs used in the primary research, with preference given to RCTs, although acknowledging that in some circumstances, different study designs may be more appropriate; in some instances, assessing the effectiveness of a treatment policy which involves a sequence of interventions that cannot be evaluated in a single study using causal pathways; identification of the main issues, controversies and questions about effectiveness and the appropriate use of interventions to be addressed in the review; the identification of the relevant outcomes that should be measured to determine effectiveness; the identification of effect modifiers, such as the characteristics of the patients and settings, choice and measurement of outcomes, or differences in the nature or delivery of interventions, or study designs, which influence the estimates of effectiveness of the intervention under investigation; the identification of particular issues related to validity, such as the specific weaknesses of the studies in the area being reviewed, and the biases to which they may be susceptible; and, finally, the identification of issues related to generalisability.

Phase 2 outlines the role of the protocol, or 'pre-determined plan', which the research and review will follow; the identification of the main questions or hypotheses the review will investigate, and the criteria by which research studies will be selected for inclusion in the review; the elaboration of the search strategy for identifying the relevant research studies; the drawing-up of basic checklists which will be used to assess the validity of the primary studies to be included, and who will assess this; the drawing-up of the data extraction sheets that will be used; and the devising of a model for synthesising the studies appropriate to producing an overall estimate of effectiveness – this can be done either using statistical analysis, or as a narrative. Phase 2 also allows for modifying of the protocol, if necessary, and for the balancing of scientific validity and comprehensiveness with savings in time and resources. Alongside this, an advisory group of consultants is set up, including relevant experts and other potential users of the review, to help clarify the specific questions which the review should address, and to provide advice about the content of the report and its dissemination.

When these two phases are complete, the reviewers move on to the bulk of the work – Phases 3–7 – which cover the reviewing methods and working arrangements to be used, and are discussed in more detail below. Phases 8 (CRD 1996, pp.59–61) and 9 (CRD 1996, p.63) are concerned with the review report, and Phase 10 (CRD 1996, pp.65–70) involves issues concerning the dissemination of the review to the relevant audience, which is undertaken with the CRD dissemination team – these will not be discussed further here.

Phase 3 (CRD 1996, pp.19–25) concerns the literature search, which is one of the major parts of a systematic review and aims to provide as extensive and comprehensive a list as possible of primary studies, both published and unpublished. The precision of the estimate of effectiveness of the treatment being evaluated depends on the volume of information obtained, and its lack of publication bias. Phase 3 also involves implementing the methods outlined for achieving a comprehensive literature search. The literature search relies heavily on the use of a range of electronic database searches, covering a range of publications in different languages, and not just limited to medical publications. The search strategies devised for searching these databases have to balance high recall, or comprehensiveness, and high precision, so as to ensure that a search is relatively comprehensive but does not result in an unmanageable volume of inappropriate references being retrieved. Emphasis is placed on the importance of retrieving published RCTs. Other search strategies include scanning the reference lists of studies retrieved through database searches, to identify other studies that may be relevant for consideration for the literature review; hand-searching key journals in the field, to find articles which may have been missed through the database searches; trying to identify 'grey literature', that is, the results of research that may have been published in reports, conference proceedings, booklets, discussion papers or other formats which are not indexed on the main databases; consultation with leading researchers and practitioners, or other subject experts, in the field; and checking national research registers for ongoing studies, whose interim results may be included, if confirmation of the validity of the studies can be obtained.

Phase 4 (CRD 1996, pp.27–30) involves determining which of the studies identified in Phase 3 should be retrieved, and which of these should be included in the final review. These decisions are made based on pre-determined written inclusion and exclusion criteria (to avoid selection or reviewer bias), which are already included in the protocol, and which in turn are based on the relevance of the study to the research question, and on the study design, or methodology. The CRD states that the selection criteria usually define the health intervention or technology in which the review is interested; the setting and relevant patient or client groups; and the outcome measures used to assess effectiveness (CRD 1996, p.27). Other inclusion criteria specify the types of study design to be included in the final analysis of the effectiveness of the treatment under scrutiny, with RCTs again identified as the preferred design, but with a recognition that not all health care has been evaluated in this way. Again, there is a balance to be made between broad and narrow inclusion criteria, which affect the manageability or generalisability of the results of the review. However, the CRD states quite specifically that if the inclusion criteria are quite liberal, it may be possible to investigate the effects of differences in the study characteristics and other effect-modifiers, using meta-regression or other statistical methods (CRD 1996, p.28). The CRD recommends that all studies are assessed and discussed by more than one reviewer, and all decisions recorded, to reduce 'reviewer bias'. The final report should include tables detailing the studies included and excluded from the review.

Phase 5 (CRD 1996, pp.31–39) involves assessing the validity of the studies selected for the review, by grading studies into a hierarchy according to their design and the reliability, bias and strength of evidence of their results (see CRD 1996, p.33 for an example of a hierarchy of evidence); and decision-making about the extent to which the findings should be incorporated into the final analysis. Preference should be given to experimental rather than observational studies; studies using random allocation rather than pseudo-random allocation to treatment; concurrent cohort studies rather than 'historical' controls; prospective rather than retrospective studies; and before-and-after studies with control groups, rather than single group studies. Validity should be based on how well a study was designed, executed and analysed, in addition to the study design used – the CRD suggests using checklists to assess all aspects of study design and execution that may affect the validity of study results, which should be included in the protocol and form part of the data extraction sheets to be used to evaluate all studies considered for inclusion in the review (CRD 1996, p.34). A statement also needs to be made in the study design exclusion criteria about the weakest form of design that will be included in the review.

Phase 6 (CRD 1996, pp.41–43) involves the actual extraction of the data from the selected studies, which is necessary for the final analysis, and is to be done as accurately and in as unbiased a way as possible. To this end the CRD suggests the use of pre-designed and pre-tested data extraction sheets, which are to be included in the original protocol. The CRD suggests these sheets include the following – bibliographic details; descriptions of the setting; study population; details concerning the exact form and delivery of the intervention; the outcome measures that were used; the results; the numbers in each patient group; dropout rates; the study methodology; other factors affecting the validity of the results; and any other comments relevant to the inclusion of the study in the review. The CRD stresses the importance of extracting raw patient numbers for the results, to allow both absolute and relative effects to be calculated. Again, the CRD stresses the importance of data extraction being performed independently by at least two people, wherever possible.

Phase 7 (CRD 1996, pp.45–58) is the last stage of the review before the writing up of the final results. At this stage the results of the primary studies selected are drawn together and synthesised, to provide an estimate of the effect of the intervention and to investigate whether the effect is roughly the same in different studies, settings and participants and, if not, to investigate apparent differences in effectiveness results. This can be done in two ways. First, a broad qualitative, narrative overview can be provided, to assess the overall evidence and the influence of various factors on the likely effectiveness of the treatment or health care studied. More weight should be given to the larger and higher quality studies than the smaller and lower quality ones. Second, by using formal statistical meta-analysis techniques, which can be classified as 'fixed effect' or 'random effects models', it may be possible to produce a quantitative estimate of effect and effect modifiers, if the review has retrieved sufficient, good-quality and fairly homogeneous studies (in terms of patients studied, intervention delivery and outcome measures). The standard approach to this has been to use summary odds ratios, and to display the overall effect together with the results of all the single studies in a graphical display (see CRD 1996, p.49, Fig.7.1). Sources of bias are investigated using 'meta-regression' to find out what the sources of variation or 'heterogeneity' between the constituent studies are, including the investigation of possible publication bias whereby only positive findings have been published.

The 29 Studies Included
in the Meta-Analysis

a1 Angliker, C.C.J., Cormier, B.M., Boulanger, P. and Malamud, B. (1973) 'A therapeutic community for persistent offenders: An evaluation and follow-up study on the first fifty cases.' *Canadian Psychiatric Association Journal 18*, 289–95.

a13 Marshall, P. (1997) 'A reconviction study of HMP Grendon therapeutic community.' *Research Findings No 53*. London: Home Office Research and Statistics Directorate.

a15 Newton, M. (1971) 'Reconviction after treatment at Grendon.' *CP Report Series B, Number 1*. London: Home Office.

a18 Rehn, G. (1979) 'Rückfall nach Sozialtherapie. Vergleichende Untersuchung aus drei Hamburger Justizvollzugsanstalten.' *Monatsschrift für Kriminologie und Strafrechtsreform 62*, 357–65.

a19 Rice, M.E., Harris, G.T. and Cormier, C.A. (1992) 'An evaluation of a maximum security therapeutic community for psychopaths and other mentally disordered offenders.' *Law and Criminal Behaviour 16*, 399–412.

a2 Auerbach, A.W. (1977) 'The Role of the Therapeutic Community "Street Prison" in the Rehabilitation of Youthful Offenders.' PhD dissertation. USA: George Washington University.

a21 Sewell, R. and Clark, C. (1982) 'An Evaluation Study of "the Annexe", a Therapeutic Community in Wormwood Scrubs Prison.' Unpublished report. London: Home Office Prison Department.

a47 Van Emmerik, J. (1987) 'Recidivism among mentally disordered offenders detained at the government's pleasure (tbr). A report of a follow-up study of patients discharged between 1974 and 1979.' In M.J.M. Brand-Koolen (ed.) *Studies on the Dutch Prison System*. Amstelveen: Kugler.

a54 McCord, W. and Sanchez, J. (1983) 'The treatment of deviant children: A twenty-five year follow-up study.' *Crime and Delinquency 29*, 238–53.

a58a Paddock III, A.L. and Scott, R.J. (1973) 'Evaluation of the Incremental Effectiveness of the Asklepieion Community on Post-incarceration Adjustment of Convicted Felons.' Unpublished report. Bakersfield: California State College.

a64 Gunn, J., Robertson, G., Dell, S. and Way, C. (1978) *Psychiatric Aspects of Imprisonment*. London: Academic Press.

a68 McMichael, P. (1974) 'After-care, family relationships and reconviction in a Scottish approved school.' *British Journal of Criminology 14*, 236–47.

a76 Cornish, D.B., Clarke, R.V.G. (1975) 'Residential treatment and its effects on delinquency.' *Home Office Research Studies 32.* London: HMSO.

a79 Hodges, E.F. (1971) 'Crime prevention by the indeterminate sentence law.' *American Journal of Psychiatry 128,* 291–95.

b12 Dolan, B., Evans, C. and Wilson, J. (1992) 'Therapeutic community treatment for personality disordered adults: Changes in neurotic symptomatology on follow-up.' *International Journal of Social Psychiatry 38,* 243–50.

b14 Dolan, B., Warren, F. and Norton, K. (1997) 'Change in borderline symptoms one year after therapeutic community treatment for severe personality disorder.' *British Journal of Psychiatry 171,* 274–79.

b20 Lehman, A. and Ritzler, B. (1976) 'The therapeutic community inpatient ward: Does it really work?' *Comprehensive Psychiatry 17,* 755–61.

b30 Rapoport, R.N. (1960) *Community as Doctor. New Perspectives on a Therapeutic Community.* London: Tavistock Publications.

b5 Copas, J.B., O'Brien, M., Roberts, J. and Whiteley, J.S. (1984) 'Treatment outcome in personality disorder; the effect of social, psychological and behavioural variables.' *Personality and Individual Differences 5,* 565–73.

b62 Tucker, L., Bauer, S., Wagner, S., Harlam, D. and Sher, I. (1987) 'Long-term hospital treatment of borderline patients: A descriptive outcome study.' *American Journal of Psychiatry 144,* 1443–48.

b7 Craft, M., Stephenson, G. and Granger, C. (1964) 'A controlled trial of authoritarian and self-governing regimes with adolescent psychopaths.' *American Journal of Orthopsychiatry 34,* 543–54.

e10 Martin, S.S., Butzin, C.A. and Inciardi, J.A. (1995) 'Assessment of a multistage therapeutic community for drug-Involved offenders.' *Journal of Psychoactive Drugs 27,* 109–16.

e11b Nielsen, A.L., Scarpitti, F.R. and Inciardi, J.A. (1996) 'Integrating the therapeutic community and work release for drug-involved offenders. The CREST program.' *Journal of Substance Abuse Treatment 13,* 349–58.

e18 Wexler, H.K., Falkin, G.P., Lipton, D.S. and Rosenblum, A.B. (1992) 'Outcome evaluation of a prison therapeutic community for substance abuse treatment.' *NIDA Research Monograph,* Issue 118. Washington: National Institute on Drug Abuse, 156–75.

e25 Graham, W.F. and Wexler, H.K. (1997) 'The Amity therapeutic community program at Donovan Prison: Program description and approach.' In De Leon, G. (ed.) *Community as Method. Therapeutic Communities for Special Populations and Special Settings.* Westport: Praeger.

e26 Lockwood, D., Inciardi, J.A., Butzin, C.A. and Hooper, R.M. (1997) 'The therapeutic community continuum in corrections.' In De Leon, G. (ed.) *Community as Method. Therapeutic Communities for Special Populations and Special Settings.* Westport: Praeger.

e28 US Bureau of Prisons, *Triad Drug Treatment Evaluation. Six-Month Report. Executive Summary.* http://www.bop.gov/orepg/oretriad6.pdf. Accessed 13 April 1998.

e6 Inciardi, J.A., Martin, S.S., Butzin, C.A., Hooper, R.M. and Harrison, L.D. (1997) 'An effective model of prison-based treatment for drug-involved offenders.' *Journal of Drug Issues 27*, 261–78.

e8 Knight, K., Simpson, D.D., Chatham, L.R. and Camacho, L.M. (1997) 'An assessment of prison-based drug treatment: Texas' in-prison therapeutic community program.' *Journal of Offender Rehabilitation 24*, 75–100.

Additional Sources of Information on Research Governance

This appendix states sources for standards in the conduct of research relating to ethics, including those relating to the use of patient and client information and research ethics committees.

General

The Human Rights Act 1998, *www.hmso.gov.uk/acts/acts1998/19980042.htm* The scope of the Act covers the articles included in the European Convention: the right to life; freedom from torture or inhuman or degrading treatment; freedom from slavery; liberty of person; right to a fair trial; prohibition against retrospective offences; right to respect for private and family life; freedom of thought, conscience and religion; freedom of expression; freedom of assembly and association; right to marry and found a family; these rights to be enjoyed without discrimination on any ground; derogation in time of war or public emergency.

Patient information

The Data Protection Act 1998 provides protection for personal data. This includes information, which by itself or in conjunction with other easily obtainable information, can identify a specific person.

Report on the Review of Patient-Identifiable Information. The Caldicott Committee/Department of Health, 1997.

For the Record: Managing Records in NHS Trusts and Health Authorities Health Service. Circular HSC 1999/053, March 1999.

The Protection and Use of Patient Information. Department of Health, 1996.

Using Confidential Patient Information in the Modern NHS. Caldicott Report and Related Guidance, 1997/98/99. *www.doh.gov.uk*

Local research ethics committees (LRECs)

Local Research Ethics Committees HSG(91)5.

Standards for Local Research Ethics Committees: A Framework for Ethical Review. NHS Training Division, 1994.

Standard Operating Procedures for Local Research Ethics Committees Comments and Examples. Christine Bendall McKenna and Co, April 1994.

Briefing pack for research ethics committee members, 1997.

Multi-centre research ethics committees (MRECs)

Ethics Committee Review of Multi-centre Research Establishment of Multi-centre Research Ethics Committees HSG(97)23.

Copies of these documents for LRECs and MRECs can be obtained from the Central Office for Research Ethics Committees (COREC) – see address below.

All relevant current regulations and references concerning policy for, and operation of, RECs will be available shortly on the Research Ethics Committees Website, currently under construction: *www.doh.gov.uk/research/recs*

Contacting research ethics committees

Addresses for MRECs and LRECs throughout the UK can be obtained from the REC Website and the Central Office for Research Ethics Committees: COREC, Room 75–77, 'B' Block, 40 Eastbourne Terrace, London W2 3QR, tel: 020 7725 3463, fax: 020 7725 3465.

MREC application forms, guidance for researchers and dates of meetings can be obtained from COREC or found on the REC Website: *www.doh.gov.uk/research/recs*

LREC application forms, local guidelines and dates of meetings are available from the administrators of each local committee.

Operational Guidelines for Ethics Committees – Committees that Review Bio-medical Research. Geneva: WHO 2000.

Personal information in medical research

www.mrc.ac.uk This guide to *Ethics and Best Practice*, together with other MRC ethics guides, is available on this Website.

Royal College of Physicians Guidelines on the Practice of Ethical Committees in Medical Research Involving Human Subjects, 3rd edition, August 1997. *publications@rcplondon.ac.uk*

Royal College of Paediatrics and Child Health Guidelines for the Ethical Conduct of Medical Research Involving Children Prepared by the Ethics Advisory Committee – August 1992. Archives of Diseases in Childhood 2000, 82: 177–82. *www.rcpch.ac.uk*

Royal College of Nursing *www.rcn.org.uk/library/library.htm* provides research ethics guidance for nurses involved in research or any investigative project involving human subjects.

Public Health Laboratory Service *www.phls.co.uk/advice/index.htm* This Website outlines the procedure for obtaining approval of PHLS Ethics Committee Involving Human Subjects.

World Health Organisation Operational Guidelines for Ethics Committees that Review Biomedical Research, 2000. *www.who.int/tdr/publications/publications/pdf/ethics.pdf*

Guidance relevant to ethics committees

Aspects of particular studies may give rise to ethical issues; researchers and ethics committees may wish to consult relevant guidance.

Consent

Consent to Treatment: Summary of Legal Rulings, HSC 1999/031.

The Department of Health's reference guide to consent for examination or treatment, 2001. *www.doh.gov.uk/consent*

General Medical Council: *Seeking Patients' Consent: The Ethical Considerations,* 1998. *www.gmc-uk.org/n_hance/good.consent.htm*

Notes

1. Various terms have been used historically, contrasting the two variants of contemporary therapeutic communities, such as democratic/autocratic; psychiatric/addiction, the programmatic ('Jones') or concept therapeutic community. These terms reflected differences in the origins as well as in the assumptions, conceptions or target populations of the treatment approach. Today, the term 'therapeutic community' more aptly embraces a coherent approach spanning different adaptations and modifications of the therapeutic community in the USA. While the qualified term 'addiction therapeutic community' emphasises the primary, target behavioural disorder, broader applications of the therapeutic community in the USA have justified further distinctions between the terms 'generic therapeutic community' and 'modified therapeutic community'.

2. The development of this manuscript was supported by the Department of Veterans Affairs Health Services Research and Development Service and by the United States National Institute on Alcohol Abuse and Alcoholism Grant AA12718.

3. 'Scientific' research approaches warn against the researcher becoming actively involved in the activity he/she is researching, because there is a fear that this will contaminate the subject matter and change things. However, this view is generally held only by positivist researchers, whose view of social research is based largely on the scientist's view of physical research. (Indeed even physical scientists now incline more and more to the view that the mere process of observation changes the things being observed.) Interpretive researchers incline to the view that, since the presence of a researcher will change things anyway, in incalculable ways, it is better for the researcher to become a competent member of the organisation he/she is studying, and use this competence to understand and explain the data collected. Moreover, it is unusual for a researcher to be exactly describing what 'actually happened' on any one occasion. The qualitative researcher is much more likely to gather various items of information together which exemplify interactional processes, and an active understanding of these processes is seen as more valuable than an accurate description of an 'uncontaminated' activity.

4. As Manning points out, it is ironic that a book which 'gained such insight from the use of the anthropologist's detached and critical perspective, has become in many ways the bible for this charismatic "faith"' (Manning 1997, p.79).

5. During a recent piece of literature research, I visited a number of democratic therapeutic communities in prisons. I soon discovered that a constant topic of ordinary staff conversation revolved around the difficulty of maintaining real democratic therapeutic community practice inside the authoritarian prison setting. I took

notes of these conversations and wrote a paper, which set out the arguments I had collected (Rawlings 1998). I did not attempt to address the problem, but simply to lay out the range of concerns, because it seemed to me that this was a good way of sorting out my own understandings. I also thought that it was a tremendously important subject, both from the point of view of prison organisation and from the point of view of the sociological understanding of conflicting cultures, and that people from both the world of prison therapeutic communities and the world of social theory would have an interest in this very focused contribution to their thinking.

6.   The term 'reflexivity' is a keyword in the language of sociology and our use of it needs an explanatory note here. We have used the term 'reflexive' throughout this chapter to mean something like 'ongoing self-reflection', a process that seems to us to characterise therapeutic communities as organisations. We think it also useful to point to the similarities between the processes of gaining knowledge used in the therapeutic community and in the pursuit of sociological research. The therapeutic community setting, as it uses an iterative process of discussion and observation in the groups and community life to build views of an individual, can be seen to enact this more complex sociological research process. (For a thorough discussion of reflexivity, see Woolgar 1988.)

7.   As Henderson Hospital is a residential therapeutic community, the term 'residents' is used in preference to the term 'patients', which implies passivity in the therapeutic process or relationship. We will use the terms 'client' and 'resident' interchangeably in this chapter even though we recognise that many therapeutic communities are not residential.

8.   Exceptions to this include researchers who reject the positivist paradigm completely, and subscribe to alternative paradigms such as 'strong' versions of social constructionism in which realism and the very notion of 'objectivity' are rejected. Without wishing to enter into philosophical debate about the validity of these different paradigms, we simply note that the scientific paradigm remains dominant in mental health research and provides the criteria against which most research is judged.

9.   The Association of Therapeutic Communities (ATC) is an international organisation, which exists to 'further the implementation of the therapeutic community approach and ideology in the psychiatric hospital and social services for the psychiatric patient and also in the appropriate related fields' (Directory of Therapeutic Communities 1995).

10.   At Grendon Underwood prison, prison officers act as facilitators in small group therapy sessions.

11.   In Rome's Communità Raymond Gledhill, the study was explained to the community by the medical director.

12.   This type of analysis was used as length-of-stay information was gathered using a categorical format.

13.   There were no significant differences between these groups in their criminal and demographic histories, or in relation to the reasons they offered for coming to

Grendon. Given their similar profiles and their exposure to the same therapeutic programmes and penal regime, the assumption was made that if a staged therapeutic process existed the response of any one of these groups at a particular point in time could be expected to be representative of the responses of the other two groups at the same moment in history. For example, it was anticipated that the responses of inmates who had been at Grendon for less than six months would broadly reflect those of inmates in the other two categories, had these men been asked the same question within the first six months of their therapy.

14. At Henderson Hospital, residents are encouraged to take responsibility for their own discharge and plan for this up to three months in advance. An unplanned discharge can occur when a resident decides to leave without giving notice, or when the community asks the person to leave. The latter usually occurs because the person has broken a community rule and/or is deemed to be unwilling to engage in therapy and community life.

15. Henderson Hospital is a tertiary-level service within the NHS and, at the time, took referrals from all of England and Wales.

Contributors

Sarah Birch is a Clinical Psychologist working for East Sussex County Healthcare NHS Trust in working age adult mental health. Before training she worked at Henderson Hospital as a researcher where she carried out the research described in her chapter in this book. She is interested in qualitative research, gender issues and all aspects of adult mental health.

Marco Chiesa, MD MRCPsych is Consultant Psychiatrist in Psychotherapy, Head of the Research Unit and of the Adult Outreach Personality Disorder Programme at Cassel Hospital, Richmond. He is Honorary Senior Lecturer at University College London and a full member of the British Psychoanalytical Society. He works part time in the NHS and runs a psychoanalytic private practice in East Sheen. He has published several articles and book chapters on borderline psychopathology, outcome research and treatment of personality disorder.

Steffan Davies is a Senior Lecturer in Forensic Psychiatry in the Division of Mental Health, University of Leicester, and Honorary Consultant Forensic Psychiatrist at Rampton High Security Hospital, Nottinghamshire Healthcare Trust. His research interests are in long-term outcomes and various forms of psychiatric treatment, health services research including economic evaluations and therapeutic environments. He has an MBA from the University of Nottingham. His clinical work is based in the Cedars Community Unit using the therapeutic community approach for patients with treatment resistant psychotic illnesses at Rampton Hospital. His other therapeutic community experience was at Francis Dixon Lodge, Leicester in the late 1990s where he began the research that contributes to this chapter.

George De Leon, PhD (Columbia) is an internationally recognized expert in the treatment of substance abuse, and acknowledged as the leading authority on treatment and research in therapeutic communities for addictions. He is the founder and Director of the Center for Therapeutic Community Research, established by a National Institute on Drug Abuse (NIDA) funded grant to the National Development and Research Institutes. He is a Clinical Professor of Psychiatry at New York University, and has published over 150 scientific papers and chapters on substance abuse, and has authored and edited four published volumes and three NIDA research monographs. He has served as special guest editor and contributing editor to several journals, including the *American Journal of Drug and Alcohol Abuse, Substance Use and Abuse, Substance Abuse*, and the *American Psychological Association Journal of Psychotherapy*. He remains active in training and programme development both nationally and internationally, and has maintained a private clinical practice in New York City for over 35 years.

Fiona Dunstan is a Chartered Counselling Psychologist who works full time in Community Forensic and Personality Disorder Services as well as doing sessional work in psychotherapy. She is employed by NW Surrey Mental Health Partnership NHS Trust. She obtained her PsychD at the University of Surrey and her research interests include social representations of personality and personality disorder, and newspaper constructions of so called 'dangerous psychopathologies'. She is currently involved in a dialectical behaviour therapy project for individuals with borderline personality difficulties, as both a group trainer and as an individual psychotherapist.

Susan Eley is a Lecturer in the Sociology, Social Policy and Criminology Section of the Department of Applied Social Science at the University of Stirling, having worked previously as a research fellow at the University of Glasgow and at the MRC Medical Sociology Unit. She is a sociologist (BA Econ Manchester, MSc Stirling, PhDMedSci Glasgow) whose current research interests include policy responses to drug users, drug use and the criminal justice system and service delivery in health and social care.

Peter Fonagy, PhD FBA is Freud Memorial Professor of Psychoanalysis and Director of the Sub-Department of Clinical Health Psychology at University College London. He is Chief Executive of the Anna Freud Centre, London. He is a clinical psychologist and a training and supervising analyst in the British Psycho-Analytical Society in child and adult analysis. His work attempts to integrate empirical research with psychoanalytic theory. He is Chairman of the Research Committee of the International Psychoanalytic Association, and a Fellow of the British Academy. He has published over 200 chapters and articles and has authored or edited several books.

Elaine Genders is Reader in Criminology at UCL. From 1997 to 2001 she was advisor to the Home Office (Prison Service Contracts and Competitions Group) on the therapeutic community element of the DCMF project for HMP Dovegate. Currently she serves as the Home Office elected independent representative on the Dovegate Therapeutic Community Committee. She is co-author (together with Elaine Player) of *Grendon: A Study of a Therapeutic Prison* and has published articles relating to the privatised mode of genesis and operation of the therapeutic community initiative at Dovegate in Punishment and Society and in the Howard Journal.

Jeremy Holmes, MD FRCPsych is Consultant Psychiatrist/Psychotherapist with North Devon Healthcare Trust and Honorary Senior Lecturer at Exeter University. He held senior positions within the Royal College of Psychiatrists and more recently he was Chairman of the Psychotherapy Faculty. His interests include personality disorder, attachment theory and the application of psychodynamic concepts to general psychiatry. He has published over 90 articles and book chapters and authored and co-edited several books.

Sigmund Karterud, MD, PhD, is Medical Director of the Department for Personality Psychiatry, Psychiatric Division, Ullevål University Hospital, Professor of Psychiatry at the University of Oslo, and training group analyst at the Institute of Group Analysis, Oslo. His doctoral dissertation concerned 'Group processes in therapeutic communities'. He is Chairman of the Board for the Norwegian Network of Psychotherapeutic Day Hospitals. He has published books on self psychology, group analysis, personality disorders and group therapies, and *Mysteries of the Self* (on Knut Hamsun's novel *Mysteries*).

Jan Lees has been a Research Associate at Francis Dixon Lodge Therapeutic Community, Leicester, UK, for the last seven years. She is also Principal Investigator on a national comparative research project, evaluating the effectiveness of 21 therapeutic communities in England and Scotland for people with personality disorders, on behalf of the Association of Therapeutic Communities, and the University of Nottingham. Publications include *Therapeutic Community Effectiveness* (with N. Manning and B. Rawlings, Centre for Reviews and Dissemination, 1999); a checklist of standards for democratic therapeutic communities (with D. Kennard, in *Therapeutic Communities*, 2001, 22, 2).

Nick Manning is Professor of Social Policy and Sociology at the University of Nottingham, UK, and Head of Research and University Liaison for the Nottinghamshire Healthcare NHS Trust. He has been involved in research on therapeutic communities for 30 years. He has published many papers and chapters, and more than 20 books including *Therapeutic Communities, Reflections and Progress* (with R.D. Hinshelwood, Routledge, 1979); *The Therapeutic Community Movement, Charisma and Routinization* (Routledge, 1989).

Frank Margison, MD, MSc, FRCPsych has been consultant psychiatrist in Gaskell Psychotherapy Centre in Manchester since 1983. He is also Medical Director of Manchester Mental Health and Social Care Trust. His research has focused on the development, teaching and evaluation of the Conversational Model of Psychotherapy. He was the Vice President of the Society for Psychotherapy Research (UK) and has been actively involved through SPR in developing Practice Research Networks.

Diana Menzies, BSc, MBBS, MRCPsych is Consultant Psychiatrist in Psychotherapy and Team Leader with Henderson Outreach Service Team and member of the Institute of Group Analysis (London). Her interest in therapeutic communities and associated research began when she worked as a psychiatry trainee at Henderson Hospital where she did a cost offset evaluation in the face of impending closure. More recent publications have been on reasons for premature leaving and the place of hope in therapy. She has also worked at Winterbourne therapeutic community.

Rudolf H. Moos earned his PhD in Psychology at the University of California at Berkeley in 1960, after which he took a Postdoctoral Fellowship in Biobehavioral Sciences at the University of California School of Medicine in San Francisco. He directed the Center for Health Care Evaluation at Stanford University and the Department of Veterans Affairs from 1964 until 2002. He is currently Senior Research Career Scientist at the Department of Veterans Affairs Health Care System, and Professor in the Department of Psychiatry and Behavioral Sciences at Stanford University in Palo Alto, California, USA. He has a long-standing interest in the development of indices of the quality of mental health treatment and in specifying their relationship to treatment outcome, and in examining the role of life context and coping factors and their interactions with treatment in the prediction of long-term adaptation.

Nicola Morant, PhD MSc is a Senior Lecturer in Social Psychology at Anglia Polytechnic University in Cambridge. Prior to this she was a Research Psychologist at Henderson Hospital, working principally on evaluating the associated Outreach Service. Her research interests broadly span social psychology and mental health issues. She has recently been involved in a number of projects using qualitative methods in mental health research. These have included work on the experiences of people leaving therapeutic communities, collaborative research with service users with a personality disorder diagnosis, the burden of care experienced by informal carers, evaluation of an innovative women's crisis centre, and patients' and relatives' experiences of schizophrenia and of a first episode of psychosis.

Kingsley Norton is Director at Henderson Hospital and Reader in Psychotherapy at St. George's Hospital Medical School. He is a Jungian analyst and has written on a range of topics, especially in the field of Personality Disorder and Therapeutic Community treatment. His main research interest is in the evaluation of treatment for PD. He is involved in the development of training for staff working with PD and is co-author of three books dealing with the treatment of PD in primary and secondary care levels, and in the medical profession in general.

Geir Pedersen, MA, is daily leader, programme designer and researcher in the Norwegian Network of Psychotherapeutic Day Hospitals. He has designed the data system and graphic output for the Network, and his main interest is psychometrics of clinical tests, in particular their relevance for personality assessment.

Elaine Player is Reader in Criminology and Criminal Justice at the School of Law, King's College London. Her research interests include therapeutic interventions in prisons and her recent publications include an evaluation of the effectiveness of the RAPt drug treatment programme Drug Treatment in Prison (with C. Martin) Waterside Press (2000). Currently she is working in the area of women and the criminal justice system and she co-authored the Wedderburn Report on the imprisonment of women, Prison Reform Trust (2000). She acted as a consultant to Premier Prisons in the initial design of Dovegate prison therapeutic community. She is a member of the research advisory group for HMP Grendon and for HMP Dovegate TC.

Barbara Rawlings is a freelance researcher, an Honorary Fellow in the Department of Sociology at the University of Manchester and a part-time tutor in research methods in the Art and Design Post-Graduate Centre at Manchester Metropolitan University. She has carried out qualitative research in a range of social care organisations, including several democratic therapeutic communities. She is a member of the Editorial Group of the ATC journal *Therapeutic Communities*, sits on the Advisory Committee of the Gartree Therapeutic Community at Gartree Prison and is a member of the Correctional Services Accreditation Panel, which works to accredit therapeutic treatments in the prisons and in the Probation Service

Øyvind Urnes, MD, is medical director of the Personality outpatient clinic, Department for Personality Psychiatry. He is a trained group analyst, and a teacher at the Institute of Group Analysis, Oslo. His current research interest is attachment types (according to the system of Pat Crittenden), and personality disorders.

Fiona Warren is based at St. George's Hospital Medical School and has worked with Henderson Hospital since 1994 on studies of outcomes and treatment process. Her research interests include the psychology of behaviours that can be viewed as harmful to the self, and the meaningful measurement of outcomes of treatment for people labelled with personality disorder.

Jane Wilson is a freelance addictions trainer based in Edinburgh. She was formerly a Research Fellow at the Scottish Drugs Training Project, University of Stirling. She has previously worked as a senior counsellor at Marin ACT (Addiction Counselling Treatment) in California, and as a Community Psychologist at the Muirhouse/Pilton Drug Project in Edinburgh. She has published a number of papers on women and HIV/AIDS; dual diagnosis; and substance abuse and therapeutic communities.

Rowdy Yates is a Senior Research Fellow (Scottish Addiction Studies) in the Department of Applied Social Science, University of Stirling. He has worked in the drugs field for more than thirty years and in 1994 was awarded the Order of Member of the British Empire (MBE) for services to the prevention of drug misuse. He is president of EWODOR (the European Working Group on Drugs Oriented Research) and Vice-President (Teaching and Research) of the EFTC (European Federation of Therapeutic Communities).

References

Alden, L.E., Wiggins, J.S. and Pincus, A.L. (1990) 'Construction of Circumplex Scales for the Inventory of Interpersonal Problems.' *Journal of Personality Assessment 55*, 521–36.

Almond, R.H. (1974) *The Healing Community*. Northvale, NJ: Jason Aronson.

American Psychiatric Association (1994) 'Global Assessment of Functioning (GAF) Scale.' In APA (ed.) *Diagnostic and Statistical Manual of Mental Disorders, Fourth Edition*. Washington, DC: American Psychiatric Association.

Anglin, M.D. and Hser, Y.I. (1990) 'Treatment of drug abuse.' In M. Tonry and J.Q. Wilson (eds) *Crime and Justice: An Annual Review of Research, Vol. 13*. Chicago: University of Chicago Press.

Appelbaum, A.H. and Munich, R.L. (1986) 'Reinventing moral treatment: The effects upon patients and staff members of a program of psychosocial rehabilitation.' *The Psychiatric Hospital 17*, 11–19.

Armstrong, D., Calnan, M. and Grace, J. (1990) *Research Methods for General Practitioners*. Oxford General Practice Series 16. Oxford: Oxford University Press.

Arnkoff, D.B., Glass, C.R., Elkin, I., Levy, J.A. and Gershefski, J.J. (1996) 'Quantitative and qualitative research can complement each other: Reply to Rennie.' *Psychotherapy Research 6*, 4, 269–76.

Artus, H.M. (1996) 'Science indicators derived from databases.' *Scientometrics 37*, 297–311.

Association of Therapeutic Communities (1995) *Directory of Therapeutic Communities*. London: Association of Therapeutic Communities.

Association of Therapeutic Communities (1999) *A Comparative Evaluation of Therapeutic Community Effectiveness for People with Personality Disorders*. At: www.therapeutic communities.org/lottery-protocol.htm

Audin, K., Mellor-Clark, J., Barkham, M., Margison, F., McGrath, G., Lewis, S., Cann, L., Duffy, J. and Parry, G. (2001) 'Practice research networks for effective psychological therapies.' *Journal of Mental Health 10*, 241–51.

Aveline, M. (2001) 'Editorial: Innovative contemporary psychotherapies.' *Advances in Psychiatric Treatment 7*, 241–42.

Bailey, C.A. (1996) *A Guide To Field Research*. Thousand Oaks, CA: Pine Forge Press.

Banister, P., Burman, E., Parker, I., Taylor, M. and Tindall, C. (1994) *Qualitative Methods in Psychology: A Research Guide*. Buckingham: Open University Press.

Barkham, M., Margison, F., Leach, C., Lucock, M., Mellor-Clark, J., Evans, C., Benson, L., Connell, J., Audin, K., and McGrath, G. (2001) 'Profile and outcomes benchmarking using the CORE-OM: Towards practice-based evidence in the psychological therapies.' *Journal of Consulting and Clinical Psychology 69*, 184–96.

Barnes, E. (ed.) (1968) *Psychosocial Nursing*. London: Tavistock Publications.

Baron, C. (1987) *Asylum to Anarchy*. London: Free Association Books.

Bateman, A. (1999) 'Effectiveness of partial hospitalisation in the treatment of borderline personality disorder: A randomised controlled trial.' *American Journal of Psychiatry 156*, 10, 1563–69.

Bateman, A. and Fonagy, P. (2000) 'Effectiveness of psychotherapeutic treatment of personality disorder.' *British Journal of Psychiatry 177*, 138–43.

Beecham, J. and Knapp, M. (1992) 'Costing psychiatric interventions.' In G. Thornicroft, C. Brewin and J. Wing (eds) *Measuring Mental Health.* London: Gaskell.

Beethforth, A., Conlan, E. and Graley, R. (1994) *Have We Got Views for You: Users' Evaluation of Case Management.* London: The Sainsbury Centre for Mental Health.

Bell, J. (1993) *Doing Your Research Project.* Second edition. Buckingham: Open University Press.

Bell, M. (1983) 'The perceived social environment of a therapeutic community for drug abusers.' *International Journal of Therapeutic Communities 4*, 262–70.

Bender, D. and Blau, A. (1937) 'The reactions of children to sexual relations with adults.' *American Journal of Orthopsychiatry 7*, 500–18.

Bennett, D., and Parry, G. (1998) 'The accuracy of reformulation in cognitive analytic therapy.' *Psychotherapy Research 8*, 84–103.

Bernstein, D.P., Ahluvalia, T., Pogge, D. and Handelsman, L. (1997) 'Validity of the Childhood Trauma Questionnaire in an adolescent psychiatric population.' *Journal of the American Academy of Child and Adolescent Psychiatry 36* (3), 340–48.

Bernstein, D., Fink, L., Handelsman, L., Foote, J., Lovejoy, M., Wenzel, K., Sapareto, E. and Ruggiero, J. (1994) 'Initial reliability and validity of a new retrospective measure of child abuse and neglect.' *American Journal of Psychiatry 151*, 8, 1132–36.

Biase, D.V., Sullivan, A.P. and Wheeler, B. (1986) 'Daytop Miniversity-Phase 2 college training in a therapeutic community: Development of self-concept among drug free addict/abusers.' In G. De Leon and J.T. Ziegenfuss (eds) *Therapeutic Communities for Addictions.* Springfield, IL: Charles C. Thomas.

Bion, W.R. (1960) *Experiences in Groups.* London: Tavistock Publications.

Birch, S., Dunstan, F. and Warren, F. (1999) 'Democratisation, reality confrontation, permissiveness and communalism. Themes or anachronisms? An examination of therapeutic agents using factor analysis.' *Therapeutic Communities 20*, 1, 43–61.

Black, T. (1999) 'Sound and fury: Grief and despair in the large group.' In P. Campling and R. Haigh (eds) *Therapeutic Communities: Past, Present and Future.* London: Jessica Kingsley Publishers.

Bloch, S., Reibstein, J., Crouch, E., Holroyd, P. and Themen, J. (1979) 'A method for the study of therapeutic factors in group psychotherapy.' *British Journal of Psychiatry 134*, 257–63.

Bloor, M.J., McKeganey, N.P. and Fonkert, J.D. (1988) *One Foot in Eden: A Sociological Study of the Range of Therapeutic Community Practice.* London: Routledge.

Bourdieu, P. and Passeron J-C. (1990) *Reproduction in Education, Society and Culture.* London: Sage Publications.

Bowlby, J. (1973) *Attachment and Loss Vol. 2 Separation: Anxiety and Anger.* London: Hogarth Press.

Bowlby, J. (1988) *A Secure Base.* London: Routledge.

Boyd, C.J., Hill, E., Holmes, C. and Purnell, R. (1998) 'Putting drug use in context: Life-lines of African American women who smoke crack.' *Journal of Substance Abuse Treatment 15* (3), 235–49.

Bratter, T., Collabolleta, E., Fossbender, A., Pennachia, M. and Rubel, J. (1985) 'The American self-help residential therapeutic community: A pragmatic treatment approach for addicted character-disordered individuals.' In T. Bratter and G. Forrest (eds) *Alcoholism and Substance Abuse.* London: Free Press.

Bridgeland, M. (1971) *Pioneer Work with Maladjusted Children: A Study of the Development of Therapeutic Education.* London: Staples Press.

Briere, J. and Zaidi, L. (1989) 'Sexual abuse histories and sequelae in female psychiatric emergency room patients.' *American Journal of Psychiatry 146,* 1602–06.

British Psychological Society (2001) *Code of Conduct, Ethical Principles and Guidelines.* Leicester: BPS Publications.

Broekaert, E., Rase, V., Kaplan, C. and Coletti, M. (1999) 'The design and effectiveness of therapeutic community research in Europe: An overview.' *European Addiction Research 5,* 21–35.

Brooks, R.G. (1996) 'EuroQol – the current state of play.' *Health Policy 36,* 53–72.

Bryman, A. (1988) *Quantity and Quality in Social Research.* London: Routledge.

Bucardo, J., Guydish, J., Acampora, A. and Werdebar, D. (1997) 'The therapeutic community model applied to day treatment of substance abuse.' In G. De Leon (ed.) *Community as Method: Therapeutic Communities for Special Populations and Special Settings.* Westport, CT: Praeger.

Burgess, R.G. (1984) *In the Field: An Introduction to Field Research.* London: Routledge.

Buston, K., Parry-Jones, W., Livingston, M., Bogan, A. and Wood, S. (1998) 'Qualitative research.' *British Journal of Psychiatry 172,* 197–99.

Callon, M. (1986) 'Some elements of a sociology of translation: Domestication of the scallops and the fishermen of St Brieuc Bay.' In J. Law (ed.) *Power, Action and Belief: A New Sociology of Knowledge?* London: Routledge and Kegan Paul.

Campbell, M.J. and Machin, D. (1999) *Medical Statistics, a Commonsense Approach.* Chichester: John Wiley and Sons.

Campling, P. and Haigh, R. (1999) *Therapeutic Communities: Past, Present, and Future.* London: Jessica Kingsley Publishers.

Caplan, C.A. (1993) 'Nursing staff and patient perceptions of the ward atmosphere in a maximum security forensic hospital.' *Archives of Psychiatric Nursing 7,* 23–29.

Center for Substance Abuse Treatment (CSAT), National Evaluation Data Services (NEDS) (1999). *The Costs and Benefits of Substance Abuse Treatment: Findings from the National Treatment Improvement Evaluation Study (NTIES).* August. Available online at www.neds.calib.com/products/pdfs/cost-ben.pdf

Chapman, C.E. (1984) 'A therapeutic community, psychosocial nursing and the nursing process.' *International Journal of Therapeutic Communities 5,* 68–76.

Chiesa, M. (1997) 'A combined inpatient/outpatient programme for severe personality disorders.' *Therapeutic Communities 18,* 297–309.

Chiesa, M., Drahorad, C. and Longo, S. (2000) 'Early termination of treatment in personality disorder treated in a psychotherapy hospital: Quantitative and qualitative study.' *British Journal of Psychiatry 177,* 107–11.

Chiesa, M. and Fonagy, P. (2000) 'Cassel personality disorder study: Methodology and treatment effects.' *British Journal of Psychiatry 176,* 485–91.

Chiesa, M., Fonagy, P., Holmes, J., Drahorad, C. and Harrison-Hall, A. (2002) 'Health service use costs by personality disorder following specialist and nonspecialist treatment: A comparative study.' *Journal of Personality Disorders 16,* 160–73.

Chiesa, M. and Iacoponi, E. (1998) 'From referral to discharge: Audit at the Cassel Hospital 1993–1998.' Unpublished.

Chiesa, M., Iacoponi, E. and Morris, M. (1996) 'Changes in health service utilization by patients with severe personality disorders before and after inpatient psychosocial treatment.' *British Journal of Psychotherapy 12*, 4, 501–12.

Clark, D.H. (1965) 'The therapeutic community concept: Practice and future.' *British Journal of Psychiatry 111*, 947–54.

Clarke, R.V.G. and Cornish, D.B. (1972) *The Controlled Trial in Institutional Research – Paradigm or Pitfall for Penal Evaluators.* London: HMSO.

Coakes, S. and Steed, L. (2001) *SPSS Analysis without Anguish.* Sydney: Wiley and Sons Australia, Ltd.

Cochrane, A.L. (1972) *Effectiveness and Efficiency: Random Reflections on Health Services.* London: Nuffield Provincial Hospital Trust.

Coleman, J.S. and Fararo, T.J. (1992) *Rational Choice Theory: Advocacy and Critique.* Newbury Park, CA: Sage.

Commissioners of Prisons (1963) *Report for 1962.* London: HMSO.

Communications (1999) Vol. 3, No. 1, July. New York: Center for Therapeutic Community Research, NDRI.

Communications (2000) Vol. 4, No. 1, Spring. New York: Center for Therapeutic Community Research, NDRI.

Comstock, B.S., Kamiliar, S.M., Thornby, J.I., Ramirez, J.V. and Kaplan, H.B. (1985) 'Crisis treatment in a day hospital: Impact on medical care-seeking.' *Psychiatric Clinics of North America 8*, 483–500.

Condelli, W.S., and De Leon, G. (1993) 'Fixed and dynamic predictors of client retention in therapeutic communities.' *Journal of Substance Abuse Treatment 10*, 11–16.

Conte, H.R., Plutchik, R., Karasu, T.B. and Jerrett, I. (1980) 'A self report borderline scale: Discriminant validity and preliminary norms.' *Journal of Nervous and Mental Disease 168*, 428–35.

Coombe, P. (1995) 'Glimpses of a Cassell Hospital outpatient group.' *Australian and New Zealand Journal of Psychiatry 29*, 309–15.

Copas, J. and Whiteley, J.S. (1976) 'Predicting success in the treatment of psychopaths.' *British Journal of Psychiatry 129*, 388–92.

Copas, J.B., O'Brien, M., Roberts, J.C. and Whitely, S. (1984) 'Treatment outcome in personality disorder: The effect of social, psychological and behavioural variables.' *Personality and Individual Differences 5*, 565–73.

CORE System Group (1998) *CORE System (Information Management) Handbook.* Leeds: CORE System Group.

Cornah, D., Stein, K. and Stevens, A. (1997) *The Therapeutic Community Method of Treatment for Borderline Personality Disorder.* Report No 67. Bristol: Research and Development Directorate, Wessex Institute for Health and Development.

Costa, P.T. and McCrae, R.R. (1992) *The NEO-PI-R Manual.* Odessa, FL: Psychological Assessment Resources.

CRD (Centre for Reviews and Dissemination) (1996) *Undertaking Systematic reviews of Research on Effectiveness.* CRD Report No. 4. York: University of York.

Crockett, R., Kirk, J.B., Manning, N. and Millard, D.W. (1978) 'Community time structure.' *Association of Therapeutic Communities Bulletin 25*, 12–17.

Cronkite, R.C. and Moos, R.H. (1978) 'Evaluating alcoholism treatment programs: An integrated approach.' *Journal of Consulting and Clinical Psychology 46*, 5, 1105–19.

Cullen, E. (1994) 'Grendon: The therapeutic prison that works.' *Journal of Therapeutic Communities 15*, 4, 301–11.

Cullen, E. (1997) 'Can prison be a therapeutic community? The Grendon template.' In E. Cullen, L. Jones and R. Woodward (eds) *Therapeutic Communities for Offenders.* Chichester: John Wiley and Sons.

Culyer, A. (1994) *Supporting Research and Development in the NHS.* London: HMSO.

Curle, A. (1947) 'Transitional Communities and Social Reconnection.' *Human Relations 1*, 1.

Davies, S. (2001) 'Economic evaluations of therapeutic community treatments of personality disorder and their influence on strategic purchasing in the NHS.' Dissertation presented in part consideration for the degree of MBA, University of Nottingham.

Davies, S. and Campling, P. (2003) 'Therapeutic community treatment of personality disorder: Service use and mortality over three years follow-up.' *British Journal of Psychiatry 182*, 44, 24–27.

Davies, S., Campling, P. and Ryan, K. (1999) 'Therapeutic community provision at regional and district levels.' *Psychiatric Bulletin 23*, 79–83.

De Leon, G. (1973) 'The Phoenix House therapeutic community: Changes in psychopathological signs.' *Archives of General Psychiatry 28*, 131–35.

De Leon, G. (1984) *The Therapeutic Community: Study of Effectiveness.* In National Institute on Drug Abuse Treatment Research Monograph Series (ADM 84-1286). Washington, DC: Superintendent of Documents, US Government Printing Office.

De Leon, G. (1985) 'The therapeutic community: Status and evolution.' *International Journal of Addictions 20*, 6–7, 823–44.

De Leon, G. (1986) 'Circumstance, motivation, readiness and suitability as correlates of treatment tenure.' *Journal of Psychoactive Drugs 18*, 203–08.

De Leon, G. (1988) 'Legal pressure in therapeutic communities.' In C.G. Leukefeld and F.M. Tims (eds) *Compulsory Treatment of Drug Abuse: Research and Clinical Practice*, NIDA Research Monograph 86 (DHHS Publication No. (Adm) 88–1578). Rockville, MD: National Institute on Drug Abuse.

De Leon, G. (1989) 'Psychopathology and substance abuse: What we are learning from research in therapeutic communities.' *Journal of Psychoactive Drugs 21*, 2, 177–88.

De Leon, G. (1991) 'Retention in drug-free therapeutic communities.' In R.W. Pickens, C.G. Leukefeld and C.R. Schuster (eds) *Improving Drug Abuse Treatment*, NIDA Research Monograph 106. Rockville, MD: National Institute on Drug Abuse.

De Leon, G. (1994a) 'The therapeutic community: Towards a general theory and model.' In F.M. Tims, G. De Leon and N. Jainchill (eds) *Therapeutic Community: Advances in Research and Application.* NIDA Research Monograph 144. Washington, DC: US DHHS.

De Leon, G. (1994b) 'Residential Therapeutic Communities in the Mainstream: Diversity and Issues.' *Journal of Psychoactive Drugs 27*, 1, 3–15.

De Leon, G. (1994c) 'Some problems with the anti-prohibitionist position on legalization of drugs.' *Journal of Addictive Diseases 13*, 2, Mar–April, 35–57.

De Leon, G. (ed.) (1997) *Community as Method: Therapeutic Communities for Special Populations and Special Settings.* Westport, CT: Greenwood Publishing Group, Inc.

De Leon, G. (2000) *The Therapeutic Community: Theory, Model, and Method.* New York: Springer Publishing Company.

De Leon, G., Hawke, J., Jainchill, N. and Melnick, G. (2000) 'Therapeutic communities: Enhancing retention in treatment using "senior professor" staff.' *Journal of Substance Abuse Treatment 19*, 1–8.

De Leon, G., Inciardi, J.A. and Martin, S.S. (1995) 'Residential drug abuse treatment research: Are conventional control designs appropriate for assessing treatment effectiveness?' *Journal of Psychoactive Drugs 27*, 1, 85–91.

De Leon, G. and Jainchill, N. (1981–82). 'Male and female drug abusers: Social and psychological status two years after treatment in a therapeutic community.' *American Journal of Drug and Alcohol Abuse 8*, 4, 465–97.

De Leon, G., Melnick, G. and Hawke, J. (2000) 'The motivation/readiness factor in drug treatment research: Implications for research and policy.' In D. McBride, R. Stephens and J. Levy (eds) *Emergent Issues in Drug Treatment, Advances in Medical Sociology.* Greenwich, CT: JAI Press, Inc.

De Leon, G., Melnick, G., Kressel, D. and Jainchill, N. (1994) 'Circumstances, motivation, readiness and suitability (the CMRS scales): Predicting retention in therapeutic community treatment.' *American Journal of Drug and Alcohol Abuse 20*, 4, 495–515.

De Leon, G., Sacks, S., Staines, G. and McKendrick, K. (2000) 'Modified therapeutic community for homeless mentally ill chemical abusers: Treatment outcomes.' *American Journal of Drug and Alcohol Abuse 26*, 3, 461–80.

De Leon, G. and Schwartz, S. (1984) 'The therapeutic community: What are the retention rates?' *American Journal of Drug and Alcohol Abuse 10*, 2, 267–84.

De Leon, G., Wexler, H.K. and Jainchill, N. (1982) 'The therapeutic community: Success and improvement rates 5 years after treatment.' *International Journal of the Addictions 17*, 747.

De Waele, J.P. and Harré, R. (1976) 'The personality of individuals'. In R. Harré, (ed.) *Personality.* Oxford: Blackwell.

Denford, J.D. (1986) 'Inpatient psychotherapy at the Cassel Hospital.' *Bulletin of the Royal College of Psychiatrists 10*, 226–69.

Denford, J.D., Schachter, J., Temple, N., Kind, P. and Rosser, R. (1983) 'Selection and outcome in in-patient psychotherapy.' *British Journal of Medical Psychology 56*, 225–43.

Denzin, N.K. and Lincoln, Y.S. (eds) (1998) *Collecting and Interpreting Qualitative Materials.* London: Sage.

Department of Health (1998a) *A First Class Service: Quality in the New NHS.* London: HMSO.

Department of Health (1998b) *The New NHS: Modern and Dependable.* London: HMSO.

Department of Health (1998c) *Modernising Mental Health Services: Safe, Sound and Supportive.* London: HMSO.

Department of Health (1999a) *National Service Framework for Mental Health: Modern Standards and Service Models.* London: HMSO.

Department of Health (1999b) *Clinical Governance: Quality in the New NHS.* London: HMSO.

Department of Health (1999c) *Guidance on Good Clinical Practice in Trials in the NHS.* London: HMSO.

Department of Health (2000) *Research and Development for a First Class Service: R and D Funding in the New NHS.* London: HMSO.

Department of Health (2001) *Research Governance Framework for Health and Social Care.* London: HMSO.

Derks, J. (1990) 'The Amsterdam Morphine Dispensing Programme: A longitudinal study of extremely problematic drug addicts in an experimental public health programme.' NcGv-series 90–93.

Derogatis, L.R. (1983) *SCL-90-R: Administration, Scoring and Procedures Manual-II for the R(evised) Version.* Towson, MD: Clinical Psychometric Research.

Derogatis, L.R. (1993) *BSI Brief Symptom Inventory.* Fourth edition. Minneapolis: NCS Pearson.

Devlin, H.B. (1993) 'Audit: A view from the Royal College of Surgeons of England.' In S.P. Frostick, P.J. Radford and W.A. Wallace (eds) *Medical Audit: Rationale and Practicalities.* Cambridge: Cambridge University Press.

Dicks, H.V. (1970) *50 Years of the Tavistock Clinic.* London: Routledge and Kegan Paul.

DoH/HO (1994) *Report of the Department of Health/Home Office Working Group on Psychopathic Disorder.* London: HMSO.

Dolan, B. (1997) 'A community based TC: The Henderson Hospital.' In E. Cullen, L. Jones and R. Woodward (eds) *Therapeutic Communities for Offenders.* London: John Wiley and Sons Ltd.

Dolan, B. and Coid J. (1993) *Psychopathic and Antisocial Personality Disorders: Treatment and Research Issues.* London: Gaskell.

Dolan, B., Evans, C. and Norton, K. (1994) 'Funding treatment of offender patients with severe personality disorder. Do financial considerations trump clinical need?' *Journal of Forensic Psychiatry 5,* 2, 263–72.

Dolan, B., Evans, C. and Norton, K. (1995) 'Multiple Axis-II diagnoses of personality disorder.' *British Journal of Psychiatry 166,* 107–12.

Dolan, B.M., Evans, C. and Wilson, J. (1992) 'Therapeutic community treatment for personality disordered adults: Changes in neurotic symptomatology on follow-up.' *International Journal of Social Psychiatry 38,* 243–50.

Dolan, B. and Norton, K. (1992) 'One year after the NHS Bill: The extra-contractual referral system and Henderson Hospital.' *Psychiatric Bulletin 16,* 745–47.

Dolan, B. and Norton, K. (1998) 'Audit and survival: Specialist in-patient psychotherapy in the NHS.' In M. Patrick and R. Davenhill (eds) *Reconstructing audit: The case of psychotherapy services in the NHS.* London: Routledge.

Dolan, B.M., Warren, F.M., Menzies, D. and Norton, K. (1996) 'Cost-offset following specialist treatment of severe personality disorders.' *Psychiatric Bulletin 20* (7), 413–17.

Dolan, B., Warren, F. and Norton, K. (1997) 'Change in borderline symptoms one year after therapeutic community treatment for severe personality disorder.' *British Journal of Psychiatry 171,* 274–79.

Dolan, B., Warren, F., Norton, K. and Murch, L. (1995) *Service Usage One Year after Specialist Treatment for Personality Disorder.* International Conference on Personality Disorder, Dublin.

Doll, R. (1998) 'Controlled trials: The 1948 watershed.' *British Medical Journal 317,* (31 October), 1217–20.

Edelson, M. (1970) *Sociotherapy and Psychotherapy.* Chicago: University of Chicago Press.

Egger, M., Davey Smith, G., Schneider, M. and Minder, C. (1997) 'Bias in meta-analysis detected by a simple, graphical test.' *British Medical Journal 315,* 629–34.

Elliott, R., Fischer, C.T. and Rennie, D.L. (1999) 'Evolving guidelines for publication of qualitative research studies in psychology and related field.' *British Journal of Clinical Psychology 38,* 215–29.

Endicott, J., Spitzer, R.L., Fleiss, J.L. and Cohen, J. (1976) 'The Global Assessment Scale.' *Archives of General Psychiatry 33,* 766–71.

Esterhuyzen, A. and Winterbotham, M. (1998) 'Surfing the interface: How to make a welfare group a microcosm of therapeutic community functioning.' *Therapeutic Communities 19,* 3.

Evans, C., Carlyle J. and Dolan, B. (1996) 'Forensic psychotherapy research.' In M. Cox and C. Cordess (eds) *Forensic Psychotherapy,* Vol. II. London: Jessica Kingsley Publishers.

Evans, C., Margison, F., and Barkham, M. (1998) 'The contribution of reliable and clinically significant change methods to evidence-based mental health.' *Evidence Based Mental Health 1,* 70–72.

Farr, R. M. and Moscovici, S. (Eds) (1984) *Social Representations.* Cambridge: Cambridge University Press.

Faulkner, A. (1997) *Knowing Our Own Minds.* London: Mental Health Foundation.

Fink, L., Bernstein, D., Handelsman, L., Foote, J. and Lovejoy, M. (1995) 'Initial reliability and validity of the Childhood Trauma Interview: A new multidimensional measure of childhood interpersonal trauma.' *American Journal of Psychiatry 152,* 1329–35.

Finkelhor, D., Hotaling, G., Levis, I. and Smith, C. (1990) 'Sexual abuse in a national survey of adult men and women: Prevalence, characteristics and risk factors.' *Childhood Abuse and Neglect 14,* 19–28.

Finney, J. and Moos, R. (1992) 'The long-term course of treated alcoholism: II. Predictors and correlates of 10-year functioning and mortality.' *Journal of Studies on Alcohol 53,* 142–53.

Finney, J.W., Noyes, C., Coutts, A. and Moos, R. (1998) 'Evaluating substance abuse treatment process models: I. Changes on proximal outcome variables during 12-step and cognitive behavioral treatment.' *Journal of Studies on Alcohol 59,* 371–80.

First, M.B., Spitzer, R.L., Gibbon, M. and Williams, J.B.W. (1995) 'The Structured Clinical Interview for DSM-III-R Personality Disorders (SCID-II): Part I. Description.' *Journal of Personality Disorders 9,* 83–91.

Flynn, C. (1993) 'The patient's pantry: The nature of the nursing task.' *Therapeutic Communities 14,* 4, 227–36.

Flynn, P.M., Kristiansen, P.L., Porto, J.V. and Hubbard, R.L. (1999) 'Costs and benefits of treatment for cocaine addiction in DATOS.' *Drug and Alcohol Dependence 57,* 167–74.

Fonagy, P. (1999) 'Attachment, the development of the self, and its pathology in personality disorders.' In J. Derksen, C. Maffei and M. Groen (eds) *Treatment of Personality Disorders.* New York: Kluwer Academic/Plenum Publishers.

Fonagy, P., Leigh, T., Steele, M.S., Steele, H., Kennedy, R., Mattoon, G., Target, M. and Gerber, A. (1996) 'The relation of attachment status, psychiatric classification, and response to psychotherapy.' *Journal of Consulting and Clinical Psychology 64,* 1, 22–31.

Fonkert, J.D. (1978) 'Reality Construction in a Therapeutic Community for Ex-Drug Addicts.' Doctoral dissertation, The Hague.

Foster, A. (1979) 'The management of boundary crossing.' In R.D. Hinshelwood and N. Manning (eds) *Therapeutic Communities: Reflections and Progress.* London: Routledge and Kegan Paul.

Foulkes, S.R. (1948) *Introduction to Group Analytic Psychotherapy.* London: Heinemann.

French, M.T., Sacks, S., De Leon, G., Staines, G. and McKendrick, K. (1999) 'Modified therapeutic community for mentally ill chemical abusers: Outcomes and costs.' *Evaluation and the Health Professions 22,* 1, 60–85.

Friis, S., Bunkan, B., Ljunggren, A.L., Moen, O. and Opjordsmoen, S. (1998) 'What are the basic dimensions of body posture? An empirical evaluation of the Comprehensive Body Examination. I.' *Nordic Journal of Psychiatry 52,* 319–26.

Friis, S., Karterud, S., Kleppe, H., Lorentzen, S., Lystrup, S. and Vaglum, P. (1982) 'Reconsidering some limiting factors of therapeutic communities: A summary of six Norwegian studies.' In M. Pines and L. Rafaelsen (eds) *The Individual and the Group: Boundaries and Interrelations.* Volume I. New York: Plenum Publishers.

Friis, S., Wilberg, T., Dammen, T. and Urnes, Ø. (1999) 'Pharmacotherapy for patients with personality disorders: Experiences from a group analytic treatment program.' In J. Derksen, C. Maffei and H. Groen (eds) *Treatment of Personality Disorders.* New York: Kluwer Academic/Plenum Publishers.

Gabbard, G., Lazar, S., Hornberger, J. and Spiegel, D. (1997) 'The economic impact of psychotherapy: A review.' *American Journal of Psychiatry 154,* 147–55.

Genders, E. and Player, E. (1995) *Grendon: A Study of a Therapeutic Prison.* Oxford: Oxford University Press.

George, C., Kaplan, N. and Main, M. (1985) *The Adult Attachment Interview.* Berkeley, CA: Department of Psychology, University of California at Berkeley.

Gerstein, D.R. and Harwood, H.J. (eds) (1990) *Treating Drug Problems Vol. 1. A Study of the Evaluation, Effectiveness, and Financing of Public and Private Drug Treatment Systems.* Institute of Medicine, Washington, DC: National Academy Press.

Giddens, A. (1985) *The Constitution of Society: Outline of the Theory of Structuration.* Oxford: Polity Press.

Gilbert, N. (1993) *Researching Social Life.* London: Sage Publications.

Glaser, A.N. (1983) 'Therapeutic communities and therapeutic communities: A personal perspective.' *International Journal of Therapeutic Communities 4,* 2, 150–62.

Glider, P., Mullen, R., Herbst, D., Davis, C. and Fleishman, B. (1997) 'Substance abuse treatment in a jail setting: A therapeutic community model.' In G. De Leon (ed.) *Community as Method: Therapeutic Communities for Special Populations and Special Settings.* Westport, CT: Praeger.

Goffman, E. (1961) *Asylums.* London: Penguin Books.

Goodwin, I., Holmes, G., Newnes, C. and Waltho, D. (1999) 'A qualitative analysis of the views of in-patient mental health service users.' *Journal of Mental Health 8,* 1, 43–54.

Grafanaki, S. (1996) 'How research can change the researcher: The need for sensitivity, flexibility and ethical boundaries in conducting qualitative research in counselling/psychotherapy.' *British Journal of Guidance and Counselling 24,* 3, 329–55.

Greenhalgh, T. (1997) *How to Read a Paper: The Basics of Evidence Based Medicine.* London: BMJ Books.

Greenhalgh, T. (1998) *Outside the Ivory Towers: Evidence Based Medicine in the Real World.* www.ucl.ac.uk/openlearning/uebpp/b5.htm

Greenwood, N., Key, A., Burns, T., Bristow, M. and Sedgwick, P. (1999) 'Satisfaction with in-patient psychiatric services: Relationship to patient and treatment factors.' *British Journal of Psychiatry 174,* 159–63.

Griffiths, P. (1995) *The Work of the Cassel Hospital.* Cassel Hospital Information Booklet for Visitors.

Griffiths, P. and Leach, G. (1998) 'Psychosocial nursing: A model learned from experience.' In E. Barnes, P. Griffiths, J. Ord and D. Wells (eds) *Face to Face with Distress: The Professional Use of Self in Psychosocial Care.* Oxford: Butterworth Heinemann.

Grove, B. (1984) 'The survival of the researcher in the therapeutic community.' *International Journal of Therapeutic Communities 5* (2), 120–26.

Gunderson, J.G. (1985) *Borderline Personality Disorder.* Washington, DC: American Psychiatric Press.

Gunderson, J.G. (1994) 'Building structure for the borderline construct.' *Acta Psychiatrica Scandinavica 89,* supplement 379, 12–18.

Gunderson, J.G. (1996) 'The borderline patient intolerance of aloneness: Insecure attachment and therapist availability.' *American Journal of Psychiatry 153,* 752–58.

Gunderson, J.G. (2001) *Borderline Personality Disorder: A Clinical Guide.* Washington, DC: American Psychiatric Press.

Gunn, J., Robertson, G., Dell, S. and Way, C. (1978) *Psychiatric Aspects of Imprisonment.* London: Academic Press.

Guthrie, E. (2000) 'Enhancing the clinical relevance of psychotherapy outcome research.' *Journal of Mental Health 9,* 3, 267–71.

Haigh, R. (1996) 'The Ghost in the Machine: The Matrix in the Milieu.' Paper presented at the ATC Windsor Conference, September.

Haigh, R. (1999) 'The quintessence of a therapeutic environment. Five universal qualities.' In P. Campling and R. Haigh (eds) *Therapeutic Communities: Past, Present and Future.* London: Jessica Kingsley Publishers.

Haigh, R. (2002) 'Therapeutic community research: Past, present and future.' *Psychiatric Bulletin 26,* 65–68.

Hammersley, M. and Atkinson, P. (1995) *Ethnography: Principles and Practice.* Second edition. London: Routledge.

Hammond, S. (1995) 'Using psychometric tests.' In G.M. Breakwell, S. Hammond and C. Fife-Schaw (eds) *Research Methods in Psychology.* London: Sage Publications.

Harré, R. (1979) *Social Being.* Oxford: Blackwell.

Harré, R. and Secord, P. (1972) *The Explanation of Social Behaviour.* Oxford: Blackwell.

Harrison, T. (2000) *Bion, Rickman, Foulkes and the Northfield Experiments. Advancing on a Different Front.* London: Jessica Kingsley Publishers.

Henwood, K. and Pidgeon, N. (1992) 'Qualitative research and psychological theorising.' *British Journal of Psychology 83,* 97–111.

Hobson, R.F. (1979) 'The messianic community.' In R.D. Hinshelwood and N. Manning (eds) *Therapeutic Communities: Reflections and Progress.* London: Routledge and Kegan Paul.

Holland, S. (1983) 'Evaluating community based treatment programs: A model for strengthening inferences about effectiveness.' *International Journal of Therapeutic Communities 4,* 4, 285–306.

Holmes, J., Montgommery, C., Chiesa, M., Harrison-Hall, A. and Drahorad, C. (2001) 'Personality disorder and quality of life.' In A. Crisp (ed.) *Every Family in the Land.* www.stigma.org.everyfamily

Homans, R. (1991) *The Ethics of Social Research.* London: Longman.

Horowitz, L.H., Rosenberg, S.E., Baer, B.A., Ureno, G. and Villasenor, V.S. (1988) 'Inventory of Interpersonal Problems; Psychometric properties and clinical applications.' *Journal of Consulting and Clinical Psychology 56,* 885–92.

Hubbard, R.L, Marsden, M.E., Rachal, J.V., Harwood, H.J., Cavanaugh, E.R. and Ginzburg, H.M. (1989) *Drug Abuse Treatment: A National Study of Effectiveness.* Chapel Hill, NC: The University of North Carolina Press.

Hubbard, R.L., Valley Rachal, J., Craddock, S.G. and Cavanaugh, E.R. (1984) 'Treatment outcome prospective study (TOPS): Client characteristics and behaviors before, during, and after treatment.' In F.M. Tims and J.P. Ludford (eds) *Drug Abuse Treatment Evaluation: Strategies, Progress, and Prospects.* NIDA Research Monograph Number 51 (DHHS Publication No. (ADM) 84–1329). Rockville, MD: National Institute on Drug Abuse.

Hughes, P.H., Coletti, S.D., Neri, R.L., Urmann, C.F., Stahl, S., Sicilian, D.M. and Anthony, J.C. (1995) 'Retaining cocaine-abusing women in a therapeutic community: The effect of a child live-in program.' *American Journal of Public Health 85,* 1149–52.

Hyler, S.E. (1994) 'Personality Diagnostic Questionnaire – IV (PDQ-IV).' Unpublished test. New York: New York State Psychiatric Institute.

Hyler, S., Reider, R.O., Spitzer, R.L. and Williams, J. (1987) *Personality Diagnostic Questionnaire – Revised.* New York: New York State Psychiatric Institute.

Imber, S.D. (1992) 'Then and now: Forty years in psychotherapy research.' *Clinical Psychology Review 12,* 199–204.

Inciardi, J.A., Martin, S.S., Butzin, C.A., Hooper, R.M. and Harrison, L.D. (1997) 'An effective model of prison-based treatment for drug-involved offenders.' *Journal of Drug Issues 27*, 2, 261–78.

Irwin, F. (1995) 'The therapeutic ingredients of baking a cake.' *Therapeutic Communities 16*, 4, 263–68.

Jacobson, N. and Truax, P. (1991) 'Clinical significance: A statistical approach to defining meaningful change in psychotherapy research.' *Journal of Consulting and Clinical Psychology 59*, 12–19.

Jainchill, N., De Leon, G. and Pinkham, L. (1986) 'Psychiatric diagnoses among substance abusers in therapeutic community treatment.' *Journal of Psychoactive Drugs 18*, 209–13.

Jainchill, N., Hawke, J. and De Leon, G. (2000) 'Adolescents in TCs: One-year posttreatment outcomes.' *Journal of Psychoactive Drugs 32*, 1, 81–94.

Jainchill, N., Yagelka, J. and Messina, M. (submitted for review) 'Development of a Treatment Environmental Risk Index (TERI): Assessing risk for client dropout.' *Psychology of Addictive Behaviors.*

Jansen, E. (ed.) (1980) *The Therapeutic Community: Outside the Hospital.* London: Croom Helm.

Jarvis, T. and Copeland, J. (1997) 'Child sexual abuse as a predictor of psychiatric co-morbidity and its implications for drug and alcohol treatment.' *Drug and Alcohol Dependence 49*, 61–69.

Jefferson, T., Demicheli, V. and Mugford, M. (2000) *Elementary Economic Evaluations in Healthcare.* Second edition. London: BMJ Books.

Jeffery, D., Burrows, M. and West, J. (1997) 'Do we really want to know? Barriers to service users' expression of their views and some ways of overcoming them.' *Clinical Psychology Forum 102*, 9–13.

Johansen, M., Karterud, S., Pedersen, G., Gude, T. and Falkum, E. (submitted) 'An Examination of the Prototype Validity of the Borderline DSM-IV Criteria.'

Johns, S. and Karterud, S. (submitted) 'Treatment Guidelines for Group Art Therapy as Part of Day Treatment Programs for Patients with Personality Disorders.'

Jones, M. (1952) *Social Psychiatry.* London: Tavistock.

Jones, M. (1968) *Beyond the Therapeutic Community.* New Haven: Yale University Press.

Jones. M. (1982) *The Process of Change.* London: Routledge and Kegan Paul.

Jones, M. (1986) 'Democratic therapeutic communities (DTCs) or programmatic therapeutic communities (PTCs) or both?' In G. De Leon and J.T. Ziegenfuss (eds) *Therapeutic Communities for Addictions.* Springfield, IL: Charles C. Thomas.

Kahn, H.A. and Sempos, C.T. (1989) *Statistical Methods in Epidemiology.* Oxford: Oxford University Press.

Kaplan, C., Broekaert, E., Frank, O. and Reichmann, S. (1999) 'Improving Psychiatric Treatment in Residential Programs for Emerging Dependency Groups: Approach and Epidemiological Findings.' Paper presented at the NIH-NIDA Community Epidemiology Work Group, Los Angeles, CA, 17 December.

Karterud, S. (1989) 'Group Processes in Therapeutic Communities.' Oslo: Doctoral dissertation.

Karterud, S. and Pedersen, G. (submitted) 'Time-limited Day Hospital Treatment. User Satisfaction of Therapeutic Components.'

Karterud, S., Pedersen, G., Bjordal, E., Brabrand, J., Friis, S., Haaseth, Ø., Haavaldsen, G., Irion, T., Leirvåg, H., Tørum, E. and Urnes, Ø. (2003) 'Day hospital treatment of patients with personality disorders. Experiences from a Norwegian treatment research network.' *Journal of Personality Disorders 17* (3), 234–62.

Karterud, S., Pedersen, G., Friis, S., Urnes, Ø., Brabrand, J., Falkum, L.R. and Leirvåg, H. (1998) 'The Norwegian Network of Psychotherapeutic Day Hospitals.' *Therapeutic Communities 19*, 1, 15–28.

Karterud, S., Pedersen, G., Urnes, Ø., Steffensen, B. (submitted) 'Cognitive-behavioral Group Treatment for Anxiety Disorders as Adjunct to a Treatment Program for Personality Disorders.'

Karterud, S. and Urnes, Ø. (submitted) 'Short Term Day Treatment Programs for Personality Disorders. What is the Optimal Composition?'

Karterud, S., Urnes, Ø. and Pedersen, G. (2001) *Personlighetsforstyrrelser. Forståelse, diagnostikk, evaluering og gruppebasert behandling*. Oslo: Pax Forlag.

Karterud, S., Vaglum, S., Friis, S., Irion, T., Johns, S. and Vaglum, P. (1992) 'Day hospital therapeutic community treatment for patients with personality disorders.' *The Journal of Nervous and Mental Disease 180*, 238–43.

Kelson, M. (1996) 'User involvement in clinical audit: A review of developments and issues of good practice.' *Journal of Evaluation in Clinical Practice 2*, 2, 97–109.

Kennard, D. (1979) 'Thinking about research in a therapeutic community.' In R.D. Hindshelwood and N. Manning (eds) *Therapeutic Communities: Reflections and Progress*. London: Routledge and Kegan Paul.

Kennard, D. (1983) *An Introduction to Therapeutic Communities*. London: Routledge and Kegan Paul.

Kennard, D. (1998) *An Introduction to Therapeutic Communities*. London: Jessica Kingsley Publishers.

Kennard, D. and Lees, J. (2001) 'A checklist of standards for democratic therapeutic communities.' *Therapeutic Communities 22*, 2, 143–51.

Kennedy, R., Tischler, L. and Haymans, A. (1986) *The Family as In-patient*. London: Free Association Books.

Kernberg, O. (1976) *Object Relations Theory and Clinical Psychoanalysis*. New York: Jason Aronson Inc.

Kernberg, O. (1984) *Severe Personality Disorders: Psychotherapeutic Strategies*. New Haven: Yale University Press.

Kisley, S. (1999) 'Psychotherapy for severe personality disorder: Exploring the limits of evidence based purchasing.' *British Medical Journal 318*, 1410–12.

Kline, P. (1998) *The New Psychometrics. Science, Psychology and Measurement*. London and New York: Routledge.

Knorr-Cetina, K.D. and Mulkay, M. (Eds) (1993) *Science Observed: Perspectives on the Soical Study of Science*. London: Sage Publications.

Koeter, M.W.J. and Hartgers, C. (1997) *Preliminary Procedure for the Computation of the Europ-ASI Composite Scores*. Amsterdam: AIAR.

Kokkevi, A. and Hartgers, C. (1995) 'Europ–ASI: European adaption of a multidimensional assessment instrument for drug and alcohol dependency.' *European Addiction Research 1*, 194–98.

Kooyman, M. (1992) *The Therapeutic Community for Addicts: Intimacy, Parent Involvement and Treatment Outcome*. Amsterdam: Swets and Zeitlinger.

Kressel, D., De Leon, G., Palij, M., and Rubin, G. (2000) 'Measuring client clinical progress in therapeutic community treatment: The therapeutic community Client Assessment Inventory (CAI), Client Assessment Summary (CAS) and Staff Assessment Summary (SAS).' *Journal of Substance Abuse Treatment 19*, 267–72.

Kressel, D., Palij, M., De Leon, G. and Rubin, G. (manuscript in submission) *Therapeutic Community Client Progress Assessment Scales: Psychometric Properties.* New York: Center for Therapeutic Community Research.

Kressel, D., Rubin, G., De Leon, G. and Palij, M. (manuscript in submission). *The Predictive Validity and Clinical Utility of Instruments Measuring Client Progress in Therapeutic Community Treatment.* New York: Center for Therapeutic Community Research.

Laing, R.D. (1971) *The Politics of the Family and Other Essays.* London: Tavistock.

Lanza, M.L., and Satz, H. (1995) 'Researcher and clinician: Role conflict and resolution.' *Group 19,* 2, 120–26.

Law, J. (1987) 'Technology and heterogeneous engineering: The case of Portuguese expansion.' In W.E Bijker, T.P Hughes and T.J. Pinch (eds) *The Social Construction of Technological Systems, New Directions in the Sociology and History of Technology.* London: MIT Press.

Law, J. (1992) 'Notes on the theory of the actor-network: Ordering, strategy, and heterogeneity.' *Systems Practice 5,* 379–93.

Law, J. and Hassard, J. (eds) (1999) *Actor Network Theory and After.* Oxford: Blackwell Publishers.

Lawson, C.A. (2000) *Understanding the Borderline Mother. Helping her Children Transcend the Intense, Unpredictable, and Volatile Relationship.* Northvale, NJ: Jason Aronson Inc.

Lees, J. (1999) 'Research: The importance of asking questions.' In P. Campling and R. Haigh (eds) *Therapeutic Communities: Past, Present and Future.* London: Jessica Kingsley Publishers.

Lees, J., Manning, N. and Rawlings, B. (1999) *Therapeutic Community Effectiveness: A Systematic International Review of Therapeutic Community Treatment for People with Personality Disorders and Mentally Disordered Offenders.* CRD Report 17. York: NHS Centre for Reviews and Dissemination, University of York.

Lewis, B.F., McCusker, J., Hindin, R., Frost, R. and Garfield, F. (1993) 'Four residential drug treatment programs: Project IMPACT.' In J.A. Inciardi, F.M. Tims and B.W. Fletcher (eds) *Innovative Approaches in the Treatment of Drug Abuse: Program Models and Strategies.* Westport, CT: Greenwood Press.

Linehan, M.M. (1997) 'Development, Evaluation and Dissemination of Effective Psychosocial Treatments: Stages of Disorder, Levels of Care, and Stages of Treatment Research.' Paper presented at the Annual General Meeting of the UK Chapter of the Society for Psychotherapy Research, Ravenscar, North Yorkshire, April.

Luborsky, L., Digner, L., Seligman, D.A., Rosenthal, R., Krause, E.D., Johnson, S., Halperin, G., Bishop, M., Berman, J. and Schweizer, E. (1999) 'The researcher's own therapy allegiances: A "wild card" in comparisons of treatment efficacy.' *Clinical Psychology: Science and Practice 6,* 1 (Spring), 95–106.

Macran, S., Ross, H., Hardy, G. and Shapiro, D. (1999) 'The importance of considering clients' perspectives in psychotherapy research.' *Journal of Mental Health 8,* 4, 325–37.

Main, T. (1946) 'The hospital as a therapeutic institution.' *Bulletin of the Menninger Clinic 10,* 66–70. (Reprinted in *Therapeutic Communities 17,* 2, 77–80.)

Main, T. (1983) 'The concept of the therapeutic community: Variations and vicissitudes.' In M. Pines (ed) *The Evolution of Group Analysis.* London: Routledge and Kegan Paul.

Main, T. (1989) *The Ailment and Other Psychoanalytic Essays.* London: Free Association Books.

Manning, N. (1976) 'Values and practice in the therapeutic community.' *Human Relations 29,* 2, 125–38.

Manning, N. (1979) 'The politics of survival: The role of research in the therapeutic community.' In R.D. Hinshelwood and N. Manning (eds) *Therapeutic Communities: Reflections and Progress.* London: Routledge and Kegan Paul.

Manning, N. (1989) *The Therapeutic Community Movement: Charisma and Routinization*. London: Routledge and Kegan Paul.

Manning, N. (1997) 'Anthropology and sociology in action.' *International Journal of Therapeutic Communities 18*, 1, 76–79.

Manning, N. (2000) 'Psychiatric diagnosis under conditions of uncertainty: Personality disorder, science, and professional legitimacy.' *Sociology of Health and Illness 22*, 5, 621–39.

Manning, N. (2002) 'Actor-networks, policy networks and personality disorder.' *Sociology of Health and Illness 24*, 5, 644–66.

Manning, N. and Lees, J. (1985) *Australian Community Care: A study of the Richmond Fellowship*. Canterbury: University of Kent.

Manning, N. and Rapoport, R.N. (1976) 'Rejection and reincorporation; a case study in social research utilisation.' *Social Science and Medicine 10*, 458–68.

Margison, F. (2000) 'Evidence based practice and practice based evidence in psychotherapy.' In C. Mace (ed.) *Evidence in the Balance*. London: Routledge.

Margison, F., Barkham, M., Evans, C., McGrath, G., Mellor-Clark, J., Audin, K. and Connell, J. (2000). 'Measurement and psychotherapy: Evidence-based practice and practice-based evidence.' *British Journal of Psychiatry 177*, 123–30.

Margison, F.R., Loebl, R. and McGrath, G. (1998) 'The Manchester experience: Audit and psychotherapy services in north-west England'. In R. Davenhill and M. Patrick (eds) *Rethinking Clinical Audit: The Case of Psychotherapy Services in the NHS*. London: Routledge.

Marlatt, A. and Gordon, J. (1985) *Relapse Prevention: Maintenance Strategies in the Treatment of Addictive Behaviour*. London: Guildford Press.

Marshall, P. (1997) 'A reconviction study of HMP Grendon Therapeutic Community.' *Research Findings 53*. London: Home Office Research and Statistics Directorate.

Martin, R.L., Cloniger, C.R., Guze, S.B. and Clayton, P.J. (1985) 'Mortality in a follow-up of 500 psychiatric outpatients: II. Cause-specific mortality.' *Archives of General Psychiatry 42*, 58–66.

Martin, S.S., Butzin, C.A., Saum, C.A. and Inciardi, J.A. (1999) 'Three-year outcomes of therapeutic community treatment for drug-involved offenders in Delaware: From prison to work release to aftercare.' *The Prison Journal 79*, 3, 294–320.

Martinson, R. (1974) 'What works? Questions and answers about prison reform.' *Public Interest 35*, 22–45.

Mays, N. and Pope, C. (1996) *Qualitative Research in Health Care*. London: British Medical Journal Publishing Group.

McGeary, K.A., French, M.T., Sacks, S., McKendrick, K. and De Leon, G. (2000) 'Service use and cost by MICAs: Differences by retention in a TC.' *Journal of Substance Abuse 11*, 2, 1–15.

McKeganey, N. (1982) 'The Social Organisation of Everyday Therapeutic Work in a Camphill Rudolf Steiner Therapeutic Community.' Unpublished PhD thesis, University of Aberdeen.

McLellan, A.T., Luborsky, L., O'Brien, C.P. and Woody, G.E. (1980) 'An improved evaluation instrument for substance abuse patients. The Addiction Severity Index.' *Journal of Nervous and Mental Disease 168*, 26–33.

McLellan, A.T., Kushner, H., Metzger, D., Peters, R., Smith, I., Grissom, G., Pettanati, H. and Argeriou, M. (1992) 'The fifth edition of the Addiction Severity Index: Historical critique and normative data.' *Journal of Substance Abuse Treatment 9*, 199–213.

McLeod, J. (1996) 'Qualitative research methods in counselling psychology.' In W. Dryden and R. Wolfe (eds) *Handbook of Counselling Psychology*. London: Sage Publications.

Mead, G.H. (1934) *Mind, Self and Society*. Chicago: University of Chicago Press.

Mead, G.H (1938) *The Philosophy of the Act.* Chicago: University of Chicago Press.

Medical Research Council (2000) *Personal Information in Medical Research.* London: Medical Research Council, www.mrc.ac.uk

Mehlum, L., Friis, S., Irion, T., Johns, S., Karterud, S., Vaglum, P. and Vaglum, S. (1991) 'Personality disorders 2–5 years after treatment: A prospective follow-up study.' *Acta Psychiatrica Scandinavica 84,* 72–77.

Melnick, G. and De Leon, G. (1999) 'Clarifying the nature of therapeutic community treatment: The Survey of Essential Elements Questionnaire (SEEQ).' *Journal of Substance Abuse Treatment 16,* 4, 307–13.

Melnick, G., De Leon, G., Hiller, M.L. and Knight, K. (2001a) 'Therapeutic communities: Diversity in treatment elements.' *Journal of Drug Use and Misuse 35,* 12–14, 1819–47.

Melnick, G., De Leon, G., Thomas, G., Kressel, D. and Wexler, H.K. (2001b) 'Treatment process in prison therapeutic communities: Motivation, participation, and outcome.' *The American Journal of Drug and Alcohol Abuse 27,* 4, 633–50.

Menzies, D., Dolan, M. and Norton, K. (1993) 'Are short term savings worth long term costs? Funding treatment for personality disorders.' *Psychiatric Bulletin 17,* 517–19.

Menzies, D., Rogers, C., McCaffrey, A., Gates, C., Franciosi, P. and Patrick, M. (in press) 'Can questionnaire-based and psychodynamic assessments of change in group psychotherapy inform each other?' *Psychology and Psychotherapy: Theory, Research and Practice.*

Merton, R.K. (1973) *The Sociology of Science: Theoretical and Empirical Investigations.* Chicago: University of Chicago Press.

Miles, M.B. and Huberman, A.M. (1994) *Qualitative Data Analysis: An Expanded Sourcebook.* Second edition. London: Sage Publications.

Mills, C. Wright (1970) *The Sociological Imagination.* Harmondsworth: Penguin.

Millstein, R. (1994) 'TCs for the Future – Views of National Leaders.' In *Proceedings of the Therapeutic Communities of America 1992 Planning Conference, Chantilly, VA: Paradigms: Past, Present and Future.* Providence, RI: Manisses Communications Group.

Mischel, W. (1968) *Personality and Assessment.* New York and London: John Wiley and Sons.

Moos, R.H. (1974a) *Evaluating Treatment Environments: A Social Ecological Approach.* New York: John Wiley and Sons.

Moos, R.H. (1974b) *The Ward Atmosphere Scale Manual.* Palo Alto, CA: Consulting Psychologists Press.

Moos, R. (1980) 'Evaluating the environments of residential care settings.' *International Journal of Therapeutic Communities 1* (4), 311–35.

Moos, R. (1996a) *Community-Oriented Programs Environment Scale Manual.* Third edition. Palo Alto, CA: Mind Garden.

Moos, R. (1996b) *Ward Atmosphere Scale Manual.* Third edition. Palo Alto, CA: Mind Garden.

Moos, R.H. (1997) *Evaluating Treatment Environments: The Quality of Psychiatric and Substance Abuse Programs.* New Brunswick, NJ: Transaction Publishers.

Moos, R., Finney, J. and Cronkite, R. (1990) *Alcoholism Treatment: Context, Process, and Outcome.* New York: Oxford University Press.

Moos, R., Finney, J., Ouimette, P. and Suchinsky, R. (1999) 'A comparative evaluation of substance abuse treatment: I. Treatment orientation, amount of care, and 1-year outcomes.' *Alcoholism: Clinical and Experimental Research 23,* 529–36.

Moos, R. and Lemke, S. (1994) *Group Residences for Older Adults: Physical Features, Policies, and Social Climate.* New York: Oxford University Press.

Moos, R.H. and Lemke, S. (1996) *Evaluating Residential Facilities. The Multiphasic Environmental Assessment Procedure.* Thousand Oaks, CA: Sage.

Moos, R. and Moos, B. (1998) 'The staff workplace and the quality and outcome of substance abuse treatment.' *Journal of Studies on Alcohol 59*, 43–51.

Moos, R., and Schaefer, J. (1987) 'Evaluating health care work settings: A holistic conceptual framework.' *Psychology and Health 1*, 97–122.

Morant, N., Dolan, B., Fainman, D. and Hilton, M. (1999) 'An innovative outreach service for people with severe personality disorders: Patient characteristics and clinical activities.' *Journal of Forensic Psychiatry 10*, 1, 84–97.

Morant, N. and King, J. (2003) 'A multi-perspective evaluation of a specialist out-patient service for people with personality disorders.' *Journal of Forensic Psychiatry and Psychology 14* (1), 44–66.

Morgenstern, J., Frey, R.M., McCrady, B.S., Labouvie, E. and Neighbors, C.J. (1996) 'Examining mediators of change in traditional chemical dependency treatment.' *Journal of Studies on Alcohol 57*, 53–64.

Morton, A. (1995) 'The enigma of non-attendance: A study of clients who do not turn up for their first appointment.' *Therapeutic Communities 16*, 2, 117–33.

Mosher, L.R. (1991) 'Soteria: A therapeutic community for psychotic persons.' *International Journal of Therapeutic Communities 12*, 53–67.

MRC (Medical Research Council) (2000) *A Framework for Development and Evaluation of RCTs for Complex Interventions to Improve Health.* London: MRC.

Mumford, E., Schlesinger, H.J., Glass, G.V., Patrick, C. and Cuerdon, T. (1984) 'A new look at evidence about cost of medical utilization following mental health treatment.' *American Journal of Psychiatry 141*, 1145–58.

Murphy, E.A., Dingwall, R., Greatbatch, D., Parker, S. and Watson, P. (1998) 'Qualitative research methods in health technology assessment: A review of the literature.' *Health Technology Assessment 2*, 16, 1–278.

Murphy, R.A. and Halgin, R.P. (1995) 'Influences on the career choice of psychotherapists.' *Professional Psychology: Research and Practice 26*, 4, 422–26.

Najavits, L.M., Weiss, R.D. and Shaw, S.R. (1997) 'The link between substance abuse and posttraumatic stress disorder in women.' *American Journal of Addictions 6*, 4, 273–83.

National Specialist Commissioning Advisory Group (1999) *Annual Report 1998–1999.* London: NHS Executive.

National Treatment Improvement Evaluation Study (NTIES) (1996) *Preliminary Report: The Persistent Effects of Substance Abuse Treatment – One Year Later.* September. Rockville, MD: US Dept of Health and Human Services, Substance Abuse and Mental Health Services Administration, Center for Substance Abuse Treatment (CSAT).

Newton, M. (1997) 'Changes in Test Scores During Treatment at Grendon.' Unpublished research paper. Grendon Underwood, Bucks: Research and Development Unit, HMP Springhill and Grendon.

NHS Executive (1996) *NHS Psychotherapy Services in England: Review of Strategic Policy.* London: Department of Health.

NHS Executive (1999) *National Service Framework for Mental Health.* London: Department of Health.

NHS Executive Information Policy Unit (2001) *The Health and Social Care Act 2001: Section 60 and 61 Background Information.* Available at www.doh.gov.uk/pu/confiden/act/ s60bg.htm

Nielsen, A. and Scarpitti, F. (1997) 'Changing the behavior of substance abusers: Factors influencing the effectiveness of therapeutic communities.' *Journal of Drug Issues 27*, 2, 279–98.

Nieminen, P. (1996) 'Therapeutic community research and statistical data analysis.' *Acta Universitatis Ouluensis Medica*. Oulu, Finland: University of Oulu Printing Center.

Nolan, T.W. (2000). 'System changes to improve patient safety.' *British Medical Journal 320*, 771–73.

Norton, K. (1992) 'Personality disordered individuals: The Henderson Hospital model of treatment.' *Criminal Behaviour and Mental Health 2*, 2, 80–191.

Norton, K. (1999) 'Joining and leaving: Processing separation, loss and re-attachment.' In P. Campling and R. Haigh (eds) *Therapeutic Communities: Past, Present and Future*. London: Jessica Kingsley Publishers.

O'Driscoll, M.P. and Evans, R. (1988) 'Organizational factors and perceptions of climate in three psychiatric units.' *Human Relations 41*, 371–88.

Ogbourne, A.C. and Melotte, C. (1977) 'An evaluation of a therapeutic community for former drug users.' *British Journal of Addiction 72*, 1, 75–82.

Paris, J. Brown, R. and Nowlis, D. (1987) 'Long term follow up of borderline patients in a general hospital.' *Comprehensive Psychiatry 28*, 530–35.

Parker, M. (1989) 'Managing separation: The Henderson Hospital leavers' group.' *International Journal of Therapeutic Communities 10*, 5–15.

Parry, G. (1996) 'Service evaluation and audit methods.' In G. Parry and F.N. Watts (eds) *Behavioural and Mental Health Research: A Handbook of Skills and Methods*. Hove: Lawrence Erlbaum/Taylor and Francis.

Parry, G. (1998) 'Psychotherapy services, healthcare policy and clinical audit.' In R. Davenhill and M. Patrick (eds) *Rethinking Clinical Audit: The Case of Psychotherapy Services in the NHS*. London: Routledge.

Parry, G. and Richardson, A. (1996) *NHS Psychotherapy Services in England. Review of Strategic Policy*. London: Department of Health.

Paul, G.L. (1967) 'Strategy of outcome research in psychotherapy.' *Journal of Consulting Psychology 31*, 2, 109–18.

Pawson, R. and Tilley, N. (1997) *Realistic Evaluation*. London: Sage Publications.

Pedersen, G. (2001) 'Assessment of self-reported symptoms and interpersonal problems: Psychometric considerations and validity of clinical use.' MA thesis. London: Warnborough University.

Pedersen, G. (2002) 'Circumplex of Interpersonal Problems (CIP): Norwegian revised version of the Inventory of Interpersonal Problems – Circumplex (IIP-C).' *Tidsskrift for Norsk Psykologforening 39*, 25–34.

Pedersen, G. and Karterud, S. (in press) 'Ward Atmosphere Scale for Therapeutic Programs (WAS-TP): Psychometric properties and clinical benefits.' *Therapeutic Communities*.

Pines, M. (1999) *Forgotten Pioneers: The Unwritten History of the Therapeutic Community Movement*. Association of Therapeutic Communities: www.therapeuticcommunities.org/journal-pines.htm

Porter, S. (1993) 'Assault experiences among drug users.' *Substance Abuse*, Bulletin 8.

Potter, J. and Wetherell, M. (1987) *Discourse and Social Psychology: Beyond Attitudes and Behaviour*. London: Sage Publications.

Price, R. and Moos, R. (1975) 'Towards a taxonomy of inpatient treatment environments.' *Journal of Abnormal Psychology 84*, 3, 181–88.

Pringle, P. and Chiesa, M. (2001) 'From the therapeutic community to the community: Developing an outreach psychosocial nursing service for severe personality disorders.' *Therapeutic Communities 22*, 215–32.

Pullen, G.P. (1982) 'Street: The 17 day community.' *International Journal of Therapeutic Communities 2*, 115–26.

Pullen, G.P. (1999) 'Schizophrenia: Hospital communities for the severely disturbed.' In P. Campling and R. Haigh (eds) *Therapeutic Communities: Past, Present and Future.* London: Jessica Kingsley Publishers.

Punch, M. (1998) 'Politics and ethics in qualitative research.' In N. Denzin and Y. Lincoln (eds) *The Landscape of Qualitative Research. Theories and Issues.* London: Sage Publications.

Ramon, S. (ed.) (2000) *A Stakeholder's Approach to Innovation in Mental Health Services – A Reader for the 21st Century.* Brighton: Pavilion Publishing.

Rapoport, R.N. *et al.* (1960) *Community as Doctor. New Perspectives on a Therapeutic Community.* London: Tavistock Publications.

Rapoport, R.N. and Manning, N. (1976) 'Rejection and re-incorporation; a case study in social research utilisation.' *Social Science and Medicine 10*, 458–68.

Rawlings, B. (1980) 'Everyday Therapy: A Study of Routine Practices in a Therapeutic Community.' Unpublished PhD thesis: University of Manchester.

Rawlings, B. (1998) 'The therapeutic community in the prison: Problems in maintaining therapeutic integrity.' *Therapeutic Communities 19*, 4, 281–94.

Rawlings, B. and Yates, R. (eds) (2001) *Therapeutic Communities for the Treatment of Drug Users.* London: Jessica Kingsley Publishers.

Reed, J. (1994) *Report of the Department of Health and Home Office Working Group on Psychopathic Disorder.* London: Department of Health, Home Office.

Rees, J.R. (1945) *The Shaping of Psychiatry by War.* London: Chapman Hall.

Research Council Streptomycin in Tuberculosis Trials Committee (1948) 'Streptomycin treatment for pulmonary tuberculosis.' *British Medical Journal ii*, 769–82.

Rigge, M. (1994) 'Involving patients in clinical audit.' *Quality in Health Care 3*, supplement, S2–S5.

Roethlisberger, F.J. and Dickson, W.J. (1939) *Management and the Worker.* Cambridge, MA: Harvard University Press.

Rosch, E.H. (1973) 'On the internal structure of perceptual and semantic categories.' In T.T. Moore (ed.) *Cognitive Development and the Acquisition of Language.* New York: Academic Press.

Rose, D. (1996) *Living in the Community.* London: The Sainsbury Centre for Mental Health.

Rose, D., Lindley, P., Ford, R. and Gawith, L. (1998) *In Our Experience: User-focused Monitoring in Mental Health.* London: The Sainsbury Centre for Mental Health.

Rosenhow, D.J., Corbett, R. and Devine, D. (1988) 'Molested as children: A hidden contribution to substance abuse?' *Journal of Substance Abuse 5*, 13–18.

Rosser, R.M., Birch, S., Bond, H., Denford, J. and Schachter, J. (1987) 'Five year follow-up of patients treated with inpatient psychotherapy at the Cassel Hospital for Nervous Diseases.' *Journal of the Royal Society of Medicine 80*, 549–55.

Roth, A. and Fonagy, P. (1996) *What Works for Whom – A Critical Preview of Psychotherapy Research (Personality Disorders).* London: Guildford Press.

Royal College of Psychiatrists (1999) *Offenders with Personality Disorder.* London: Royal College of Psychiatrists (CR71).

Royal College of Psychiatrists (2001) *Guidelines for Researchers and for Research Ethics Committees on Psychiatric Research Involving Human Participants.* London: Gaskell.

Sackett, D.L., Rosenberg, W.M., Gray, J.A., Haynes, R.B. and Richardson, W.S. (1996) 'Evidence-based medicine: What it is and what it isn't.' *British Medical Journal 312*, 71–72.

Sackett, D.L. and Wennberg, J.E. (1997) 'Choosing the best research design for each question (editorial).' *British Medical Journal 315*, 1636.

Salkovskis, P. (1995) 'Demonstrating specific effects in cognitive and behavioural therapy.' In M. Aveline and D.A. Shapiro (eds) *Research Foundations for Psychotherapy Practice.* Chichester: John Wiley and Sons.

Sanders, B. and Giolas, M. (1991) 'Dissociation and childhood trauma in psychologically disturbed adolescents.' *American Journal of Psychiatry 148* (1), 50–54.

Schimmel, P. (1997) 'Swimming against the tide? A review of the therapeutic community.' *Australian and New Zealand Journal of Psychiatry 31*, 120–27.

Schoenberg, E. (ed.) (1972) *A Hospital Looks At Itself.* Oxford: Cassirer.

Scottish Drugs Training Project (1998) *The Connection: Proceedings of a Conference on Childhood Sexual Abuse and Adult Dependence.* Stirling: Scottish Drugs Training Project.

Sechrest, L., West, S., Phillips, M., Redner, R. and Yeaton, W. (1979) 'Some neglected problems in evaluation research: Strength and integrity of treatments.' In L. Sechrest, S. West, M. Phillips, R. Redner and W. Yeaton (eds) *Evaluation Studies Review Annual.* Beverly Hills, CA: Sage.

Seglen, P.O. (1997) 'Why the impact factor of journals should not be used for evaluating research.' *British Medical Journal 314*, 498–502.

Seligman, M.E.P. (1995) 'The effectiveness of psychotherapy: The *Consumer Reports* study.' *American Psychologist 50*, 12, 965–74.

Shapiro, D.A., Barkham, M., Rees, A., Hardy, G.E., Reynolds, S. and Startup, M. (1995) 'Decisions, decisions, decisions: Determining the effects of treatment method and duration on the outcome of psychotherapy for depression.' In M. Aveline and D.A Shapiro (eds) *Research Foundations for Psychotherapy Practice.* Chichester: John Wiley and Sons.

Shaw, I. (1999) *Qualitative Evaluation.* London: Sage Publications.

Sheehan, D.V., Lecrubier, Y., Janavs, J., Knapp, E., Weiller, E. and Bonora, L.I. (1994) *Mini International Neuropsychiatric Interview (M.I.N.I.).* Tampa, FL and Paris, France: University of South Florida Institute for Research in Psychiatry and INSERM-Hôpital de la Salpétrière.

Shine, J. (1997) 'Appraisal and coping processes used by staff in a prison based therapeutic community to deal with stress.' *Therapeutic Communities 18*, 4, 271–82.

Shine, J. (ed.) (2000) *A Compilation of Grendon Research.* Aylesbury: HMP Grendon.

Simpson, D.D. (1979) 'The relation of time spent in drug abuse treatment to posttreatment outcome.' *American Journal of Psychiatry 136*, 1449–53.

Simpson, D.D. (1997) 'Effectiveness of drug abuse treatment: A review of research from field settings.' In J.A. Egertson, D.M. Fox and A.I. Leshner (eds) *Treating Drug Abusers Effectively.* Cambridge, MA: Blackwell Publishers of North America.

Simpson, D.D. and Curry, S.J. (eds) (1997) 'Special issue: Drug Abuse Treatment Outcome Study (DATOS).' *Psychology of Addictive Behaviors 11.*

Simpson, D.D. and Joe, G.W. (1993) 'Motivation as a predictor of early dropout from drug abuse treatment.' *Psychotherapy 30*, 2, 357–68.

Simpson, D.D., Joe, G.W., Fletcher, B.W., Hubbard, R.L. and Anglin, M.D. (1999) 'Treatments for cocaine addiction: A national evaluation of outcomes.' *Archives of General Psychiatry 56*, 507–14.

Simpson, D.D., Joe, G.W., Rowan-Szal, G.A. and Greener, J. (1997) 'Drug abuse treatment process components that improve retention.' *Journal of Substance Abuse Treatment 14*, 6, 565–73.

Simpson, D.D. and Sells, S.B. (1982) 'Effectiveness of treatment for drug abuse: An overview of the DARP research program.' *Advances in Alcohol and Substance Abuse 2*, 7–29.

Simpson, T.L., Westerberg, V.S., Little, L.M. and Trujillo, M. (1994) 'Screening for childhood physical and sexual abuse among outpatient substance abusers.' *Journal of Substance Abuse Treatment 11*, 4, 347–58.

Slade, M. and Priebe, S. (2001) 'Are randomised controlled trials the only gold that glitters?' *British Journal of Psychiatry 179*, 286–87.

Smith, J.H., Harré, R. and van Langenhove, L. (1995) *Semi-structured Interviewing and Qualitative Analysis: Rethinking Methods in Psychology*. London: Sage Publications.

Sperry, L., Brill, P.L., Howard, K.I. and Grissom, G.R. (1996) 'From clinical trials outcomes research to clinically relevant research on patient progress.' In L. Sperry, P.L. Brill, K.I. Howard and G.R. Grissom (eds) *Treatment Outcomes in Psychotherapy and Psychiatric Interventions*. New York: Brunner Mazel.

Spitzer, R.L. (1983) 'Psychiatric diagnoses: Are clinicians still necessary?' *Comprehensive Psychiatry 24*, 399–411.

Spitzer, R.L., Williams, J.B. and Gibbon, M. (1987) 'Structured Clinical Interview for DSM-III-R (SCID).' New York: New York State Psychiatric Institute, Biometric Research Department.

Spitzer, R.L., Williams, J., Gibbon, M. and First, M. (1990) *Structured Clinical Interview for DSM-III-R*. Washington DC: American Psychiatric Press.

Squier, R.W. (1994) 'The relationship between ward atmosphere and staff attitude to treatment in psychiatric in-patient units.' *British Journal of Medical Psychology 67*, 319–31.

Stafford, B. (2002) 'Being more certain about Random Assignment in Social Policy Evaluations.' *Social Policy and Society 1*, 4, 275–84.

Steiner, H., Haldipur, C. and Stack, L. (1982) 'The acute admission ward as a therapeutic community.' *American Journal of Psychiatry 139*, 897–901.

Stevens, S., Arbiter, N. and Glider, P. (1989) 'Female residents: Expanding their role to increase treatment effectiveness.' *International Journal on the Addictions 4*, 285–306.

Stevens, S. and Glider, P. (1994) 'Therapeutic communities: Substance abuse treatment for women.' In F.M. Tims, G. De Leon and N. Jainchill (eds) *Therapeutic Community: Advances in Research and Application*. NIDA Research Monograph 144 (NIH Publication Number 94–3633). Rockville, MA: National Institute on Drug Abuse.

Stevens, S.J., Chong, J. and Erickson, J.R. (1997) 'Homelessness and substance abuse: The efficacy of modified residential and nonresidential therapeutic community models.' In G. De Leon (ed.) *Community as Method: Therapeutic Communities for Special Populations and Special Settings*. Westport, CT: Praeger.

Stone, M., Stone, D. and Hurt, S. (1987) 'Natural history of borderline patients treated by intensive hospitalization.' *Psychiatric Clinics of North America 10*, 185–206.

Strauss, A.L. and Corbin, J. (1990) *Basics of Qualitative Theory Research. Grounded Theory Procedures and Techniques*. London: Sage Publications.

Strauss, A. and Corbin, J. (1994) 'Grounded theory methodology: An overview.' In M. Miles and A. Huberman (eds) *Qualitative Data: An Expanded Sourcebook*. Second edition. London: Sage Publications.

Suddards L. and Wilks, R. (1996) 'Care in the Community: An Evaluation of Therapeutic Community Practice.' Paper presented at the ATC Windsor Conference, September.

Sugarman, B. (1974) *Daytop Village: A Therapeutic Community*. New York: Holt, Rinehart and Winston.

Sugarman, B. (1986) 'Structure, variations, and context: A sociological view of the therapeutic community.' In G. De Leon and J.T. Ziegenfuss (eds) *Therapeutic Communities for Addictions: Readings in Theory, Research and Practice*. Springfield, IL: Charles C. Thomas.

Tajfel, H. (ed.) (1982) *Social Identity and Intergroup Relations.* Cambridge: Cambridge University Press.

Talboy, E.S. (1998) *Therapeutic Community Experiential Training: Facilitator Guide.* Kansas City, MO: Mid-America Addiction Technology Transfer Center. www.mattc.org

Taylor, F.H. (1963) 'The treatment of delinquent psychopaths.' *The Howard Journal 1*, 1–9.

Temple, N., Patrick, M., Evans, H., Holloway, F. and Squire, C. (1996) 'Interpretive group psychotherapy and dependent day hospital patients – an exploratory study.' *International Journal of Social Psychiatry 43*, 116–28.

Thompson, B. and Daniel, L. (1996) 'Factor analytic evidence for the construct validity of scores: An historical overview and some guidelines.' *Educational and Psychological Measurement 56*, 2, 197–208.

Thompson, S.G. and Sharp, S.J. (1999) 'Explaining heterogeneity in meta-analysis: A comparison of methods.' *Statistics in Medicine 18*, 2693–2708.

Timko, C. (1994) *Residential Substance Abuse and Psychiatric Programs Inventory (RESPPI) Handbook for Users.* Palo Alto, CA: Centre for Health Care Evaluation, VA HSR&D Field Program, Department of Veterans Affairs Medical Centre.

Timko, C. (1995) 'Policies and services in residential substance abuse programs: Comparisons with psychiatric programs.' *Journal of Substance Abuse 7*, 43–59.

Timko, C. (1996) 'Physical characteristics of residential psychiatric and substance abuse programs: Organizational determinants and patients' outcomes.' *American Journal of Community Psychology 24*, 173–92.

Timko, C. and Moos, R. (1998) 'Determinants of the treatment climate in psychiatric and substance abuse programs: Implications for improving patient outcomes.' *Journal of Nervous and Mental Disease 186*, 96–103.

Timko, C., Moos, R. and Finney, J. (2000) 'Models of matching patients and treatment programs.' In K. Craik, R. Price, and W.B. Walsh (eds) *New Directions in Person-Environment Psychology.* Second edition. Hillsdale, NJ: Lawrence Erlbaum.

Timmins, N. (2001) *The Five Giants. A Biography of the Welfare State.* London: Harper Collins.

Tims, F.M., De Leon, G. and Jainchill, N. (eds) (1994) *Therapeutic Community: Advances in Research and Application.* NIDA Monograph 144 (NIH Publication No. 94–3633). Washington, DC: Superintendent of Documents, US Government Printing Office.

Tims, F.M. and Ludford, J.P. (eds) (1984) *Drug Abuse Treatment Evaluation: Strategies, Progress and Prospects.* National Institute on Drug Abuse Research Monograph 51 (DHHS Publication No. (ADM) 84–1329). Rockville, MD: National Institute on Drug Abuse.

Trauer, T., Bouras, N. and Watson, J.P. (1987) 'The assessment of ward atmosphere in a psychiatric unit.' *International Journal of Therapeutic Communities 8*, 199–205.

Tuxford, J. (1961) *Treatment as a Circular Process.* London: King Edward's Hospital Fund.

Vaglum, P., Friis, S., Karterud, S., Mehlum, L. and Vaglum, S. (1993) 'Stability of the severe personality disorder diagnosis: A 2–5 year prospective study.' *Journal of Personality Disorders 7*, 4, 348–53.

Verhaest, S., Pierloot, R. and Janssens, G. (1982) 'Comparative assessment of two different types of therapeutic communities.' *International Journal of Social Psychiatry 28*, 46–52.

Warren, F. and Dolan, B. (eds) (2001) *Perspectives on Henderson Hospital.* Second edition. Sutton: Henderson Hospital.

Warren, F., Preedy-Fayers, K., McGauley, G., Pickering, A., Norton, K., Geddes, J.R. and Dolan, B. (2003) *Review of Treatments for Severe Personality Disorder.* London: Home Office. Online publication, 30/03 www.homeoffice.gov. uk/rds/onlinepubs1.html

Weissman, M.M. (1975) 'The assessment of social adjustment.' *Archives of General Psychiatry 32*, 357–65.

Weitzman, E. and Miles, M.B. (1995) *Computer Programs for Qualitative Data Analysis: A Software Sourcebook.* London: Sage Publications.

Wells, K.B. (1999) 'Treatment research at the crossroads: The scientific interface of clinical trails and effectiveness research.' *American Journal of Psychiatry 156*, 1, 5–10.

Wendt, R., Mosher, L., Matthews, S. and Menn, A. (1983) 'Comparison of two treatment environments for schizophrenia.' In J.G. Gunderson, O.A. Will and L.R. Mosher (eds) *Principles and Practice of Milieu Therapy.* New York: Jason Aronson.

Wesby, R., Menzies, D., Dolan, B. and Norton, K. (1995) 'A survey of psychological types in a therapeutic community.' *Therapeutic Communities 16*, 4, 229–38.

Westen, D. and Shedler, J. (1999a) 'Revising and assessing Axis II, Part I: Developing a clinically and empirically valid assessment method.' *American Journal of Psychiatry 156*, 258–72.

Westen, D. and Shedler, J. (1999b) 'Revising and assessing Axis II, Part II: Toward an empirically based and clinically useful classification of personality disorders.' *American Journal of Psychiatry 156*, 273–85.

Wexler, H. (1997) 'Therapeutic communities in American prisons.' In E. Cullen, L. Jones and R. Woodward (eds) *Therapeutic Communities for Offenders.* Chichester: John Wiley and Sons.

Wexler, H., Melnick, G., Lowe, L. and Peter, J. (1999) 'Three-year reincarceration outcomes for Amity in-prison therapeutic community and aftercare in California.' *The Prison Journal 79*, 3, 321–36.

Whiteley, J.S. (1970) 'The response of psychopaths to a therapeutic community.' *British Journal of Psychiatry 166*, 517–29.

Whiteley, J.S. and Collis M. (1987) 'Therapeutic factors applied to group psychotherapy in a therapeutic community.' *International Journal of Therapeutic Communities 8*, 1, 21–31.

Whiteley, J.S. and Gordon, J. (1979) *Group Approaches to Psychiatry.* London: Routledge.

Wilberg, T., Dammen, T. and Friis, S. (2000) 'Comparing Personality Diagnostic Questionnaire – 4+ (PDQ-4) with Longitudinal, Expert, All Data (LEAD) Standard Diagnoses in a sample with high prevalence of Axis I and Axis II disorders.' *Comprehensive Psychiatry 41*, 295–302.

Wilberg, T., Friis, S., Karterud, S., Mehlum, L., Urnes, Ø. and Vaglum, P. (1998b) 'Outpatient group therapy. A valuable supplement to day treatment for patients with borderline personality disorder? A three years follow-up study.' *Nordic Psychiatric Journal 52*, 213–21.

Wilberg, T., Karterud, S., Pedersen, G., Urnes, Ø., Irion, T., Brabrand, J., Haavaldsen, G., Leirvåg, H., Johnsen, K., Andreasen, H., Hedmark, H. and Stubhaug, B. (submitted) 'Outpatient group psychotherapy following day treatment of patients with personality disorders. Experiences from a multicenter quality assurance system.'

Wilberg, T., Karterud, S., Urnes, Ø., Pedersen, G. and Friis, S. (1998a) 'Outcomes of poorly functioning patients with personality disorders in a day treatment program.' *Psychiatric Services 49*, 1462–67.

Wilberg, T., Urnes, Ø., Friis, S., Irion, T., Pedersen, G. and Karterud, S. (1999a) 'One-year follow-up of day treatment for poorly functioning patients with personality disorders.' *Psychiatric Services 50*, 1326–30.

Wilberg, T., Urnes, Ø., Friis, S., Pedersen, G. and Karterud, S. (1999b) 'Borderline and avoidant personality disorders and the five-factor model of personality: A comparison of DSM-IV diagnoses and NEO-PI-R.' *Journal of Personality Disorders 13*, 226–40.

Wills, D. (1967) *The Hawkspur Experiment.* London: Allen and Unwin.

Wilson, J. (1985) 'Leaving home as a theme in a therapeutic community.' *International Journal of Therapeutic Communities 6*, 2, 71–78.

Wilson, S. and Mandelbrote, B. (1978) 'The relationship between duration of treatment in a therapeutic community for drug abusers and subsequent criminality.' *British Journal of Psychiatry 132*, 487–91.

Woolgar, S. (1988) *Knowledge and Reflexivity: New Frontiers in the Sociology of Knowledge.* London: Sage Publications.

Yablonsky, L. (1965) *Synanon: The Tunnel Back.* New York: Macmillan.

Yalom, I. (1975) *The Theory and Practice of Group Psychotherapy.* New York: Basic Books.

Yandow, V. (1989) 'Alcoholism in women.' *Psychiatric Annals 19*, 5, 243–47.

Young, E. (1990) 'The role of incest issues in relapse.' *Journal of Psychoactive Drugs 22* (2), 249–58.

Zeitlyn, B. (1967) 'The therapeutic community – fact or fantasy.' *British Journal of Psychiatry 113*, 1083–86.

Subject Index

Author Index